# The Best of
# Byerly's

## A RECIPE COLLECTION

*from the Test Kitchen of*  *Home Economists*

*THIS BOOK IS DEDICATED TO BYERLY'S "BUILDERS"...*

*...to the Byerly's Home Economists for their many
long hours and diligent efforts that went into this cookbook;*

*...to our employees, past and present, who have worked
as a team to promote quality and service, and*

*...to all of you, friends and supporters for
the past quarter of a century.*

Managing Editor:  **Judy Crocker**

Home Economists:
**Linda Day Anderson
Judy Crocker
Carol Froke
Leisha Ingdal
Sharon Johnson
Lois Kemp
Betty Pierce
Merrilyn Tauscher**

Food Editor:  **Betsy Norum**

Copywriter:  **Heather Randall King**

Nutritional Data:  **Nutrition & Food Associates, Inc.**

Graphic Design and Art Direction:
Cover:  **Bergh Jensen & Associates, Robert Jensen**
Text:  **Calton Design, Inc., Bob Calton**

Photography:  **Marvy! Advertising Photography**

Color Separations:  **R&S Litho Inc., Thomas Dreyer**

Food Stylists:
**Florence French
Barb Standal**

Illustration:  **Bob Calton**

Production and Printing:  **Northstar Printing under the direction of
James Whiting & Stephen Dusek**

Greetings,

My career in the food business began back in high school when I worked part-time delivering groceries. It was an enlightening experience for me. Often, when my customers weren't home, the key was left under the doormat and I was entrusted with the job of placing the order in the kitchen and putting away perishables. During those days of very personal store-to-door service, I soon learned the fundamentals of building a trusting business relationship — quality and service. Since then, I have found them to be a powerful partnership.

Quite frankly, it was precisely those two fundamentals which drew me to Byerly's. The philosophy of this upscale supermarket was one which I could relate to with enthusiasm. From the beginning there was a tremendous emphasis on listening — being sensitive to customer comments. Today, with nine stores, we are still committed to giving customers what they need and want.

Our first cookbook, in fact, was published in direct response to hundreds of customer requests. With sales of over 100,000 copies, "The Best of Byerly's" has proven to be a resounding success. It is available in bookstores across the country and we are delighted that many copies have become keepsakes of foreign visitors.

It was barely off the presses when we began receiving requests for a sequel. And so, with great pleasure, we unveil Volume II — a truly contemporary collection of recipes and menus attuned to today's lifestyles. Continuing the tradition of excellence found in Volume I, it showcases exciting food and serving trends. And, it reflects our quest for more healthful dining and streamlined culinary techniques.

As we mark our 25th anniversary, we celebrate this milestone with gratitude for accomplishments, never forgetting that you are an integral part of our success. Looking ahead, we envision conscientious growth and community involvement underscored by a commitment to improving quality of life by offering a unique, enjoyable shopping experience. But first and foremost, our vision is a continued pledge to offer the highest quality products and innovative services to you, our valued customers.

Best wishes as you transform groceries from Byerly's into the inviting recipes and menus in this anniversary collection.

Tom Harberts

BYERLY'S...since 1968

"Extraordinary! Distinctive! Innovative! Exotic! Friendly and convenient!" — just a few of the accolades awarded Byerly's by customers, visitors and the media since the first supermarket opened in Golden Valley, Minnesota 25 years ago. *People* and *Time* magazines — internationally renowned newspapers like *The Wall Street Journal* and *The New York Times* and nationally televised shows like *Good Morning, America* and *The Today Show* — all and more have showcased Byerly's upscale style, unique offerings and trend-setting approach to the retail food industry.

Today, with nine stores in Minnesota and more on the drawing board, Byerly's imposing interiors feature ultra-wide, carpeted aisles, warm lighting from chandeliers and a host of other amenities which attract weekly visitors from across the country and around the world.

In addition to old-fashioned friendly service and competitive pricing, customers are treated to a multitude of one-stop shopping features including: an enticingly eclectic deli with meats and imported cheeses sliced to order; an in-store bakery complete with specialty breads, cakes for all occasions and French pastries; a complete salad bar; an extensive line of hot entrées; fish and seafood market with over 70 varieties; a vast U.S.D.A. prime meat selection; a produce section abundant with home-grown as well as exotic imported fruits and vegetables and ice cream, soft-serve yogurt and espresso bars.

Each Byerly's offers complimentary services of an in-store home economist, special helps for shoppers with dietary restrictions, an FTD florist, banking and postal services and a 24-hour restaurant. The St. Louis Park flagship store boasts even more attractions and services — a pharmacy, gift gallery, photo lab and culinary arts school plus specialty shops for wine and spirits, gourmet candies and cards.

With over 30,000 separate items available in each store, Byerly's continually seeks innovative products and services to satisfy customer desires. From freshly-baked bagels to Waterford crystal, from homemade soups to made-to-order fruit baskets for gifting, Byerly's makes grocery shopping an enjoyable, unforgettable experience.

As Byerly's Home Economists, it is our pleasure to work closely with customers in planning important occasions and offering ideas for family menus as well as answering questions about nutrition and a wide range of other food-related topics. This personal association began 25 years ago and has offered us valuable direction and guidance in designing "The Best of Byerly's — Volume II."

Our response to your requests comes in the form of this creative collection of recipes...from appetizers to desserts, from comforting family meals to sophisticated special occasion menus. Look for seasonal serving ideas, an abundance of make-ahead recipes tailored to all timetables, "enlightened" dishes to promote wholesome choices, recipes to serve a few or a crowd and many other innovative suggestions.

If you enjoyed our first cookbook, you will find this new one an exciting addition to your repertoire of good food and entertaining.

*The Home Economists at Byerly's*

# GUIDELINES FOR PRODUCTS AND TECHNIQUES USED IN RECIPES

▼

Recipes in this cookbook were developed using fresh, high quality ingredients, accurate measurements, and specific sizes of cooking utensils. Whole packages or containers of food were used whenever possible to avoid waste. The following guidelines also will help assure success.

### Ingredients

Baking Powder and Baking Soda:   Check for freshness dates.

Beef:   Use U.S.D.A. prime grade. Roasting times may vary when other grades are used.

Broth:   Use canned, undiluted broths (unless otherwise indicated).

Brown Sugar:   Always pack.

Convenience Products:   Use when they make preparation easier without compromising quality (example: prepared minced garlic or chopped jalapeño peppers).

Eggs:   Use Grade AA "large" (unless otherwise indicated).

Flour:   Use all-purpose flour.

Lemon or Lime Juice:   Use fresh squeezed or frozen juice.

Milk:   Use whole or 2% milk (unless otherwise indicated).

Powdered Sugar:   Use it unsifted (unless otherwise indicated).

Sugar:   Use white cane or beet sugar.

Sherry and other wines:   Purchase from a liquor store. Do not substitute cooking sherry or cooking wine.

### Measuring

Dry ingredients and solid fats:   Measure in appropriate graduated measuring cups and level off.

Flour:   Stir in the canister, lightly spoon into appropriate graduated measuring cups and level off.

Liquids:   Measure in clear measuring cup with markings on the side.

When to measure:   This is determined by the wording used in the ingredient list. For example, "one cup peanuts, chopped" means to measure, then chop, while "one cup chopped peanuts" means to chop, then measure.

## Procedures and Equipment

Greasing pans:   Use solid shortening, butter or margarine (unless otherwise indicated).

Kitchen supplies:   Common supplies like foil, waxed paper, paper baking cups, wooden picks and no-stick cooking spray are not included in the ingredient lists. Less common supplies such as parchment paper or wooden skewers are listed with the ingredients.

Microwave recipes:   Microwave ovens used for testing were 650-700 watts. Additional cooking time may be necessary if using an oven with lower wattage.

Ovens:   Heat 10 minutes before baking or roasting.

Pan sizes:   Using the specified pan or dish size and type is extremely important for recipe success.

Serving sizes:   Number of servings given with recipes relates to nutritional considerations. Adjust if necessary to suit family appetites and needs.

Testing for doneness:   The test for doneness is given first before approximate cooking time. Check doneness at the minimum time indicated in a range like "20 to 30 minutes."

Thermometers:   To test meat doneness, use an instant-read type of thermometer (unless otherwise indicated).

Bundt® is a registered trademark of Northland Aluminum, Minneapolis, Minnesota.

# TABLE OF CONTENTS

# MENUS FOR ALL SEASONS

**As** the seasons come and go, they reflect our ever changing tastes for the wide variety of foods that nature provides. Lazy summer days coax us outdoors for casual ambiance and hot-off-the-coals creations. Fall finds us moving inside and scenting the kitchen with the aroma of apple pie, lunch box cookies and duckling dinners. As we cozy up around the fireplace for holiday celebrations and Super Bowl gatherings, it's hot drinks, robust ragouts and rich desserts that prove most satisfying. Then, hooray for spring and the celebrations it brings! Showers, graduations and wedding receptions are the perfect occasions for festive entrées, a kaleidoscope of fruit salads and desserts, the first tender garden vegetables and congratulatory cakes.

Our menus are designed not only to showcase seasonal foods and honor specific occasions, they are planned for maximum ease in preparing and serving. The cook is uppermost in our minds as we temper any last-minute details with plenty of do-ahead convenience. Each menu provides balance, complementary colors, textures and flavors plus appealing contrasts in hot and cold. A suggested number of servings has been given for each menu. In some cases you will need to increase the recipe to meet these amounts. For best results, prepare each recipe singly, rather than doubling. Feel free to mix and match, adding your own personal trademarks along the way.

We have gathered a collection of menus for all seasons...for all reasons. We wish you much pleasure in preparing and serving each recipe with confidence.

# "Souper" Bowl "Sundae"

Let the game begin! Your guests have the best seats in the house with kick-off-the-shoes comfort and the promise of a hearty supper, win or lose. As "coach" you know timing is everything — in the game and in the kitchen. So that there's no interference with important plays, place pre-game and first half beverages and nibblers within arm's reach of the action. At half time, have your guests ladle up the sumptuous sampler of soups and pass the breads and crackers. Then, celebrate the winning touchdown with an all-star medley of super sundae fixings artfully arranged for help-yourself convenience.

**CHICKEN 'N CHUTNEY SPREAD**
**VEGETABLE CRUDITÉS 'N TORTELLINI TRAY**
**FRESH BASIL DIP**
**ASSORTED BEER    SPARKLING WATER**
**BEAUJOLAIS**

---

**WILD RICE SOUP**
**LENTIL SOUP OR BLACK BEAN SOUP**
**TOMATO VEGETARIAN SOUP**
**CHEESE 'N HERB FRENCH BREAD    FOCACCIA    ASSORTED CRACKERS\***

---

**MAKE YOUR OWN SUNDAE BAR**
**COFFEE**

---

*Serves Twelve*

*Countdown menu*
*page 28*

**\*Recipe not included.**

1

# WINTER WONDERLAND PARTY

For the chilliest month of the year, create a cozy atmosphere
with warm hospitality. Whether you're hosting a New Year's Day get-
together, an après ski or skating party, a Twelfth Night
celebration or simply a relaxing fireside postlude to the holiday hustle,
this menu with its casual elegance is superb. Since January
brings us back to busy routines, there are ample do-ahead options.
Dishes adapt flexibly to a fork buffet or sit-down service.
From the warmed Brie to the flavored coffee, you will delight in these
creative chill-chasers for frosty evenings.

CHUTNEY 'N BRIE
CITRUS SAUTERNE PUNCH

---

BERRY BEEF RAGOUT
BOWTIE PASTA
CARROTS 'N AMARETTO
TOSSED GREEN SALAD*
CRUSTY ROLLS*
BEAUJOLAIS

---

NUTCRACKER SWEET
MACADAMIA NUT AND CREAM-FLAVORED COFFEE
TEA

---

*Serves Twelve*

*Recipe not included.

# A Romantic Table for Two

This tantalizing toast to Valentinc's Day, an anniversary, an engagement celebration or any other enchanted tête-à-tête features a "heart-y" and handsome menu with elegant embellishments. Pamper that one special guest with gourmet selections streamlined with our step-by-step, foolproof directions. Set a leisurely pace to savor each course to the fullest, and serve the salad European-style following the entrée, if you wish. Dessert and coffee would be lovely served graciously in the living room or before the fire. An evening to remember for incurable romantics.

**HERB 'N NUT BRIE**
**CHAMPAGNE**

---

**RACK OF LAMB WITH TOMATOES PROVENCALE**
OR
**VEAL CUTLETS ORIENTAL**
**ROSEMARY NEW POTATOES**
**BUTTERED BROCCOLI SPEARS***
**PIGNOLI AND PEAR SALAD**
**CLOVERLEAF DINNER ROLLS***
**CABERNET**

---

**FLAMING CARAMBOLA SUNDAE**
**JAMAICAN BLUE MOUNTAIN COFFEE**

---

*Serves Two*

*Recipe not included.

# BLACK TIE GOURMET AFFAIR

Elegance everywhere you look — gleaming silver, damask
linens, flickering candles and fresh flowers. The stage is set for a
memorable evening and a marvelous menu. While
guests are raising their glasses to the festive ambiance and raving about
the hors d'oeuvres, you have only a few final touches to add
before inviting everyone to the table. Your reputation as a fabulous
cook is assured when you confidently present each dish,
resplendent with complementary flavors, textures and colors. Toasts to
the hosts are guaranteed!

**SAVORY PHYLLO SQUARES**
**CAVIAR SPREAD**
**MERRY BERRY PUNCH**

---

**INDIVIDUAL BEEF WELLINGTON**
**DUCHESS DO-AHEAD POTATOES**
**CINNAMON-SPICED CARROTS**
**APPLES 'N GREENS**
**BRIOCHE***
**PINOT NOIR**

---

**CHOCOLATE PECAN PIE**
**VANILLA-FLAVORED COFFEE**
**TEA**

---

*Serves Eight*

*Recipe not included.

# SUNRISE BRUNCH

▼

With the sun's rays becoming warmer every day, it's easier to
"rise and shine," especially for a sensational spread like this. Most
brunches fall between mid-morning and early afternoon.
Because guests usually come famished, savvy hosts are well organized
for prompt serving. Except for mixing the mimosas as guests
arrive, baking the do-ahead eggs and tossing the salad, the timetable is
streamlined and stress-free. Fresh fruit, one of spring's
special gifts, is showcased in both salad and dessert.

**MIMOSAS À LA ASTI SPUMANTE**
**ASSORTED FRUIT JUICES***

---

**INDIVIDUAL EGGS MORNAY**
**FRESH FRUIT SALAD**
**APPLE NUT COFFEECAKE     ASSORTED MINI-MUFFINS***
**DANISH PASTRIES***

---

**FRUITY YOGURT BREAKFAST TART**
**FRENCH ROAST COFFEE**

---

*Serves Twelve*

*Recipe not included.

# A Springtime Gathering

For the special occasions that burst forth when the first
daffodil blooms, we feature succulent spring lamb as the centerpiece
of this festive menu. Eagerly, we replace heavier
wintertime fare with lighter, brighter selections like tangy Golden Fruit
Punch, ginger-sparked Carrot Soup, rice with citrus zest,
sunny orange-studded salad and mint-refreshed peas. Use this
wonderful repast to welcome back "snowbirds,"
celebrate spring holidays, mark a confirmation or baptism, or simply to
delight in the season of renewal and each other's company.

PARTY PÂTÉ
ASSORTED CRACKERS*
GOLDEN FRUIT PUNCH

---

CARROT SOUP

---

ROAST LEG OF LAMB
RICE 'N LEMON
SPRING PEAS
ARTICHOKE 'N ORANGE TOSSED SALAD
BUTTERFLUFF DINNER ROLLS*
CABERNET

---

SHERRY BUNDT POUND CAKE WITH
SHERRY CREAM SAUCE
AMARETTO-FLAVORED COFFEE

---

*Serves Ten*

*Recipe not included.

# GRADUATION CELEBRATION

▼

After the tassels are tossed and the strains of "Pomp and Circumstance" have faded, it's time to celebrate! This menu and teenaged appetites are made for each other. The casual-chic flexibility makes this suitable for an open house serving style to be readied ahead and replenished as necessary. The Beef 'n Salsa mixture can be kept warm in an attractive slow cooker or chafing dish with baskets of buns close by. Avoid congestion by placing the punch and appetizers on a separate table away from heartier foods. To show off the graduation cake and other sweets, arrange them on yet another table or sideboard along with coffee, cups, plates and dessert forks.

NO-BAKE CRACKER SNACKER

WONTON CHIPS

FRUITY TROPICAL PUNCH

———

BEEF 'N SALSA BUNWICHES

OR

SMOKED TURKEY AND BEEF ROLL-UPS

ASSORTED SMALL BUNS*

DILL POTATO SALAD

FRUIT PLATTER

ALMOND DIP OR CITRUS FRUIT DIP

———

GRADUATION CAKE*

APRICOT OATMEAL BARS    CHOCOLATE CHEESECAKE BARS

ASSORTED CARBONATED BEVERAGES

COFFEE

———

*Serves Twenty-Four*

*Recipe not included.

# COME FOR THE WEEKEND BRUNCH

When you have houseguests, it's always a gracious gesture to invite some good friends or family members over to enliven the weekend and add their welcome. The accent is on informality, and the inviting menu is one that hosts can handle with finesse, thanks to advance preparation. The country-style casserole and muffins bake while you and your guests are enjoying the zesty eye-opening Bloody Marys. The divine dessert requires only garnishing before making a grand entrance.

**PEPPAR BLOODY MARYS**

---

**COUNTRY BREAKFAST CASSEROLE**
**FROSTY FRUIT CUP**
**CORN MUFFINS WITH MAPLE BUTTER**

---

**LEMON CURD PAVLOVA**
**FLAME ROOM BREAKFAST BLEND COFFEE**

---

*Serves Eight to Ten*

# SPRING LUNCHEON AT ONE

The merry month of May brings the joy of sampling the first
young asparagus and rhubarb, not to mention the bright berries of the
season. It would be folly not to incorporate them in a
stellar spring luncheon. No matter how busy you are, this carefree menu
makes it possible for you to go ahead and fête a new
neighbor, officers of a club, a bride-to-be or a houseguest. Walnuts
and Crème Fraîche add unique richness to ever-popular
chicken salad, and a garnish of fresh tarragon sprigs completes the posh
presentation. The dessert is too pretty to cut before everyone
gets a chance to admire it, so why not serve it right at the table while
a friend does coffee-pouring honors?

**CRAN-ORANGE PUNCH**

---

**CHICKEN 'N WALNUT SALAD**
**ASPARAGUS 'N RASPBERRY SALAD**
**LEMON POPOVERS**
**RIESLING**

---

**STRAWBERRY RHUBARB TART**
**HAZELNUT-FLAVORED COFFEE**

---

*Serves Eight*

# TEA AT THREE

Formal without being stuffy, an afternoon tea evokes fond
memories of another era and offers the perfect excuse to display
Grandmother's lace tablecloth and tea cup collection.
This refined gathering provides a tasteful tribute to mark a special
occasion, honor a new daughter-in-law, celebrate the special
bond between mothers and daughters or mark the end of another
school year with a teacher's tea. The mid-afternoon hour
invites an array of dainty, beautiful-to-behold, sweet and savory bites.
Serving both hot and iced tea is a splendid way to satisfy
every taste and weather eventuality. Invite several friends to share
pouring duties so you are free to greet guests, make
introductions and handle other hosting duties with ease.

**CRANBERRY 'N ORANGE SCONES**
**MOCK DEVONSHIRE CREAM**
**ASSORTED FINGER SANDWICHES***
**SMOKED SALMON 'N CUCUMBER TEA SANDWICHES**
**WATERCRESS 'N EGG SANDWICHES**

---

**COOKIE BON BONS**
**FRUIT TARTS**
**LEMON CURD MINI-TARTS**
**SHORTBREAD...TRADITIONAL**
**ICED PEACHY MINT TEA**
**EARL GREY TEA**
**LEMON SLICES    MILK**
**COFFEE**

---

*Serves Twenty*

*Sunshine Brunch menu*
*page 5*

*Recipe not included.

# WEDDING IN THE GARDEN

Hosting such an unforgettable occasion is truly a labor of
love. Mother Nature furnishes the setting and you complete the idyllic
scene with a picture-perfect menu. This sophisticated yet
simply-prepared spread serves twenty, but is easily expanded for more.
Because it is such a special, and no doubt busy day, consider
engaging help for perfect timing, streamlined serving and speedy
clean-up. These recipes are appropriate for noon
through dinner receptions and will complement both formal and
informal ceremonies. The flavorful dishes are also wonderful
for posh parties all summer long.

**GRAPES\* ASSORTED CHEESES\* CRACKERS\***
**SHERBET PUNCH**

---

**TANDOORI CHICKEN**
**RICE 'N CHUTNEY SALAD**
**FRUIT PLATTER**
**SPINACH SALAD**
**ASSORTED DINNER ROLLS\***
**GEWURZTRAMINER**

---

**WEDDING CAKE\***
**ASTI SPUMANTE**
**COFFEE     TEA**

---

*Serves Twenty*

*A Taste of
Scandinavia menu
page 24*

**\*Recipe not included.**

# CELEBRATION BUFFET

You will be amazed at the ease with which this first class
feast can be readied for twenty-four. With a subtle Italian accent,
generous helpings of fresh seasonal vegetables and
fruits, and the inclusion of convenience products and trendy ingredients
for contemporary flair, this menu speaks to a myriad of
celebrations. Whether you're hosting a rehearsal dinner, a
housewarming, a special anniversary, a birthday or a
pull-out-all-the-stops send-off for a friend who is moving, you can count
on this collection of recipes to make a memorable impact.

**PESTO 'N CROSTINI**
**RASPBERRY SLUSH**

---

**BEEF TENDERLOIN SUPREME**
**PENNE PASTA TOSS**
**VEGETABLE MEDLEY**
**FOCACCIA**
**MERLOT**

---

**KIWI SQUARES**
**CHOCOLATE TRUFFLES**
**COLOMBIAN SUPREMO COFFEE**

---

*Serves Twenty-Four*

# MILESTONE BIRTHDAY PARTY

Celebrate zest for life at any age by throwing a party to make
the guest of honor feel young at heart. This benchmark birthday
buffet can be served with casual ambiance any time of
the year. If a surprise party is part of the plan, this menu would be easy
to execute. A bit of foreign intrigue is present in the guise of
the Spanish Tapenade, Italian tortellini tray and colorful insalata. Use
the gaily decorated birthday cake for a centerpiece, if
you wish, and tune up for a rousing "Happy Birthday" as the candles
are extinguished.

TAPENADE
VEGETABLE CRUDITÉS 'N TORTELLINI TRAY
FRESH BASIL DIP
ASSORTED BEER    BEAUJOLAIS    SPARKLING WATER

———

BRISKET BUNWICHES
MINI KAISER ROLLS*
FRUIT PLATTER
ALMOND DIP OR CITRUS FRUIT DIP
TOSSED INSALATA

———

BIRTHDAY CAKE*
ICE CREAM BALLS
BLACK FOREST CHOCOLATE-FLAVORED COFFEE

———

*Serves Twenty-Five*

*Recipe not included.

# STAR-SPANGLED FOURTH OF JULY

Friends and family gather for an all-American holiday to rally
'round the flag and enjoy a Texas-style barbecue. This mid-summer
feast is a sure-fire way to satisfy hearty appetites before
the fireworks begin. Absolutely everything is done ahead except for
grilling the chicken and Texas Garlic Toast. It's the carefree
menu you've been hankering for, with just a splash of zesty
southwestern flavors to savor in the shade of backyard
trees. If the day's a scorcher, beat the heat and lessen the time over a
hot grill by partially cooking chicken in the microwave.

**SOUTHWESTERN BLACK BEAN DIP**
**RASPBERRY OR STRAWBERRY SLUSH**

---

**CHICKEN ON THE GRILL**
**POTATO SALAD VINAIGRETTE**
OR
**SPAGHETTI SALAD**
**MELON AND JICAMA STAR KABOBS**
**TEXAS GARLIC TOAST**
**ICED TEA    LEMONADE**

---

**TRIPLE BERRY SHORTCAKE**
**COFFEE**

---

*Serves Twelve*

# DINNER ON THE DECK

There's something about summer! Food takes on added
flavor when it's cooked and eaten under a bright blue sky. Grilling is
part of the fun and entertainment of this outdoor
dinner. Sip a frosty Peach Slush while grilling pre-cooked Buffalo Wings
to golden perfection. Then bring on the salmon steaks and
veggie kabobs, which cook side by side for about the same amount of
time. Choose between two desserts: frozen Banana Split
Dessert or Fresh Peach and Strawberry Tart. What a great time of the
year to sit on the deck and leisurely sip iced coffee after a
delicious meal.

**BUFFALO WINGS**
**PEACH SLUSH**

---

**SALMON...DILLED AND GRILLED**
**POTATO 'N VEGGIE KABOBS**
**SUN-DRIED TOMATOES 'N GREENS**
**BAGEL STICKS***

---

**BANANA SPLIT DESSERT**
**OR**
**FRESH PEACH AND STRAWBERRY TART**
**SPICED AND ICED COFFEE**

---

*Serves Eight*

*Recipe not included.

# MINNESOTA MEDLEY

Before the calendar flips from summer to fall, celebrate
Minnesota's unique bounty with a down-home heartland cookout.
What's for dinner? Wild rice harvested from northern
lakes; corn, potatoes and sunflower seeds raised with care in rolling
fields or backyard gardens; and ruby red raspberries plucked
in their prime from Albert Lea to International Falls. Although these
foods are traditional favorites, we've added some
innovations to replace the "ho-hum" with "how about a second
helping?" For the finale, you may wish to serve a Minnesota
Sundae — vanilla ice cream ladled with pure maple syrup and
sprinkled with sunflower nuts...a real treat! This menu is
a perfect example of how easily the basics can be enhanced, with a few
simple additions, to become very special indeed.

**WILD RICE HAMBURGERS**
**JO JO POTATOES**
**CORN ON THE COB**
**BROCCOLI SALAD**
**FRESH SLICED TOMATOES***
**MINNESOTA BEER**

---

**FRESH RASPBERRY PIE**
OR
**MINNESOTA SUNDAES**
**A TASTE OF MINNESOTA BLEND COFFEE**

---

*Serves Four*

*Recipe not included.

# SUMMER NIGHT FIESTA

Import the sights, sounds and flavors of old Mexico and
sunny Spain to your own backyard. Invite your amigos for a lively
evening of lights, music, colorful decorations and, of
course, a fiesta feast served buffet-style. This definitely is the occasion for
using your most colorful pottery and table accessories. Lights
strung from trees, glowing votive candles and/or flaming torches, vivid
paper flower centerpieces and background mariachi
music are the passports to a party with pizzazz. Give guests ample time
to enjoy the abundant hors d'oeuvres before serving the
Chalupa. Cap the evening with cake, coffee and sweets from a pinata.
Your guests will say "muchas gracias."

**EMPANADAS**
**PICO DE GALLO     GUACAMOLE**
**FIESTA TORTE**
**MARGARITAS     CERVEZA**

---

**CHALUPA**
**ASSORTED TOPPINGS**

---

**MEXICAN CHOCOLATE CAKE**
**PINEAPPLE 'N COCONUT CAKE**
**COFFEE**

---

*Serves Eight to Twelve*

# HEART-HEALTHY GRILLING

▼

Here's a sensational (and sensible) salute to great grilling
without guilt. Featured are lean, trimmed beef, fresh fruits and
vegetables, and special additions that say "yes" to less
fat and cholesterol. Our menu includes two all-time favorites, sirloin
steak and potato salad. Easy recipe modifications do not
sacrifice the traditional flavors you've come to enjoy.

**PEPPERED BEEF TOP SIRLOIN STEAK**
**EASY ENLIGHTENED POTATO SALAD**
**FRESH FRUIT BOWL\***
**BREAD OR BAGEL STICKS\***

---

**LEMON-GO-LIGHTLY MERINGUE CAKE**
**COFFEE    TEA**

---

*Serves Eight*

# ELEGANTLY "ENLIGHTENED"

▼

The response has become familiar. You invite guests for
dinner only to learn that they "would love to come, but..." they are
on a low-sodium, low-cholesterol or other restricted
diet. Rather than pass up the opportunity for a convivial evening, turn to
this tailor-made menu. It respects the needs of your friends
with healthful products, smart substitutions and preparation that does
not sacrifice flavor or good looks. You can confidently
serve this meal with pride, and don't be a bit surprised if satisfied diners
request the recipes.

**CRAB CLAWS    COCKTAIL SAUCE**

---

**HERBED PORK TENDERLOIN WITH APRICOT GLAZE**
**WILD RICE MUSHROOM BAKE**
**HERBED SUMMER SQUASH**
**SALAD GREENS\*    CREAMY GARLIC SALAD DRESSING**
**PARTY PERFECT POPOVERS**

---

**BERRY FILLED MERINGUES**
**COFFEE    TEA**

---

*Serves Six*

**\*Recipe not included.**

# A FAMILY GATHERING...ITALIAN STYLE

Fun-loving Italians, like families everywhere, need no special occasion to gather 'round the table for a robust spread punctuated with lots of laughter and conversation. This menu is as full-bodied as a Chianti from the Tuscany vineyards and as traditional as "O Solo Mio." All of the recipes, except the Focaccia, can be assembled ahead. In southern Italy, a small serving of Cannelloni might be offered as a first course and prelude to a veal or poultry entrée. However, with our simplified American style of dining, not to mention our love of pasta, we elevate it to main dish status surrounded by complementary co-stars. Choose one of the refreshing desserts as the perfect finale before saying "Ciao!"

**ITALIAN CHEESE CRUST TOPPERS**
**CAMPARI**

---

**CANNELLONI**
**OLIVE MEDLEY**
**TOSSED GREEN SALAD\***
**FOCACCIA**
**CHIANTI**

---

**SPUMONI TORTONI**
**OR**
**TIRAMISU**
**ITALIAN ESPRESSO COFFEE**

---

*Serves Twelve*

**\*Recipe not included.**

# FALL FEST FOR FRIENDS

Bid a fond farewell to summer. The kids are back in school,
and the timing is perfect to swing into fall with an informal supper
and chance to chat. So the hosts won't miss any of the
socializing, we have planned a stout-hearted sampler that is a do-ahead
delight. There's a nip in the air, so the chili or soup is on
the hearty side. It is accompanied by Corn Muffins, also satisfyingly
filling. The perfect fall dessert, Apple Harvest Cake, is
served with warmed Caramel Sauce. If you're planning a "cooperative
supper," you will find each dish quite adaptable to a
potluck mode.

**DEVILED EGGS**
**HUMMUS**
**SPARKLING FALL CIDER**

---

**BEEF 'N BEAN CHILI**
**OR**
**BLACK BEAN SOUP**
**VEGETABLE CRUDITES***
**CORN MUFFINS**

---

**APPLE HARVEST CAKE WITH CARAMEL SAUCE**
**COFFEE**

---

*Serves Eight*

*Dinner On The Deck menu*
*page 15*

*Recipe not included.

# GOURMET CLUB DINNER

With an ace up your sleeve like this menu, you will be ready,
willing and able to happily host your autumnal Gourmet Club
gathering. Plan your own upscale rendition of
Oktoberfest with continental creativity and a German-accented entrée.
Dividing up the recipes to be served makes it an elegant but
fairly easy menu to execute. The Party Pâté appetizer is a winner with
popular appeal and tasteful presentation. There are
some last minute details necessary before serving these stylish recipes,
so why not enlist the aid of another club member to make
short work of the final flourishes?

**PARTY PÂTÉ**

**CHAMPAGNE**

---

**GOAT CHEESE AND GREENS**

---

**ROAST DUCK WITH RASPBERRY SAUCE**

**BROCCOLI 'N CAULIFLOWER SAUTÉ**

**SPATZLE***

**SOUR DOUGH ROLLS***

**PINOT NOIR**

---

**DOUBLE DUTCH MOCHA MOUSSE IN LACY DESSERT CUPS**

**SWISS MOCHA ALMOND-FLAVORED COFFEE**

---

*Serves Eight*

*Wedding In*
*The Garden menu*
*page 11*

**\*Recipe not included.**

# THANKSGIVING FROM THE HEARTLAND

Celebrate this American day of thanksgiving and feasting with
a marvelous melding of family traditions. The "star" of this regal
repast is, of course, turkey and dressing. Colorful
accompaniments offer inviting diversity and do-ahead convenience — a
refreshingly tart molded salad, creamy mashed potatoes,
unique vegetable combinations and two popular pies. This is a day
when your microwave becomes your best friend, heating
and reheating side dishes so they are piping hot. All in all, it is a
bountiful and beautiful menu.

**SPICY LINGONBERRIES ON CAMEMBERT**
**RIESLING**

---

**TURKEY BREAST WITH SAGE DRESSING**
**CREAMY MASHED POTATOES     TURKEY GRAVY**
**YAMS 'N ESCALLOPED APPLES**
**SUGAR SNAP PEAS 'N CARROTS**
**SHERRIED CRANBERRY MOLD**
**WHITE MOUNTAIN DINNER ROLLS***
**BEAUJOLAIS OR RIESLING**

---

**PUMPKIN PIE     PUMPKIN PIE TOPPERS**
**SOUR CREAM RAISIN PIE**
**COFFEE**

---

*Serves Six to Eight*

*Recipe not included.

# GREAT BEGINNINGS AND GRAND FINALES

What's your favorite part of a meal? Half of you will say
"hors d'oeuvres," the other half will claim desserts. Well, why not
incorporate both favorites into an opulent open house?
Everyone will be well fed with an international array of savory tidbits
followed by a divine dessert buffet to satiate any sweet tooth.
We suggest this for November entertaining before the parade of other
holiday parties begins. Consider it for an Election Night
gathering, for instance, or a neighborhood party. Or plan a gala evening
to benefit a favorite charity, candidate or arts organization.
We recommend engaging help to serve food and beverages, replenish
platters and handle baking and reheating tasks. After all,
you want to have fun, too!

APRICOT 'N BRANDY BRIE

SHRIMP BOIL     COCKTAIL SAUCE

GARLICKY SUN-DRIED TOMATO APPETIZER

CRACKER BREAD ROLL-UPS

OLIVE MEDLEY

CAPONATA     CROSTINI

MUSHROOM 'N GORGONZOLA BUNDLES

SAVORY PHYLLO SQUARES

MEATBALLS 'N LINGONBERRIES

SLICED BEEF TENDERLOIN WITH HORSERADISH SAUCE*

STUFFED BELGIAN ENDIVE 'N RADICCHIO

ASSORTED BEER     SPARKLING WATER

BEAUJOLAIS

OR

GEWURZTRAMINER

_____

CHOCOLATE DECADENCE     RASPBERRY SAUCE

AMARETTO CAKE

LEMONY LEMON CAKE

FROSTED DRIED APRICOTS 'N ALMONDS

COFFEE

_____

*Serves Twenty-Five*

*Recipe not included.

# A Taste Of Scandinavia

Here in Minnesota where Scandinavians abound, we revel in celebrating special ethnic holidays with an elaborate feast for the eyes as well as the palate — the abundant smorgasbord. Traditionally, there are three tables — one for appetizers, one for entrées, and one for desserts and coffee. As foods are consumed, platters are replenished to entice everyone to help themselves to seconds (and thirds). If you haven't experienced the variety and subtle mingling of flavors and textures presented with a menu of this type, you are in for a treat!

**Mini Smorrebrod**

**Aquavit**

---

**Scandinavian Meatballs**

**Pork Loin Roast with Lingonberry Sauce**

**Parsley Buttered New Potatoes***

**Pickled Cucumbers**

**Sweet 'n Sour Red Cabbage**

**Lefse***     **Flat Bread***

**Merlot**

---

**Almond 'n Coffee Torte**

**Cream Cake**

**Swedish Nuts**

**Scandinavian Blend Coffee**

---

*Serves Eighteen to Twenty-Four*

*Recipe not included.

# TRIM THE TREE

Create your own personal Currier and Ives-style party by
inviting close friends to share in trimming the tree. With the evergreen
securely in place and decorations unpacked and ready,
guests can go to work on decorating and building appetites for this
exciting menu. The entrée, for example, is one you will want
to make again and again. The vegetable and salad medleys feature
some surprise ingredients to make them particularly
festive, and the dessert is sinfully rich — ideal for December indulgence.
Why not follow dinner with a lively singing of carols? Then,
reward tree trimmers with a gift from your kitchen — a small jar of
preserves or relish, a mini-loaf of quick bread, or a
sampler of holiday cookies or candies.

**HOLIDAY WREATH CHEESE SPREAD**
**BERRY HOT CIDER**

---

**PARMESAN DIJON CHICKEN**
**PECAN RICE**
**SUGAR SNAP PEAS 'N ONIONS**
**APPLES 'N GREENS**
**ASSORTED BAGEL STICKS***
**CHARDONNAY**

---

**BLACK FOREST CAKE**
**COFFEE**

---

*Serves Eight*

*Recipe not included.

# 'TIS THE SEASON

December is THE month for sharing and celebrating. The challenge faced by every host is to arrive at an innovative menu that isn't too taxing to prepare. Planning, of course, is essential. As you review the selections, you will note many convenient do-aheads, some of which can be frozen weeks before the date. Other dishes can be assembled the night before, leaving party day free for final embellishments. Since most calorie counting is cast aside until January, sweet splurges are spotlighted and served with flavored coffee.

**PISTACHIO 'N PHYLLO PINWHEELS**
**LAYERED APPETIZER TORTA**
**CHARDONNAY**

---

**COMPANY CHICKEN 'N ARTICHOKES**
**BUTTERED NOODLES OR RICE***
**SUN-DRIED TOMATOES 'N GREENS**
**CRANBERRY CHUTNEY***
**FINGER ROLLS***
**CHARDONNAY**

---

**CHOCOLATE 'N CRANBERRY COOKIES**   **FRUITCAKE BARS**
**MINNESOTA SNOWBALLS**   **SHORTBREAD HEART COOKIES**
**IRISH CREAM-FLAVORED COFFEE**
**TEA**

---

*Serves Ten to Twelve*

*Recipe not included.

# DAZZLING HOLIDAY DINNER

For many families, this is the most important dinner of the
year. This spectacular spread for twelve lives up to great expectations,
from the first bite of the chic Caviar Spread to the last
satisfying sip of Espresso. Every recipe is impressive in its own right. The
show-stopping crown roast, for example, is amazingly easy to
prepare and artfully garnished. Since the rosy-hued Campari Ice is
served as a palate cleanser, a tiny scoop for each person
is quite adequate. Both desserts get high marks for handsome
appearance and hassle-free preparation. All told, this is a
dazzling banquet befitting the most glorious of holidays.

**CAVIAR SPREAD**
**CHAMPAGNE**

---

**SPINACH AND BOSTON LETTUCE SALAD**

---

**CAMPARI ICE**

---

**CROWN ROAST OF PORK**
**STUFFING BALLS**
**GREEN BEANS 'N RED PEPPERS**
**TEA BISCUITS\***
**PINOT NOIR**

---

**ICE CREAM BOMBE**
**OR**
**DOUBLE CHOCOLATE COOKIE ROLL**
**ESPRESSO**

---

*Serves Twelve*

\*Recipe not included.

# NEW YEAR'S EVE COUNTDOWN

▼

What a festive way to bid farewell to the old and welcome
the new! Whether you are going all out for a black tie celebration or
favor a more casual approach, this menu is appropriate.
Timing can be planned two ways. You may choose to serve dinner in its
entirety and let gala champagne toasts usher in the New
Year. Or, once the clock strikes that magic hour, you can follow up
midnight toasts with coffee and dessert. So that
everyone can enjoy this special evening together (including hosts), most
of the food preparation can be completed ahead of time. The
exceptions are tossing the salad and a few simple baking and
reheating tasks. What a relaxed and resplendent
beginning to a new year!

GARLICKY SUN-DRIED TOMATO APPETIZER
CRACKER BREAD ROLL-UPS
GEWURZTRAMINER

---

CHICKEN 'N PISTACHIO ROLL-UPS
WILD AND BROWN RICE ACCOMPANIMENT
GREEN BEANS 'N SESAME SEEDS
CITRUS SALAD TOSS
ASSORTED KNOT DINNER ROLLS*
GEWURZTRAMINER

---

CHOCOLATE HAZELNUT CHEESECAKE
HAZELNUT-FLAVORED COFFEE

---

*Serves Twelve*

*Recipe not included.

# MENU ORCHESTRATION

▼

You've selected your party theme and menu. Now it's time to fine-tune your plans, from the guest list to the serving style. We have developed some helpful guides to take the worry and guesswork out of even the simplest details. You can entertain with confidence and ease by referring to our five different table-setting guides. The number of people you are serving, your seating arrangement and menu items will help you to determine whether a formal table setting or buffet service would be best, or whether one or two serving lines would be the easiest way to handle your crowd.

The party organizer at the end of the chapter can be duplicated for each event you plan. Attach copies of the recipes to this sheet so that everything you need will be in one place. This will also make it easy to prepare and organize your grocery list! If the party is a success, why not make a file for future reference? Many busy people repeat the same menu several times with different guest lists. It makes entertaining progressively easier each time. Your guests are sure to give you a standing ovation and demand an encore. Bravo!

## INDIVIDUAL FORMAL PLACE SETTING

▼

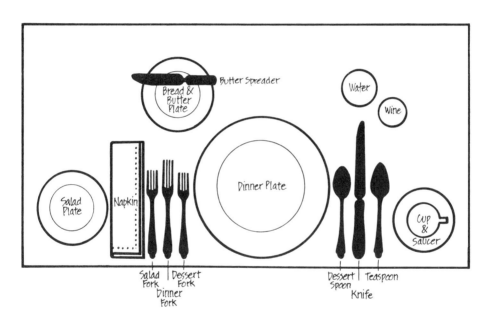

Although there is some room for personal preference, most formal settings are arranged in this manner. Options include replacing the bread and butter plate with the salad plate if bread or rolls are not being served. If salad is served as a first course, it can be placed on or in the position of the dinner plate. If salad is served European-style following the entrée, it is placed in the center after the dinner plate has been removed. The dessert spoon and/or fork can be placed horizontally above the top of the dinner plate rather than at its side. Cups and saucers may be on the table throughout the meal or brought in later when coffee and/or tea is served. The dinner knife is placed with the cutting edge facing the plate and with the handle bottom aligned with the bottom edge of the dinner plate. Glasses are placed above the dinner knife moving outward in the order beverages will be poured.

# LARGE GROUP TEA TABLE

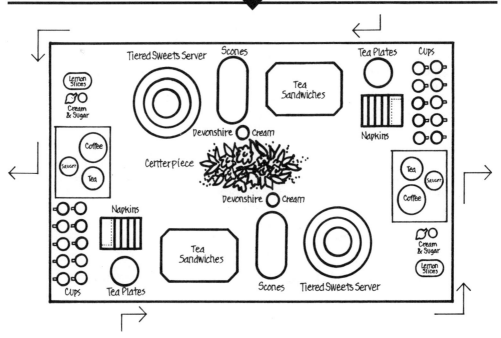

This arrangement places duplicate dishes on each side of the table for efficient serving. Coffee and tea service are at both ends of the table along with cream, sugar, lemon slices, cups and napkins. Saucers are unnecessary since the cups will be placed on the tea plates. If preferred, beverage service can be at one end only or arranged with coffee at one end, tea at the other. The key is streamlined, graceful service where everyone has easy access to beverages, food and dishes. Eye-appeal is very important, so create an elegant, uncrowded arrangement with one or two showy centerpieces, depending on table size.

# SMALL GROUP BUFFET TABLE

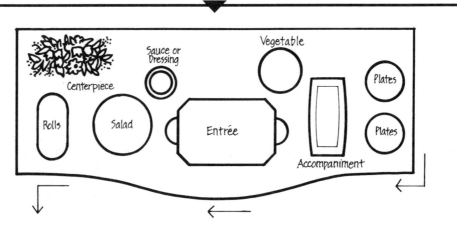

For smaller groups of eight to twenty, single-line buffet service combined with sit-down dining provides comfort and convenience. Guests pick up their plates from one end of the table and proceed along one side of the table, kitchen counter or formal dining room buffet table. After helping themselves, they sit at tables set with silverware, glassware and napkins. The centerpiece is placed where it can be admired, but does not interfere with food service.

# LARGE GROUP SINGLE-LINE BUFFET TABLE

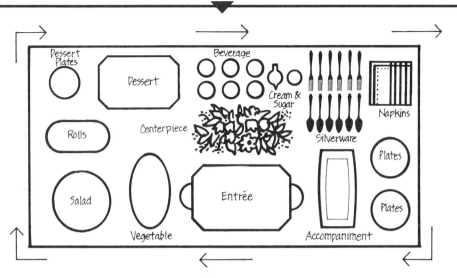

A table large enough to hold dinner and dessert plates, glassware, napkins and silverware as well as food is arranged so guests move in a single line around the entire table. Plates come first followed by food (main course and other foods from hot to cold) and, finally, glasses or cups, silverware and napkins. Food should be easily eaten with just a fork if small tables or lap trays are unavailable. Ample room for circulating around the table is important for smooth traffic flow.

# LARGE GROUP DOUBLE-LINE BUFFET TABLE

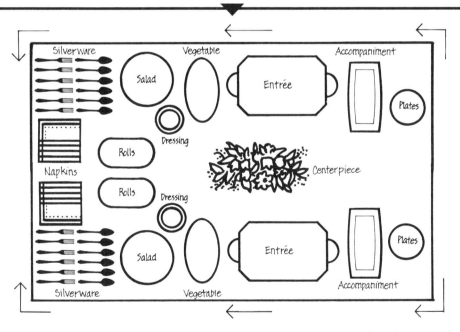

For smooth circulation of large groups, duplicate dishes are placed across from each other with a double stack of plates at one end of the table. Napkins and silverware are arranged neatly for easy pickup at the opposite end. It is helpful if foods that need slicing are cut ahead of time and reassembled to appear whole or artfully arranged on platters. Proper serving utensils should be readily available for each dish. For this diagram, dessert and beverage service are at a separate table. They may be placed at the left end of this table, if desired.

# THE PARTY ORGANIZER

▼

Event: _____ Theme: _____ Date: _____ Time: _____

| Menu | Things To Do | Table Appointments |
|---|---|---|
| Appetizers: | Freeze Ahead Foods: | China: |
| Main Dish: | | Glassware: |
| Potato, Pasta or Rice: | 2 Days Before: | Silver: |
| Vegetable: | | Linens: |
| Salad: | The Day Before: | Centerpiece: |
| Bread: | | Candles: |
| Dessert: | On The Day: | Serving Pieces: |
| Beverages: | | Place Cards/Favors: |
| Garnishes: | Last Minute: | Bar Supplies: |

| Guest List | RSVP | Guest List | RSVP |
|---|---|---|---|
| | | | |

# Appetizers

**A**ppetizers, canapés, hors d'oeuvres, snacks...whatever you choose to call them, they have taken on a whole new look. For the creative cook, appetizers reflect the excitement of experimenting with new products, international influences, fresh herbs and exotic seasonings.

We invite you to be bold in your exploration, because the rewards are rich. Sun-dried tomatoes, phyllo dough, black beans, radicchio and cracker bread may not yet be part of your recipe repertoire. They soon will be, however, because you won't want to miss out on a single bite.

This savory collection includes a variety of spreads, pick-up and eat appetizers and Italian, Mexican or French palate-pleasers to meet the needs of any occasion. Some are filling enough for a light and luscious lunch or mini-meal. Others are designed just to take the edge off before a special dinner. Appetizers are so much fun to make and so appealing to guests you may decide to host an open house, cocktail buffet, or appetizer and dessert party.

# HOLIDAY WREATH CHEESE SPREAD

▼

*Have fun varying garnishes for other holidays – red pepper or pimento hearts for Valentine's Day or shamrocks cut from green peppers for a St. Pat's party.*

2 (8-ounce) packages cream cheese, softened
1 (3-ounce) package cream cheese, softened
1 (7-ounce) bottle roasted sweet red peppers, drained, divided
1 teaspoon minced garlic

½ teaspoon salt
10 slices bacon, crisply fried, crumbled
½ cup smoked almonds, coarsely chopped
¼ cup sliced green onions
– snipped fresh parsley
– crackers

In food processor, process cream cheese, ½ of the roasted red peppers, garlic and salt until smooth. Add bacon, almonds and green onions; process just until combined. Refrigerate 1 hour. On serving platter, spoon cheese mixture into a circle. With hands, form into a smooth wreath shape (mixture will be soft). Cover with parsley. Cut remaining roasted red peppers into thin strips for ribbon and a bow; arrange on wreath. Refrigerate, covered, until firm. Serve with crackers.

*Amount: 3½ cups.*

**Variation:** Substitute 1 (5-ounce) can chunk breast of chicken drained, flaked for bacon.

# LAYERED APPETIZER TORTA

▼

*Prepared pesto streamlines this contemporary crowd-pleaser. The green and red layered look makes a stylish statement on a cocktail holiday buffet table.*

3 (8-ounce) cartons light cream cheese, softened
¼ cup margarine or butter, softened
3 tablespoons milk
½ teaspoon white pepper
1 (7-ounce) carton pesto, drained

2 tablespoons Italian bread crumbs
1 (8-ounce) jar marinated sun-dried tomatoes, drained, finely chopped
– snipped fresh parsley
– bread rounds or crackers

Line 8½ × 4½-inch baking pan with foil. Beat cream cheese, margarine, milk and white pepper until smooth. Spread 1 cup cream cheese mixture evenly in lined pan. Combine pesto and bread crumbs; carefully spread over cream cheese layer. Spread with another 1 cup cream cheese, then sprinkle with tomatoes. Spread with remaining cream cheese mixture. Refrigerate, covered, several hours or overnight. Unmold onto serving platter; smooth top. Garnish with parsley. Serve with bread rounds.

*18 to 24 servings.*

*Holiday Wreath
Cheese Spread
page 33*

# GARLICKY SUN-DRIED TOMATO APPETIZER

▼

*This "new" garlic is blended with sun-dried tomatoes and baked with cheese to make a perfect topper for French bread slices.*

1 (1½-ounce) package Dr. Saki garlic, peeled
2 (3-ounce) packages sun-dried tomatoes, coarsely chopped
2 (14½-ounce) cans ⅓ less salt chicken broth

2 (4-ounce) packages crumbled feta or (3.5-ounce) packages goat cheese
2 baguettes French bread, cut into ½-inch slices

Heat oven to 375°. Combine garlic and tomatoes in food processor; process until finely chopped. Spoon into quiche pan or 10-inch pie plate. Pour chicken broth over tomato mixture. Bake 50 minutes; stir. Sprinkle with cheese. Continue baking until heated through (about 15 minutes).

To Serve: Spread tomato mixture on bread slices.

*12 to 16 servings.*

**Tip:** Feta cheese will remain in crumbled pieces. Goat cheese will melt and give a creamy texture.

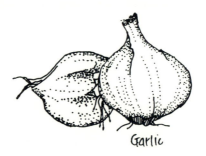

Garlic

# CHICKEN 'N CHUTNEY SPREAD

▼

*Exotic, easy and the epitome of elegance – a molded make-ahead gilded with chutney and sparked with curry.*

1 envelope unflavored gelatin
½ cup milk
1 teaspoon instant chicken bouillon
1½ to 2½ teaspoons curry powder
¼ teaspoon garlic salt
¼ teaspoon Tabasco
1 (12-ounce) carton lowfat cottage cheese

1 (3-ounce) package cream cheese, softened
3 (5-ounce) cans chunk breast of chicken, drained, flaked
1 (10-ounce) jar colonial chutney (Chut-nut), divided
½ cup finely chopped red bell pepper
¼ cup sliced green onions
– lavosh

Lightly oil 4-cup mold. In small saucepan, sprinkle gelatin over milk. Let stand until softened (about 5 minutes). Stir constantly over low heat until gelatin is dissolved. Stir in bouillon, curry, garlic salt and Tabasco; remove from heat. In food processor, process cottage cheese and cream cheese together until smooth. Add chicken, ½ cup of the chutney, red pepper, onions and gelatin mixture; process on and off until mixture is just combined but still chunky. Pour into oiled mold. Refrigerate, covered, until firm (2 to 3 hours).

To Serve: Unmold onto serving platter; spread remaining chutney over top. Serve with lavosh.

*Amount: 4 cups.*

# TAPENADE

▼

*A taste trip to Provençe is yours with every bite of this boldly-seasoned spread. Process carefully in the second step to maintain a sturdy texture with recognizable chunks of olive and onion.*

¼ cup drained capers
¼ cup olive oil
2 tablespoons snipped fresh
  cilantro leaves
1 tablespoon lemon juice
1 tablespoon minced garlic
2 teaspoons anchovy paste

1 (3¼-ounce) can tuna packed
  in oil, drained
1 (2½-ounce) bottle Spanish
  pitted olives, drained
1 (2¼-ounce) can sliced ripe
  olives, drained
½ cup sliced green onions
– assorted crackers

Combine capers, olive oil, cilantro, lemon juice, garlic, anchovy paste and tuna in food processor; process just until blended. Add olives and green onions; pulse just until combined. (Mixture should be chunky). Spoon into serving bowl. Refrigerate, covered, several hours or overnight. Serve with crackers.

*Amount: 2 cups.*

# PEPPERONI PARTY DIP

▼

*Bright bits of pepperoni give this baked creamy cheese dip plenty of party pizazz. Prepared cheese spread and pizza sauce make this a super-easy partner for your favorite dippers.*

1 (8-ounce) carton herb and
  garlic cream cheese
1 (8-ounce) package reduced-
  fat cream cheese, softened
¼ teaspoon crushed red pepper
½ cup pizza sauce

½ (3½-ounce) package sliced
  pepperoni, chopped
⅓ cup sliced green onions
½ cup shredded mozzarella
  cheese (2 ounces)
– raw vegetables
– crackers or cocktail bread

Heat oven to 350°. Combine flavored cream cheese, cream cheese and red pepper until smooth. Spread evenly in 9-inch quiche dish or pie plate. Spread pizza sauce over cheese mixture. Sprinkle with pepperoni and onions; top with mozzarella cheese. Bake until mixture is heated through and cheese is melted (about 15 minutes). Serve with raw vegetables, crackers or bread.

*8 to 10 servings.*

# HUMMUS

▼

*This economical and effortless Mid-Eastern appetizer is puréed into a versatile spread for breads, crackers, cucumber slices and sturdy leaves of Belgian endive.*

1 (15-ounce) can garbanzo
  beans (chick peas), drained
¼ cup Tahini
3 tablespoons chopped onion
2 tablespoons olive oil
3 tablespoons lemon juice

1 to 1½ teaspoons minced garlic
½ teaspoon ground cumin
⅛ teaspoon salt
– dash pepper
– paprika
– snipped fresh parsley
– pita bread

In food processor, purée garbanzo beans, Tahini, onion, olive oil, lemon juice, garlic, cumin, salt and pepper. Spoon into serving bowl; garnish with paprika and parsley. Serve with pita bread wedges.

*Amount: 2 cups.*

# PARTY PÂTÉ

▼

*Spicy pork sausage sparks this make-ahead French attraction. Flavors will mature during chilling and seasonings will become appealingly subtle.*

1 (12-ounce) package frozen
   ground hot pork sausage,
   thawed
¼ pound chicken livers, rinsed,
   chopped
½ cup chopped onion
3 slices bacon, chopped
1 teaspoon minced garlic
¾ cup Burgundy wine
2 tablespoons dry bread
   crumbs

2 eggs
1 tablespoon cornstarch
½ teaspoon salt
¼ teaspoon pepper
– leaf lettuce
1 (3-ounce) package cream
   cheese, softened
– coarsely cracked pepper
   melange
– assorted cocktail breads and
   crackers

Grease 7½ × 2½ × 2-inch loaf pan. Heat oven to 350°. In medium skillet, combine sausage, chicken livers, onion, bacon and garlic. Cook over medium-high heat, stirring occasionally, until cooked through (10 to 12 minutes). Drain well; cool. In food processor, process meat mixture and wine until smooth and creamy. Add bread crumbs, eggs, cornstarch, salt and pepper; continue processing until well blended. Pour mixture into greased pan; cover with foil. Place pan in shallow baking pan; pour hot water around loaf pan to a depth of ½ inch. Bake until set (about 1 hour). Cool about 45 minutes. Refrigerate, covered, several hours or overnight.

To Serve: Arrange leaf lettuce on serving plate. Run blade of knife around edge of pâté. Unmold onto serving plate. Spread top of pâté with cream cheese; sprinkle with pepper. Serve with breads and crackers.

*Amount: 2½ cups.*

# BRIE...BEYOND THE BASICS

▼

*Brie or Camembert can be used interchangeably for all three unique variations.*

**Apricot 'n Brandy Brie:** Place 1 (8-ounce) Brie round in center of microwavable plate. Microwave (LOW, 10% power) 2½ to 3½ minutes, rotating plate ½ turn after 1 minute. Let stand 3 minutes. Poke holes in top of Brie with tines of fork. Combine ⅓ cup apricot preserves and 2 tablespoons brandy in microwavable dish. Microwave (MEDIUM, 50% power) 1 minute. Pour over Brie; garnish with grapes.

**Chutney 'n Brie:** Place 1 (8-ounce) Brie round in center of microwavable plate. Microwave (LOW, 10% power) 2½ to 3½ minutes, rotating plate ½ turn after 1 minute. Let stand 3 minutes. In 1-cup glass measure, microwave (MEDIUM, 50% power) ½ cup chutney 1 minute. Pour over Brie; sprinkle with roasted salted nuts and sliced green onion.

**Herb 'n Nut Brie:** Combine 2 teaspoons butter and 2 tablespoons sliced almonds in microwavable cup. Sprinkle with ⅛ teaspoon each of tarragon and thyme, crumbled. Microwave (HIGH) 1 minute. Spoon over 1 (4½-ounce) Brie round on microwavable plate. Microwave (MEDIUM, 50% power) until cheese softens (about 1 minute).

# VEGETABLE CRUDITÉS 'N TORTELLINI TRAY

*Crisp crudités are partnered with al dente tortellini for a showy spread of dippers.*

1 (2-pound) head cauliflower
1 (2-pound) bunch broccoli
2 (8-inch) zucchini squash
2 (8-inch) yellow summer squash
1 (1¾-pound) jicama, peeled

1 (9-ounce) package fresh spinach tortellini with chicken and prosciutto
1 (9-ounce) package fresh egg tortellini with chicken and prosciutto
1 cup Italian dressing
– Fresh Basil Dip (below)
– frilled wooden picks

Cut cauliflower and broccoli into 1 to 1½-inch florets. Cut squash into ¼-inch slices. Cut jicama into ¼-inch slices, then into 4 × ¼-inch strips. Refrigerate vegetables in separate containers. Cook tortellini according to package directions; drain. Marinate pasta in Italian dressing. Refrigerate, covered, several hours. Prepare dip.

To Serve: Spoon dip into attractive bowl in center of large tray. Arrange vegetables in separate sections around bowl, alternating colors. Drain tortellini; insert pick in center of each. Arrange in a section on tray.

*20 to 30 servings.*

**Fresh Basil Dip:** Combine 1½ cups each of mayonnaise and reduced-fat sour cream, ½ cup each of freshly grated Romano Cheese and minced fresh basil and 2 teaspoons each minced fresh oregano and minced garlic. Refrigerate, covered, several hours or overnight.

*Amount: 3 cups.*

# NO-BAKE CRACKER SNACKER

*Here's a crunchy, well-seasoned munchie to have on hand for snacking or packing in festive tins for hostess gifts or college student "care packages."*

2 (6-ounce) boxes corn bugle snacks, original flavor
1 (9½-ounce) box mini-round cheese-flavored crackers
1 (10-ounce) package soup and oyster crackers
1 (6-ounce) package original flavor tiny goldfish crackers

4 cups pretzel sticks
2 teaspoons dried dill weed
1 teaspoon lemon pepper
¼ teaspoon garlic powder
1 (0.4-ounce) package original Ranch salad dressing mix
¾ cup buttery flavor popcorn oil

In large roaster, combine bugle snacks, all crackers and pretzels. In small bowl, combine dill, lemon pepper, garlic powder and salad dressing mix. Sprinkle evenly over dry snacks. Slowly add oil, stopping occasionally to gently toss with rubber spatula or wooden spoon. Store at room temperature in covered container for up to 1 week.

*Amount: 24 cups.*

# SOUTHWESTERN BLACK BEAN DIP

▼

*Black beans mingle magnificently with colorful accompaniments – a feast for the eyes as well as the palate.*

| | |
|---|---|
| 1 (8-ounce) package bacon, coarsely chopped | ½ cup chopped red bell pepper |
| 1 small onion, chopped (½ cup) | ½ cup chopped yellow bell pepper |
| 2 (15-ounce) cans Cuban-style black beans, drained | ¼ cup thinly sliced green onions, including some tops |
| 1 tablespoon chili powder | 4 ounces colby-jack cheese, shredded (1 cup) |
| 1 teaspoon red pepper sauce | 1 tablespoon snipped fresh cilantro |
| 1 (6-ounce) carton frozen avocado dip, thawed | |
| ¼ cup reduced-fat sour cream | – blue and white corn tortilla chips |

In large skillet, fry bacon until crisp; remove from pan and drain, reserving drippings. Return 2 teaspoons bacon drippings to skillet; add onion and sauté until tender. In medium bowl, mash beans; stir in bacon, onion, chili powder and red pepper sauce. Mound bean mixture in center of 9-inch quiche pan or serving platter; spoon avocado dip and sour cream on top. Sprinkle with bell peppers, green onions, cheese and cilantro. Serve with tortilla chips.

*10 to 15 servings.*

# PICO DE GALLO

▼

*When garden-fresh tomatoes are ripe for the picking, 'tis the season for showcasing their incomparable flavor with this zesty relish. Cilantro, or fresh coriander, is known for its unique pungent flavor.*

| | |
|---|---|
| 5 large ripe tomatoes, chopped | ⅓ cup chopped fresh cilantro |
| ½ cup chopped green onions | 1 teaspoon snipped fresh oregano |
| 1 to 2 jalapeño peppers, seeded, minced | ¼ teaspoon salt |
| 1½ teaspoons minced garlic | ⅛ teaspoon pepper |
| ¼ cup lemon juice | – tortilla chips (optional) |

Combine all ingredients except tortilla chips. Refrigerate, covered, several hours. Serve with tortilla chips or as a topping on Mexican dishes.

*Amount: 6 cups.*

# GUACAMOLE

▼

*This "butter pear" makes a great accompaniment for Mexican-inspired entrées, a topper for garden fresh tomatoes or a sandwich spread with your favorite meats or poultry, cheeses and lettuce.*

| | |
|---|---|
| 4 medium ripe avocados, peeled, seeded, coarsely chopped | 2 tablespoons lemon juice |
| | 1½ teaspoons seasoned salt |
| | ½ cup salsa |

Process all ingredients in food processor until smooth and well blended. Cover tightly with plastic wrap touching spread; refrigerate up to 2 hours before serving.

*Amount: 2½ cups.*

# FIESTA TORTE

▼

*Whether you're celebrating Cinco de Mayo or another occasion, this festive appetizer is bound to turn any party into a fiesta.*

2 (8-ounce) packages cream cheese, softened
1 (8-ounce) package shredded sharp Cheddar cheese (2 cups)
1 (1¼-ounce) package taco seasoning mix
1 (16-ounce) carton sour cream, divided

3 eggs
1 (4-ounce) can diced green chiles, drained
½ cup diced red bell pepper
½ cup hot salsa
1 (6-ounce) carton frozen avocado dip, thawed
– diced tomato
– tortilla chips

Heat oven to 350°. In large mixer bowl, beat cream cheese, Cheddar cheese and taco seasoning until fluffy. Stir in 1 cup of the sour cream; set remainder aside. Beat in eggs, one at a time, blending well after each addition. Fold in chiles and red pepper. Pour into 8½ or 9-inch springform pan. Bake until center of torte is just about firm (40 to 45 minutes). Cool on wire rack 10 minutes. Combine remaining sour cream with salsa; spread over top of torte. Continue baking until partially set around edges (5 to 8 minutes longer). Cool on wire rack 30 minutes. Refrigerate several hours or overnight.

To Serve: Run sharp knife carefully around edge of pan. Release side of pan; place on serving plate. Spread avocado dip over top of torte; garnish with tomato. Serve with tortilla chips.

*20 to 25 servings.*

# EMPANADAS

▼

*Festive foldovers of spicy ground beef encased in a rich cottage cheese pastry. They freeze beautifully and are a boon to busy cooks who keep them frozen for impromptu baking and entertaining.*

¾ cup margarine or butter
2½ cups flour
1 (12-ounce) carton small curd cottage cheese
7 to 8 tablespoons cold water
1 pound lean ground beef
½ cup minced onion
1½ teaspoons salt

½ teaspoon cayenne
½ teaspoon chili powder
¼ teaspoon pepper
¼ teaspoon garlic salt
– zipper closure food storage bag
– Pico de Gallo (page 38) or
– salsa (optional)

Cut margarine into flour with pastry blender until mixture resembles coarse crumbs. Gently stir in cottage cheese. Sprinkle in water, 1 tablespoon at a time, stirring until all flour is moistened. Gather dough into 2 flat balls. Refrigerate, covered, about 30 minutes. Brown ground beef in skillet with onion, salt, cayenne, chili powder, pepper and garlic salt; cool. (Ground beef mixture needs to be finely chopped.) On lightly floured surface, roll one ball of dough to about ¼-inch thickness. Cut with 2-inch round cookie cutter. Spoon 1 teaspoon meat mixture in center of dough circle; fold over to form a half circle. Seal edges with fork. Freeze on baking sheets until firm; transfer to food storage bag. Freeze up to 2 months.

To Bake: Heat oven to 400°. Place frozen empanadas on lightly greased baking sheet. Bake until golden brown (about 25 minutes). Serve immediately with Pico de Gallo or salsa, if desired.

*Amount: about 5 dozen appetizers.*

# OLIVE MEDLEY

▼

*A tantalizing, tri-colored selection of olives with a robust marinade! An attractive selection for a large party appetizer or buffet table relish.*

| | |
|---|---|
| 1 (14-ounce) jar plain queen green olives | ½ cup olive oil |
| 1 (16-ounce) jar Calamata olives | 2 cloves garlic, slivered |
| 1 (16-ounce) jar Greek black olives | 1 tablespoon fresh rosemary, stems removed |
| 1 medium lemon | ½ teaspoon coarsely ground black pepper |
| | 3 small dried hot chiles |
| | ½ cup sliced green onions |

Drain olives. Remove peel from lemon in strips. In medium bowl, combine lemon strips with remaining ingredients; stir in olives. Refrigerate, covered, several hours or overnight.

To Serve: Remove olives from liquid with slotted spoon; arrange in serving bowl.

*Amount: 6 cups.*

**Tip:** Olives may be stored, undrained, up to 3 days.

# CAPONATA

▼

*Bring rich Mediterranean flavors to your appetizer repertoire by combining the understated eggplant with a pleasurable potpourri of enhancements.*

| | |
|---|---|
| ¼ cup olive oil | ½ cup Spanish pitted olives, drained, sliced |
| 1 teaspoon sugar | 2 tablespoons small capers, drained |
| 1½ cups chopped onions | 2 tablespoons red wine vinegar |
| 1 (30-ounce) jar spaghetti sauce | 1 tablespoon snipped fresh basil |
| 3 cups finely chopped eggplant | 1½ teaspoons minced garlic |
| 1 green bell pepper, chopped (1 cup) | – Crostini (below) |
| ½ cup shredded carrot | |

In large skillet, heat oil and sugar over medium heat; stir in onions. Reduce heat to medium-low; continue cooking onions until caramelized (about 15 minutes), stirring often. Stir in remaining ingredients, except Crostini. Simmer, stirring occasionally, until vegetables are tender (15 to 20 minutes). Refrigerate, covered, several hours or overnight.

To Serve: Spoon Caponata into serving bowl; spread on Crostini.

*Amount: 4 cups.*

# CROSTINI

▼

*Have these crisp golden rounds on hand to serve with all manner of savory spreads. An appealing, versatile alternative to crackers, they are especially tasty topped with Caponata and pâtés.*

| | |
|---|---|
| 1 baguette French bread | ⅓ cup olive oil |

Heat oven to broil. Slice baguette into ¼-inch slices. Brush both sides with olive oil; arrange on baking sheet. Broil 6 inches from heat source until golden brown (about 2 minutes). Turn, continue broiling until golden brown (1½ to 2 minutes). Remove to wire rack to cool. Store in airtight container up to 5 days.

*Amount: about 55 slices.*

**Tip:** Watch closely to prevent burning.

# ITALIAN CHEESE CRUST TOPPERS

*These versatile pre-baked cheese pizza crusts, serve as a fabulous foundation for a multitude of toppings and spreads. Assemble ahead, if desired and bake just before serving.*

Arrange 1 or more 6-inch pre-baked cheese pizza crusts on baking sheet. Layer with any topping combination below (amounts given are for 1 crust). Refrigerate, covered, several hours or overnight, if desired.

To Serve: Heat oven to 450°. Uncover crust; bake until cheese is melted and bubbly (8 to 11 minutes). Cut into wedges; serve immediately.

*1 cheese pizza crust.*

**Asparagus, Pepper and Cheese:**
- ½ cup shredded Monterey Jack cheese
- ½ teaspoon minced garlic
- 5 spears frozen asparagus, thawed, drained
- 1 roasted sweet red pepper, drained, cut into strips (from 14-ounce jar)
- 1 tablespoon freshly grated Parmesan cheese

**Three Cheese and Tomato:**
- ¼ cup shredded Swiss cheese
- ¼ cup shredded mozzarella cheese
- ¼ cup freshly grated Parmesan cheese
- 3 marinated sun-dried tomatoes, drained, chopped
- ½ tablespoon snipped fresh basil
- ¼ teaspoon minced garlic

**Hot Pepper:**
- ½ cup shredded Monterey Jack cheese
- 2 tablespoons hot pepper rings, drained

**Honey Mustard and Prosciutto:**
- 1 tablespoon honey mustard
- ½ cup shredded colby-jack cheese
- 1 thin slice prosciutto, julienne-cut

**Creamy Lobster:**
- 2 tablespoons cocktail sauce
- ¼ cup salad style imitation lobster
- ¼ cup shredded fontina cheese

**Chicken, Peppers and Pine Nuts:**
- ½ cup shredded fontina cheese
- 1½ teaspoons snipped fresh basil
- ½ teaspoon minced garlic
- 1 thin slice cooked chicken breast, julienne-cut
- 2 tablespoons sweet fried peppers with onions
- 1 tablespoon pine nuts

Basil

# MUSHROOM 'N GORGONZOLA BUNDLES

▼

*Tender pastry "bundles" encase a marvelous mushroom-cheese filling. Prepared puff pastry makes preparation a breeze and gives these appetizers special-occasion status.*

24 (1-inch) mushrooms
½ (17¼-ounce) package frozen puff pastry, thawed

4 ounces Gorgonzola cheese
1 egg, slightly beaten

Lightly grease baking sheet. Heat oven to 400°. Rinse and pat mushrooms dry; twist off stems. On lightly floured surface, roll puff pastry into a rectangle approximately 10 × 15-inches. Cut pastry into 2½-inch squares. Fill each mushroom cap with a rounded ½ teaspoon Gorgonzola cheese. Place 1 filled mushroom in center of each pastry square. Draw all 4 corners up to form a small bundle. Carefully pinch center together to form a small knob. Brush each bundle lightly with egg. Bake on greased baking sheet until golden brown (about 10 minutes).

*Amount: 24 appetizers.*

**Tip:** Bundles may be prepared up to 12 hours ahead. Refrigerate, covered. Remove from refrigerator 30 minutes before baking. Brush with beaten egg. Bake as directed.

# STUFFED BELGIAN ENDIVE 'N RADICCHIO

▼

*These unique greens, though different, are very compatible in this exceptionally pretty appetizer platter.*

1 (8-ounce) package provolone cheese, diced (¼ inch)
4 ounces hard salami, diced (¼ inch)
1 (7-ounce) jar roasted sweet red peppers, drained, coarsely chopped
2 tablespoons olive oil

1½ tablespoons lemon juice
1 tablespoon snipped fresh basil
½ teaspoon pepper
2 heads Belgian endive (16 leaves)
1 small head radicchio (16 leaves)

In medium bowl, combine all ingredients except endive and radicchio. Refrigerate, covered, several hours. Separate, wash and drain endive and radicchio leaves. If necessary, trim radicchio. Spoon 1 tablespoon cheese mixture into each leaf; arrange on serving platter. Refrigerate, covered, up to 2 hours.

*Amount: 32 appetizers.*

*Belgian endive is a small enlongated head of tightly packed leaves with a slightly bitter flavor. It is grown in complete darkness to prevent it from turning green.*

*Radicchio is an Italian red leafed chicory with burgundy-red leaves and creamy white stalks and veins. The leaves are tender but firm with an appealing slightly bitter flavor.*

*Radicchio*

# DEVILED EGGS

▼

*Readily available refinements transform this classic family favorite into an always-appreciated appetizer or meal accompaniment.*

12 eggs, hard-cooked, peeled
½ cup mayonnaise
1 teaspoon prepared mustard
¼ teaspoon seasoned salt
⅛ teaspoon cayenne

1 (1-quart) size zipper closure food storage bag
– leaf lettuce
– snipped fresh herbs or caviar (optional)

Cut eggs in half lengthwise; scoop out yolks and set whites aside. Mash yolks with fork or pastry blender until fine. Combine with mayonnaise, mustard, salt and cayenne until well mixed. Spoon mixture into food bag; seal. Snip hole in corner of bag. Pipe yolk mixture into egg white halves. Arrange on lettuce-lined serving plate. Garnish with herbs or caviar.

### *Amount: 24 appetizers.*

**Variations:**  Any one of the following can be stirred into yolk mixture
• 1 tablespoon curry powder
• 2 tablespoons chutney
• 2 tablespoons snipped fresh chervil, cilantro or dill

# PISTACHIO 'N PHYLLO PINWHEELS

▼

*Collect compliments with these pistachio-studded pinwheels. Preparing these tasty morsels ahead and freezing them makes for hassle-free serving on party day.*

⅓ cup finely chopped onion
1 teaspoon minced garlic
1 tablespoon butter
1 (8-ounce) package cream cheese, softened
2 egg yolks
8 drops Tabasco

¼ teaspoon Worcestershire
2 teaspoons lemon juice
½ cup finely chopped pistachios
9 phyllo sheets, thawed
½ cup butter, melted
2 to 4 tablespoons finely chopped pistachios

Sauté onion and garlic in 1 tablespoon butter until soft (2 to 4 minutes). Beat cream cheese, egg yolks, Tabasco, Worcestershire and lemon juice until smooth; stir in onion mixture and ½ cup chopped pistachios. Unroll phyllo; arrange 9 sheets between pieces of waxed paper. Cover waxed paper with damp towel to prevent drying. Remove 1 phyllo sheet, place on another piece of waxed paper; brush with butter. Cover with 2 more phyllo sheets, brushing each with butter. Spoon ⅓ of pistachio mixture along long end of phyllo; roll up tightly, jelly roll fashion, beginning with filled end. Brush roll with butter; wrap in plastic wrap. Refrigerate. Repeat with remaining phyllo and filling to make 2 more rolls.

To Bake: Grease 10 × 15-inch jelly roll pan. Heat oven to 375°. Cut rolls into ¾ to 1 inch pieces; place filling side up, 1-inch apart on greased jelly roll pan. Sprinkle with remaining pistachios. Bake until golden brown (12 to 15 minutes). Serve warm.

### *Amount: 4 to 5 dozen appetizers.*

**Tip:**  Filled phyllo rolls can be wrapped in foil and frozen. Thaw, cut and bake as directed. To reheat baked appetizers, arrange 12 in a circle on microwavable plate. Microwave (HIGH) 1 minute.

# SAVORY PHYLLO SQUARES

▼

*Hot, bite-size squares with an unexpected "crust" of buttery, layered phyllo sheets. "Fresh" is the password here with freshly grated cheese, fresh herbs and garden fresh cherry tomatoes.*

¼ cup butter or margarine, melted
½ teaspoon minced garlic
7 phyllo sheets, thawed
½ cup freshly grated Parmesan or Romano cheese

1 (8-ounce) carton 4 cheese gourmet blend
2 tablespoons snipped fresh basil
2 teaspoons snipped fresh oregano
1 cup thinly sliced onion rings
5 cherry tomatoes, sliced

Heat oven to 375°. Combine butter and garlic; brush baking sheet with butter mixture. Unfold phyllo sheets on flat surface. Place 1 phyllo sheet on baking sheet. Brush with butter; sprinkle with 1 tablespoon Parmesan cheese. Repeat until all phyllo and butter are used. Sprinkle with remaining Parmesan cheese and cheese blend. Sprinkle with herbs, onion rings and tomato slices. Bake until phyllo edges are golden brown (15 to 20 minutes). Cut into squares. Serve warm.

*Amount: 30 (3 × 2½-inch) appetizers.*

# CRACKER BREAD ROLL-UPS

▼

*This hearty appetizer is equally engaging as a sandwich alternative for luncheon and supper menus.*

1 (8-ounce) package cream cheese, softened
1 tablespoon prepared white horseradish
2 teaspoons Dijon mustard
½ teaspoon salt
¼ teaspoon pepper

½ (17-ounce) package soft cracker bread, room temperature
1 pound thinly sliced deli Italian roast beef
18 spinach leaves, stems removed
1 red bell pepper, cut into julienne strips

Combine cream cheese, horseradish, mustard, salt and pepper. Cut 1 round of cracker bread in half. Spread ⅓ cup cream cheese mixture on cracker bread half. Arrange ⅓ roast beef slices over surface up to 1-inch of rounded edge. Top beef with 6 spinach leaves. About 1-inch from straight edge, arrange several red pepper strips in a row. Starting at straight edge, roll up tightly, jelly-roll fashion. Place roll on plastic wrap; wrap tightly. Repeat with remaining filling ingredients and 2 more cracker bread halves. Refrigerate several hours or overnight.

To Serve: Cut rolls into 1-inch slices.

*Amount: 36 (1-inch) slices.*

**Variation:** Substitute 2 (4-ounce) packages soft spreadable cheese with garlic and herbs for cream cheese, horseradish, mustard, salt and pepper in recipe above. Combine cheese with 8-ounces imitation crab, flaked, and 2 to 3 teaspoons milk. Omit beef. Spread ⅓ cheese-crab mixture on each cracker bread half. Top with spinach leaves and red pepper strips.

*Cracker bread is an Armenian tradition. Soft cracker bread, right out of the package, makes delicate yet durable appetizers and creative sandwiches.*

# BUFFALO WINGS

▼

*Overnight marinating is the first step in preparing these hot and hearty drumettes. Whether you grill or bake, you will have cooked up a winner to spice up any get-together.*

¾ cup cider vinegar
¼ cup lemon juice
2 tablespoons vegetable oil
1 tablespoon Worcestershire
1 tablespoon minced garlic
1 to 2 teaspoons Louisiana hot sauce
2 tablespoons sugar
1 teaspoon ground cumin
1 teaspoon celery salt

1 teaspoon coarsely ground pepper
½ teaspoon crushed red pepper
4 pounds chicken wing drumettes
1 jumbo zipper closure food storage bag
1 (16-ounce) jar blue cheese dressing
– celery sticks

In large bowl, combine vinegar, lemon juice, oil, Worcestershire, garlic, hot sauce, sugar, cumin, celery salt and peppers. Rinse chicken; drain and pat dry. Place chicken in food storage bag. Pour marinade over chicken; seal bag. Refrigerate overnight, turning bag occasionally.

**Grill Method:** Prepare grill. Place chicken wings and marinade in rectangular microwavable baking dish; cover with waxed paper. Microwave (HIGH) until exterior is no longer pink (10 to 15 minutes), stirring twice to rearrange. Spray grill rack with no stick cooking spray. Using direct heat cooking method, arrange hot chicken wings on grill, 4 to 5 inches above medium-hot coals. Grill chicken, uncovered, turning constantly until crispy and golden brown (20 to 25 minutes).

**Oven Method:** Heat oven to 350°. Spray broiler pan rack with no stick cooking spray. Arrange drained chicken wings on rack. Bake until browned and cooked through (45 to 50 minutes).

Serve hot with blue cheese dressing as a dipping sauce, and with celery sticks.

*Amount: about 40 wings.*

**Tip:** For a little "zing," use 1 teaspoon Louisiana hot sauce!
For a moderate amount of "zing," use 1½ teaspoons Louisiana hot sauce!!
For a lot of "zing," use 2 teaspoons Louisiana hot sauce!!!

# MEATBALLS 'N LINGONBERRIES

▼

*With a mingling of Scandinavian and German flavors and just a dash of French mustard, these lightly glazed meatballs will bring international intrigue to a holiday open house buffet table.*

1 pound bulk pork sausage
1 pound lean ground beef
1 (8-ounce) can sauerkraut, drained, chopped (1 cup)
¾ cup minced onion
1½ cups soft rye bread crumbs
1 egg, slightly beaten

1 teaspoon caraway seed
1 teaspoon ground cardamom
1 teaspoon salt
¼ teaspoon pepper
1 (14-ounce) jar lingonberries in sugar
¼ cup chili sauce
2 teaspoons Dijon mustard

Heat oven to 375°. Combine sausage, ground beef, sauerkraut, onion, bread crumbs, egg, caraway seed, cardamom, salt and pepper until thoroughly mixed. Shape rounded teaspoonfuls of mixture into 1-inch balls. Arrange on 10 × 15-inch jelly roll pan. Bake 10 minutes. Spoon meatballs into 2-quart casserole. Refrigerate, covered.

To Serve: Heat oven to 350°. Combine lingonberries, chili sauce and mustard in small saucepan. Bring to a boil; pour over meatballs. Bake, uncovered, until bubbly (25 to 30 minutes), stirring after 15 minutes and just before serving.

*Amount: about 90 meatballs.*

# MINI SMORREBROD

▼

*A sumptuous Scandinavian specialty of artistically arranged ingredients to please every palate. Wonderful for light luncheon fare with chilled soup or on a tea table as well as for canapes.*

Select cocktail bread. Butter evenly and thickly. Arrange any of the following to completely cover bread in an attractive design:

- Pickled herring over lettuce leaf; garnish with green onion rings and slivers of tomato.

- Thinly sliced roast beef over leaf lettuce; garnish with gherkin and mustard pickle slices.

- Lettuce leaf topped with sliced hard-cooked egg and a layer of tiny cooked shrimp; garnish with a sprig of fresh dill.

- Spread bread with a mixture of softened cream cheese, chopped nuts and chopped radishes; garnish with sliced grape.

- Spread bread with liver pâté; garnish with sliced pickled mushrooms, tomato slice and a sprig of fresh dill or parsley.

- Lettuce leaf topped with thin slice of Swiss cheese and cooked shrimp; garnish with black caviar.

- Lettuce leaf topped with alternating cooked cold asparagus spears and long chunks of crabmeat; garnish with lemon curl.

# HORS D'OEUVRES...IN A HURRY

▼

*Company's coming and you're caught by surprise! Speedy and sumptuous snacks can be supplied on very short notice with a few simple ingredients. With very little fuss, you can present a festive welcome.*

**Caviar Spread:** Spread 1 (2-ounce) jar red or black caviar, drained, on top of 1 (8-ounce) block of cream cheese. Sprinkle with ¼ cup sliced green onions. Serve with crackers.

**Wonton Chips:** Heat oven to 350°. Cut wonton skin in half diagonally. Brush with melted butter; sprinkle with freshly grated Parmesan cheese and Greek seasoning. Bake until crisp (7 to 9 minutes).

**Crab Claws:** Claws are usually sold frozen and ready to eat. Heat according to package directions and serve with melted butter or cocktail sauce for dipping.

**Mini Filled Cups:** Fill mini cream puffs, frozen puff pastry cups or mini croustades with deli ham spread, chicken salad, tuna or flavored cream cheese. Garnish with herb sprigs or green or ripe olive slices.

**Pesto 'n Crostini:** Combine 1 (6-ounce) carton pesto, drained, with 1 (8-ounce) carton whipped cream cheese and ¼ cup chopped toasted pine nuts (pignoli). Refrigerate, covered, 1 hour. Serve with Crostini (page 40).

**Fruit and Cheese Platter:** Three wedges of soft spreadable cheese served with small clusters of red, green and black grapes and lavosh crackers.

**Smoked Salmon Strips:** Place salmon strips on crackers that have been spread with herb cream cheese.

**Spicy Lingonberries on Camembert:** Stir ½ teaspoon ground cardamom into 1 (10-ounce) jar lingonberries. Place Camembert on lettuce-lined plate; top with berries and serve with crackers.

# Soups & Stews

Simple and soothing, chilled and refreshing, rich and restorative — in a word, soup! Every day is a perfect day to prepare and serve soup because of the infinite varieties to suit each season, time of day, role on the menu, personal taste and available ingredients.

The best soups and stews contain the freshest, most flavorful ingredients available, judicious seasonings and full-bodied chicken or beef broth. We suggest preparing these two basic stocks at your convenience and keeping them on hand in the freezer for impromptu additions to soup kettle, stew pot, slow cooker or Dutch oven.

Before bringing bowls to the table, add a final festive touch — an appropriate garnish. Choose a creative topper that will add color, texture, contrast, flavor and/or seasoning. Then, serve with pride.

# STRAWBERRY YOGURT SOUP

▼

*Invite this rosy cooler, reminiscent of Scandinavian fruit soups, to your summer table, either as a first course or a light dessert.*

1 (16-ounce) package frozen strawberries, thawed, drained
2 tablespoons powdered sugar
1 (8-ounce) carton vanilla lowfat yogurt

1 tablespoon frozen orange juice concentrate, thawed
¼ teaspoon almond extract
– vanilla lowfat yogurt
– ground nutmeg

In food processor or blender, process strawberries, powdered sugar, 1 carton yogurt, orange juice concentrate and almond extract until smooth. Refrigerate, covered, until very cold. Ladle into soup bowls; top each with a dollop of yogurt and a sprinkle of nutmeg.

*Amount: 3 cups.*

# CARROT SOUP

▼

*Dry sherry and gingerroot add intrigue to this light soup. It makes a perfect fireside sipper served in mugs or first course served in bowls.*

¼ cup margarine or butter
1 large onion, chopped (1⅓ cups)
2 tablespoons finely minced gingerroot
1½ teaspoons minced garlic

2 pounds carrots, sliced ½-inch thick (4 cups)
4 (14½-ounce) cans ⅓-less-salt chicken broth
1 cup dry sherry
– snipped fresh chives

In large Dutch oven, melt margarine. Sauté onion, gingerroot and garlic until tender (about 10 minutes). Stir in carrots, chicken broth and sherry. Bring to a boil. Reduce heat; simmer, uncovered, until carrots are soft (45 to 50 minutes). In blender or food processor, process half of soup; repeat with remainder. Refrigerate, covered, several hours or overnight. Reheat just before serving. Garnish with chives.

*Amount: 8 cups.*

# BRIE SOUP

▼

*Ladle this rich, satiny-smooth do-ahead soup into soup bowls and serve it immediately before the apple pieces begin to darken.*

¼ cup margarine or butter
½ cup chopped onion
½ cup thinly sliced celery
¼ cup flour
1½ cups milk

2 (10½-ounce) cans chicken broth
12 ounces Brie with rind, cubed
1 Granny Smith apple, finely chopped

In large saucepan, melt margarine. Sauté onion and celery until tender (4 to 5 minutes). Blend in flour. Stir in milk and chicken broth. Cook over medium heat, stirring occasionally, until sauce comes to a boil; boil and stir 1 minute. Stir in cheese until melted. Process in food processor or blender until smooth. Refrigerate, covered, several hours or overnight. Return to saucepan; stir in apple. Cook over medium-low heat until soup is heated through and apples are slightly softened (about 20 minutes). Serve immediately.

*Amount: 5 cups.*

*Beef 'n Bean Chili*
*page 54*

# CHICKEN BROTH

▼

*Basics are never boring when they are as important as this one to every cook's recipe repertoire. This makes a superior stock to add whenever chicken broth or stock is required.*

| | |
|---|---|
| 1 (5 to 6-pound) stewing chicken, halved | 2 ribs celery, cut into 2-inch chunks |
| 2 large carrots, cut into 2-inch chunks | ½ cup chopped fresh parsley |
| 1 large parsnip, peeled, cut up | 12 cups water |
| 1 large onion, quartered | 1 tablespoon salt |
| | 12 peppercorns |
| | 2 tablespoons chicken base |
| | – cheesecloth |

Combine all ingredients except chicken base and cheesecloth in 5-quart Dutch oven. Bring to a boil; reduce heat and simmer until chicken is tender (about 2 hours). Remove chicken; cool slightly. Refrigerate. (When chicken is cool, remove from bones; refrigerate or freeze for future use.) Stir chicken base into broth. Cook, uncovered, over medium-low heat about 30 minutes. Strain broth through cheesecloth-lined strainer into large bowl. Refrigerate broth, leaving fat layer on surface until ready to use. Cover broth when cool.

*Amount: about 8 cups.*

**Tip:** Chicken broth can be stored, tightly covered, in refrigerator 1 to 2 days or in freezer 1 month.

# CHICKEN NOODLE SOUP

▼

*Where is it written that you have to be "under the weather" to appreciate the rich homemade goodness of this made-from-scratch classic? When you have the broth and cooked poultry, preparation is streamlined.*

| | |
|---|---|
| 8 cups Chicken Broth (this page) | 1 cup chopped onion |
| 3 large carrots, sliced | ¼ teaspoon pepper |
| 2 large ribs celery, chopped | 2 cups dry egg noodles |
| | 4 cups cubed cooked chicken |

Bring chicken broth to a boil in large Dutch oven. Stir in vegetables and pepper. Simmer, covered, until vegetables are tender (20 to 30 minutes). Meanwhile, cook egg noodles according to package directions in boiling water with 1 teaspoon salt. Drain. Stir noodles and chicken into soup; heat through.

*Amount: 14 cups.*

**Variation:** One (9-ounce) package fresh pasta or one (12-ounce) package frozen egg noodles can be substituted for dry egg noodles. Cook according to package directions; drain. Stir into soup.

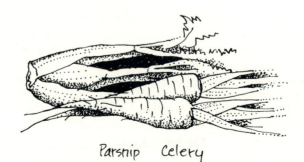

Parsnip   Celery

# BEEF BROTH

*This stock is the basis for a multitude of sauces, stews and soups – a very useful activity when you have extra time to spend in the kitchen.*

2 whole cloves
2 medium onions, quartered
2 ribs celery with leaves, cut into 2-inch pieces
1 carrot, sliced
2 pounds center-cut beef shank bones
2 pounds beef marrow bones
12 cups water
1 (7½-ounce) can whole tomatoes, undrained, cut up

1½ teaspoons salt
½ teaspoon dried thyme, crumbled
¼ teaspoon dried marjoram, crumbled
5 peppercorns
2 sprigs fresh parsley
½ teaspoon minced garlic
1 bay leaf
– cheesecloth
¾ teaspoon salt (optional)

Heat oven to 450°. Insert 1 whole clove in each of 2 onion quarters. Place onions, celery, carrot, beef shank and marrow bones in large roasting pan. Bake, uncovered, until bones are deeply browned (about 45 minutes), turning bones and vegetables occasionally. Transfer ingredients from roasting pan to 8-quart stockpot. Discard fat in roasting pan. Stir 2 cups of the water into roasting pan; heat and scrape to loosen any browned meat drippings. Pour hot liquid and 10 cups remaining water over bones and vegetables. Bring to a boil. Simmer, partially covered, 30 minutes.

Skim off any foam that rises to surface. Stir in tomatoes, 1½ teaspoons salt, thyme, marjoram, peppercorns, parsley, garlic and bay leaf. Simmer, partially covered, an additional 3 hours. Remove bones. (Remove meat from bones; refrigerate or freeze for future use.) Strain broth through cheesecloth-lined strainer into large bowl. Stir in ¾ teaspoon salt. Refrigerate broth, leaving fat layer on surface until ready to use. Cover broth when cool.

*Amount: about 8 cups.*

**Tip:** Beef broth can be stored, tightly covered, in refrigerator 1 to 2 days or in freezer 1 month.

# FRENCH ONION SOUP

*This European classic is the perfect showcase for your homemade beef stock. The irresistible aroma of this simmering will lure diners to the table. Enjoy it as the French do – topped with toasted bread and melted cheese.*

1½ pounds yellow onions, thinly sliced (about 7 cups)
¼ cup butter
½ teaspoon salt
1 teaspoon sugar
7 cups Beef Broth (this page)
2 teaspoons Worcestershire

⅛ teaspoon Tabasco
⅛ teaspoon pepper
– French bread, cut into 1-inch slices
– shredded Swiss or Gruyère cheese
– freshly grated Parmesan cheese

Cook onions in butter over low heat 15 minutes. Stir in salt and sugar; increase heat to medium-low. Cook, stirring almost continuously, until even, deep golden brown (25 to 30 minutes). Stir in beef broth, Worcestershire, Tabasco and pepper; simmer 30 to 40 minutes. Arrange bread on baking sheet; broil until lightly toasted on both sides. Sprinkle with Swiss cheese; broil until cheese is melted.

To Serve: Spoon soup into bowls, place bread on top and sprinkle with Parmesan.

*Amount: 9 cups.*

# HOT AND SOUR SOUP

▼

*This piquant Asian favorite has plenty of personality – the seasonings see to that! It features several ingredients considered basic to Chinese cooking – bamboo shoots, fresh gingerroot, dried mushrooms and scallions or green onions.*

½ ounce dried black
  mushrooms (½ cup)
½ pound boneless, skinless
  chicken breast, cut into
  julienne strips
2 tablespoons Oriental sesame
  oil
2 (14½-ounce) cans ⅓-less-salt
  chicken broth
½ cup canned sliced bamboo
  shoots, cut into julienne
  strips
¼ cup white vinegar
2 tablespoons soy sauce

1 teaspoon sugar
1 tablespoon minced
  gingerroot
⅛ to ¼ teaspoon cayenne
  pepper
¼ teaspoon pepper
8 ounces tofu, cut into ½-inch
  cubes
2 tablespoons cornstarch
2 tablespoons water
2 eggs, slightly beaten
3 tablespoons sliced green
  onions, including some
  green tops

Cover mushrooms with warm water and soak until soft (about 30 minutes); drain. Remove and discard tough stems. Cut mushrooms into thin strips. In Dutch oven, sauté chicken strips in sesame oil until chicken is tender (3 to 4 minutes). Stir in chicken broth; heat to boiling. Stir in mushrooms, bamboo shoots, vinegar, soy sauce, sugar, gingerroot, peppers and tofu. Heat soup over medium heat just until simmering. Combine cornstarch and water; stir into soup. Cook over medium heat, stirring constantly, until soup thickens slightly and all ingredients are heated through (about 5 minutes). Remove from heat; gradually stir in eggs. Serve in small bowls. Garnish with green onions.

*Amount: 6 cups.*

# TOMATO VEGETARIAN SOUP

▼

*Make a satisfying meatless meal out of this crowd pleaser. Chock full of colorful vegetables and pleasantly seasoned with dried herbs, it needs only crusty rolls, bread sticks or crackers as an accompaniment.*

2 ribs celery, diced
1 medium green bell pepper,
  diced
2 medium carrots, diced
1 medium zucchini, diced
¼ cup olive oil
1 (10-ounce) package frozen
  chopped broccoli, thawed,
  drained
1 (8-ounce) package frozen
  cauliflower, thawed, drained,
  chopped

3 (28-ounce) cans tomatoes,
  undrained, cut up
1 (46-ounce) can tomato juice
1 tablespoon salt
½ teaspoon pepper
3 tablespoons sugar
1½ teaspoons dried oregano,
  crumbled
1½ teaspoons dried basil,
  crumbled
½ teaspoon dried rosemary,
  crumbled
1 (10-ounce) package frozen
  tiny peas, thawed, drained

In 7-quart Dutch oven, sauté celery, green pepper, carrots and zucchini in oil (5 to 6 minutes). Stir in broccoli and cauliflower; sauté until vegetables are crisp-tender (about 5 minutes longer). Stir in remaining ingredients except peas. Bring to a boil; simmer, covered, 20 minutes. Stir in peas; simmer, covered, 10 minutes longer.

*Amount: about 22 cups.*

# TURKEY MINESTRONE SOUP

*Here's a tasty and nutritious use for a meaty turkey carcass. It is transformed into a hearty soup in under 2 hours and makes enough for a crowd or several flavorful family meals.*

1 meaty turkey carcass
¼ cup chicken base
1 bay leaf
10 cups water
2 (14½-ounce) cans stewed tomatoes, undrained
1 (15½-ounce) can great northern beans, drained
1 (15-ounce) can garbanzo beans, drained

2 potatoes, peeled, cubed (2 cups)
1 large onion, chopped (2 cups)
1½ teaspoons minced garlic
1 tablespoon dried basil, crumbled
½ teaspoon salt (optional)
¼ teaspoon pepper
½ cup broken dry spaghetti
1 (9-ounce) package frozen Italian green beans

Combine turkey carcass, chicken base, bay leaf and water in large stockpot or Dutch oven. Bring to a boil; reduce heat. Simmer, covered, 1 hour. Remove turkey carcass from broth; cool. Strain broth; return broth to stockpot. Remove turkey from bones; discard bones. Chop turkey; return to broth. Stir in tomatoes, beans, potatoes, onion, garlic, basil, salt and pepper. Bring to a boil; reduce heat and simmer 20 minutes. Stir in spaghetti and green beans; continue cooking until potatoes and pasta are tender (about 10 minutes).

*Amount: 18 to 20 cups.*

# COCK A LEEKIE

*Generations of Scots have savored this stewed chicken and leeks combination. There's nothing to rival it on a bone-chilling day, no matter where you live.*

1 (5-pound) stewing chicken, cut up
2 cups chopped onions
¼ cup snipped fresh parsley
1 cup sliced celery
¼ cup chopped celery leaves
4 teaspoons salt
½ teaspoon pepper

1 tablespoon sugar
10 cups water
2 tablespoons barley
3 to 4 leeks, cleaned and sliced (4 cups)
3 medium potatoes, peeled and cubed (about 3 cups)
– snipped fresh parsley

Combine chicken, onions, ¼ cup parsley, celery, celery leaves, salt, pepper, sugar and water in stockpot or Dutch oven. Bring to a boil; reduce heat and simmer, covered, until chicken is tender (about 2 hours). Remove chicken from broth; cool. Remove meat from bones; discard bones. Cut chicken into thin slices; return to broth with barley, leeks and potatoes. Simmer, covered, until barley and potatoes are tender (35 to 45 minutes). To Serve: Ladle into soup bowls; garnish with snipped parsley.

*Amount: 15 cups.*

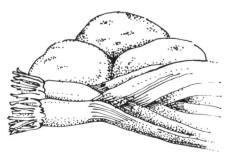

*Potatoes Leeks*

# CHICK PEA SOUP

▼

*Chick peas, popular in many European countries in soups and salads and in the Middle East in stews and spreads, are congenial with all manner of seasonings. We think you will be impressed with this departure from the old standbys.*

| | |
|---|---|
| 1 (1-pound) package dried chick peas | 2 bay leaves |
| 2 (46-ounce) cans chicken broth | 2 teaspoons minced garlic |
| 1 (1½ to 2-pound) beef soup bone | 2 cups chopped onions |
| 1 (1½ to 2-pound) ham shank | 2 carrots, shredded |
| ⅛ teaspoon curry powder | 2 cups diced potato (peeled or unpeeled) |
| | 2 cups finely shredded Napa cabbage |

Cover chick peas with water; soak overnight. Drain. In 4-quart Dutch oven, combine chick peas, chicken broth, soup bone, ham shank, curry powder, bay leaves, garlic, onions and carrots. Bring to a boil; reduce heat and simmer, covered, 3 hours. Stir in potato and cabbage; simmer 1 hour longer. Remove soup bone and ham shank. Cut meat into small pieces; discard bones. Return meat to soup. Discard bay leaves.

*Amount: about 10 cups.*

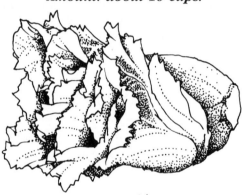

Napa Cabbage

# LENTIL SOUP

▼

*High in protein, lentils need no soaking before adding their considerable charm to European-style soups such as this.*

| | |
|---|---|
| 1 (16-ounce) package dried lentils | 1 (14½-ounce) can diced tomatoes |
| 2 tablespoons olive oil | 2 (46-ounce) cans chicken broth |
| ½ cup chopped Canadian bacon | ¾ cup uncooked rosamarina pasta |
| 1 cup chopped onion | ½ teaspoon salt |
| 1 cup chopped celery | ¼ teaspoon pepper |
| 2 cups thinly sliced carrots | – freshly grated Parmesan cheese |
| 1½ teaspoons minced garlic | |

Rinse lentils in strainer. Heat oil in Dutch oven. Cook bacon, onion, celery, carrots and garlic 5 minutes, stirring occasionally. Stir in lentils, tomatoes and chicken broth. Simmer, covered, 45 minutes. Stir in rosamarina, salt and pepper. Simmer, covered, until lentils and rosamarina are tender (about 15 minutes). Ladle into soup bowls; sprinkle with Parmesan.

*Amount: 16 cups.*

# BLACK BEAN SOUP

*Although the preparation is reminiscent of navy bean soup, the warm, sweet flavor of cumin and the unique consistency of the beans create quite another product. Oft-used in southwestern fare, black beans are frequently paired with ham or pork in soups, stews and other dishes.*

2 (12-ounce) packages dried black beans
2 tablespoons olive oil
3 cups chopped onions
1 tablespoon minced garlic
1 large smoked ham shank
2 (46-ounce) cans chicken broth
7 teaspoons ground cumin

1 tablespoon dried basil, crumbled
1 teaspoon salt
½ teaspoon pepper
⅛ teaspoon cayenne pepper
1 red bell pepper, diced
1 tablespoon brown sugar
4 carrots, chopped
– Crème Fraîche

Cover beans with water; soak overnight. Drain. Heat oil in large Dutch oven. Sauté onions and garlic until vegetables are tender (about 5 minutes). Stir in beans, ham shank, broth, cumin, basil, salt, pepper and cayenne. Bring to a boil; reduce heat to medium. Cook, uncovered, until beans are very tender (1½ to 2 hours). Remove ham shank; cool slightly. Pull off meat and shred. Return meat to Dutch oven with bell pepper, brown sugar and carrots; simmer 30 minutes. Ladle into soup bowls; top each with a dollop of Crème Fraîche.

*Amount: 14 cups.*

# WHITE CHILI

*You must try this lighter, whiter version of one of America's favorite casual dishes. Once chicken is cooked, canned beans and chiles mean quick-to-the-table preparation.*

1½ pounds split chicken breasts with ribs, skin removed
1 teaspoon olive oil
1 teaspoon minced garlic
1 cup chopped onion
1 (19-ounce) can cannellini beans, undrained
1 (15-ounce) can Great Northern beans, undrained

2 (4-ounce) cans diced green chiles, undrained
2 tablespoons snipped fresh cilantro
2 teaspoons ground cumin
¼ teaspoon salt
¼ teaspoon cayenne pepper
– shredded colby or Monterey Jack cheese
– tortilla chips

In large saucepan, add chicken to boiling salted water (3 cups water, 1 teaspoon salt). Reduce heat to low; simmer, covered, until chicken is fork-tender and juices run clear (20 to 25 minutes). Remove chicken from bones; cut into 1-inch pieces. Heat oil in Dutch oven; sauté garlic and onion over medium heat until onion is tender (4 to 5 minutes). Stir in chicken and remaining ingredients except cheese and tortilla chips; heat through. Ladle into soup bowls; sprinkle with cheese and crushed tortilla chips.

*Amount: 6 cups.*

Cilantro

# BEEF 'N BEAN CHILI
▼

*An upscale version of the everyday variety of chili uses stew meat instead of ground beef. No browning of the meat is required, just simple, slow simmering for maximum flavor and tenderness. Serve with colorful condiments artfully arranged in small bowls.*

- 2 pounds beef stew meat
- 2 cups chopped onions
- 1 tablespoon minced garlic
- ⅓ cup chili powder
- 2 tablespoons sugar
- 1 tablespoon ground cumin
- 4 teaspoons Louisiana hot sauce
- 1 teaspoon dried oregano, crumbled

- 1 teaspoon salt
- 1 (28-ounce) can crushed tomatoes with added purée
- 2 (15-ounce) cans pinto beans, drained
- 1 (15-ounce) can garbanzo beans, drained
- 1 (15-ounce) can kidney beans, drained
- – Quick Chili Bowls (below) (optional)

**CHILI CONDIMENTS**

- 1 (4-ounce) package shredded sharp Cheddar cheese (1 cup)
- 1 (4-ounce) package shredded Monterey Jack cheese (1 cup)

- 2 (2¼-ounce) cans sliced ripe olives, drained
- 1 (8-ounce) carton sour cream
- 1 (6-ounce) carton frozen guacamole, thawed
- 1 (½-ounce) package fresh cilantro, stems removed
- – sliced green onions
- – tortilla chips

Cut beef into bite-size pieces. Combine beef, onion, garlic, chili powder, sugar, cumin, hot sauce, oregano, salt and tomatoes in large Dutch oven. Bring to a boil; reduce heat. Simmer, partially covered, 1½ hours, stirring occasionally. Stir in beans. Simmer, uncovered, 30 minutes longer. Serve in Quick Chili Bowls or soup bowls, with condiments.

*8 servings.*

**Quick Chili Bowls:** Form and bake 2 (5.6-ounce) packages salad shells according to package directions. Spoon chili into shells just before serving.

**Tip:** Salad shells are found in the dairy department. They can be prepared 2 days ahead. Store in loosely covered container.

# POP-IN-THE-OVEN STEW
▼

*You can depend on this lazy-day delight to provide a marvelous meal with little effort. There's no need to brown the meat, no need to stir while baking. It's a no-fuss feast requiring few accompaniments.*

- 2 pounds boneless beef stew meat, cut into 1½-inch cubes
- 8 ribs celery, cut into 1-inch chunks
- 8 carrots, cut into 2-inch chunks
- 6 potatoes, peeled, quartered
- 2 large onions, peeled, cut up
- 1 cup water

- 1 (28-ounce) can whole tomatoes, undrained
- 1 teaspoon instant beef bouillon
- ⅓ cup instant tapioca
- 2 teaspoons salt
- ¼ teaspoon pepper
- 1 teaspoon dried basil, crumbled
- 1 teaspoon minced garlic

Combine all ingredients in Dutch oven. Bake, covered, in a 325° oven until meat and vegetables are tender (2½ to 3 hours).

*8 servings.*

**Variation:** Two (12-ounce) jars brown home-style gravy can be substituted for the tomatoes.

# EGGS & CHEESE

**E**ggs and cheese — truer "comfort foods" are hard to find. A grilled cheese sandwich or a scrambled egg are homey staples we have savored since childhood. Over the years as our palates have become more sophisticated, we have enlivened our menus with creative egg and cheese recipes and fresh approaches to wholesome preparation.

Our tribute to these two beautiful basics includes festive recipes with international flair like Eggs Benedict à la Crab, "eggstra" special brunch dishes like Country Breakfast Casserole, best bets for entertaining like Individual Eggs Mornay and Dilled Three Cheese Quiche and flavor-filled family favorites like Tortilla Breakfast Bundles and Brunch Pizza.

Whether you are feeding a lazy day brunch bunch or planning an elegant ladies' luncheon, you will find plenty of imaginative, nutritious ideas for showcasing eggs, cheese and your own special culinary skills.

# COUNTRY BREAKFAST CASSEROLE

▼

*A creamy, mild cheese and potato mixture is enlivened with spicy sausage and a splash of salsa.*

2 (12-ounce) packages frozen hot pork sausage, thawed
1 (2-pound) package frozen southern-style hash brown potatoes
1 cup minced onion, (1 medium)
2 cups milk
2 (8-ounce) packages shredded colby-jack cheese (4 cups), divided
½ teaspoon salt
6 eggs, slightly beaten
1 (12-ounce) carton salsa

Grease 9 × 13-inch glass baking dish. In medium skillet, brown sausage; drain. In large bowl, combine sausage, hash browns, onion, milk, 3 cups of the cheese, salt and eggs. Pour mixture into greased baking dish. Top with remaining 1 cup cheese. Refrigerate, covered, several hours or overnight.

Heat oven to 350°. Bake, uncovered, until knife inserted near center comes out clean (50 to 55 minutes). Let stand 10 minutes, covered. Cut into squares and serve warm with salsa.

*8 to 10 servings.*

# FRENCH TOAST...OVEN STYLE

▼

*Convenience plus a choice of creative toppings.*

4 eggs, beaten
1 cup milk
2 tablespoons sugar
1 teaspoon vanilla
1 teaspoon grated orange peel
¼ teaspoon ground cinnamon
12 diagonal slices French bread (1 inch thick)
– melted margarine or butter
1 large zipper closure freezer storage bag
– Orange Butter or Fluffy Cream (below) or, strawberry pourable fruit, warmed

In large bowl, combine eggs, milk, sugar, vanilla, orange peel and cinnamon. Arrange bread slices on 10 × 15-inch jelly roll pan. Pour egg mixture over bread and let stand until partially absorbed; turn slices and allow bread to completely absorb remaining mixture. Place in freezer, uncovered, until firm (about 1 hour). Using wide spatula, loosen slices from pan. Place slices in freezer storage bag; seal and freeze until needed.

To Bake: Grease 10 × 15-inch jelly roll pan. Heat oven to 450°. Place frozen slices on greased pan. Brush top side of each slice with melted margarine. Bake 8 minutes. Turn slices; brush with margarine. Continue baking until lightly browned (about 8 minutes). Top with Orange Butter, Fluffy Cream or pourable fruit.

*4 to 6 servings.*

**Orange Butter:** Combine ½ cup softened butter, 2 tablespoons grated orange peel and 1 tablespoon thawed frozen orange juice concentrate until well blended. Refrigerate until ready to serve.

*Amount: ½ cup.*

**Fluffy Cream:** Combine ⅓ cup powdered sugar and ¼ cup reduced-fat sour cream; fold into 1 cup thawed frozen whipped topping. Refrigerate until ready to serve.

*Amount: about 1⅔ cups.*

*Beefy Chèvre Sandwich*
*page 59*

# BRUNCH PIZZA

▼

*Begin with the convenience of crescent rolls or a pizza crust mix and top with an appealing array of colors, textures and flavors.*

1 (8-ounce) package crescent rolls or 1 (6½-ounce) package pizza crust mix
1 (12-ounce) package frozen regular pork sausage, thawed
⅓ cup sliced green onions
¼ cup chopped green bell pepper
¼ cup chopped red bell pepper

1 (4-ounce) package shredded mozzarella cheese (1 cup)
1 cup frozen hash brown potatoes, thawed
4 eggs
¼ cup milk
¼ cup snipped fresh parsley
¼ teaspoon salt
⅛ teaspoon pepper
⅛ teaspoon ground nutmeg
⅓ cup freshly grated Parmesan cheese

Heat oven to 350°. On lightly floured surface, roll out crescent roll dough or pizza crust (mixed according to package directions) to fit a 12-inch pizza pan or 11-inch quiche pan. Press dough on bottom and up side of pan, forming a rim. In medium skillet, cook sausage until no longer pink, stirring to crumble; drain. Add green onions and bell peppers; sauté until soft, stirring occasionally. Spoon sausage mixture into prepared crust. Sprinkle mozzarella cheese over top; distribute potatoes over cheese. Beat together eggs, milk, parsley, salt, pepper and nutmeg; pour over mixture in crust. Sprinkle with Parmesan cheese. Bake until set and lightly browned (40 to 45 minutes). Cut into wedges. Serve immediately.

*4 servings.*

# INDIVIDUAL EGGS MORNAY

▼

*Mornay sauce is a popular French addition to egg and vegetable dishes. Here it graces do-ahead company fare gilded with a butter-crumb topping.*

4 tablespoons margarine or butter, divided
⅓ cup chopped red bell pepper
⅓ cup chopped green onions
12 eggs, beaten
1 (4½-ounce) jar sliced mushrooms, drained
2 tablespoons flour
1 teaspoon chicken bouillon granules
1½ cups milk

2 ounces fancy shredded Swiss cheese (½ cup)
¼ cup freshly grated Parmesan cheese
⅛ teaspoon ground nutmeg
1½ cups soft bread crumbs
¼ cup margarine or butter, melted
3 tablespoons freshly grated Parmesan cheese
2 tablespoons snipped fresh parsley

Grease 6 (10-ounce) custard cups. In large skillet, melt 2 tablespoons of the margarine; sauté red pepper and green onions until onions are crisp-tender. Stir in eggs; cook over medium heat until eggs are slightly firm. Stir in mushrooms; set aside. Melt remaining 2 tablespoons margarine in small saucepan; blend in flour and chicken bouillon. Gradually stir in milk. Cook over medium heat, stirring constantly, until mixture comes to a boil; boil and stir 1 minute. Stir in cheeses and nutmeg until smooth. Fold sauce into scrambled eggs; spoon into greased custard cups. Combine bread crumbs, ¼ cup melted margarine, 3 tablespoons Parmesan cheese and parsley; sprinkle over eggs. Refrigerate, covered, several hours or overnight.
Heat oven to 350°. Bake until topping is golden brown (30 to 35 minutes).

*6 servings.*

**Tip:** Three (8-ounce) cartons low cholesterol egg substitute, thawed, if necessary and skim milk may be substituted for eggs and milk.

# CHEESY APPLE QUICHE

▼

*Tart apple cubes mingle magnificently with spices and Swiss cheese for a unique quiche variation. Garnish it with a "fan" of red and green unpeeled apple slices.*

| | |
|---|---|
| 1 (10-inch) unbaked pie shell | 2 tablespoons margarine or |
| 1¾ cups fancy shredded Swiss | butter |
| cheese (7 ounces), divided | 1½ teaspoons flour |
| 2 cups peeled, cubed Granny | ½ teaspoon ground cinnamon |
| Smith apples | ¼ teaspoon ground nutmeg |
| ¼ cup minced shallots | 4 eggs, beaten |
| | 2 cups half-and-half |
| | 1 teaspoon salt |

Prepare pie shell. Heat oven to 350°. Sprinkle ¼ cup of the cheese in pie shell. Bake pie shell 10 minutes on lowest oven rack; cool. In medium skillet, sauté apples and shallots in margarine until soft (8 to 10 minutes); stir in flour, cinnamon and nutmeg. Spread apple mixture evenly in pie shell; sprinkle with remaining 1½ cups cheese. In 4-cup glass measure, whisk eggs, half-and-half and salt together. Place pie pan on lowest oven rack; pour egg mixture over apples and cheese. Bake until firm and knife inserted near center comes out clean (about 60 minutes). Let stand 10 minutes, covered. Cut into wedges. Serve warm.

*6 to 8 servings.*

# DILLED THREE CHEESE QUICHE

▼

*Fresh dill, readily available in the produce department, enhances a trio of mild cheeses in this easy crowd-sized pleaser.*

| | |
|---|---|
| 1 (15-ounce) package | ½ cup freshly grated Parmesan |
| refrigerated all ready pie | cheese |
| crusts | ½ cup chopped green onions |
| 1 cup shredded Gruyére | ½ teaspoon salt |
| cheese (4 ounces) | ¼ teaspoon pepper |
| 3 cups half-and-half | ¼ teaspoon mace |
| 8 eggs | 1 (4-ounce) package fancy |
| 1 (½-ounce) package fresh dill, | shredded Swiss cheese |
| snipped | (1 cup) |

Follow directions on pie crust package for standing, unfolding and flouring crusts. Arrange 1 crust, floured side down, on half of a 10 × 15-inch jelly roll pan, gently stretching pastry into corners to line pan. Repeat with other crust on remaining half of pan. Trim overlap in center of pan; use trimmings to fill in around edges. Pinch pastry edges together firmly, patting and smoothing out seams. Trim pastry evenly, extending edge slightly above pan; flute edge. Refrigerate pastry-lined pan 15 minutes.

Heat oven to 350°. Line pastry with foil and fill with dried beans or rice to weigh it down. Bake on the lowest oven rack 15 minutes. Remove from oven; remove beans and foil. Bake crust an additional 8 to 10 minutes; do not brown. Remove from oven; sprinkle Gruyére cheese over hot crust.* Whisk together half-and-half, eggs, dill, Parmesan cheese, green onions, salt, pepper and mace. Place crust on lowest oven rack. Pour filling mixture into crust; sprinkle with Swiss cheese. Continue baking until set and light golden brown (about 30 minutes longer). Cool slightly; cut into squares. Serve warm.

*10 servings or 48 appetizer squares.*

**Tip:** *Recipe can be prepared to this point one day ahead. Cover crust and store at room temperature.

# TORTILLA BREAKFAST BUNDLES

▼

*This terrific, totable, tortilla-wrapped treat will win over non-breakfast eaters in a hurry.*

1 (12-ounce) package regular ground pork sausage
¾ cup milk
6 eggs
½ cup sliced green onions
1 teaspoon salt
½ teaspoon pepper

2 tablespoons margarine or butter
6 (8-inch) soft flour tortillas
1 (8-ounce) package shredded colby and Monterey Jack cheese (2 cups)
1 (8-ounce) jar mild salsa

In medium skillet, cook sausage until no longer pink, stirring to crumble; drain. In 2-cup glass measure, whisk milk and eggs together until thoroughly combined; stir in green onions, salt and pepper. In medium skillet, melt margarine. Add egg mixture; cook over medium-low heat until thickened but still moist (3 to 5 minutes).

To Serve: Divide sausage, scrambled eggs and cheese equally among each of 6 tortillas; top with desired amount of salsa. Roll up.

*3 to 6 servings.*

# EGGS BENEDICT À LA CRAB

▼

*Packaged hollandaise sauce adds convenience plus food safety, since you don't have to use raw eggs.*

6 eggs
1 tablespoon margarine or butter

1 (8-ounce) package imitation king crabmeat, flake style
1 (0.9-ounce) package hollandaise sauce mix
3 English muffins, split and toasted

In large skillet, poach eggs in simmering water about 10 minutes or until firm, basting with water to set tops. In small saucepan, melt margarine; add crabmeat and cook over low heat until heated through (2 to 3 minutes). Prepare hollandaise sauce mix according to package directions.

To Serve: Divide crabmeat equally among English muffin halves; spoon half of sauce over crabmeat. Top with poached eggs and remaining sauce.

*3 to 6 servings.*

# BLUEBERRY OVEN PANCAKE

▼

*An appealing alternative to blueberry muffins.*

¾ cup fresh or frozen blueberries
1½ teaspoons granulated sugar
3 tablespoons margarine or butter

4 eggs
½ cup flour
¼ teaspoon salt
½ cup milk
1 tablespoon powdered sugar
– maple syrup (optional)

Heat oven to 425°. Rinse berries; drain. Sprinkle with granulated sugar. Spray 10-inch oven-proof skillet with no stick cooking spray. Melt margarine in skillet, rotating to coat pan side. Beat eggs, flour, salt and milk in medium bowl until smooth. Stir excess margarine from skillet into egg mixture. Gently fold in blueberries; pour into skillet. Bake until puffy and edges are crisp and browned (20 to 25 minutes). Sprinkle with powdered sugar; cut into wedges. Serve immediately with syrup.

*4 servings.*

# EGG AND CHEESE BAKE...ITALIAN STYLE

*An Italian accent and do-ahead convenience make this superb strata the star of any luncheon or supper menu.*

| | |
|---|---|
| 10 slices Vienna bread, crusts removed, cubed (7 cups) | 8 eggs |
| 1 pound mild Italian sausage | 3½ cups milk |
| ½ cup chopped onion (1 small) | 2 teaspoons salt |
| 1 (8-ounce) package shredded mozzarella cheese (2 cups) | 2 teaspoons Italian herb seasoning |
| ½ cup freshly grated Parmesan cheese | ¼ cup snipped fresh parsley |
| | 1 (30-ounce) jar spaghetti sauce |

Butter 9 × 13-inch glass baking dish; cover bottom with half of bread cubes. In medium skillet, brown sausage and onion; drain. Layer sausage over bread cubes. Combine cheeses; sprinkle evenly over bread cubes. Layer with remaining bread cubes. In large bowl, whisk together eggs, milk, salt and Italian seasoning; pour evenly over casserole. Garnish with parsley. Refrigerate, covered, several hours or overnight.

Heat oven to 350°. Bake, uncovered, until knife inserted near center comes out clean (50 to 55 minutes). Let stand 10 minutes, covered. In 4-cup microwavable container, microwave (HIGH) spaghetti sauce until heated through (4 to 5 minutes). Cut strata into squares and serve with warm sauce.

*8 to 10 servings.*

# BEEFY CHÈVRE SANDWICH

*Trendy ingredients and garden-fresh vegetables meld magnificently in an upscale French bread sandwich.*

| | |
|---|---|
| 1 (6-ounce) package Wisconsin goat cheese | 1 teaspoon minced garlic |
| 6 marinated sun-dried tomatoes | 1 (16-inch) loaf French bread |
| ⅓ cup thinly sliced red onion | 1 pound thinly sliced Italian roast beef |
| 4 large fresh basil leaves | 2 small tomatoes, thinly sliced |
| | 12 large spinach leaves |
| | 6 radicchio leaves |

In food processor, process cheese, sun-dried tomatoes, onion, basil and garlic until smooth, scraping down side of bowl as necessary. Halve bread lengthwise; hollow out loaf, leaving 1-inch shell. Spread cheese mixture evenly in both halves. Layer roast beef in bottom half of bread. Arrange tomato slices over beef, overlapping slightly. Top with spinach and radicchio leaves, overlapping slightly. Cover with top half of bread; press together lightly. Cut loaf diagonally into 1½-inch slices.

*6 to 8 servings.*

**Tip:** Sandwich may be assembled 2 hours ahead, wrapped tightly and refrigerated. Bring to room temperature before serving.

Spinach

# MUENSTER APPLE STACK

▼

*Tart apple slices and sprouts add tantalizing texture and the cashew-onion mayo gives a gourmet touch.*

- 4 slices heavy grain bread
- – Cashew Mayonnaise (below)
- 4 leaf lettuce leaves

- 4 slices Muenster cheese
- 1 Granny Smith apple, thinly sliced
- ½ cup alfalfa sprouts

Spread each bread slice with ¼ of Cashew Mayonnaise; top with lettuce leaf, 1 cheese slice, ¼ of apple slices and 2 tablespoons alfalfa sprouts. Wrap in plastic wrap; refrigerate 2 or more hours.

*4 sandwiches.*

**Cashew Mayonnaise:** Combine ½ cup mayonnaise, ¼ cup coarsely chopped cashews and 1 tablespoon finely minced green onion.

# CINNAMON-RAISIN YOGURT CHEESE SPREAD

▼

*Try this fruit-sparked spread as a healthful, lowfat alternative to cream cheese.*

- – cheesecloth or coffee filters
- 2 (8-ounce) containers vanilla lowfat yogurt (without added gelatin)

- 2 tablespoons coarsely chopped dried cranberries or cherries
- 2 teaspoons sugar
- 1 teaspoon grated orange peel

Place large strainer lined with double thickness of cheesecloth or coffee filters over large bowl. In small bowl, combine yogurt, cranberries, sugar and orange peel; spoon into prepared strainer. Cover with plastic wrap; refrigerate until liquid has drained and yogurt is spreadable (8 to 10 hours).

To Serve: Transfer mixture to small bowl; discard cheesecloth or filters and accumulated liquid. Serve on bagels, toast, scones or English muffins.

*Amount: 1 cup.*

# SAVORY SANDWICH SPREADS

▼

*These innovative combinations are sure to beat the lunch time blahs!*

**Smoky Ham and Cheese Spread:** In food processor, combine ½ pound ham, cut into chunks; ½ pound Swiss cheese, cut into chunks; 1 (4-ounce) jar drained, sliced pimientos; 3 tablespoons mayonnaise; 1 tablespoon milk; and 1 large green onion, cut into pieces. Process until almost smooth. Refrigerate, covered up to 3 days. Spread on rye bread.

*Amount: 2½ cups.*

**Nutty Cheese Spread:** In medium bowl, combine ½ (8-ounce) container soft pineapple cream cheese; 1 small pear, chopped; 1 medium carrot, shredded; ¼ cup chopped pecans; ¼ cup raisins; and ¼ teaspoon ground nutmeg. Refrigerate, covered, several hours or up to 3 days. Spread on bread or crackers.

*Amount: 2 cups.*

**Cream Cheese and Fruit Spread:** In 4-cup microwavable glass measuring cup, combine ½ cup diced, dried fruits and raisins and ½ cup orange juice. Microwave (HIGH) until fruit is plump and mixture boils (2 to 3 minutes). Cool completely (about 20 minutes). Place 1 (8-ounce) package unwrapped cream cheese on microwavable plate. Microwave (MEDIUM, 50% power) 1 minute. Let stand 2 minutes. In medium bowl, combine cream cheese with fruits and ½ teaspoon ground cinnamon. Refrigerate, covered, until of spreading consistency. Spread on nut breads.

*Amount: about 1½ cups.*

# FISH & SEAFOOD

Are the fish biting? Yes, indeed! Let us lure you into the kitchen with the promise of a fresh catch — familiar or exotic, fresh water or salt water. Take your choice, knowing that whatever you select comes with the bonus of impressive quantities of protein and significant amounts of vitamins and minerals.

You will find most varieties amazingly adaptable to many preparation methods and to an enticing array of sauces, marinades, pestos and salsas. We've included old-fashioned favorites like Salmon Loaf, haute cuisine Sole En Phyllo and continental classics like Coquilles Saint Jacques. In addition, you can reel in some trendy tantalizers with our selections for Tilapia Dijonnaise and Herbed Catfish Sandwiches.

Whether you bake, broil, grill, poach, saute or microwave, you will find each "fish story" has a happy ending. And, you never have to bait a hook!

# SALMON EN PAPILLOTE

*Hearts of parchment encase salmon steaks to seal in juices from the fish and savory mushroom topping. Accompaniments can be quite simple as this will be the star attraction.*

| | |
|---|---|
| 4 (8 to 10-ounce) salmon steaks, 1 inch thick | – parchment paper |
| 1 tablespoon snipped fresh tarragon | 4 teaspoons lemon juice |
| 1 tablespoon snipped fresh thyme | ½ teaspoon salt |
| 2 tablespoons snipped fresh parsley | ⅛ teaspoon pepper |
| | 4 ounces fresh mushrooms, thinly sliced (about 1⅓ cups) |
| | 2 teaspoons grated lemon peel |
| | 4 teaspoons dry sherry |

Heat oven to 450°. Rinse salmon steaks; pat dry with paper towels. Combine tarragon, thyme and parsley; set aside. Fold 13 × 15-inch piece of parchment in half crosswise to make a rectangle 7½ × 13 inches. Draw a half-heart, beginning and ending at folded edge. Cut out heart. Repeat with 3 more pieces of parchment. Unfold hearts; place each steak on a heart, about 1 inch from center fold line with rounded edge of steak in upper rounded section of heart, keeping at least 1 inch from edges.

Brush each steak with 1 teaspoon lemon juice. Combine salt and pepper; sprinkle evenly over steaks. Top each with about ⅓ cup mushrooms and ½ teaspoon lemon peel; drizzle with 1 teaspoon sherry. Seal according to directions below. Place packets in shallow baking pan. Bake until salmon is slightly opaque in center (about 15 minutes). To check for doneness: Insert tip of sharp knife straight down through paper into thickest part of steak. Twist knife into steak to determine if salmon is opaque. With knife tip barely inserted in the slit, gently lift paper so packet is puffed again. Serve or continue to bake.

To Serve: Place one packet on each of 4 dinner plates. Cut each packet open by slashing a large "X" on top.

*4 servings.*

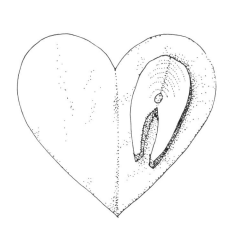

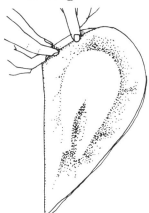

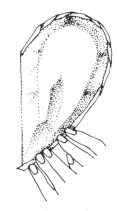

Fold empty half of heart over fish, lining up edges. Do not press down top of packet.

Beginning at top of heart, hold edges together and fold parchment over ¼ inch, creasing with fingers. Fold this first section over again and crease. Move along crease about 1 inch and fold over edge ¼ inch.

Continue folding and creasing once every inch to the bottom tip of the heart. Fold the tip under.

*Swordfish Steaks with Citrus Salsa page 68*

# BROILED SALMON FILLETS

▼

*The versatility of salmon makes it an ideal partner for savory herb-sparked toppings like the trio presented here. Combine topping ingredients several hours ahead for peak flavor.*

Heat broiler. Rinse 2 (6 to 8-ounce) salmon fillets; pat dry with paper towels. Arrange skin side down on lightly greased broiler pan. Brush with olive oil; spread with one of toppings (below). Broil 4 inches from heat until salmon just flakes with a fork (about 10 minutes per inch of thickness, measured at its thickest part). Garnish with Lemon and Lime Twists (below).

*2 servings.*

**Toppings:**

**Lemon Pepper:**  Combine ½ teaspoon lemon and pepper seasoning salt and 1 teaspoon snipped fresh dill.

**Mustardy Lime:**  Combine 1 tablespoon natural seed mustard, 1 teaspoon grated lime peel, 2 tablespoons lime juice, ¼ teaspoon salt and ⅛ teaspoon pepper.

**Tarragon:**  Combine 1 tablespoon lime juice, 1½ tablespoons snipped fresh tarragon, ¼ teaspoon salt and ⅛ teaspoon pepper.

# SALMON...DILLED AND GRILLED

▼

*Prepared dill dip coats salmon before and during grilling for added moisture and enhanced flavor. For variety, try other steaks of the same thickness and similar texture, like halibut, swordfish and tuna.*

| | |
|---|---|
| 4 salmon steaks, 1 inch thick | 2 tablespoons drained small |
| 1 cup prepared dill dip |    capers |
| 1 teaspoon minced garlic | – Lemon Twists (below) |
| | – fresh dill sprigs |

Rinse salmon steaks; pat dry with paper towels. Arrange salmon steaks in large shallow glass dish. In small bowl, combine dill dip, garlic and capers. Spread ½ cup sauce mixture over both sides of steaks. Refrigerate salmon and remaining sauce, covered, 1 hour. Prepare grill. Spray grill rack with no stick cooking spray. Using direct heat cooking method, arrange steaks on grill rack 4 to 5 inches over medium-hot coals. Grill, uncovered, until salmon is slightly opaque in center (15 to 20 minutes), turning once. Garnish with Lemon Twists and dill. Serve with reserved sauce mixture.

*4 servings.*

## LEMON, LIME OR ORANGE TWISTS

▼

Cut lemon, lime or orange crosswise into thin slices. Make one cut in each slice from the center out to the edge.

Single Twist: Twist ends of one slice in opposite directions.

Double Twist: Place 2 similar size slices of citrus fruit together, lining up slits; twist ends in opposite directions. If desired, add a fresh herb sprig.

# SALMON STEAKS 'N CUCUMBER SAUCE

*A complementary herbed cucumber sauce tastefully tops quickly microwaved salmon steaks.*

| | |
|---|---|
| 1 (8-ounce) carton reduced-fat sour cream | ½ teaspoon dried basil, crumbled |
| ⅔ cup finely chopped seeded cucumber | ⅛ teaspoon white pepper |
| 2 tablespoons minced shallot | 4 (8 to 10-ounce) salmon steaks, 1 inch thick |
| 2 tablespoons snipped fresh parsley | 1 cup water |
| ¾ teaspoon salt, divided | ½ cup dry sherry |
| | 1 small onion, sliced |
| | 2 sprigs fresh parsley |
| | ¼ teaspoon pepper |

Combine sour cream, cucumber, shallot, snipped parsley, ½ teaspoon of the salt, basil and white pepper. Refrigerate, covered. Rinse salmon steaks; pat dry with paper towels. In 12-inch microwavable dish, arrange salmon steaks in a circle with wide edge toward outside. In 4-cup glass measure, combine water, sherry, onion, parsley sprigs, pepper and remaining ¼ teaspoon salt. Microwave (HIGH) until mixture boils (3½ to 4½ minutes). Pour hot mixture over salmon. Cover with vented plastic wrap. Microwave (MEDIUM-HIGH, 70% power) until slightly opaque in center (8 to 10 minutes). Carefully lift salmon from poaching liquid to heated platter or dinner plates. Top each steak with a dollop of cucumber sauce. Serve immediately. Pass remaining sauce.

*4 servings.*

**Variation:**

**Lemon Asparagus Sauce:** Omit reduced-fat sour cream, cucumber, shallot, snipped parsley, ½ teaspoon of the salt, basil and white pepper in recipe above. Microwave salmon steaks in poaching liquid as directed above; keep warm. Prepare 1 (1.8-ounce) package lemon dill sauce mix according to microwave package directions; set aside, covered. Combine ½ pound fresh asparagus, diagonally cut into 1½-inch pieces, and 2 tablespoons water in microwavable casserole; cover. Microwave (HIGH), stirring once, until crisp-tender (3 to 4 minutes); drain. Stir into lemon dill sauce. Serve over salmon steaks.

# SALMON LOAF

*From our collection of "comfort foods" comes this wonderful rendition of a tasty old-timer. Bake potatoes along with the salmon loaf, if you wish, and serve creamed peas on the side or spooned over the loaf.*

| | |
|---|---|
| 1 (14¾-ounce) can red salmon | 3 tablespoons snipped fresh parsley |
| 2 cups soft bread crumbs | ¼ teaspoon salt |
| ⅓ cup minced onion | ½ teaspoon dried dill weed |
| ¼ cup milk | ⅛ teaspoon pepper |
| 2 eggs, slightly beaten | – Creamed Peas (below) |
| 1 tablespoon lemon juice | |

Heat oven to 350°. Drain salmon, reserving 2 tablespoons liquid. Flake salmon in large bowl. Add reserved liquid and remaining ingredients except Creamed Peas; mix well. Pat into well greased 3¾ × 7½-inch loaf pan. Bake until knife inserted in center comes out clean (about 50 minutes). Remove from oven; let stand 5 minutes. Loosen salmon loaf from sides of pan; remove to serving platter. Serve with Creamed Peas.

*4 to 6 servings.*

**Creamed Peas:** Melt 3 tablespoons margarine or butter in saucepan; blend in 3 tablespoons flour, ¼ teaspoon salt and dash of white pepper. Gradually stir in 1½ cups milk. Cook over medium heat, stirring constantly, until mixture comes to a boil; boil and stir 1 minute. Stir in 1 cup frozen baby peas, thawed and drained; heat through (2 to 3 minutes).

# POACHED SALMON STEAKS

▼

*This sumptuous entrée could be voted "most likely to succeed" at your next dinner party.*

| | |
|---|---|
| 2 medium carrots | 2 tablespoons coarse salt |
| 1 leek | 1 teaspoon grated lemon peel |
| 1 stalk celery | 2 cloves garlic, unpeeled |
| 5 green onions | 25 peppercorns |
| 2 shallots | – bouquet garni (below) |
| 2 cups dry white wine | 4 salmon steaks, 1 inch thick |
| 6 cups water | – Lemon Dill Sauce (below) |
| | – fresh parsley sprigs |

Wash and peel vegetables; cut into ½-inch slices. Combine vegetables, wine, water and seasonings in large saucepan; simmer 20 minutes. Strain; discard vegetables and seasonings. Reserve 1¼ cups pan liquid for Lemon Dill Sauce. Heat remaining liquid in large skillet. Rinse salmon steaks; pat dry with paper towels. Add salmon steaks and simmer, covered, until salmon is slightly opaque in center (8 to 10 minutes). With wide spatula remove steaks; drain well. Place on warm platter. Spoon Lemon Dill Sauce over each steak. Garnish platter with parsley.

*4 servings.*

**Bouquet Garni:** In a cheesecloth bag, combine 6 sprigs parsley, ½ bay leaf, ¼ teaspoon dried fennel seed and ¼ teaspoon dried thyme; tie bag shut.

**Lemon Dill Sauce:**

| | |
|---|---|
| 3 tablespoons margarine or butter | ½ cup whipping cream |
| 3 tablespoons flour | 2 tablespoons lemon juice |
| 1¼ cups reserved pan liquid | ½ teaspoon salt |
| | ½ teaspoon dill weed |

In medium saucepan melt margarine. Blend in flour; gradually stir in pan liquid and cook, stirring constantly, until thickened. Stir in whipping cream, lemon juice, salt and dill weed; heat through.

*Amount: 2 cups.*

**Tip:** The vegetable stock used for poaching and as a sauce base may be made a day ahead of cooking the salmon. Refrigerate, covered.

# ARTICHOKE-SALMON MELTS

▼

*The unique combination of sandwich ingredients goes together quickly and will be devoured just as fast.*

| | |
|---|---|
| 1 (6-ounce) jar marinated artichoke hearts, drained, reserving marinade | 2 soft French rolls, sliced in half lengthwise |
| 1 (14¾-ounce) can red salmon, drained and flaked | 1 medium tomato, cut into 8 slices |
| ⅓ cup prepared dill dip | 4 ounces fontina cheese, grated |

Cut artichoke hearts in half. In medium microwavable bowl, combine artichoke hearts, 1 tablespoon marinade, salmon and dill dip. Brush cut surface of rolls with remaining marinade. Heat broiler; place rolls on broiler pan and broil until golden brown (2 to 3 minutes). Microwave (HIGH) salmon mixture until slightly warm (45 to 60 seconds). Spread salmon mixture evenly on 4 roll halves. Arrange 2 tomato slices on each; sprinkle with grated cheese. Broil 5 inches from heat source until cheese is slightly brown (3 to 5 minutes).

*4 servings.*

# HERBED CATFISH SANDWICHES

*Spicy cornmeal-coated fillets are quickly fried and tucked into poor boy buns for a delicious double-quick dinner. Serve with colorful fresh fruit kabobs.*

| | |
|---|---|
| 4 (4 to 6-ounce) catfish fillets | ½ cup flour |
| 1 egg | ¼ cup vegetable oil |
| ¼ cup milk | ½ cup mayonnaise |
| ½ cup yellow cornmeal | 1 tablespoon dill pickle relish |
| 1 teaspoon cayenne pepper | 4 poor boy buns, sliced in half |
| 1 teaspoon garlic powder | lengthwise |
| ¾ teaspoon salt | 1 cup shredded lettuce |
| ½ teaspoon lemon and pepper | 1 medium tomato, cut into |
| seasoning salt | 8 slices |
| ¼ teaspoon dried thyme, | – Fruit and Jicama Star Kabobs |
| crumbled | (below) |

Rinse catfish; pat dry with paper towels. Beat egg and milk together. In shallow dish, combine cornmeal, cayenne pepper, garlic powder, salt, seasoning salt and thyme. Coat fillets lightly in flour; dip into egg mixture. Dredge in seasoned cornmeal mixture. In heavy skillet, heat oil over medium heat. Fry 2 breaded fillets until crisp and golden brown on one side (3 to 4 minutes); turn fillets. Cook until fish just flakes with a fork (about 3 minutes); drain on paper towels. Repeat with remaining fillets. Meanwhile, combine mayonnaise and pickle relish; spread on cut sides of buns. Place 1 fried fillet inside each bun; divide lettuce and tomato evenly over catfish. Serve hot with Fruit and Jicama Star Kabobs.

*4 servings.*

## FRUIT AND JICAMA STAR KABOBS

Arrange a watermelon ball, a pineapple wedge, a cantaloupe ball and a strawberry on a wooden skewer. Using a 1-inch star-shaped cookie cutter, cut a star from ½-inch thick slice of jicama. Top skewer with a jicama star. If desired, substitute a slice of carambola (star fruit) for jicama.

# TILAPIA DIJONNAISE

*We think you will applaud the mild, slightly sweet flavor of tilapia. The high moisture content of this fish requires slightly longer cooking to make it flaky.*

| | |
|---|---|
| 1½ pounds tilapia fillets | 2 tablespoons snipped fresh |
| ½ cup Dijon mustard | basil |
| ⅓ cup olive oil | 1 tablespoon snipped fresh |
| ⅓ cup white wine | chives |
| 3 tablespoons lemon juice | 1 tablespoon minced shallots |
| | – fresh basil sprigs |

Rinse fillets; pat dry with paper towels. Arrange in glass baking dish. Combine remaining ingredients except basil sprigs; pour over fillets, turning to coat. Refrigerate, covered, 1 hour. Heat broiler. Arrange fillets on lightly oiled broiler pan. Broil 4 inches from heat until fish flakes easily with a fork (5 to 7 minutes). Garnish with basil sprigs. Serve immediately.

*4 servings.*

# CATFISH ITALIAN STYLE

▼

*Favorite Mediterranean flavors are featured in this unique presentation of a popular farm-raised fish.*

| | |
|---|---|
| 2 teaspoons vegetable oil | ⅛ teaspoon cayenne pepper |
| 3 tablespoons chopped green onions | ¼ cup diced tomato |
| | 1½ pounds catfish fillets |
| ½ teaspoon minced garlic | ¾ teaspoon salt |
| ½ cup tomato juice | ¼ teaspoon white pepper |
| ¼ cup white wine | ⅓ cup flour |
| ¼ teaspoon dried basil, crumbled | 2 tablespoons vegetable oil |
| | 2 tablespoons margarine or butter |
| ⅛ teaspoon dried thyme, crumbled | ¼ cup freshly shredded Parmesan cheese |

In medium saucepan, heat 2 teaspoons oil. Stir in onions and garlic; sauté over medium heat until tender (2 to 3 minutes). Stir in tomato juice, wine, basil, thyme and cayenne pepper; simmer, stirring occasionally, until reduced to a thick sauce (7 to 8 minutes). Stir in tomato. Meanwhile, rinse fillets; pat dry with paper towels. Sprinkle with salt and white pepper; coat with flour. In large skillet, heat 2 tablespoons oil and margarine over medium heat. Sauté fillets, turning once, until fish just flakes with a fork (7 to 8 minutes). Remove fillets to heated serving platter. Spoon sauce over fish; sprinkle with Parmesan cheese.

*4 servings.*

# RASPBERRY-SAUCED WALLEYE OR SOLE

▼

*When fresh raspberries are in season, sample this simple but sensational entrée.*

| | |
|---|---|
| 1½ pounds walleye or sole fillets | 2 tablespoons vegetable oil |
| ½ teaspoon salt | 2 tablespoons margarine or butter |
| ⅛ teaspoon pepper | – Raspberry Sauce (below) |
| ⅓ cup flour | – fresh whole raspberries |

Rinse fillets; pat dry with paper towels. Sprinkle with salt and pepper; coat with flour. In large skillet, heat oil and margarine over medium heat. Sauté fillets, turning once, until fish just flakes with a fork (7 to 8 minutes for walleye; 3 to 4 minutes for sole). Remove to heated serving platter; top with warm Raspberry Sauce. Garnish with raspberries.

*4 servings.*

**Raspberry Sauce:** Crush ½ cup fresh raspberries. Stir in 2 tablespoons snipped fresh thyme, 1 cup dry sherry and ½ teaspoon sugar; let stand 1 hour. Strain mixture into small saucepan; stir in 2 tablespoons minced shallots. Simmer, uncovered, until reduced to 3 to 4 tablespoons (about 15 minutes). Whisk in ½ cup butter, 2 tablespoons at a time. Stir in ¼ teaspoon salt and ⅛ teaspoon white pepper.

*Amount: about ¾ cup.*

*Keep fresh fish or thawed frozen fish in the coldest part of the refrigerator. Cook within one or two days.*

# SOLE EN PHYLLO

▼

*Our explicit, step-by-step instructions make this exquisite gift-wrapped entrée amazingly easy to prepare.*

1 (8-ounce) package imitation crabmeat, flaked
½ cup chopped fresh mushrooms
1 tablespoon minced shallots
1 tablespoon snipped fresh parsley
1 cup soft bread crumbs
1 tablespoon dry sherry
½ teaspoon dried dill weed, crumbled
½ teaspoon salt
⅛ teaspoon white pepper
6 sole fillets (about 1 pound)
½ cup margarine or butter, melted
12 phyllo sheets, thawed according to package directions
1 (1.8-ounce) package lemon dill sauce mix
¼ cup margarine or butter
½ cup milk
– Phyllo Bows (below)
– fresh dill sprigs

In medium bowl, combine crabmeat, mushrooms, shallots, parsley, bread crumbs, sherry, dill weed, salt and pepper. Rinse sole; pat dry with paper towels. Spoon equal portion of crab mixture on centers of each sole fillet; fold ends of each fillet over filling, overlapping ends.

Heat oven to 375°. Brush melted margarine lightly on 1 phyllo sheet; top with second sheet; brush with melted margarine. (Cover remaining phyllo sheets with slightly dampened towel until used.) Fold in half to make an 8½ × 14-inch rectangle. Place 1 stuffed sole fillet in center of folded phyllo. Fold long sides of phyllo over top of fillet, overlapping slightly. Fold phyllo ends over fillet to overlap. Arrange wrapped fillet, seam side down, in ungreased 9 × 13-inch baking pan. Brush with melted margarine. Repeat with remaining fillets and phyllo. Bake until golden brown (25 to 30 minutes).

Meanwhile, prepare lemon dill sauce mix according to package directions using ¼ cup margarine and ½ cup milk.

To Serve: Pour ¼ cup lemon dill sauce on each of 6 heated dinner plates; top with phyllo-wrapped sole. Place 1 Phyllo Bow on each serving; garnish with dill sprig. Serve immediately.

### *6 servings.*

**Tip:** To prepare ahead, cover phyllo-wrapped fish with plastic wrap; refrigerate up to 24 hours. Bake 5 to 10 minutes longer.

## PHYLLO BOWS

▼

Heat oven to 375°. Place 1 thawed sheet of phyllo on lightly dampened towel; brush with melted margarine. Cut into 6 strips 2¾ × 14 inches long. Starting at narrow ends, crimp center of each strip together with fingers down the length of strip to form a bow. Arrange on ungreased baking sheet. Bake until golden brown (6 to 9 minutes). Remove to wire rack to cool. Bows may be stored overnight in airtight container.

# SWORDFISH OR TUNA STEAKS WITH CITRUS SALSA

▼

*Fiesta flavors ignite firm-textured fish steaks for an imaginative, colorful presentation.*

1 (8-ounce) can pineapple tidbits
1½ tablespoons firmly packed brown sugar
1½ tablespoons lemon juice, divided
¾ teaspoon salt, divided
¼ teaspoon pepper
1½ to 2 pounds swordfish or tuna steaks

1 (11-ounce) can mandarin orange segments, drained, coarsely chopped
2 green onions, thinly sliced
1 tablespoon chopped hot red jalapeño peppers
1 tablespoon snipped fresh cilantro
¼ teaspoon cayenne pepper

Drain pineapple, reserving 1 tablespoon juice. In small bowl, combine reserved pineapple juice, brown sugar, ½ tablespoon of the lemon juice, ½ teaspoon of the salt and pepper. Rinse swordfish; pat dry with paper towels. Remove skin from fish. Arrange fish in glass baking dish. Pour marinade over fish, turning to coat. Refrigerate, covered, 30 minutes. In medium microwavable bowl, combine pineapple, 1 remaining tablespoon lemon juice, remaining ¼ teaspoon salt, orange segments and remaining ingredients.

Prepare grill. Spray grill rack with no stick cooking spray. Using direct heat cooking method, arrange fish on grill rack 4 to 5 inches over medium-hot coals. Grill, uncovered, until slightly opaque in center (about 10 minutes per inch of thickness measured at its thickest part), turning once.

To Serve: Microwave (HIGH) pineapple mixture until heated through (1½ to 2 minutes). Arrange fish on heated serving platter; top with citrus salsa.

*4 servings.*

# BAKED TROUT WITH CAPER WINE SAUCE

▼

*This very simple method of baking produces picture-perfect results. Add a caper-seasoned wine sauce and you have a gourmet feast.*

4 (8 to 10-ounce) whole boneless rainbow trout, heads and tails removed, butterflied
1 tablespoon olive oil
¼ teaspoon salt
⅛ teaspoon pepper

⅓ cup slivered almonds, chopped
3 tablespoons margarine or butter
3 tablespoons drained capers
¼ cup dry white wine
1 teaspoon minced garlic
1 tablespoon snipped fresh parsley

Heat oven to 450°. Rinse trout; pat dry with paper towels. Arrange trout, skin side down, on lightly oiled shallow baking pan; brush with olive oil. Sprinkle with salt, pepper and almonds. Bake until trout just flakes with a fork (6 to 7 minutes). Meanwhile, combine margarine, capers, wine and garlic in small saucepan. Bring to a boil over high heat. Boil, stirring constantly, 1 minute. Arrange trout on heated platter. Spoon caper wine sauce over trout; sprinkle with parsley.

*4 servings.*

# PEACHY ORANGE RUFFIE

▼

*For a change of pace, try this preparation method and sauce with catfish, too. Delicious!*

| | |
|---|---|
| 1 (12-ounce) jar peach preserves | 1 tablespoon dried thyme, crumbled |
| 2 tablespoons lemon juice | 1½ teaspoons salt |
| 1 teaspoon minced gingerroot | ½ teaspoon pepper |
| 2 pounds orange ruffie fillets | ¼ cup vegetable oil, divided |
| ½ cup flour | ¼ cup margarine or butter, divided |
| | ½ cup coarsely chopped pecans |

In small microwavable bowl, combine peach preserves, lemon juice and gingerroot; set aside. Rinse fillets; pat dry with paper towels. Combine flour, thyme, salt and pepper; coat fillets with mixture. In large skillet, heat 2 tablespoons of the oil and 2 tablespoons of the margarine over medium heat. Add pecans; stir until slightly browned (1 to 2 minutes). Remove pecans with slotted spoon to paper towels to drain. Arrange half of fillets in skillet; sauté over medium heat until lightly browned (3 to 4 minutes). Turn fillets; sauté until fillets just flake with a fork (2 to 3 minutes). Remove fillets to heated platter; cover. Add remaining 2 tablespoons oil and 2 tablespoons margarine to skillet. Sauté remaining fillets as above. Microwave (HIGH) peach sauce, stirring once, until heated through (about 2 minutes).

To Serve: Top each fillet with 2 to 3 tablespoons peach sauce; sprinkle with pecans.

*6 servings.*

# SNAPPER AND FENNEL DELUXE

▼

*Here, we team snapper with the pleasing, mild anise flavor of fennel. Enjoy this divine entrée for two.*

| | |
|---|---|
| 2 (6-ounce) snapper fillets | 1 small onion, thinly sliced (½ cup) |
| ¼ teaspoon salt, divided | 2 tablespoons white wine |
| ¼ teaspoon pepper, divided | ½ cup half and half |
| 3 tablespoons margarine or butter, divided | 2 teaspoons balsamic vinegar |
| 1 fennel bulb (about ¾-pound), trimmed and thinly sliced | ⅛ teaspoon dried fennel seed |
| | – fennel leaves |

Rinse fillets; pat dry with paper towels. Season with ⅛ teaspoon of the salt and ⅛ teaspoon of the pepper; set aside. In medium skillet, melt 2 tablespoons of the margarine; add sliced fennel and onion. Cook, covered, over medium heat until fennel is just tender (6 to 8 minutes), stirring occasionally. Stir in wine; cook 1 minute. Whisk in half-and-half, vinegar, remaining salt and pepper and fennel seed. Cook and whisk over medium heat 1 minute. Transfer mixture to bowl; keep warm. In same skillet, melt remaining 1 tablespoon margarine. Sauté snapper fillets over medium-high heat until fillets just flake with a fork (about 3 minutes per side). Divide fennel and onion mixture between 2 heated dinner plates; place 1 fillet on each. Garnish with fennel leaves.

*2 servings.*

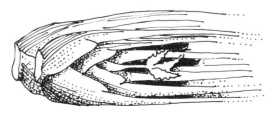

Fennel

# CHILLED HALIBUT STEAKS
# WITH MUSTARD DILL SAUCE

▼

*Poaching is one of the best methods of cooking halibut, particularly with the warm, mellow flavor of sherry added to the stock. The marvelous Mustard Dill Sauce adds even more character to this choice chilled entree.*

| | |
|---|---|
| 2 cups dry sherry | 1 lemon, thinly sliced |
| 2 cups water | 1 small onion, sliced |
| 2 teaspoons instant chicken bouillon | ¼ teaspoon dried dill weed |
| ½ teaspoon salt | 4 halibut steaks, 1 inch thick |
| ¼ teaspoon pepper | – Scored Citrus Slices (below) |
| | – Mustard Dill Sauce (below) |

In 10 to 12-inch skillet, bring sherry, water, chicken bouillon, salt, pepper, lemon and onion slices and dill weed to a boil; boil 3 minutes. Rinse halibut; pat dry with paper towels. Arrange steaks in single layer in liquid; simmer, covered until halibut is slightly opaque in center (6 to 8 minutes). Uncover; let cool in liquid 5 minutes. Carefully remove halibut to serving platter. Refrigerate, covered, several hours or overnight. Garnish with Scored Citrus Slices. Serve cold with Mustard Dill Sauce.

### *4 servings.*

**Mustard Dill Sauce:** Combine 2 tablespoons snipped fresh parsley, 1 tablespoon minced shallot, 1 teaspoon dried dill weed, 1 (8-ounce) carton plain lowfat yogurt, 2 tablespoons mayonnaise, 1 teaspoon Dijon mustard, 1 teaspoon lemon juice and ¼ teaspoon salt; mix well. Refrigerate, covered, several hours or overnight.

## SCORED CITRUS SLICES

▼

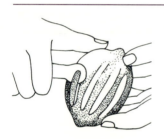

Hold bent "U-shaped" edge of citrus stripper against orange, lemon or lime. Firmly press down on citrus peel while pulling stripper toward you. Remove peel in long, "parallel" strips from top of fruit to bottom, leaving about ½ inch between each cut.

Cut fruit crosswise into thin slices.

Layer two or three different fruit slices together or arrange alternately around edge of platter.

# NUT-BUTTERED HALIBUT

▼

*Nut butters give five-star status to broiled fish steaks. They are added during the final minutes of broiling and cooked to a luscious-looking golden brown.*

| | |
|---|---|
| 1½ to 2 pounds halibut steaks, 1 inch thick | ¼ cup lemon juice |
| ½ teaspoon salt (optional) | 1 tablespoon vegetable oil |
| ¼ teaspoon pepper (optional) | – Pistachio Herb Butter or Hazelnut Butter (below) |
| | – fresh basil sprigs (optional) |

Rinse halibut; pat dry with paper towels. Sprinkle with salt and pepper. Combine lemon juice and oil; brush both sides of steaks with mixture. Heat broiler. Arrange steaks on lightly oiled broiler pan. Broil 4 inches from heat 5 minutes. Turn steaks; brush with lemon mixture. Broil 2 minutes; spread each steak with about 2 tablespoons flavored butter of choice. Continue broiling until steaks are slightly opaque in center and butter begins to brown (1½ to 2½ minutes). Transfer steaks to heated serving platter. Garnish with basil. Serve immediately.

*4 servings.*

**Pistachio Herb Butter:** Process ¼ cup shelled pistachio nuts and 10 large fresh basil leaves in blender until coarsely chopped. Add ½ cup softened butter, 1 tablespoon minced shallots, 1 teaspoon lemon juice and ½ teaspoon minced garlic. Process until well blended. Refrigerate, covered, several hours.

*Amount: ½ cup.*

**Hazelnut Butter:** Process ¼ cup roasted hazelnuts in blender until coarsely chopped. Add ½ cup softened butter, 2 tablespoons minced green onions and 1 tablespoon grated lemon peel. Process until well blended. Refrigerate, covered, several hours.

*Amount: ½ cup.*

**Tip:** To roast hazelnuts (filberts), heat oven to 275°. Spread nuts in single layer in shallow pan. Roast until skins crack (20 to 30 minutes). To remove skins, rub nuts while warm with a rough cloth (some of skins will remain).

# CARIBBEAN FILLETS WITH PINEAPPLE SALSA

▼

*Grouper or mahi-mahi fillets are crowned with a tropical salsa that's fruity and sweet. Count on the microwave to cook fish superbly.*

| | |
|---|---|
| 1½ pounds mahi-mahi or grouper fillets | 1 lime |
| 2 tablespoons margarine or butter | 1 teaspoon snipped fresh cilantro |
| | – Pineapple Salsa (below) |
| | – Lime Twists (page 62) |

Rinse fillets; pat dry with paper towels. Measure margarine into shallow microwavable dish. Microwave (HIGH) until margarine is melted (30 to 45 seconds). Squeeze juice from lime into dish; dip both sides of fillet in lime mixture to coat. Arrange single layer of fillets in dish, skin side down, with thicker portions to outside. Tuck under thin ends of fillets so fish will be uniform in thickness. Sprinkle with cilantro. Cover with plastic wrap; vent one corner. Microwave (HIGH) 3 minutes; rearrange fillets. Cover, microwave (HIGH) until fish is slightly translucent in center (2 to 4 minutes). Let stand, covered, until fish is opaque throughout (3 to 5 minutes). Transfer fillets to heated platter. Top each serving with Pineapple Salsa and Lime Twist.

*4 servings.*

**Pineapple Salsa:** In 2-cup glass measure, combine 1 (15½-ounce) can well-drained crushed pineapple, 2 tablespoons cream of coconut, 1 teaspoon grated lime peel and 1 tablespoon lime juice. Microwave (HIGH) until heated through (about 1½ minute).

*Amount: about 1 cup.*

# FISH STEAKS...BASICS

▼

*No matter which cooking method you choose, don't overcook fish. Fish is done when the flesh has just begun to turn from translucent to opaque and is firm, but still moist.*

Thaw fish, if frozen. Rinse steaks; pat dry with paper towels.

**To Bake:** Heat oven to 450°. Place steaks in greased baking dish. Drizzle with melted margarine or butter. Sprinkle with salt, pepper and favorite seasonings. Bake until fish is slightly opaque in center (about 10 minutes per inch of thickness measured at its thickest part*).

**To Broil:** Heat broiler. Place steaks on greased broiler pan. Cook 4 inches from heat until fish is slightly opaque in center (about 10 minutes per inch of thickness measured at its thickest part), turning once and brushing several times during cooking with vegetable oil, margarine, butter or basting sauce.

**To Grill:** Prepare grill. Spray grill rack with no stick cooking spray. Using direct heat cooking method, arrange fish on grill rack 4 to 5 inches over medium-hot coals. Grill, uncovered, until slightly opaque in center (about 10 minutes per inch of thickness measured at its thickest part), turning once and brushing several times during cooking with vegetable oil, margarine, butter or basting sauce.

**To Poach:** Cover fish with hot salted water. Add several onion and lemon slices, a handful of parsley and several peppercorns. Simmer, covered, until fish is slightly opaque in center (about 10 minutes per inch of thickness measured at its thickest part).

***The "10 minute rule"** is a good general guide for judging the cooking time for fish. For example, a 1-inch thick fish steak should be cooked a total of 10 minutes; a ¾-inch thick fish steak should be checked for doneness after 7 to 8 minutes of cooking.

# GRILLED BLACKENED FISH

▼

*In a cast iron skillet on the grill, fish is prepared in creatively Cajun fashion. Fillets at least ½ inch thick are essential for this method of cooking. Since heat is intense, be prepared with long, fireproof oven mitt and long-handled spatula.*

| | |
|---|---|
| 1½ pounds (½ to ¾-inch thick) firm-fleshed fish fillets or steaks | ½ cup margarine or butter, melted |
| | 5 tablespoons Cajun seasoning for blackened redfish |

Place grill rack directly on lava rocks or ceramic briquets; turn gas grill to high. Place a 12-inch cast iron skillet directly on grill rack. Close grill cover; heat until skillet is white hot (about 20 minutes). Meanwhile, rinse fish; pat dry with paper towels. Pour melted margarine into an 8 or 9-inch pie plate. Pour seasoning into similar size plate. When skillet is ready, dip both sides of fish into melted margarine, then into seasoning mix, coating all fish surface. Wearing long, fireproof oven mitt and using long handled spatula, place fish in hot skillet. Cook 2½ minutes uncovered; turn. Continue cooking, uncovered, until fish just flakes with a fork (2 to 2½ minutes longer). Remove to heated platter; serve immediately.

*4 servings.*

**Tip:** To cook fish on a charcoal grill, remove grill rack; place 12-inch cast iron skillet directly on hot coals. Close grill cover; allow to heat until skillet is white hot (20 to 25 minutes). Coals must still be very hot when ready to grill fish. Proceed as in recipe above.

# SKEWERED SHRIMP

▼

*Curry powder gives a golden glow to the shrimp as well as a rich, exotic flavor. Serve these with a rice pilaf and a crisp green salad.*

| | |
|---|---|
| 4 (12-inch) wooden skewers | 1 teaspoon minced garlic |
| ½ cup margarine or butter, melted | ½ teaspoon onion powder |
| | ½ teaspoon salt |
| 1½ to 2 teaspoons curry powder | 1¼ pounds "15 to 20 count" |
| 1½ teaspoons dried dill weed, crumbled | (large) shell-on, uncooked shrimp |

Soak wooden skewers in water at least 30 minutes. Prepare grill. Combine margarine, curry powder, dill weed, garlic, onion powder and salt. Shell and devein shrimp, leaving tail attached. Rinse; pat dry with paper towels. Thread shrimp on skewers; brush with margarine mixture. Spray grill rack with no stick cooking spray. Using direct heat cooking method, arrange skewers on grill rack 4 to 5 inches over medium-hot coals. Grill, uncovered, turning and brushing with margarine mixture, until shrimp are opaque throughout (5 to 7 minutes).

*4 servings.*

# SHRIMP 'N CHICKEN KABOBS...SZECHWAN STYLE

▼

*An attention-getting "Asian" marinade imparts fabulous flavor to plump chicken pieces, jumbo shrimp and fresh vegetables.*

| | |
|---|---|
| ¾ pound "10 to 12 count" (jumbo) shell-on, uncooked shrimp | 2 tablespoons minced green onions |
| ½ pound boneless skinless chicken breast, cut into 1¼-inch cubes | 1 tablespoon chili puree with garlic |
| | 1 teaspoon Oriental sesame oil |
| 1 large zipper closure food storage bag | 1 teaspoon minced gingerroot |
| | 4 (12-inch) wooden skewers |
| 2 tablespoons rice wine vinegar | 1 red bell pepper, cut into 1½-inch squares |
| 2 tablespoons vegetable oil | 2 to 3 small zucchini, cut into ¾-inch slices |
| 2 tablespoons soy sauce | 8 whole fresh mushrooms |

Shell and devein shrimp, leaving tail attached. Rinse; pat dry with paper towels. Place shrimp and chicken in food storage bag. Combine vinegar, vegetable oil, soy sauce, green onions, chili puree, sesame oil, and gingerroot; pour over shrimp and chicken. Seal bag; refrigerate 1 to 2 hours, turning bag occasionally. Soak wooden skewers in water at least 30 minutes. Remove shrimp and chicken from marinade; reserve marinade. Alternately thread shrimp, chicken and vegetables on skewers. Prepare grill. Spray grill rack with no stick cooking spray. Using direct heat cooking method, arrange kabobs on grill rack 5 inches over medium-hot coals. Brush with reserved marinade. Grill, uncovered, until shrimp and chicken are opaque throughout (6 to 10 minutes), turning once and brushing with reserved marinade halfway through cooking. Serve immediately.

*4 servings.*

*Chili puree with garlic is a hot, spicy sauce made from chili peppers. It is widely used in Szechwan (Sichuan) and Hunan recipes. Refrigerate after opening.*

# SHRIMP BOIL

▼

*Careful timing is crucial to keep these subtly-seasoned shrimp tender and tasty.*

| | |
|---|---|
| 6 cups water | 2 teaspoons salt |
| 1 teaspoon minced garlic | 1 pound "21 to 25 count" |
| 1 lemon, sliced | (large) shell-on, uncooked |
| 1 small onion, quartered | shrimp |
| 1 tablespoon seasoning for seafood | – lemon wedges |

In 4-quart Dutch oven, combine all ingredients except shrimp and lemon wedges. Bring to a boil over high heat. Reduce heat; simmer, covered 20 minutes. Rinse shrimp; drain. Split shrimp down back; remove veins and legs, not shells. Return seasoned water to a rolling boil; add shrimp. Cover and immediately remove from heat. Let stand until shells turn pink and shrimp is opaque throughout (about 3 minutes).

To Serve: Arrange hot shrimp on serving platter. Garnish with lemon wedges. Remove shells as eaten. Dip shrimp in Clarified Butter (page 77), if desired.

*3 servings.*

**Tip:** For Shrimp Cocktail, rinse cooked shrimp in cold water; refrigerate. Serve over crushed ice with seafood cocktail sauce.

# BUTTERFLIED HERBED SHRIMP

▼

*A marinade infused with aromatic fresh herbs permeates shrimp before cooking and then serves as a basting sauce during broiling step. Presentation is dramatic for gourmet guest appeal.*

| | |
|---|---|
| 1 pound "10 to 12 count" (jumbo) shell-on, uncooked shrimp | 1 (½-ounce) package fresh cilantro, snipped (5 tablespoons) |
| ⅓ cup lemon juice | 3 tablespoons snipped fresh parsley |
| ¼ cup olive oil | 2 teaspoons minced garlic |
| 1 (½-ounce) package fresh basil, snipped (5 tablespoons) | ½ teaspoon salt |
| | ⅛ teaspoon white pepper |
| | 1 large zipper closure food storage bag |
| | – Lemon Twists (page 62) |

Shell shrimp, leaving tail attached. Make a deep cut nearly all the way through shrimp down the entire length of the back; rinse out vein. Pat dry with paper towels. Press shrimp flat into butterfly shape. Combine lemon juice, oil and seasonings in food storage bag. Add shrimp; seal bag. Refrigerate 1 to 2 hours, turning bag occasionally. Heat broiler. Arrange shrimp on broiler pan; reserve marinade. Broil shrimp 4 inches from heat until shrimp are opaque throughout (3½ to 4½ minutes), brushing with reserved marinade halfway through cooking. Garnish with Lemon Twists. Serve immediately.

*3 servings.*

*Shrimp "count", usually listed on the package, tells you the number of shrimp in a pound. This "count" is included in our recipes to assist you in determining the correct size shrimp to purchase. We suggest you rely on the "count", since size descriptions (jumbo, large, medium, small) can vary from one supplier to another.*

# SEAFOOD AND PASTA WITH SAFFRON SAUCE

▼

*Saffron is a rather powerful spice, so little is needed to add distinctive flavor and color. This is a handsome entrée with European flair.*

| | |
|---|---|
| 1 (0.2-gram) vial saffron, crushed | ½ cup minced shallots |
| 1 cup dry sherry | 1 cup chicken broth |
| ½ pound "40 to 50 count" (medium) shelled, deveined uncooked shrimp | 1½ cups whipping cream |
| | 3 carrots, sliced diagonally (2 cups) |
| ½ pound bay scallops | 1 (9-ounce) package fresh fettuccine |
| ¼ cup olive oil | |
| 2 teaspoons minced garlic | ½ pound snow peas, ends and strings removed |
| ½ teaspoon salt | |
| ¼ teaspoon pepper | 6 green onions, including some tops, sliced diagonally (¾ cup) |

Soak saffron in sherry for 10 minutes. Rinse shrimp and scallops; pat dry with paper towels. In large skillet, heat olive oil over medium heat; stir in shrimp, scallops, garlic, salt and pepper. Cook, stirring occasionally, until shrimp and scallops turn opaque (2 to 4 minutes). With slotted spoon, remove to heated platter; cover. Pour saffron-sherry mixture, shallots, chicken broth and whipping cream into skillet; stir in carrots. Bring to a boil over high heat; boil, stirring occasionally, until liquid is reduced by half (12 to 14 minutes). Cook pasta according to package directions, adding ½ teaspoon salt to water; drain. Add cooked pasta, snow peas, onions, shrimp and scallops to sauce; simmer until heated through (about 3 minutes). Spoon onto heated serving platter. Serve immediately.

*4 to 5 servings.*

# SHRIMP CREOLE

▼

*Creole sauce, a Louisiana specialty, builds on a tomato base with bold seasonings and chopped vegetables. Plump shrimp add even more flavor to this dinner party dandy.*

| | |
|---|---|
| 2 pounds "28 to 34 count" (medium) shelled, deveined uncooked shrimp | 2 (28-ounce) cans whole tomatoes, undrained, chopped |
| ¼ cup safflower oil | 2 small bay leaves |
| 2 cups chopped onions | 1 tablespoon paprika |
| 1 cup chopped green bell pepper | ½ to ¾ teaspoon cayenne pepper |
| 1 cup sliced celery | 2 teaspoons salt |
| 1½ teaspoons minced garlic | 2 cups uncooked long-grain rice, cooked |
| | – snipped fresh parsley |

Rinse shrimp; pat dry with paper towels. Heat oil in heavy 4 to 5-quart Dutch oven. Sauté onion, green pepper, celery and garlic 5 minutes, stirring occasionally. Stir in tomatoes, bay leaves, paprika, cayenne pepper and salt. Simmer 15 minutes. Stir in shrimp; continue to simmer until shrimp turn opaque (3 to 5 minutes). Discard bay leaves.

To Serve: Spoon Shrimp Creole over cooked rice; garnish with parsley. Serve immediately.

*8 servings.*

# SEAFOOD LASAGNA

▼

*Here's a whole new look for lasagna–lighter, more delicately flavored and with an elegant rather than casual presentation. It's splendid as a luncheon or supper dish.*

- 1 pound "40 to 50 count" (medium) shelled, deveined uncooked shrimp
- 1 pound bay scallops
- 2 tablespoons margarine or butter
- 1 cup chopped onions
- ½ teaspoon minced garlic
- 1 (12-ounce) carton cottage cheese
- 1 (8-ounce) package cream cheese, softened
- 2 eggs
- 1 tablespoon dried basil, crumbled

- ¼ teaspoon salt
- ⅛ teaspoon white pepper
- 2 (10¾-ounce) cans cream of mushroom soup with ⅓ less salt
- ⅓ cup dry sherry
- 1 (8-ounce) package flake-style imitation crabmeat
- ½ cup freshly grated Parmesan cheese, divided
- 2 sheets fresh pasta or 1 (8-ounce) package dry lasagna noodles
- 2 tablespoons snipped fresh parsley

Cook shrimp and scallops in salted water (1 quart water, 1 teaspoon salt) over medium heat until opaque throughout (about 3 minutes); drain. Cut shrimp in half. Melt margarine in skillet; sauté onion and garlic until onion is tender. Stir in cottage cheese, cream cheese, eggs, basil, salt and pepper. Combine soup, sherry, cooked shrimp and scallops, crabmeat and ¼ cup of the Parmesan cheese. Arrange 1 sheet of fresh pasta, folded crosswise, in bottom of buttered 8x12-inch glass baking dish. (Or, cook dry pasta according to package directions; drain. Place one layer of cooked lasagna noodles in baking dish.) Spread one half of cheese mixture and half of seafood mixture over pasta. Repeat layers. Sprinkle with remaining ¼ cup Parmesan cheese. Refrigerate, covered, up to 24 hours.

Heat oven to 325°. Bake, uncovered, until bubbly in center (65 to 70 minutes). Sprinkle with parsley. Let stand 10 minutes, covered, before cutting into squares.

*12 servings.*

# MUSSELS

▼

*Mussels, which enjoy widespread popularity in Europe, are increasing in favor on American menus. For those unfamiliar with this tender mollusk, the following recipe is a good one to try!*

- 5 dozen mussels
- 2 tablespoons salt
- 1 large leek, thinly sliced
- 2 large shallots, chopped
- 1½ cups dry white wine
- ¾ cup water

- 2 teaspoons salt
- ⅛ teaspoon pepper
- ½ cup margarine or butter
- 1 large tomato, diced
- 1 tablespoon snipped fresh parsley
- – crusty French bread

Rinse mussels in cold water, discarding any that are open. With stiff brush, scrub mussels to remove dirt and beards. Transfer to a large bowl; cover with water and 2 tablespoons salt. Let stand 30 minutes. Drain; transfer to 3-quart saucepan. Stir in leek, shallots, wine, water, 2 teaspoons salt and pepper. Cook, covered, over high heat until mussels open (6 to 8 minutes), stirring after 4 minutes to bring mussels on bottom to top. Remove mussels with slotted spoon to individual serving bowls, discarding unopened mussels. Cover with foil to keep hot. Boil liquid 3 minutes. Reduce heat to medium, stir in margarine and tomato; heat through. Pour over mussels; garnish with parsley. Serve with crusty bread.

*4 to 6 servings.*

# COQUILLES SAINT JACQUES

▼

*This classic dish presents the delectable shell fish bathed in a rich, creamy wine sauce. "Coquille" denotes a small shell-shaped baking dish or the actual shell of the scallop.*

| | |
|---|---|
| 1 pound fresh mushrooms, sliced | ¼ teaspoon dried savory, crumbled |
| 5 tablespoons margarine or butter, divided | ⅛ teaspoon pepper |
| 2 tablespoons lemon juice | 1 pound bay scallops, rinsed, drained |
| ½ cup dry white wine | 3 tablespoons flour |
| ½ cup water | 1 cup half-and-half |
| 1 bay leaf | ½ cup fresh bread crumbs |
| ½ teaspoon salt | 1 tablespoon margarine or butter, melted |

Heat oven to 400°. In medium skillet, combine mushrooms, 2 tablespoons of the margarine and lemon juice. Cook over medium heat, stirring often, until all of the liquid evaporates; set aside. In large saucepan, combine wine, water, bay leaf, salt, savory and pepper; bring to a boil over high heat. Reduce heat to medium; add scallops. Simmer 3 minutes. Drain, reserving ¾ cup broth.

In medium saucepan, melt remaining 3 tablespoons margarine; stir in flour until smooth. Gradually whisk in reserved scallop broth and half-and-half. Cook over medium heat, stirring constantly, until mixture comes to a boil; boil and stir 1 minute. Stir in scallops and mushrooms; spoon into 4 individual baking dishes. Combine bread crumbs and 1 tablespoon melted margarine; spoon on top. Bake until bubbly and crumbs are golden brown (about 10 minutes).

*4 servings.*

**Tip:** To serve as an appetizer, spoon scallop mixture into 8 sea shells. Bake as above.

*Scallops come in several sizes. Bay scallops are much smaller than sea scallops and their meat is sweeter and more tender.*

# OVEN STEAMED KING OR SNOW CRAB LEGS

▼

*Invite your friends over for a "finger food" dinner of crab legs, corn on the cob and crusty French bread. Since the crab is already cooked, oven time is purposely brief to heat without toughening.*

Heat oven to 450°. Thaw crab legs, if frozen; rinse. Arrange in shallow baking pan. Add hot water to fill pan ⅛ inch deep. Cover with foil. Bake until just heated through (7 to 10 minutes).

To Serve: Arrange crab on serving platter; garnish with lemon wedges. Serve hot with Clarified Butter (below), and have nut crackers ready to split shells.

**Clarified Butter:** Melt butter completely over low heat. Remove from heat; let stand a few minutes, allowing milk solids to settle to the bottom. Skim foam from top. Pour off clear liquid (clarified butter); discard milk solids.

**Tip:** Purchase ¾ to 1 pound king crab legs or 1 pound snow crab legs per serving.

# HERB BUTTERS

▼

*Most fish fans favor varieties which are delicately flavored. Herb butters add complimentary flavors to enhance these species and help keep flesh moist during cooking.*

Brush these herb butters on fish during cooking and just before serving.

**Basil-Oregano Butter:** In small mixer bowl, beat ½ cup softened butter, 1 tablespoon dry sherry, 2 tablespoons snipped fresh basil, 2 tablespoons snipped fresh oregano, ½ teaspoon minced garlic and a dash salt and pepper. Refrigerate, covered, several hours. Soften butter before using.

*Amount: ½ cup.*

**Cilantro Butter:** In small mixer bowl, beat ½ cup softened butter, 1 (½-ounce) package fresh cilantro (snipped), 3 tablespoons lemon juice, 1 teaspoon minced garlic, ⅛ teaspoon salt and ⅛ teaspoon white pepper. Refrigerate, covered, several hours. Soften butter before using.

*Amount: ½ cup.*

**Dill Butter:** In small mixer bowl, beat ½ cup softened butter with 1 tablespoon dry sherry, 3 tablespoons snipped fresh dill, 1 tablespoon snipped fresh parsley, 1 teaspoon minced onion, 2 teaspoons lemon juice and a dash of salt and pepper. Refrigerate, covered, several hours. Soften butter before using.

*Amount: ½ cup.*

**Tarragon Butter:** In small mixer bowl, beat ½ cup softened butter, 1 tablespoon dry sherry, 3 tablespoons snipped fresh tarragon and a dash of salt and pepper. Refrigerate, covered, several hours. Soften butter before using.

*Amount: ½ cup.*

# CILANTRO PESTO

▼

*Thankfully, the traditional mortar and pestle method of preparing pesto is unnecessary to produce satisfying results. Let the food processor streamline the melding process and then enjoy this pesto with swordfish, tuna and other flavorful fish steaks.*

4 (½-ounce) packages fresh cilantro (2 cups cilantro leaves)
1 to 2 teaspoons minced garlic

½ (2-ounce) bottle pignoli nuts (¼ cup)
¾ cup olive oil
¾ cup freshly grated Parmesan cheese
¼ teaspoon salt

Place cilantro leaves, garlic and pignoli nuts in food processor bowl; process until finely chopped. Add oil in slow, steady stream with motor running. Add cheese and salt; process until well combined. Serve at room temperature or slightly heated.

*Amount: 1¾ cups.*

# MEAT

▼

Shopping around for some good news?
You have come to the right place — the meat department.
Thanks to improved breeding and feeding practices, today's
fresh beef and pork cuts are even leaner than a decade ago.
This is reason enough to cook your way through this chapter
with enthusiasm! You will find entertaining specialties, helpful
roasting charts and easy family fare. Because do-aheads are
always on the most-wanted list, several have been included.
Plus, look forward to numerous over-the-coal creations
featuring a variety of beef and pork cuts.

Become acquainted with the qualities of
the various cuts and how each should best be prepared to
achieve moist, tender results. We encourage you to rely on a
meat thermometer whenever possible as it's the best check for
doneness.

The recipes in this chapter were
designed with care to provide the important basics of meat
cookery as well as contemporary creations with foreign flair.
They are sure to please, one and all.

# ROAST BEEF

▼

***Roasting is a very uncomplicated method of arriving at succulent results. Choose prime meat and follow this timetable.***

Place refrigerated roast, fat side up, on rack in shallow roasting pan. If desired, rub all meat surfaces with Herbed Garlic Rub (below). Insert meat thermometer in thickest part of meat with tip not touching bone or fat. **Do not add water; do not baste; do not cover.** For smaller roasts in each weight category, use the higher cooking times. Allow ⅓ to ½ pound per serving for boneless roasts; allow about ¾ pound per serving for roasts with bone.

Roasts will be easier to carve if allowed to stand, covered with foil, 10 to 15 minutes after removing from oven. If roast is to stand, remove from oven when thermometer registers 5° less than desired doneness (10° less for 11 to 14-pound roasts). Internal temperature will rise 5 to 10° during standing.

### TIMETABLE FOR BEEF ROASTS
Roast in a 325° oven unless otherwise indicated.

| Cut | Approximate Weight (pounds) | Internal Temperature Reading on Meat Thermometer | Approximate Cooking Time (minutes/pound) |
|---|---|---|---|
| Standing Rib | 3 to 4 | 140° (rare) | 30 to 33 |
| | | 160° (medium) | 36 to 38 |
| | 5 to 7 | 140° (rare) | 26 to 29 |
| | | 160° (medium) | 33 to 35 |
| | 8 to 10 | 140° (rare) | 18 to 23 |
| | | 160° (medium) | 24 to 30 |
| | 11 to 14 | 140° (rare) | 14 to 17 |
| | | 160° (medium) | 18 to 22 |
| Rolled Rib or Rolled Rump | 3 to 4 | 140° (rare) | 31 to 34 |
| | | 160° (medium) | 36 to 38 |
| | 5 to 7 | 140° (rare) | 24 to 28 |
| | | 160° (medium) | 28 to 34 |
| | 8 to 10 | 140° (rare) | 20 to 22 |
| | | 160° (medium) | 22 to 25 |
| | 11 to 12 | 140° (rare) | 18 to 19 |
| | | 160° (medium) | 20 to 21 |
| Round Tip | 3 to 4 | 140° (rare) | 30 to 32 |
| | | 150° (medium-rare) | 35 to 37 |
| | 6 to 8 | 140° (rare) | 22 to 24 |
| | | 150° (medium-rare) | 25 to 27 |
| Rib Eye (Roast to 350°) | 4 to 6 | 140° (rare) | 19 to 21 |
| | | 160° (medium) | 22 to 24 |
| | | 170° (well) | 25 to 26 |
| Tenderloin (Roast at 425°) | 2 to 4 | 140° (rare) | 35 to 40 (total time) |
| | | 150° (medium) | 40 to 50 (total time) |

**Herbed Garlic Rub:** Combine 1 teaspoon garlic powder, ½ teaspoon paprika, ½ teaspoon each dried chervil, tarragon and thyme, crumbled and ½ teaspoon coarse ground pepper. This makes enough seasoning for a 4 to 6-pound beef roast.

*Uncooked beef roasts can be stored in the refrigerator 3 to 5 days or in the freezer 6 to 12 months when wrapped in vapor and moisture proof wrap.*

*Rack of Lamb*
*with Tomatoes Provençale*
*page 92*

# BERRY BEEF RAGOUT
▼

*The French define "ragout" as a "highly seasoned stew". We define this as fabulous! Beef cubes tenderize as they cook in a cranberry-sparked sweet-sour sauce and are served over bow tie pasta.*

| | |
|---|---|
| 4 pounds beef top round, cut into 1-inch cubes | 4 medium onions, thinly sliced (about 4 cups) |
| ¼ cup vegetable oil | 1 (12-ounce) package fresh cranberries, coarsely chopped (about 3⅓ cups) |
| 2 teaspoons salt | |
| ½ teaspoon pepper | |
| 1 teaspoon dried thyme, crumbled | ¾ cup firmly packed brown sugar |
| 2 teaspoons minced garlic | ½ cup flour |
| 1½ cups dry red wine | 2 (16-ounce) packages dry bow tie-shaped pasta |
| 1 (14½-ounce) can beef broth | – vegetable oil |
| 2 tablespoons red wine vinegar | ¼ cup margarine or butter |
| 2 tablespoons tomato paste | 1 tablespoon poppy seed |
| | – snipped fresh parsley |

In large Dutch oven, brown half of meat in half of oil until well browned; remove meat. Repeat with remaining meat and oil. Pour off any excess oil. Return all meat to Dutch oven. Stir in salt, pepper, thyme, garlic, wine, broth, vinegar, tomato paste and onions. Bring mixture to a boil. Reduce heat; simmer, covered, until meat is tender (about 1 hour), stirring occasionally. Refrigerate, uncovered until cool; cover and refrigerate several hours or overnight. Combine cranberries, brown sugar and flour; refrigerate, covered. Cook pasta in salted water (8 quarts water, 2 teaspoons salt) 10 minutes. Drain; rinse with cold water. Transfer to large bowl; toss with small amount of oil; cover top edge of pasta with plastic wrap; refrigerate.

To Serve: About 30 minutes before serving, reheat ragout to boiling, stirring often. Stir in cranberry mixture. Simmer until ragout is thickened (about 10 minutes), stirring occasionally. Bring water to a boil in large Dutch oven; stir in bow ties. Heat until almost tender (about 5 minutes). Drain; toss with margarine and poppy seed. Spoon pasta into heated serving bowl. Spoon ragout into another heated serving bowl; garnish with parsley.

*12 servings.*

**Variation:** Four pounds boneless pork can be substituted for beef.

# PEPPERED TENDERLOINS WITH CHEESE TOPPER
▼

*Prime cuts of beef are seasoned, broiled and crowned with a savory cheese mixture. Here's a recipe to remember when you need a special but speedy entrée.*

| | |
|---|---|
| ¼ cup semi-soft herb and garlic cheese | ½ teaspoon seasoned pepper |
| 1 tablespoon freshly grated Parmesan cheese | 4 beef tenderloin steaks, 1 inch thick (about 4 ounces each) |
| 1 tablespoon minced shallot | ½ teaspoon salt, divided |
| | – snipped fresh chives |

Heat broiler. Combine cheeses and shallot. Press an equal amount of pepper into both sides of steaks. Arrange steaks on lightly oiled broiler pan. Broil 5 inches from heat 5 minutes. Season with ¼ teaspoon of the salt. Turn and broil second side of steaks (2 to 3 minutes). Season with remaining ¼ teaspoon salt. Top each steak with 1 tablespoon cheese mixture. Broil an additional 1 to 2 minutes. Sprinkle each steak with chives. Serve immediately.

*4 servings.*

# BACON-WRAPPED TENDERLOINS

▼

*The zippy sauce will be a hit not only with these grilled steaks, but with beef roasts as well.*

| | |
|---|---|
| ½ cup prepared horseradish | 6 bacon slices |
| ¼ cup Dijon mustard | – dash salt |
| 4 beef tenderloin steaks | – dash pepper |
| (1¼ inches thick) | |

Prepare grill. In small bowl, combine horseradish and mustard; set aside. Flatten tenderloins with a meat mallet to ¾-inch thickness. Wrap 1½ bacon slices around outer edge of each tenderloin, securing with wooden picks. Spray grill rack with no stick cooking spray. Using direct heat cooking method, arrange tenderloins on grill rack 4 to 5 inches over medium coals. Grill, covered, to desired doneness (8 to 10 minutes), turning once. Sprinkle with salt and pepper. Arrange on serving platter; top with dollop of horseradish sauce.

*4 servings.*

## GRILLING BY DIRECT AND INDIRECT HEAT

▼

**Direct Heat Cooking Method:** This method of heat distribution is used for fast cooking of flat meats such as steaks, chops, hamburgers and kabobs, plus fish steaks and fillets. Coals are placed in a pyramid-shaped mound in the base of the grill, then spread out when hot. The food is placed on the grill rack directly over the coals to absorb their full heat.

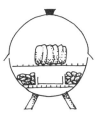

**Indirect Heat Cooking Method:** This method of heat distribution is used to cook larger cuts of meat such as roasts, ham, turkey and meats that require longer cooking at lower temperatures. Equal amounts of charcoal are placed on either side of an aluminum foil drip pan, which is centered in the bottom of the grill. The food is placed on the grill rack just over the drip pan. If using a gas grill, follow manufacturer's directions.

# GREEN PEPPERCORN SAUCE

▼

*A spoonful of this sumptuous sauce drizzled over simply grilled, roasted or broiled meats and fish immediately transforms the entrée into festive fare.*

| | |
|---|---|
| 3 tablespoons margarine or butter | 2 tablespoons green peppercorns in brine, rinsed and drained |
| 3 tablespoons minced shallots | 1 teaspoon instant beef bouillon |
| 1 cup whipping cream | 1 teaspoon Dijon mustard |
| 3 tablespoons dry vermouth | ¼ teaspoon dried thyme, crumbled |

In 2-quart saucepan, melt margarine; add shallots. Sauté over medium-high heat until golden brown (about 5 minutes), stirring occasionally. Stir in remaining ingredients; bring to a boil. Boil, stirring occasionally, until thickened (6 to 8 minutes).

*Amount: about 1 cup.*

# INDIVIDUAL BEEF WELLINGTON

▼

*This blue ribbon specialty of upscale restaurants becomes an easy do-it-at-home entrée using individual fillets rather than the traditional uncut tenderloin.*

½ cup minced shallots
2 tablespoons margarine or butter
1 (8-ounce) package fresh mushrooms, minced
½ cup chopped fresh parsley
1 tablespoon Dijon mustard
½ teaspoon dried thyme, crumbled
¼ teaspoon salt
¼ teaspoon pepper
1 (4¼-ounce) can liver pâté (optional)

4 (5 to 5½-ounce) beef tenderloin fillets
¼ cup margarine or butter
– dash salt
– dash pepper
3 tablespoons flour
1 (10½-ounce) can beef consommé
⅓ cup Madeira wine
1 (17¼-ounce) package frozen puff pastry sheets, thawed according to package directions
1 egg, beaten
1 teaspoon water

Sauté shallots in 2 tablespoons margarine over medium heat until tender (4 to 5 minutes). Stir in mushrooms and parsley; sauté until all liquid is absorbed (8 to 10 minutes). Stir in mustard, thyme, ¼ teaspoon each salt and pepper; cool. Stir in pâté; set aside. Sauté fillets in ¼ cup margarine over medium heat until internal temperature registers 130 to 135° (3 to 4 minutes per side). Remove fillets and sprinkle each with dash of salt and pepper; set aside. Blend flour into pan drippings; cook 3 minutes, stirring constantly. Stir in consommé and Madeira. Bring to a boil, stirring constantly; boil 1 minute. Stir 1 tablespoon sauce into mushroom mixture. Cover remaining sauce; refrigerate.

On lightly floured surface, roll each sheet of puff pastry to ⅛-inch thickness; cut each pastry sheet in half. Spoon ¼ of mushroom mixture onto center of each piece of pastry; top with steak. Fold pastry overlapping only enough to seal; trim if necessary. Pinch edges to seal, moistening slightly with water. Place seam side down on well-greased baking sheet. Refrigerate, covered, several hours.

To Bake: Heat oven to 400°. Combine egg and water; brush over pastry. Pierce top of pastry several times with wooden pick to allow steam to escape. Bake, uncovered, until golden brown (about 25 minutes). Heat remaining Madeira sauce; spoon over fillets, if desired.

*4 servings.*

# SALISBURY STEAK

▼

*This budget-friendly old favorite offers superlative flavor and streamlined preparation.*

1 (10¾-ounce) can golden mushroom soup, divided
1½ pounds ground beef
½ cup cracker or dry bread crumbs
1 egg, slightly beaten
⅓ cup diced onion

⅓ cup diced green bell pepper (optional)
¼ teaspoon salt
⅛ teaspoon pepper
1 tablespoon vegetable oil
2 tablespoons red wine
¼ cup water
1 teaspoon Worcestershire

In medium bowl, combine about ¼ can soup with ground beef, crumbs, egg, onion, green pepper, salt and pepper until thoroughly blended; shape into 6 patties. Heat oil in large skillet; brown patties over medium heat until browned on both sides (6 to 8 minutes total). Drain excess fat. Combine remaining soup with wine, water and Worcestershire; spoon over patties. Simmer, covered, 10 to 15 minutes.

*6 servings.*

# GRILLED TOP ROUND STEAK

▼

*This easy marinade works wonders to flavor and tenderize an economical cut of meat. It's sure to become a favorite!*

| | |
|---|---|
| 1 (2-pound) beef top round steak (about 1¼ inches thick) | ¼ cup red wine |
| | ¼ cup soy sauce |
| | 1 teaspoon minced garlic |
| 1 large zipper closure food storage bag | 1 teaspoon dried rosemary, crumbled |
| ¼ cup olive oil | ¼ teaspoon cracked pepper |
| | – Onion Mum (below) |

Place steak in food storage bag. Combine remaining ingredients except Onion Mum; pour over meat. Seal bag; refrigerate overnight, turning bag occasionally. Drain and reserve marinade.

To Grill: Prepare grill. Spray grill rack with no stick cooking spray. Using direct heat cooking method, arrange steak on grill rack 4 to 5 inches over medium-hot coals. Grill, covered, to desired doneness (12 to 18 minutes), turning once and brushing once with reserved marinade. Carve steak on the diagonal across the grain into thin slices. Arrange on serving platter. Garnish with Onion Mum.

*5 to 6 servings.*

## ONION MUM

▼

| | | |
|---|---|---|
| Select an evenly shaped onion. Trim stem and root ends; peel off outer skin. | With root end down, make a series of cuts to slice onion into quarters, then into eighths, and so on. Keep all cuts about ¼ inch from the root end. | Refrigerate in ice water until onion opens; drain. |

# CAJUN CHUCK ROAST

▼

*Meat marinates then simmers to perfection in this trendy and tantalizing treatment of traditional chuck roast.*

| | |
|---|---|
| 1 (3 to 4 pound) boneless beef chuck roast | ½ cup water |
| | 1 to 2 teaspoons cajun meat magic spice |
| 1 large zipper closure food storage bag | 2 tablespoons honey |
| ¾ cup ketchup | 2 teaspoons Worcestershire |
| ½ cup cider vinegar | ½ to 1 teaspoon Tabasco |

Place roast in food storage bag. In small saucepan, combine remaining ingredients; bring to a boil. Reduce heat; simmer 10 minutes. Cool. Pour marinade over meat; seal bag. Refrigerate several hours or overnight, turning bag several times. Drain and reserve marinade.

Heat oven to 325°. Place roast in large roaster or Dutch oven. Pour ½ cup of the reserved marinade over roast; cover. Refrigerate remaining marinade. Bake until tender (2½ to 3 hours). Remove meat from pan; carve on the diagonal across the grain into thin slices. Heat remaining reserved marinade to a boil; serve with sliced roast.

*6 to 8 servings.*

# SCANDINAVIAN MEATBALLS

▼

*Gently spiced meatballs are oven-baked for convenience and then bathed in a delectable dill sauce. This do-ahead classic deserves star billing at your next smorgasbord.*

| | |
|---|---|
| 1 cup minced onion | 1 teaspoon dried dill weed, |
| 4 tablespoons margarine or | divided |
|    butter, divided | ¼ teaspoon pepper |
| 2½ pounds meat loaf mixture | ¼ teaspoon ground nutmeg |
|    (ground beef, pork and veal) | ¼ teaspoon ground allspice |
| 1 cup fresh bread crumbs | ¼ teaspoon ground cardamom |
| 3 eggs, slightly beaten | ⅓ cup flour |
| 1½ cups half-and-half | 2 (10½-ounce) cans beef broth |
| 2 teaspoons salt | 1 cup whipping cream |

Spray 10 × 15-inch jelly roll pan with no stick cooking spray. Heat oven to 400°. In small skillet, cook onion in 1 tablespoon of the margarine until soft. In large bowl, combine onion with meat loaf mixture, crumbs, eggs, half-and-half, salt, ½ teaspoon of the dill weed, pepper, nutmeg, allspice and cardamom. (Mixture will be very soft.) Shape into 1½-inch balls; arrange on coated jelly roll pan. Bake until cooked through and lightly browned (14 to 16 minutes).

Meanwhile, melt remaining 3 tablespoons margarine in large skillet; stir in flour. Gradually whisk in beef broth. Cook over medium heat, stirring constantly, until mixture thickens. Stir in whipping cream and remaining ½ teaspoon dill weed; simmer 5 minutes. (Have gravy finished when meatballs come out of oven.) Scrape meatballs and browned bits into gravy; stir to combine. Spoon into 3-quart casserole. Refrigerate, covered, several hours or overnight.

To Serve: Heat oven to 325°. Bake casserole until heated through (40 to 50 minutes).

*Amount: about 5 dozen.*

**Tip:** If meatballs are not refrigerated before baking, reduce baking time to 30 minutes.

# BEEF 'N MANGO STIR-FRY

▼

*Here's a tropical twist for sirloin strips that's creative and colorful. While meat is marinating, prepare other ingredients so stir-frying step can be completed without interruption.*

| | |
|---|---|
| 1 pound boneless beef sirloin | 3 tablespoons vegetable oil |
|    steak, thinly sliced | 8 ounces fresh mushrooms, |
| ¼ cup soy sauce |    sliced |
| 1 tablespoon dry sherry | 1 medium onion, sliced |
| 2 teaspoons grated gingerroot |    (1 cup) |
| 1 teaspoon minced garlic | ¼ pound pea pods, ends and |
| ⅛ teaspoon white pepper |    strings removed |
| 1 large zipper closure food | 4 green onions, including |
|    storage bag |    some tops, cut into 1-inch |
| ½ cup beef broth |    pieces |
| 2 tablespoons cornstarch | 1 large ripe mango, peeled, |
| 2 tablespoons oyster sauce |    cubed (1½ cups) |
| | – hot cooked rice |

Combine steak, soy sauce, sherry, gingerroot, garlic and white pepper in food storage bag; seal bag. Refrigerate 1 hour, turning occasionally. Combine beef broth, cornstarch and oyster sauce; set aside. In large skillet, heat oil over medium-high heat; add mushrooms, stir-fry 2 to 3 minutes. Remove mushrooms with slotted spoon. Add steak mixture with marinade and sliced onions; stir-fry over medium-high heat until beef is lightly browned (2 to 4 minutes). Stir cornstarch mixture and pea pods into beef; cook and stir until mixture thickens and boils. Stir in green onions, mango and mushrooms; cook until heated through. Serve immediately over hot rice.

*4 servings.*

# BEEFY CHILE RELLENOS CASSEROLE

*Assorted toppings add the finishing touch to this hearty do-ahead casserole. Serve with a grapefruit-avocado salad and crusty rolls.*

5 (4-ounce) cans whole green chiles, drained
1 pound lean ground beef
1 medium onion, chopped (1 cup)
1 teaspoon minced garlic
3 teaspoons ground cumin, divided
1 (1.25-ounce) package taco seasoning, divided
½ teaspoon salt
1 (8-ounce) package shredded Monterey Jack cheese (2 cups)

1 (8-ounce) package shredded sharp Cheddar cheese (2 cups)
4 eggs, beaten
1 (12-ounce) can evaporated milk
1 tablespoon flour
1 (15-ounce) can tomato sauce
– sour cream
– raisins
– toasted slivered almonds
– pitted ripe olive slices

Grease 9 × 13-inch glass baking dish. Split chiles lengthwise; remove seeds. Pat chiles dry with paper towels. In heavy skillet, cook and stir ground beef with onion and garlic until meat is no longer pink; drain. Stir in 1 teaspoon of the cumin, 2 tablespoons of the taco mix and salt. Arrange half of chiles in a single layer in greased baking dish; top with beef mixture and another layer of chiles. Sprinkle cheeses over chiles. Combine eggs, milk and flour; pour over cheeses. Stir remaining 2 teaspoons cumin and remaining taco mix into tomato sauce. Cover casserole and tomato sauce; refrigerate up to 24 hours.

To Bake: Heat oven to 325°. Spread seasoned tomato sauce evenly over casserole. Bake until bubbly in center (about 60 minutes). Serve with sour cream, raisins, almonds and olives.

*10 to 12 servings.*

**Tip:** If casserole is not refrigerated before baking, reduce baking time to 50 minutes.

# TEX-MEX MEAT LOAVES

*Microwave preparation makes these individual meat loaves ideal for after work dinner-on-the-double.*

½ pound lean ground beef
¼ cup uncooked rolled oats
1 egg, slightly beaten
2 tablespoons medium picante sauce

1 teaspoon instant minced onion
¼ teaspoon chili powder
¼ teaspoon salt
⅓ cup medium picante sauce
¼ cup shredded sharp Cheddar cheese

Combine ground beef, oats, egg, 2 tablespoons picante sauce, onion, chili powder and salt; shape into 2 (2 × 4-inch) loaves. Place in microwavable baking dish; cover with waxed paper. Microwave (HIGH), rotating dish ¼ turn every 2 minutes, until instant read thermometer reads 160° (4 to 5 minutes). Spoon ⅓ cup picante sauce into 1-cup glass measure. Microwave (HIGH) 30 seconds. Spoon evenly over loaves; top with cheese. Microwave (HIGH) until cheese is melted (about 45 seconds).

*2 servings.*

*An instant read thermometer takes only seconds to register the temperature of both large and small cuts of meat and poultry. Remove food from heat source before inserting this type of thermometer into food.*

# ROSEMARY 'N PEPPER CRUSTED PORK ROAST

▼

*Whether you grill or bake this herb-crusted roast, watch meat thermometer carefully during last 15 minutes to avoid overcooking.*

| | |
|---|---|
| 1 (2½ to 3-pound) boneless double loin pork roast | 4 teaspoons dried rosemary, crumbled |
| 2 tablespoons coarsely ground or cracked pepper | 2 teaspoons salt |
| | 1 teaspoon garlic salt |

Remove netting from roast; separate into 2 single loins. Combine remaining ingredients; rub on surface of pork.

**Grill Method:** Prepare rack. Spray grill rack with no stick cooking spray. Using indirect heat cooking method, center loins on grill rack over drip pan 4 to 5 inches opposite medium-hot coals. Grill, covered, until meat thermometer registers 155° (50 to 60 minutes), turning once. Remove pork from grill; cover loosely with foil and allow to stand 10 minutes before slicing.

**Oven Method:** Heat oven to 350°. Prepare pork as above with seasonings. Arrange loins 2 inches apart on broiler pan or on rack in shallow pan. Roast until meat thermometer registers 155° (50 to 60 minutes). Cover loosely with foil and allow to stand 10 minutes before slicing.

*8 to 10 servings.*

# PORK LOIN ROAST WITH LINGONBERRY SAUCE

▼

*Redolent with spices, a boneless pork loin roast cooks to mouth watering tenderness. The crowning touch is a wine-laced lingonberry sauce – a refreshingly tart contrast to the mildly flavored meat.*

| | |
|---|---|
| 1 (4 to 6-pound) boneless double loin pork roast | ½ teaspoon garlic powder |
| 1 teaspoon dry mustard | ½ teaspoon white pepper |
| 1 teaspoon salt | ½ teaspoon ground cardamom |
| | – Spicy Lingonberry Sauce (below) |

Heat oven to 325°. Place pork on rack in shallow roasting pan. Combine mustard, salt, garlic powder, white pepper and cardamom; rub into roast. Roast, uncovered, until meat thermometer registers 155° (29 to 33 minutes per pound). Cover loosely with foil; let stand 10 minutes before carving. Serve with Spicy Lingonberry Sauce.

*14 to 20 servings.*

**Spicy Lingonberry Sauce:** In saucepan, combine 1 (.50 to .60 pound) carton lingonberries, drained, ¼ cup sauterne wine, 2 tablespoons lemon juice, ½ to ¾ cup sugar, 2 teaspoons grated lemon peel and 1 teaspoon grated orange peel; bring to a boil. Reduce heat; simmer until thickened (15 to 20 minutes), stirring occasionally.

*Amount: 1 to 1½ cups.*

*Take care not to overcook pork, which is much leaner today than in the past. The recommended internal temperature for very lean pork cuts is 160°. There may be just a hint of pink in the center. Cook larger cuts to 155°, then let stand, covered, allowing juices to set and internal temperature to reach 160°.*

# SWEET-AND-SOUR PORK

▼

*American palates adore this colorful Oriental specialty. The presentation is picture perfect.*

- 3 tablespoons soy sauce, divided
- 1 tablespoon dry sherry
- 4 tablespoons cornstarch, divided
- ¼ teaspoon salt
- 1½ pounds boneless lean pork, cut into 1-inch cubes
- 3 tablespoons vegetable oil
- 1 (20-ounce) can pineapple chunks in own juice
- ½ teaspoon minced garlic
- ⅓ cup firmly packed brown sugar
- 2 tablespoons Hoisin sauce
- ⅓ cup cider vinegar
- 1 green bell pepper, cut into julienne strips
- 1 (6-ounce) jar maraschino cherries, drained (½ cup) (optional)
- – hot cooked rice

Combine 1 tablespoon of the soy sauce, sherry, 2 tablespoons of the cornstarch and salt; stir in pork. Marinate 30 minutes. In wok or large skillet heat oil to 350°. Fry half of pork until browned and crisp (4 to 5 minutes); remove pork with slotted spoon. Repeat with remaining pork; drain off all but 1 tablespoon oil. Return pork to wok. Drain pineapple; reserve ½ cup juice. Combine remaining 2 tablespoons of the cornstarch and reserved pineapple juice; pour into wok. Stir in remaining 2 tablespoons soy sauce, garlic, brown sugar, Hoisin sauce and vinegar. Cook over medium heat, stirring constantly, until sauce comes to a boil; boil and stir 1 minute. Stir in pineapple, green pepper and cherries; heat through (about 5 minutes). Serve over rice.

*4 to 6 servings.*

# GLAZED PORK LOIN RIBS

▼

*Preparation for these meaty down-home back ribs begins the day before serving when the snappy ginger-garlic glaze ingredients are combined and refrigerated.*

- 2 tablespoons cornstarch
- ⅔ cup firmly packed brown sugar
- ⅔ cup soy sauce
- 1 (2.5-ounce) box crystallized ginger slices
- 1 teaspoon minced garlic
- ¼ cup apple cider vinegar
- 2 cups water
- 4 pounds pork loin back ribs
- 1 teaspoon beau monde seasoning
- – Scored Citrus Slices (page 70)

Combine cornstarch, brown sugar, soy sauce, crystallized ginger, garlic and vinegar in blender container; process until ginger is finely chopped. Refrigerate glaze, covered, about 24 hours. Bring water to a boil in large Dutch oven. Cut ribs into serving-size portions. Arrange ribs in single layer in water; stir in beau monde. Simmer, covered, 30 minutes; drain.

**Grill Method:** Prepare grill. Spray grill rack with no stick cooking spray. Using direct heat cooking method, arrange meaty side of ribs on grill rack 5 inches from low to medium-low coals. Grill, uncovered, until browned (5 to 8 minutes). Brush browned side with glaze, turn; grill until browned (4 to 6 minutes). Continue grilling until heated through (10 to 15 minutes longer), turning often and brushing with glaze. Arrange ribs on heated platter; brush with remaining glaze. Garnish with Scored Citrus Slices.

**Oven Method:** Heat oven to 325°. Arrange simmered ribs in single layer in shallow baking pan. Bake, covered, 30 minutes. Brush with glaze. Bake until tender (about 30 minutes longer), brushing with glaze every 15 minutes.

*4 servings.*

# APPLE SPICED PORK MEDALLIONS

▼

*These very tender pork cuts are quickly sautéed and then briefly simmered in a savory onion-apple mixture. For a special autumn menu, team with golden acorn squash or ruby red cabbage.*

| | |
|---|---|
| 1 pound pork tenderloin | 3 tablespoons vegetable oil, |
| 1 teaspoon dried thyme, |    divided |
|    crumbled | ½ cup minced onion |
| 1 teaspoon ground ginger | 1 large Golden Delicious |
| 1 teaspoon ground cinnamon |    apple, unpeeled, coarsely |
| ¼ teaspoon ground nutmeg |    chopped (2 cups) |
| ¼ teaspoon pepper | 1 cup apple cider |
| ½ teaspoon salt | 1½ teaspoons cornstarch |
| | 1 tablespoon apple cider or |
| |    water |

Separate tenderloin into 2 single tenderloins. Cut each tenderloin crosswise into 4 medallions; flatten slightly with palm of hand. Combine thyme, ginger, cinnamon, nutmeg, pepper and salt; coat medallions with spice mixture. Heat 2 tablespoons of the oil in large skillet. Sauté pork over medium heat until brown (about 2 minutes per side). Remove from skillet; cover and set aside. Add remaining 1 tablespoon oil to skillet; stir in onion and apple. Sauté until onion is tender (2 to 4 minutes). Pour in 1 cup cider; heat to simmer. Return pork medallions to skillet. Simmer, covered, 5 minutes. Arrange pork in circle around edge of serving platter. Spoon apple mixture into center of platter, leaving juices in skillet; cover platter. Dissolve cornstarch in 1 tablespoon cider; slowly stir into juices and continue cooking over medium-high heat until thickened (3 to 5 minutes). Pour sauce over pork medallions; serve immediately.

*4 servings.*

# PORK CHOPS DIJON

▼

*Company's coming and time is short? This elegant entrée, which belies its speedy preparation, features a piquant mustard sauce spooned over sautéed pork chops.*

| | |
|---|---|
| 4 boneless pork loin chops, | 2 teaspoons minced gingerroot |
|    ¾ inch thick | 2 teaspoons Dijon mustard |
| 2 tablespoons flour | 2 teaspoons natural seed |
| 1 tablespoon margarine or |    mustard |
|    butter | ¼ teaspoon salt |
| ½ cup chicken broth | ⅛ teaspoon pepper |
| 2 tablespoons dry sherry | – Orange Twists (page 62) |
| ¼ cup minced shallots | – fresh parsley sprigs |

Coat pork chops with flour. In medium skillet, melt margarine; add pork chops. Sauté over medium heat until brown on both sides (3 to 4 minutes per side – pork will have a hint of pink in center). Remove chops to heated platter; keep warm. Pour broth and sherry into skillet; bring to a boil, loosening brown particles from skillet. Add shallots and gingerroot; cook, stirring frequently, 2 minutes. Stir in mustards, salt and pepper. Spoon sauce over chops. Garnish with Orange Twists and parsley sprigs.

*4 servings.*

# GINGER-GARLIC PORK CHOPS

▼

*These grilled chops are irresistible! Take care not to overcook them so the meat will remain moist as well as tender.*

| | |
|---|---|
| 4 (1¼-inch thick) boneless pork loin chops | 1 cup low-sodium soy sauce |
| 1 large zipper closure food storage bag | 1 tablespoon minced garlic |
| | 1 tablespoon minced gingerroot |

Trim any excess fat from chops. Arrange in food storage bag. Combine remaining ingredients; pour over chops. Seal bag; refrigerate 12 to 24 hours, turning bag occasionally. Drain and reserve marinade.

To Grill: Prepare grill. Spray grill rack with no stick cooking spray. Using direct heat cooking method, arrange chops on grill rack 4 to 5 inches over medium coals. Grill, covered, until browned and just a hint of pink remains in center (14 to 18 minutes total), turning and brushing once with reserved marinade.

*4 servings.*

# CROWN ROAST OF PORK

▼

*This regal entrée requires little attention while roasting and makes a stunning tableside presentation.*

Order in advance from meat department: 1 (7 to 9-pound) pork rib crown roast.

To Roast: Heat oven to 325°. Place refrigerated roast, bone tips up, on lightly oiled broiler pan. Insert meat thermometer in thickest part of meat with tip not touching bone or fat. Cover bone ends with foil. Roast, uncovered, until internal temperature registers 160° (about 1¾ hours total). Remove from oven. Cover roast loosely with foil; let stand 10 minutes.

To Serve: Carefully transfer roast to heated serving platter. Remove strings. Replace foil on bone ends with paper frills. Carve tableside, slicing meat between ribs.

*10 to 14 servings.*

# RUM GLAZED HAM

▼

*Only three ingredients blend into a rich, rum-flavored orange glaze.*

| | |
|---|---|
| 1 (3 to 4-pound) boneless fully cooked ham half | 1 cup orange marmalade |
| | ½ cup dark rum |
| | 1 tablespoon dry mustard |

Heat oven to 325°. Insert meat thermometer into center of ham. Place ham on rack in shallow pan. Cover pan tightly with foil, leaving thermometer dial exposed. Bake 1¼ hours. Combine marmalade, rum and mustard; brush ham with mixture. Continue baking, uncovered, until meat thermometer registers 135° (20 to 30 minutes longer), brushing once with glaze. Let ham stand, covered loosely with foil, 10 minutes before slicing. If desired, heat remaining glaze; drizzle over platter of ham slices before serving.

*12 to 16 servings.*

# GRILLED HAM STEAKS WITH PINEAPPLE SLICES

▼

*You never knew "fast food" could be so delicious! This colorful entrée requires only minutes on the grill and is brightened with sunny pineapple slices brushed with a brown sugar glaze.*

¼ cup margarine or butter, melted
1 tablespoon snipped fresh thyme or 1 teaspoon dried thyme, crumbled

½ teaspoon lemon and pepper seasoning salt
2 (1-pound) ham steaks, ½ inch thick
– Grilled Pineapple Slices (below)

Prepare grill. Combine margarine, thyme and lemon and pepper seasoning salt. Trim fat from outer edge of ham steaks; brush both sides with thyme-salt mixture. Spray grill rack with no stick cooking spray. Using direct heat cooking method, arrange ham steaks on grill rack 4 to 5 inches over medium coals. Grill, covered, 4 minutes; baste with thyme-salt mixture. Continue grilling, covered, until heated through (about 3 minutes). Serve with Grilled Pineapple Slices.

*5 to 6 servings.*

**Grilled Pineapple Slices:** Slice 1 peeled, cored pineapple into 6 slices. In 1-cup glass measure, combine ⅓ cup firmly packed brown sugar, 2 tablespoons margarine, 2 tablespoons rum and ¼ teaspoon ground cinnamon. Microwave (HIGH) 1 minute. Brush both sides of pineapple with glaze mixture. Using direct heat cooking method, arrange pineapple slices next to ham slices over medium coals. Grill, turning frequently and brushing with glaze mixture, until glazed and heated through (6 to 8 minutes).

*Determining Charcoal Temperatures: Cautiously hold your hand, palm side down, over the coals at about grill rack level. Then, count the number of seconds you can comfortably hold that position and you will have an indicator of the temperature of the coals: 5 seconds = low; 4 seconds = medium; 3 seconds = medium-hot; and 2 seconds = hot.*

# SCALLOPED POTATOES AND HAM

▼

*A little leftover ham goes a long way in this classic "meat and potatoes" casserole. It's just as welcome on today's menus as it was when Grandma brought it to the table.*

3 pounds potatoes (8 medium)
¼ cup margarine or butter
¼ cup flour
3 cups milk
1½ teaspoons salt
⅛ teaspoon pepper

¾ cup chopped onion
1½ pounds baked ham, cut into 1½-inch cubes
1 tablespoon margarine or butter, melted
½ cup soft bread crumbs

Heat oven to 325°. Peel and cut potatoes into slices about ⅛ inch thick. Immediately place in cold water to cover. Melt ¼ cup margarine in medium saucepan; blend in flour. Gradually stir in milk. Cook over medium heat, stirring constantly, until mixture comes to a boil; boil and stir 1 minute. Stir in salt and pepper. Drain potatoes thoroughly. Layer half of potatoes, onion, ham and white sauce in greased 3-quart casserole; repeat layers. Combine 1 tablespoon margarine and bread crumbs; sprinkle over potatoes. Bake, covered, 45 minutes. Uncover; bake until potatoes test done when pierced with fork (35 to 45 minutes longer).

*6 servings.*

# ROAST LEG OF LAMB

▼

*A traditional rite of spring is showcasing leg of lamb on special dinner menus. Because lamb should be served piping hot, have accompaniments table-ready when you begin carving.*

Heat oven to 325°. Allow ½ to ¾ pound of bone-in lamb per person; allow ⅓ pound of boneless lamb per person. If desired, season roast with a mixture of 1½ teaspoons minced garlic, 1 tablespoon paprika, 1½ teaspoons dried rosemary, crumbled, 2 teaspoons salt and ½ teaspoon pepper. Cut slits in roast with point of knife; press seasoning mixture into slits. Place roast, fat side up, on rack in shallow roasting pan. Insert meat thermometer in thickest part of meat with tip not touching bone or fat. Roast to desired doneness. **Do not add water; do not baste; do not cover.**

Roasts will be easier to carve if allowed to stand, covered with foil, 10 to 15 minutes after removing from oven. If roast is to stand, remove from oven when thermometer registers 5° less than desired doneness. Internal temperature will rise 5 to 10° during standing.

| Cut | Approximate Weight (pounds) | Internal Temperature Reading on Meat Thermometer | Approximate Cooking Time (minutes/pound) |
|---|---|---|---|
| Leg | 5 to 7 | 140° (rare)<br>150° (medium-rare)<br>160° (medium) | 17 to 19<br>20 to 23<br>24 to 27 |
| Leg, shank half | 3 to 4 | 140° (rare)<br>150° (medium-rare)<br>160° (medium) | 23 to 26<br>27 to 30<br>31 to 34 |
| Leg, sirloin half | 4 to 5 | 140° (rare)<br>150° (medium-rare)<br>160° (medium) | 19 to 22<br>23 to 26<br>27 to 29 |
| Leg, boneless | 4 to 7 | 140° (rare)<br>150° (medium-rare)<br>160° (medium) | 21 to 23<br>24 to 26<br>27 to 29 |

# BRAISED LAMB SHANKS

▼

*Browning the shanks seals in juices and adds to the attractive appearance of this savory meat and vegetable medley.*

¼ cup vegetable oil
6 lamb shanks (5 to 6 pounds)
2 cups sliced onions
1 cup sliced celery
1 cup sliced carrots
1 beef bouillon cube
1 cup boiling water
1 (15-ounce) can tomato sauce
3 tablespoons ketchup
¼ teaspoon sugar

1 teaspoon salt
½ teaspoon dried rosemary, crumbled
¼ teaspoon garlic powder
¼ teaspoon pepper
1 bay leaf
2 (9-ounce) packages frozen whole green beans, thawed, drained
5 medium red potatoes, peeled, cut into chunks

Heat oil in Dutch oven; brown shanks in 2 batches. Remove shanks and all but 2 to 3 tablespoons oil. Sauté onions, celery and carrots until golden (about 5 minutes). Dissolve bouillon cube in boiling water; add to vegetables with tomato sauce, ketchup, sugar, salt, rosemary, garlic powder, pepper, bay leaf and lamb shanks. Simmer, covered, until shanks are tender (about 1 hour), stirring occasionally. Stir in green beans and potatoes. Simmer, covered, until vegetables are tender (20 to 25 minutes). Remove bay leaf. Arrange lamb shanks and vegetables on large serving platter. Serve with pan juices.

*6 servings.*

# RACK OF LAMB WITH TOMATOES PROVENÇALE

▼

*Addictive aroma, fantastic flavor and magnificent presentation...what more can one ask from an entrée for VIP occasions? The bonus is an uncomplicated preparation with a demi-glace sauce from a mix.*

1 (7-rib) French-cut rack of lamb (1½ to 1¾ pounds)
½ teaspoon cracked pepper
¾ teaspoon dried basil, crumbled, divided
½ teaspoon dried rosemary, crumbled

¼ teaspoon dried thyme, crumbled
– Tomatoes Provençale (below)
1 (1.2-ounce) package demi-glace sauce mix
2 tablespoons brandy
2 tablespoons margarine or butter

Heat oven to 375°. Remove frills from rib ends, if necessary. Place meat, bone side down, in shallow roasting pan. Combine cracked pepper, ½ teaspoon basil, rosemary and thyme; pat mixture over meat. Cover exposed rib ends with strip of foil. Roast until thermometer registers 145 to 150° (35 to 45 minutes) for medium-rare. Prepare Tomatoes Provençale; arrange around lamb after 15 to 20 minutes of roasting time. Prepare demi-glace sauce mix according to package directions. Stir in brandy; margarine and remaining ¼ teaspoon of basil. Cover; set aside. When lamb is removed from oven, cover with foil and let stand 5 to 10 minutes.

To Serve: Place frills on bone ends; arrange lamb on platter with Tomatoes Provençale. Reheat demi-glace; drizzle part of sauce over lamb. Carve into individual ribs; pass remaining sauce.

*2 servings.*

**Tomatoes Provençale:** Remove core from 1 large tomato; cut in half crosswise. Combine 2 tablespoons dry bread crumbs, 1 tablespoon dried basil, crumbled, 1 tablespoon grated Romano cheese, dash salt, dash pepper, 2 teaspoons olive oil and ½ teaspoon minced garlic. Sprinkle crumb mixture equally on cut surfaces of tomato halves.

# LAMB CHOPS WITH COUSCOUS STUFFING

▼

*Couscous, a fine semolina made from wheat germ, is enhanced with a tart kumquat mixture for a unique lamb chop stuffing.*

1 (10-ounce) jar kumquats
1 cup chicken broth
⅓ cup chopped celery
¼ cup sliced green onions
⅛ teaspoon pepper
1¼ cups couscous
2 tablespoons orange-flavored liqueur

½ (2-ounce) bottle pignoli nuts (¼ cup), toasted
8 lamb loin chops, 1 inch thick
2 tablespoons orange marmalade
1 teaspoon Worcestershire
1 tablespoon margarine or butter
1 tablespoon water

Drain kumquat syrup into saucepan. Reserve 4 kumquats for garnish; chop remaining kumquats. Stir chopped kumquats, chicken broth, celery, green onions and pepper into reserved syrup. Bring to a boil. Reduce heat; simmer, covered, 5 minutes. Remove from heat; stir in couscous. Cover; let stand 5 minutes. Stir in liqueur and pignoli. Trim any fat and "tails" from lamb chops. Cut a pocket in each chop by cutting horizontally almost to bone through meaty part of chop. Spoon 2 to 3 tablespoons couscous mixture into each pocket.

Heat broiler. Combine orange marmalade and Worcestershire; brush glaze over chops. Broil 3 inches from heat for 5 to 8 minutes. Turn; brush with glaze. Broil to desired doneness (5 to 9 minutes longer).

Meanwhile, combine margarine, water and remaining couscous in microwavable bowl. Microwave (HIGH), covered, until heated through (1 to 2 minutes). Arrange couscous on heated platter, top with lamb chops; garnish with reserved kumquats. Serve immediately.

*4 servings.*

# SAVORY VEAL CHOPS

▼

*The herbed artichoke and mushroom sauce is a perfect partner for these browned veal chops.*

| | |
|---|---|
| 4 veal loin chops, 1 inch thick | 1 (9-ounce) package frozen |
| ¾ teaspoon salt, divided | artichoke hearts, thawed |
| ¼ teaspoon pepper | 1 cup sliced fresh mushrooms |
| ¼ cup flour | ¾ cup dry white wine |
| 3 tablespoons olive oil, divided | 2 tablespoons snipped fresh |
| 1 tablespoon thinly sliced | marjoram |
| green onions | 1 cup half-and-half |
| 1 teaspoon minced garlic | – fresh marjoram sprigs |

Trim any excess fat from chops. Sprinkle chops with ½ teaspoon of the salt and pepper; lightly coat both sides with flour. In large heavy skillet, heat 2 tablespoons of the oil over medium heat. Add chops; cook until of medium doneness (13 to 15 minutes), turning once or twice to brown evenly. Remove chops to heated platter; keep warm. Add remaining 1 tablespoon oil, green onions and garlic to skillet. Cook and stir over medium heat 1 minute. Add artichokes, mushrooms, wine and snipped marjoram. Cook, 6 minutes, stirring occasionally and scraping browned particles from pan. Increase heat to high. Whisk in half-and-half. Cook and whisk until thickened (4 to 6 minutes). Stir in remaining ¼ teaspoon salt and accumulated juices from veal platter. Spoon vegetable sauce over chops; garnish with marjoram sprigs.

*4 servings.*

# VEAL CUTLETS ORIENTAL

▼

*Here, tender, thin veal steaks are quickly sautéed and bathed in an enchanting ginger-infused wine sauce. It's a sensational entrée for two!*

| | |
|---|---|
| 1 tablespoon olive oil | ¼ cup dry white wine |
| 1 tablespoon margarine or | 1 green onion, including some |
| butter | tops, thinly sliced |
| ½ teaspoon minced garlic | 1 teaspoon grated fresh |
| 4 thinly sliced veal round | gingerroot |
| steaks (2 to 3 ounces each) | ½ teaspoon Oriental sesame oil |
| ¼ teaspoon salt | 1 tablespoon minced fresh |
| ⅛ teaspoon white pepper | parsley |
| | – Onion Brushes (below) |

In large heavy skillet, heat olive oil and margarine over medium heat. Stir in garlic; cook 1 minute. Add veal; cook until lightly browned (2 to 3 minutes), turning once. Remove veal to heated platter; sprinkle with salt and white pepper. Add wine, onion and gingerroot to skillet; increase heat to high. Cook and stir 1 minute, scraping browned bits from bottom of pan. Remove pan from heat; stir in sesame oil. Return veal to skillet; coat all slices with sauce. Arrange veal on 2 heated dinner plates; spoon any remaining sauce over veal. Sprinkle with parsley. Garnish each plate with an Onion Brush. Serve immediately.

*2 servings.*

## ONION BRUSHES

▼

Trim off root end of green onion. Then, remove green top, leaving a 3-inch section.

With tip of a paring knife, cut 1-inch-long parallel slits from each end, leaving the center uncut. Cut as many slits as possible to make the fluffiest brush.

Refrigerate in ice water until ends curl and brush is ready to be used. (Ends will curl in a few minutes.)

# MARINADE POTPOURRI

▼

*Marinades that contain an acid ingredient such as lemon juice, wine or vinegar, will help tenderize meat in addition to flavoring it.*

Refrigerate marinades in zipper closure food storage bags for ease in handling. Allow ½ cup marinade per pound of meat. Marinate up to 24 hours, turning occasionally.

**Beer Mustard:** Combine 1 cup beer, ¼ cup each minced green onion and vegetable oil, 3 tablespoons Dijon mustard, 1 teaspoon minced garlic, ½ to 1 teaspoon salt and ¼ teaspoon pepper.

*Amount: about 1⅓ cups.*

**Burgundy 'n Onion:** Combine ¾ cup Burgundy, 3 tablespoons vegetable oil, 2 tablespoons chopped green onion, 2 teaspoons brown sugar, 1 teaspoon each minced garlic and salt and ¼ teaspoon pepper.

*Amount: about 1 cup.*

**Teriyaki:** Combine ½ cup soy sauce, ¼ cup honey or white corn syrup, ½ teaspoon minced garlic and ¼ teaspoon ground ginger.

*Amount: about ¾ cup.*

**Thyme 'n Lemon:** Combine ⅓ cup each lemon juice, soy sauce, olive oil and minced green onion, 1 tablespoon dried thyme, crumbled and ½ teaspoon each salt and pepper.

*Amount: about 1⅓ cups.*

# GRILLING TOPPERS

▼

*Here's a trio of toppers to add pizzazz to grilled meats and poultry.*

**Barbecue Sauce:** Combine ½ cup ketchup, ¼ cup firmly packed brown sugar, 1 tablespoon vinegar, 1 teaspoon salt, ½ teaspoon dried sage, 1 teaspoon prepared mustard and ¼ teaspoon cayenne pepper. Brush on ribs, hamburgers, pork or chicken during last few minutes of grilling.

*Amount: about ¾ cup.*

**Fruit Glaze:** Combine 1 (13-ounce) jar pineapple preserves, 1 (10-ounce) jar apple jelly, ¼ cup Dijon mustard and 2 tablespoons horseradish. Brush on ribs, chicken or fish during last few minutes of grilling.

*Amount: about 2 cups.*

**Spicy Garden Salsa:** In 2-quart microwavable bowl, combine 1 cup ketchup, 1 seeded and chopped tomato, 1 chopped green bell pepper, 2 tablespoons each minced onion, brown sugar, Worcestershire and steak sauce, ½ teaspoon garlic powder and ¼ teaspoon Tabasco. Cover with plastic wrap; vent one corner. Microwave (HIGH), stirring once, 10 minutes. Let stand 15 minutes. (Sauce thickens upon standing.) Serve over grilled steaks, ribs, hamburgers or chicken.

*Amount: about 2½ cups.*

# POULTRY

**P**oultry comes with perks aplenty! Favorites in American kitchens, chicken and turkey are highly revered for their mild flavor and congeniality with all manner of seasonings and flavors.

Poultry choices have changed significantly since the days of the inevitable "chicken every Sunday" dinner or the "holiday turkey". We have a selection of cuts and parts to suit every style of cooking and serving, from ground to quartered, drumsticks to wings, or breasts to thighs. Turkey entices us as cutlets, fillets and tenderloins as well as in more familiar forms. Select from many skinless and boneless cuts or parts. For elegant meals, select young ducklings or Cornish game hens.

This potpourri of recipes is designed to showcase poultry for maximum year-round enjoyment. You will find deluxe and down-home recipes, intriguing international specialities, tempting casseroles, hearty roll-ups, superb sandwiches and marinades extraordinaire. Recipes are streamlined to suit snug timetables and promote do-ahead ease.

# CHICKEN 'N PISTACHIO ROLL-UPS

▼

*Pistachio nuts accent the stuffing, and a generous portion of sherry contributes to an enticing sauce for this four star entrée.*

| | |
|---|---|
| **6 whole boneless, skinless chicken breasts, halved** | **1 (8-ounce) carton fresh mushrooms, chopped** |
| **¾ teaspoon salt** | **½ cup chopped pistachio nuts** |
| **¼ teaspoon pepper** | **¾ cup soft bread crumbs** |
| **3 tablespoons margarine or butter** | **– Sherry Wine Sauce (below)** |
| | **– chopped pistachio nuts** |
| | **– snipped fresh parsley** |

Heat oven to 350°. With rolling pin, flatten chicken between waxed paper, to an even thickness. Sprinkle with salt and pepper. In small skillet, melt margarine. Sauté mushrooms and ½ cup chopped pistachios over medium heat until all liquid evaporates. Stir in bread crumbs; cool. Divide mixture into 12 equal portions; spoon 1 portion onto center of each breast half. Roll up jelly-roll fashion. Arrange, seam side down, in 9 × 13-inch glass baking dish. Spoon Sherry Wine Sauce over rolls. Refrigerate, covered, up to 24 hours. Bake, uncovered, until chicken is tender and juices run clear (about 40 minutes), basting once or twice.

To Serve: Arrange on heated serving platter. Spoon sauce over chicken. Garnish with remaining chopped pistachios and parsley.

*12 servings.*

**Sherry Wine Sauce:** In small saucepan, combine 4 teaspoons cornstarch and 1 cup dry sherry until smooth. Stir in ½ cup melted margarine or butter, ½ cup apricot preserves and ½ cup colonial chutney (Chut-nut). Cook over medium heat, stirring constantly, until thickened.

# RASPBERRY SAUCED CHICKEN BREASTS

▼

*Speedy stovetop preparation and an exceptionally delicious sauce give this entrée high marks from our staff.*

| | |
|---|---|
| **4 boneless, skinless chicken breast halves** | **¼ cup minced shallots** |
| **¼ teaspoon salt** | **¼ cup raspberry vinegar** |
| **2 tablespoons margarine or butter** | **¼ cup chicken broth** |
| | **¼ cup half-and-half** |
| | **1 tablespoon tomato paste** |
| | **– fresh raspberries** |

Flatten chicken breasts slightly; sprinkle chicken with salt. Melt margarine in large skillet. Sauté chicken over medium heat until lightly browned (about 4 minutes per side). Remove chicken from skillet. Stir shallots into drippings. Cook, covered, over low heat until tender (8 to 10 minutes), stirring occasionally. Stir in vinegar; cook, uncovered, over medium heat, stirring occasionally, until liquid is reduced to 1 tablespoon. Whisk in chicken broth, half-and-half and tomato paste; simmer 1 minute. Return chicken and juices to skillet. Simmer, uncovered, basting often, until chicken is no longer pink when cut in thickest part (5 to 7 minutes). Arrange on warmed serving platter; spoon sauce evenly over chicken. Garnish with raspberries.

*2 to 4 servings.*

*Chicken Fajitas*
*page 99*

# PARMESAN DIJON CHICKEN

▼

*This crunchy coating is just piquant enough to add unique flavor and texture to succulent chicken breasts. Prepare up to eight hours before baking for added convenience.*

2 cups fine, fresh bread crumbs (3 to 4 slices)
¾ cup freshly grated Parmesan cheese
¼ cup chopped fresh parsley
1 teaspoon minced garlic

⅔ cup Dijon mustard
3 tablespoons dry white wine
10 boneless, skinless chicken breast halves
¼ cup margarine or butter, melted

Dry bread crumbs at room temperature for several hours. Combine bread crumbs, Parmesan cheese, parsley and garlic. In shallow pan, combine mustard and wine. Dip chicken pieces in mustard mixture; roll in crumb mixture to coat. Arrange in 9 × 13-inch glass baking dish. Refrigerate, covered, up to 8 hours.

To Serve: Heat oven to 350°. Drizzle with melted margarine. Bake, uncovered, until chicken is tender and juices run clear (50 to 60 minutes).

*8 to 10 servings.*

# COMPANY CHICKEN 'N ARTICHOKES

▼

*When entertaining with panache, serve this delicately seasoned do-ahead that will have guests clamoring for the recipe.*

6 large whole boneless chicken breasts, halved (4½ to 5 pounds)
2 (14½-ounce) cans clear chicken broth with ⅓ less salt
2 (14-ounce) cans quartered artichoke hearts, drained
2 tablespoons margarine or butter
12 ounces fresh mushrooms, sliced

1 large red bell pepper, diced
⅓ cup margarine or butter
½ cup flour
¼ teaspoon salt
⅛ teaspoon pepper
1 cup half-and-half
½ cup freshly grated Parmesan cheese
2 tablespoons dry sherry
½ teaspoon dried rosemary, crumbled

In large skillet, simmer chicken breasts, in a single layer, in chicken broth, covered, until chicken is tender and juices run clear (15 to 20 minutes). Remove chicken, cool slightly; remove skin. Arrange chicken in 9 × 13-inch glass baking dish. Reserve 1½ cups chicken broth for sauce. Spoon artichoke hearts over chicken. In medium skillet, melt 2 tablespoons margarine; sauté mushrooms and red pepper until all liquid has evaporated. Set aside.

In small saucepan, melt ⅓ cup margarine; blend in flour, salt and pepper. Gradually stir in reserved chicken broth and half-and-half. Bring to a boil, stirring constantly; boil and stir 1 minute. Gradually stir in Parmesan cheese until cheese is melted. Stir in sherry and rosemary; pour sauce over chicken. Sprinkle mushrooms and red pepper evenly over sauce. Refrigerate, covered, several hours or overnight.

To Bake: Heat oven to 325°. Bake, covered, 1 hour; uncover and bake until heated through (about 15 minutes).

*10 to 12 servings.*

# HONEY MUSTARD CHICKEN

▼

*A colorful bouquet of fresh vegetables is microwaved with boneless chicken breasts for an on-the-double dinner.*

2 tablespoons margarine or
   butter
1 (6-inch) zucchini, cut into
   2 × ½-inch strips (1 cup)
1 (6-inch) yellow summer
   squash, cut into 2 × ½-inch
   strips (1 cup)
1 medium red bell pepper, cut
   into 2 × ½-inch strips (1 cup)

4 boneless, skinless chicken
   breast halves (about
   1½ pounds)
3 tablespoons honey
2 tablespoons Dijon mustard
2 teaspoons soy sauce
½ to 1 teaspoon curry powder
¼ teaspoon pepper
– snipped fresh parsley

In 1-quart microwavable bowl, microwave margarine (HIGH) until melted (30 seconds). Stir in vegetables. In 12-inch round microwavable dish, arrange chicken breasts, rib side up, with thicker edges toward outside. Combine honey, mustard, soy sauce, curry powder and pepper; spoon half of mixture evenly over chicken. Cover with waxed paper. Microwave (HIGH) 5 minutes. Turn chicken pieces over, keeping thickest part toward outside of dish. Spoon on remaining sauce. Arrange vegetables in center of dish; cover. Microwave (HIGH) until chicken juices run clear and vegetables are crisp-tender (4½ to 5 minutes).

To Serve: Spoon juices over vegetables and chicken; sprinkle with parsley.

*4 servings.*

Zucchini

# CHICKEN DIJON FETTUCCINE

▼

*Dijon mustard with its blend of spices and white wine lends subtle, sought-after flavor to elegant dishes like this one.*

3 whole boneless, skinless
   chicken breasts (about
   2 pounds)
1½ teaspoons salt
¼ teaspoons pepper
¼ cup margarine or butter

1 pint whipping cream
⅓ cup Dijon mustard
2 tablespoons snipped fresh
   chives
¼ cup chopped fresh parsley
¾ pound dry fettuccine

Cut chicken breasts into 1-inch pieces. Sprinkle with salt and pepper. Melt margarine in large skillet; sauté chicken until no longer pink (4 to 7 minutes). Remove chicken from skillet. Stir cream and mustard into drippings; bring to a boil. Reduce heat; simmer until slightly thickened (about 8 minutes). Return chicken to skillet; add chives and parsley. Cook over low heat, stirring occasionally, until heated through; do not boil. Cook fettuccine according to package directions in boiling water with 1 teaspoon salt. Drain well; transfer to large heated platter. Gently toss with hot chicken mixture. Serve immediately.

*6 servings.*

**Tip:** Sauce may be made ahead and refrigerated. Reheat in heavy saucepan, stirring frequently.

# CHICKEN FLORENTINE WITH MUSHROOM SAUCE

▼

*Spinach, teamed with rich distinctive fontina cheese and toasted almonds, is baked along with the chicken producing a terrific entrée for two.*

2 boneless, skinless chicken breast halves (5 to 6 ounces each)
2 teaspoons margarine or butter
2 tablespoons finely chopped onion
1 (5-ounce) package frozen chopped spinach, thawed, drained
1 ounce fontina cheese, shredded (¼ cup)
2 tablespoons slivered almonds, toasted

– dash ground nutmeg
1 tablespoon margarine or butter, melted
**Mushroom Sauce**
1 tablespoon margarine or butter
1⅓ cups sliced fresh mushrooms
½ teaspoon instant chicken bouillon
½ cup water
1½ teaspoons lemon juice
½ cup whipping cream
¼ cup dry sherry
⅛ teaspoon white pepper

Lightly butter 7 × 11-inch glass baking dish. Heat oven to 350°. Flatten chicken breasts between waxed paper with rolling pin to ¼-inch thickness. In small skillet, melt 2 teaspoons margarine; sauté onion until tender. Remove from heat; stir in spinach, cheese, almonds and nutmeg. Divide mixture in half; slightly mound each half in buttered baking dish. Place 1 chicken breast half over each mound; brush with melted margarine. Bake until chicken is tender and juices run clear (30 to 35 minutes).

**Mushroom Sauce:** In medium saucepan, melt 1 tablespoon margarine; sauté mushrooms until all liquid has evaporated (about 5 minutes). Combine instant bouillon and water; stir bouillon and remaining ingredients into mushrooms. Bring to a boil over medium-high heat; boil, stirring constantly, until sauce is reduced to ⅔ cup and is slightly thickened (7 to 9 minutes). Using a wide spatula, place chicken and spinach on dinner plates; spoon sauce over chicken.

*2 servings.*

# CHICKEN ON THE GRILL

▼

*For a lighter but tasty alternative to heavier, sweeter basting sauces, try this brushed-on favorite for grilled chicken.*

1 cup vinegar
½ cup water
½ cup margarine or butter

1½ teaspoons salt
2 (2½ to 3-pound) chicken fryers, quartered

Prepare grill. In small saucepan, combine vinegar, water, margarine and salt; heat until margarine is melted and salt is dissolved. Keep hot on grill. Brush chicken on both sides with sauce. Arrange chicken, bone side down, on grill 5 inches from medium coals. Every 10 to 15 minutes, brush chicken generously with sauce and turn. Grill until golden brown and juices run clear (1 to 1½ hours).

**To Precook in the Microwave:** Prepare grill. Arrange pieces of one chicken in single layer on microwavable dish with meatier portions toward edge of dish. Microwave (HIGH), covered, 10 minutes, turning pieces over after 5 minutes. Repeat with remaining chicken. Using direct heat cooking method, immediately arrange chicken on grill rack 5 inches from medium coals. Grill, covered, until juices run clear (15 to 25 minutes), turning and basting every 10 to 15 minutes until last 5 minutes. For Gas Grill: Heat grill on medium about 10 minutes; reduce to medium-low. Arrange chicken on grill. Grill, covered, until juices run clear (20 to 25 minutes), turning and basting until last 5 minutes.

*6 to 8 servings.*

# CHICKEN FAJITAS

▼

*Now's the time to try this restaurant favorite at home. Grill or broil to
suit your personal style, and use chicken or turkey to suit your taste.*

- large zipper closure food
  storage bag
½ cup fresh lime juice
1 teaspoon minced garlic
½ teaspoon salt
½ teaspoon dried oregano,
  crumbled
1 tablespoon snipped fresh
  cilantro
⅛ teaspoon Tabasco
6 boneless, skinless chicken
  breast halves
1 large red onion, sliced,
  separated into rings

1 red bell pepper, cut into
  julienne strips
1 green bell pepper, cut into
  julienne strips
1 yellow bell pepper, cut into
  julienne strips
6 to 8 (8-inch) flour tortillas

Toppings:
- pico de gallo or salsa
- chunky guacamole
- sour cream
- shredded sharp Cheddar
  cheese

In food storage bag, combine lime juice, garlic, salt, oregano, cilantro and
Tabasco; add chicken. Seal bag. Refrigerate 4 hours, turning bag occasionally.
Remove chicken from bag; reserve marinade.

**To Grill:** Prepare grill. Combine onion and bell pepper strips in heavy duty
aluminum foil; seal. Heat marinade to boiling. Grill onion-pepper packet and
chicken 5 inches from medium coals for 10 minutes. Turn packet and chicken;
brush chicken with reserved marinade. Continue grilling chicken until juices
run clear (15 to 17 minutes). Wrap tortillas in foil; add to grill during last
10 minutes. Remove chicken; slice diagonally into strips. Cover with foil to
keep warm.

**To Broil:** Broil chicken 4 inches from heat for 4 minutes; turn, broil until
juices run clear (4 to 5 minutes). Slice diagonally into strips; cover with foil to
keep warm. In large skillet, heat 3 tablespoons oil; stir-fry onion and peppers
until crisp-tender (4 to 5 minutes). Stir in chicken strips; heat through.

To Serve: Fill warmed tortillas with chicken strips, onion-pepper mixture and
toppings. Roll up; serve immediately.

*Amount: 6 to 8 fajitas.*

**Variation:** One (1 to 1½-pound) package turkey breast tenderloin can be
substituted for chicken breasts. Grill or broil as above until juices run clear
(about 20 minutes total).

# CITRUS CHICKEN

▼

*A zesty trio of citrus juices mingle in a sherry-sparked marinade which
bathes the chicken for several hours before broiling.*

6 boneless chicken breast
  halves
1 teaspoon salt
¼ teaspoon pepper
1 medium orange

1 medium lemon
1 medium lime
2 tablespoons dry sherry
1 tablespoon minced shallots
- watercress

Sprinkle chicken with salt and pepper. Grate and measure 2 teaspoons orange
peel. Squeeze juice from orange, lemon and lime. Combine juices, peel, sherry
and shallots. Arrange chicken in shallow glass dish; pour juice mixture over
chicken. Refrigerate, covered, 4 or more hours, turning chicken occasionally.

To Broil: Position oven rack so broiler will be 5 to 6 inches from heat; heat
broiler. Arrange chicken, skin side down, on broiler pan; reserve marinade.
Broil chicken 7 minutes, brushing with reserved marinade twice. Turn chicken;
brush with marinade. Broil until juices run clear (about 5 minutes). Remove to
heated platter. Garnish with watercress.

*4 to 6 servings.*

# CHICKEN MARSALA

▼

*Top quickly sautéed chicken breasts for two with a Marsala wine-laced sauce.*

2 tablespoons flour
¼ teaspoon salt
⅛ teaspoon pepper
2 boneless, skinless chicken breast halves (5 to 6 ounces each)

1 tablespoon olive oil
1 tablespoon margarine or butter
¾ cup Marsala wine
1 to 2 tablespoons snipped fresh parsley

Combine flour, salt and pepper; coat chicken. In skillet, heat oil and margarine until hot and foamy. Sauté chicken over medium heat until golden brown on both sides. Stir in wine. Simmer, covered, until chicken is no longer pink when cut in thickest part (about 10 minutes). Remove chicken to platter; keep warm. Over medium-high heat, boil liquid in skillet, scraping skillet to loosen brown particles, until liquid is reduced to about ¼ cup. Stir in parsley. Pour over chicken. Serve immediately.

*2 servings.*

**Variation:**

**Chicken Picatta:** Substitute ¼ cup water and 3 tablespoons lemon juice for Marsala wine.

# CANNELLONI

▼

*The use of ground chicken rather than beef gives a lighter touch to this Italian classic. Freshly grated Parmesan cheese blends well while shredded is better for melting.*

1 pound frozen ground chicken Italian style, thawed
1 small onion, chopped (½ cup)
1 teaspoon minced garlic
1 tablespoon olive oil
½ cup freshly grated Parmesan cheese
¼ cup snipped fresh parsley
½ teaspoon ground nutmeg

1 (1.6-ounce) package Alfredo sauce mix
1 (30-ounce) jar spaghetti sauce, divided
2 sheets fresh egg pasta for lasagna or 1 (13-ounce) package frozen lasagna sheets, thawed
¼ pound thinly sliced prosciutto
½ cup freshly shredded Parmesan cheese

In large skillet, brown ground chicken, onion and garlic in olive oil. Stir in ½ cup grated Parmesan cheese, parsley and nutmeg. Prepare Alfredo sauce according to package directions. Stir ⅓ cup sauce into chicken mixture; reserve remainder. Spread half of spaghetti sauce in bottom of 9 × 13-inch baking pan. Cut pasta sheets in half lengthwise. Divide each half into thirds (or in half if thawed sheets are used), forming 12 squares. Cut 1 slice prosciutto to fit width of 1 pasta square. Top with 2 rounded tablespoons chicken mixture. Roll pasta into tube; arrange, seam side down, in sauce. Repeat with remaining squares. Pour remaining spaghetti sauce over pasta. Drizzle top with reserved Alfredo sauce. Refrigerate, covered.

Heat oven to 400°. Bake, covered, 15 minutes. Remove cover; continue baking until bubbly (15 to 25 minutes longer). Sprinkle with ½ cup shredded Parmesan cheese. Let stand, covered, 10 minutes before serving.

*Amount: 12 cannelloni.*

**Tip:** One pound ground chicken combined with ¼ teaspoon pepper, ¼ teaspoon crushed red pepper, 1 teaspoon fennel seed and 1 teaspoon paprika can be substituted for 1 pound ground chicken, Italian style.

# CHICKEN 'N HERB PIZZA FILLING

▼

*Fresh herbs and vegetables plus a generous addition of garlic impart robust flavors to this unique chicken pizza.*

- Basic Pizza Crust or Whole Wheat Pizza Crust (page 164)
- 3 tablespoons olive oil
- 2 whole chicken breasts, skinned, boned, cut into ¾-inch cubes
- 3 tablespoons snipped fresh basil
- 2 tablespoons snipped fresh oregano
- 2 tablespoons snipped fresh cilantro
- 2 teaspoons minced garlic
- ¾ teaspoon salt
- 1 medium onion, thinly sliced, separated into rings
- 1 red bell pepper, cut into julienne strips
- 1 green bell pepper, cut into julienne strips
- 6 ounces fontina cheese, shredded (1½ cups)
- 1 (8-ounce) package shredded mozzarella cheese (2 cups)
- ¼ cup pignoli nuts

Prepare 2 pizza crusts (page 164). Heat oven to 425°. In large skillet, heat olive oil over medium heat. Stir in chicken, basil, oregano, cilantro, garlic and salt; cook 5 minutes, stirring occasionally. Stir in onion and bell peppers. Continue cooking until chicken is no longer pink (3 to 5 minutes), stirring occasionally. Layer 2 pizza crusts with equal amounts of fontina cheese, chicken herb mixture, mozzarella cheese and pignoli nuts. Bake until crust is golden brown (15 to 20 minutes), rotating pans on oven racks halfway through baking time.

*Amount: 2 (12-inch) pizzas.*

**Stuffed Pizza:** Prepare Basic Pizza Crust or Whole Wheat Pizza Crust (page 164). Grease one pizza pan; sprinkle with cornmeal. Heat oven to 425°. Roll out 2 (12-inch) pizza crusts. Place one crust on greased pizza pan. Spread with Chicken 'n Herb Pizza Filling. Cover with second crust. Press two edges firmly together. Prick top crust with tines of fork. Bake in oven until crust is golden brown (about 20 minutes).

**Pizza Foldover (Calzone):** Prepare pizza crust and pizza pan as in Stuffed Pizza. Heat oven to 425°. Roll out 1 (12-inch) pizza crust. Place crust on greased pizza pan. Spread Chicken 'n Herb Pizza Filling on half of crust. Fold other half of crust over filling. Prick top crust with tines of fork. Bake in oven until golden brown (about 20 minutes).

# CHEESY CHICKEN SANDWICH

▼

*Olé for a super supper sandwich with south-of-the-border spiciness and microwave quick preparation. Even the buns have a zesty spread!*

- 4 boneless, skinless chicken breast halves (4 ounces each)
- ¼ to ½ teaspoon salt
- ⅛ teaspoon pepper
- ½ cup salsa
- 4 slices pepper cheese
- ¼ cup margarine or butter, softened
- 1 teaspoon minced garlic
- ⅛ teaspoon chili powder
- ⅛ teaspoon ground cumin
- 4 Kaiser rolls, sliced horizontally
- leaf lettuce
- 1 avocado, peeled, sliced
- salsa

Flatten chicken breasts slightly. Arrange chicken breast halves in circle near outer edge of round microwavable plate. Cover with plastic wrap; vent one corner. Microwave (HIGH) 3 minutes. Turn over and rearrange. Sprinkle with salt and pepper; top each chicken breast half with 2 tablespoons salsa. Cover; microwave (HIGH) until chicken is no longer pink when cut in thickest part (2 to 3 minutes). Top each chicken breast with 1 cheese slice; cover. Microwave (HIGH) 1 minute. Combine margarine, garlic, chili powder and cumin. Spread evenly on bottom of rolls; top with lettuce leaf, chicken breast, avocado slices and top of roll. Serve with salsa.

*4 sandwiches.*

# SAVORY BAKED CHICKEN AND VEGETABLES

▼

*Something for everyone – simple preparation, handsome presentation, fabulous flavor and a continental allure that makes it ideal for parties.*

3½ pounds chicken pieces, skinned
½ (16-ounce) package frozen small whole onions, thawed
1 (15-ounce) can artichoke hearts, drained, halved
1 large green or red bell pepper, cut into julienne strips
½ cup dry sherry
2 tablespoons flour

½ cup chicken broth
3 tablespoons snipped fresh thyme
1 tablespoon snipped fresh parsley
¾ teaspoon minced garlic
1 teaspoon salt
¼ teaspoon pepper
1 (4-ounce) package shredded Monterey Jack cheese (1 cup)

Heat oven to 375°. Arrange chicken pieces in single layer in greased 9 × 13-inch baking dish. Arrange onions, artichoke hearts and bell pepper evenly over chicken. Combine sherry and flour until smooth. Bring chicken broth to a boil; stir in thyme, parsley, garlic, salt and pepper. Gradually blend in flour mixture. Cook over medium heat, stirring constantly, until thickened; boil and stir 1 minute. Pour sauce over chicken and vegetables. Bake, covered, until chicken is tender and juices run clear (50 to 55 minutes). Sprinkle with cheese. Bake, uncovered, until cheese is melted (about 5 minutes).

*4 to 5 servings.*

# GINGERED CHICKEN

▼

*Exotic seasonings penetrate chicken pieces during several hours of refrigeration prior to broiling.*

1 (3.5-pound) chicken fryer, cut up
4 cloves garlic
2 ounces gingerroot, peeled, cut into ¼-inch slices
1½ (½-ounce) packages fresh cilantro

1 tablespoon grated orange peel
½ teaspoon salt
½ teaspoon pepper
¼ cup orange juice
2 tablespoons salad vinegar
4 teaspoons vegetable oil
– Orange Twists (page 62)
– fresh cilantro sprigs

With sharp knife, make diagonal cuts about ¼ inch apart over entire skin of chicken. With food processor running, drop garlic, gingerroot and cilantro through feed tube; process until finely minced. Drop in orange peel, salt and pepper. Combine orange juice and vinegar; pour through feed tube. With processor running, gradually add oil. Rub mixture into cuts and over entire surface of chicken. Arrange in single layer in glass dish. Refrigerate, covered, 3 or more hours.

To Broil: Position oven rack so broiler will be 5 to 6 inches from heat; heat broiler. Arrange chicken on broiler pan, skin side up; broil 10 minutes. Turn, broil 10 minutes longer. Turn pieces again; continue broiling until chicken is no longer pink when cut in thickest part of thigh (6 to 10 minutes). If necessary, rearrange chicken on broiler pan to prevent pieces from becoming too dark. Transfer to heated platter; garnish with orange twists and cilantro.

*4 servings.*

# CHICKEN 'N PESTO

▼

*A thick fresh basil pesto transforms chicken breasts into a marvelous entrée. It's table-ready in just minutes thanks to microwave preparation.*

1 (½-ounce) package fresh
  basil leaves (1 cup)
1 (1-ounce) bottle pignoli nuts
  (¼ cup)
1 large clove garlic
¼ teaspoon salt

¼ cup olive oil
¾ cup freshly grated Parmesan
  cheese
3 tablespoons hot water
4 split chicken breasts with
  ribs

Combine basil, pignoli, garlic and salt in food processor or blender; process until combined. With processor running, gradually add oil. Add Parmesan cheese and water; process until well blended. Set aside until mixture is consistency of thick spread. Remove skin from chicken breasts. Spread half of pesto mixture on rib side of chicken. Arrange in 2-quart microwavable dish. Spread top and sides of chicken with remaining pesto. Cover with waxed paper. Microwave (HIGH) 6 minutes. Turn dish one-quarter turn; microwave (HIGH) until juices run clear when cut at thickest part (6 to 8 minutes). Let stand, covered, 6 to 7 minutes.

*4 servings.*

*"great*  ✶ CHICKEN 'N DUMPLINGS ✶ *awesome"*

▼

*Plenty of tender chicken and vegetables with the bonus of plump, fluffy dumplings for a mouth-watering country-style suppertime treat.*

1 (3 to 3½-pound) chicken
  fryer, cut up
2 tablespoons vegetable oil
2 ribs celery, cut into ½-inch
  slices
1 small onion, sliced (½ cup)
3 chicken bouillon cubes

3 cups water
1 bay leaf
1 to 1½ teaspoons salt
¼ teaspoon pepper
6 carrots, cut into 1-inch
  pieces
⅓ cup flour
½ cup cold water
– Fluffy Dumplings (below)

In Dutch oven or large skillet, brown chicken in oil. Add celery, onion, bouillon, water, bay leaf, salt and pepper. Bring to a boil; simmer, covered, over low heat 25 minutes. Add carrots, simmer until tender (about 20 minutes). Skim off excess fat. Combine flour and cold water; stir until well blended. Stir into chicken mixture; bring to a boil. Drop Fluffy Dumplings by tablespoonfuls over top of chicken mixture. Simmer, covered (without lifting lid), 15 minutes. Dumplings are done when no longer doughy underneath.

*4 to 6 servings.*

**Fluffy Dumplings:** In mixing bowl, combine 1½ cups flour, 2 teaspoons baking powder, ½ teaspoon salt, ⅛ teaspoon ground nutmeg and 1 tablespoon minced fresh parsley. Stir in ⅔ cup milk, 1 slightly beaten egg and 2 tablespoons vegetable oil just until dry ingredients are moistened.

*Amount: 8 to 10 dumplings.*

# DEVILED CHICKEN

▼

*Just the right combination of herbs and spices enlivens oven-baked chicken pieces. Perfect served hot or cold for casual gatherings.*

½ cup fine dry bread crumbs
3 tablespoons snipped fresh parsley
4 teaspoons onion powder
4 teaspoons curry powder
1½ teaspoons salt
½ teaspoon garlic powder
½ teaspoon paprika

½ teaspoon coarsely ground pepper
⅓ cup milk
1 tablespoon sharp and creamy mustard
3 pounds chicken breasts and drumsticks (about 4 breasts and 6 drumsticks), with or without skin

Heat oven to 375°. Combine crumbs, parsley, onion powder, curry powder, salt, garlic powder, paprika and pepper in shallow pan. Combine milk and mustard; dip chicken pieces in milk mixture. Roll in crumb mixture. Arrange chicken on greased 10 × 15-inch jelly roll pan. Bake until juices run clear when cut in thickest part of breasts (40 to 45 minutes). (Skinless chicken requires less baking time). Serve hot or cold.

*6 servings.*

# CRANBERRY ORANGE CHICKEN

▼

*Tangy cranberry orange crushed fruit is combined with other convenience ingredients for a mixture that does double duty as a marinade and a sauce. So easy and so tasty!*

1 (12-ounce) carton cranberry orange crushed fruit for chicken or 1 (16-ounce) can whole berry cranberry sauce
½ (2.4-ounce) box dry onion soup mix (1 envelope)

1 (8-ounce) bottle French dressing
⅓ cup orange juice
6 split chicken breasts with ribs (7 to 8 ounces each)
– Orange Twists (page 62)
– fresh parsley sprigs

Combine cranberry orange crushed fruit, soup mix, French dressing and orange juice. Arrange chicken in a single layer in 9 × 13-inch glass baking dish. Pour cranberry mixture evenly over chicken. Refrigerate, covered, several hours or overnight.

Heat oven to 350°. Bake, covered, 45 minutes. Remove cover; continue to bake until tender and instant read thermometer registers 170° (10 to 20 minutes). Arrange on platter; garnish with orange twists and parsley. Skim fat from sauce; spoon sauce over chicken.

*6 servings.*

• *Cranberries are one of three native North American fruits. (Concord grapes and blueberries are the other two.)*

cranberry

# CHICKEN...ROASTED

*The best of the basics – a plump roasting chicken sprinkled inside and out with savory seasonings and baked to perfect tenderness.*

| | |
|---|---|
| 1 (4½-pound) roasting chicken | 1 clove garlic, peeled, crushed |
| ½ teaspoon salt | 1 small onion, peeled, |
| ¼ teaspoon pepper |    quartered |
| 1 teaspoon dried rosemary or | – safflower oil |
|    thyme, crumbled | – kitchen twine or cotton string |
| | – Pan Gravy (below) (optional) |

Heat oven to 325°. Remove neck and giblets from chicken cavities, if present. Clean cavities, removing extra fat. Rinse chicken with cold water; drain. Pat dry with paper towels. Combine salt, pepper and rosemary. Divide mixture in half; sprinkle half into cavities, reserving remainder. Arrange garlic and onion in cavity. Run string under and around body, tying wings to body. Tie legs together in same manner. Place, breast side up, on rack in shallow roasting pan. Brush bird with oil. Evenly sprinkle on remaining salt and rosemary mixture. Insert meat thermometer into thickest part of inner thigh, not touching bone. Roast 1 hour. Remove from oven, carefully cut string holding drumsticks together (so thighs will cook evenly). Return chicken to oven. Roast until meat thermometer reaches 185° or until juices run clear (15 to 30 minutes longer). Drain juices from cavity into roasting pan. Remove chicken and rack from pan; cover chicken with foil. Let stand 10 minutes; meanwhile, make Pan Gravy. Carve chicken; serve with Pan Gravy.

*4 to 5 servings.*

**Pan Gravy:** Drain off fat in roasting pan, reserving ¼ cup and browned particles. Blend in ¼ cup flour. Cook over medium heat, stirring constantly, until bubbly and lightly browned. Gradually stir in 2 cups chicken broth. Cook, stirring constantly, until gravy boils and thickens. Season to taste with salt and pepper.

*Amount: 2¼ cups.*

**Tip:** One (3½-pound) whole fryer chicken can be substituted for the roasting chicken.

# CHICKEN BREASTS

*Use our simple guidelines for baking or poaching chicken to use in salads, casseroles or sandwiches.*

**Baked Chicken Breasts:** Heat oven to 350°. Arrange boneless chicken breasts or split breasts with ribs flat in shallow pan. Do not let pieces touch. Brush lightly with oil, salt and pepper. Cover with foil. Bake until juices run clear (about 35 minutes for boneless breasts, 50 minutes for split breasts with ribs).

**Poached Chicken Breasts:** Place 3 pounds whole chicken breasts, split; 1 unpeeled onion, washed, quartered; 5 sprigs fresh parsley; 8 peppercorns; 2 teaspoons dried thyme, crumbled; 2 bay leaves; 1 tablespoon salt and 1 cup white wine in large kettle or Dutch oven. Add enough water to cover. Bring to a boil, covered; reduce heat and simmer until juices run clear (30 to 40 minutes). Remove from heat; let stand 30 minutes. Remove chicken. Refrigerate, covered, several hours.

*Amount: 3 pounds boneless chicken breasts = 6 cups cubed.*
*3 pounds split chicken breasts with ribs = 4 cups cubed.*

# CORNISH GAME HENS WITH POTATOES AND ONIONS

*Herbed Cornish hens and a duo of complementary vegetables bake simultaneously for virtually carefree preparation.*

½ cup margarine or butter
1 teaspoon dried basil, crumbled
½ teaspoon paprika
½ teaspoon garlic powder
½ teaspoon dried thyme, crumbled
½ teaspoon salt
⅛ teaspoon pepper

2 frozen Cornish game hens, split lengthwise (at meat counter), thawed, giblets removed
4 medium russet potatoes, quartered lengthwise
2 medium onions, quartered
– cherry tomatoes
– fresh parsley sprigs

Heat oven to 450°. Melt margarine; stir in basil, paprika, garlic powder, thyme, salt and pepper. Place hens, skin side up, on 10 × 15-inch jelly roll pan. Arrange potatoes and onions around hens; brush all with margarine mixture. Bake until meat near thigh bone is no longer pink and potatoes are tender (30 to 35 minutes). Arrange on serving platter; garnish with cherry tomatoes and parsley.

*4 servings.*

# ROAST DUCK WITH RASPBERRY SAUCE

*This may well be the most delectable poultry entrée you have ever sampled! While the ducklings are roasting to golden, crisp-skinned goodness, prepare the raspberry liqueur-laced gourmet sauce.*

2 (4 to 5-pound) ducklings
2 tablespoons margarine or butter, divided
3 tablespoons sugar
⅓ cup raspberry vinegar
1 carrot, chopped
1 medium onion, chopped

1 tomato, chopped
1 (10½-ounce) can chicken broth
2 tablespoons cornstarch
¼ cup raspberry-flavored liqueur
1 cup fresh raspberries, divided

Thaw ducklings if frozen. Heat oven to 425°. Remove giblets and trim ducklings of all excess fat. Place ducklings on broiler pan; prick skin with fork in many places. Insert meat thermometer into thickest part of the inner thigh, not touching bone. Roast until meat thermometer registers 180 to 185° (1 to 1¼ hours). Meanwhile, melt 1 tablespoon margarine in 2-quart saucepan. Stir in sugar; cook over medium heat until mixture is melted and brown, stirring occasionally. Stir in vinegar; cook over medium-high heat until reduced by half (8 to 10 minutes). In skillet, melt remaining 1 tablespoon margarine. Sauté carrot, onion and tomato 4 to 5 minutes, stirring often. Stir in chicken broth; bring to a boil. Reduce heat; simmer 8 to 10 minutes. Strain broth into reduced vinegar mixture. Combine cornstarch and liqueur until smooth; stir into vinegar mixture. Cook over medium heat, stirring constantly, until mixture comes to a boil; boil and stir 1 minute. (Have sauce hot when ducklings are finished roasting.)

To Serve: Drain fat from cavities of ducklings. Arrange ducklings on serving platter; brush with raspberry sauce. Stir half of the raspberries into remaining sauce; serve in gravy boat. Garnish platter with remaining raspberries.

*4 to 5 servings.*

# TURKEY BREAST WITH SAGE DRESSING

▼

*Here's traditional turkey and all the trimmings with streamlined preparation, less time in the oven and no sacrifice of flavor. It's perfect for small gatherings or those who love white meat only.*

¾ cup margarine or butter
1 medium onion, chopped (1 cup)
1½ cups chopped celery
¼ cup chopped fresh parsley
1 tablespoon dried rubbed sage
12 cups dry bread cubes
1½ teaspoons salt
¼ teaspoon pepper

1 teaspoon dried thyme, crumbled
½ teaspoon dried marjoram, crumbled
½ teaspoon ground nutmeg
½ to 1¼ cups chicken broth
1 (4 to 6-pound) turkey breast, thawed if frozen
2 (18 × 24-inch) pieces heavy duty foil
– vegetable oil
– Turkey Gravy (below)

Heat oven to 325°. Melt margarine in large skillet; sauté onion, celery, parsley and sage until onion and celery are tender. Combine bread cubes with salt, pepper, thyme, marjoram and nutmeg in large bowl. Stir in margarine mixture. Pour in enough chicken broth to moisten cubes. Rinse turkey breast; drain. Pat dry with paper towels. Place double thickness of foil on broiler pan rack. Pierce center portion of foil in a few places. Mound about 4 cups dressing in oval shape on foil. Place turkey breast on dressing. Spoon remaining dressing evenly around breast. Roll foil and crimp around base of breast, covering dressing completely. Brush breast with oil. Roast, uncovered, until instant read thermometer registers 170 to 175° in turkey breast and 160 to 165° in dressing (2¼ to 2½ hours). Let stand, covered, about 15 minutes. Spoon dressing into serving bowl; carve turkey. Serve with Turkey Gravy.

*8 to 10 servings.*

# TURKEY GRAVY

▼

*Here's a no-fuss gravy that's as flavorful as those made with the turkey drippings.*

2 (14½-ounce) cans ⅓-less-salt chicken broth
2 celery ribs, cut into 2-inch pieces
2 carrots, cut into 2-inch pieces
1 medium onion, quartered

6 whole peppercorns
1 small bay leaf
6 tablespoons margarine or butter
6 tablespoons flour
¼ teaspoon browning and seasoning sauce
¼ teaspoon salt

Combine broth, celery, carrots, onion, peppercorns and bay leaf in medium saucepan. Cook, uncovered, over medium heat 20 minutes. Strain broth; discard vegetables and seasonings. Melt margarine in medium skillet; blend in flour. Cook until mixture is slightly browned; gradually stir in seasoned broth, browning and seasoning sauce and salt. Cook over medium heat, stirring constantly, until mixture comes to a boil; boil and stir 1 minute.

*Amount: 3 cups.*

# TURKEY BREAST...GLAZED AND GRILLED

▼

*The exciting difference here is a rich raspberry glaze that permeates the meat with delicate flavor. Precooking the turkey in the microwave trims grilling time.*

| | |
|---|---|
| 1 (2½ to 3-pound) fresh turkey breast half with bone | ¼ cup olive oil |
| ½ cup raspberry vinegar | ½ cup seedless raspberry jam |
| | – fresh raspberries (optional) |

Prepare grill. Rinse turkey; drain and pat dry with paper towels. Place breast, skin side down, in square glass casserole; cover with waxed paper. Microwave (MEDIUM-HIGH, 70% power) 15 minutes, turning skin side up halfway through cooking time. In small bowl, combine raspberry vinegar, olive oil and raspberry jam; set aside. Spray grill rack with no stick cooking spray. Using indirect heat cooking method, center hot turkey breast on grill rack 4 to 5 inches above drip pan that has been placed opposite medium-hot coals. Grill, covered, until meat thermometer registers 170 to 175° (1¼ to 1½ hours). Using half of glaze, brush turkey breast several times during last half of cooking time. Let stand, covered, about 15 minutes. Slice. Heat reserved glaze to boiling in microwave. Garnish turkey breast slices with glaze and raspberries.

*4 to 6 servings.*

# TENDER TURKEY THIGHS

▼

*Superb lightly-sauced turkey thighs are browned and partially baked, then new potatoes are added for the last half hour of cooking.*

| | |
|---|---|
| 4 turkey thighs | 1 teaspoon dry mustard |
| 2 tablespoons vegetable oil | 1 teaspoon paprika |
| 1 (10¾-ounce) can chicken broth | ¼ teaspoon dried basil, crumbled |
| 1 cup chopped fresh mushrooms | ¼ teaspoon dried sage leaves, crumbled |
| 1 cup sliced green onions including some tops (2 bunches) | ⅛ teaspoon pepper |
| | 12 small new potatoes |
| ½ cup dry sherry | 3 tablespoons cornstarch |
| 1½ teaspoons salt | 3 tablespoons water |
| | 2 tablespoons snipped fresh parsley |

Heat oven to 350°. In Dutch oven, brown turkey in oil; drain. Combine chicken broth, mushrooms, onions, sherry, salt, mustard, paprika, basil, sage and pepper; pour over turkey. Bake, covered, 1 hour, turning once. Add potatoes to turkey. Bake, covered, until thighs are tender and potatoes are easily pierced with fork (30 to 35 minutes). Arrange turkey and potatoes on serving platter; cover to keep warm. Combine cornstarch and water until smooth. Bring pan juices to a boil; stir in cornstarch mixture. Bring to a boil, stirring constantly; boil 1 minute. Pour about 1 cup gravy over turkey and potatoes; sprinkle with parsley. Pass remaining gravy.

*4 servings.*

# TURKEY TENDERLOIN WITH SAUCE

▼

*What's for dinner? This speedy stovetop meal is the delicious answer. Its enticing flavor is complemented by your choice of salsa or topping.*

| | |
|---|---|
| 1 tablespoon vegetable oil | – freshly ground pepper |
| 1 tablespoon margarine or butter | ¼ cup chicken broth |
| 2 (10 to 12-ounce) turkey tenderloins | ¼ cup dry white wine |
| | – Pineapple Salsa (page 71) (optional) |
| ¼ teaspoon salt | – Easy Bearnaise Sauce (below) (optional) |

Combine oil and margarine in medium skillet. Sauté tenderloins over medium heat until brown on both sides (5 to 7 minutes total). Sprinkle with salt and pepper; add broth and wine. Simmer, covered, over low heat until tender and juices run clear (15 to 20 minutes). Meanwhile, prepare Pineapple Salsa or Easy Bearnaise Sauce according to package directions.

To Serve: Slice ½ inch thick; arrange on heated platter and top with choice of sauce.

*4 to 6 servings.*

**Easy Bearnaise Sauce:** Prepare 1 (0.9-ounce) package Bearnaise Sauce Mix according to package directions. Spoon over turkey; garnish with 2 tablespoons drained capers.

# MARINADES FOR POULTRY

▼

*Basil, with its sweet, clove-like aroma and flavor, marries particularly well with the mild flavor of poultry. To retain an appealingly firm texture, marinate poultry no more than 12 hours.*

**Balsamic 'n Basil:** Combine ⅔ cup olive oil, ½ cup balsamic vinegar, ¼ cup snipped fresh basil, 2 tablespoons each snipped fresh chives and minced onion, ½ teaspoon salt and ¼ teaspoon white pepper.

*Amount: about 1 cup.*

**Basil 'n Citrus:** Combine ½ cup each olive oil and snipped fresh basil, ⅓ cup lemon juice, 2 tablespoons snipped fresh chives, 1 teaspoon salt and ½ teaspoon white pepper.

*Amount: about 1 cup.*

**Tips:**
- Allow ½ cup marinade per pound of poultry.
- Marinate in zipper closure food storage bag, for ease in handling; turn bag occasionally.
- Always marinate in refrigerator.

**Turkey Thawing Tips:**
- To Thaw In Refrigerator: Leave in original wrap. Place on tray in refrigerator, allow twenty-four hours for every five pounds of turkey. (This is the preferred method.)
- To Thaw In Cold Water: Leave in original wrap. Place turkey in sink. Cover with cold water, changing water frequently, allow ½ hour per pound of turkey.

# POULTRY PRONTO

▼

*It's easy to be a gourmet cook when you use these clever, quick and tasty tricks with ready-to-cook or ready-to-eat poultry.*

**Chicken Dijon:** Heat broiler. Combine 2 tablespoons Dijon mustard, ½ teaspoon minced garlic, ¼ teaspoon salt and ⅛ teaspoon pepper. Spread half of mixture evenly over 1 side of 4 boneless, skinless chicken breast halves. Arrange chicken on oiled broiler pan. Broil 4 to 5 inches from heat 5 minutes. Turn chicken; spread with remaining mustard mixture. Broil until juices run clear (3 to 5 minutes).

*2 to 4 servings.*

**Easy Glazed Chicken:** Bring home a hot rotisserie chicken from the deli. Place on microwavable dish. Brush with a mixture of ¼ cup honey, ¼ cup softened margarine and 2 teaspoons dry mustard (or brush with bottled sweet-sour, barbecue or picante sauce). Microwave (MEDIUM, 50% power) until heated through (2 to 3 minutes).

*4 servings.*

**Barbecued Chicken Bunwiches:** Remove skin from deli rotisserie chicken; cut meat into bite-size pieces. Combine with 1½ cups barbecue sauce. Spoon into 2-quart casserole. Refrigerate, covered, several hours or overnight.

To Serve: Heat oven to 325°. Bake barbecued chicken until heated through (about 40 minutes). Spoon onto mini Kaiser rolls.

To Heat in Microwave: Cover with plastic wrap; vent one corner. Microwave (HIGH) until heated through (8 to 9 minutes), stirring once.

*Amount: 10 to 14 mini-bunwiches.*

**Deli Delight:** Slice 1 twin French bread loaf (8-ounce) in half lengthwise. Drain liquid from 1 (6-ounce) jar marinated artichoke hearts into small bowl; whisk in 1 teaspoon minced garlic and 1 tablespoon olive oil; drizzle 2 tablespoons of mixture on cut surfaces of bread. Arrange 1 thinly sliced tomato on bottom half of loaf; sprinkle with 2 tablespoons snipped fresh basil. Top with 8 slices deli roast turkey, 8 slices deli salami, 6 thin slices red onion and quartered artichokes. Drizzle with remaining marinade mixture; top with 4 slices deli Cheddar cheese. Place top of loaf on filling; press down lightly. Cut diagonally into 6 slices.

*6 servings.*

**Grilled Turkey and Cheese:** Combine 1 tablespoon Dijon mustard, 1½ tablespoons mayonnaise and ⅛ teaspoon tarragon; spread on 2 slices of bread. Top one slice with sliced turkey and cheese and the other bread slice. Butter outside of sandwich; grill until toasted and cheese is melted.

*1 sandwich.*

# SALADS & DRESSINGS

In the course of culinary seasons, salads bring eternal springtime. Today salads are the answer for a first course, side dish, main event or aprés entrée. What other menu makers are as versatile, as nutritious and as ready to accommodate the quest for light or hearty, chilled or warm, make-ahead or last minute, savory or sweet?

Intriguing combinations of dewy-fresh variety greens and herbs, bold or subtly flavored vinegars and distinctive oils have put salads squarely in the spotlight. Complementary contrasts are enhanced by colorful fruits with global personalities, by pasta and by marinated and grilled meats or fish.

Whether tossed, arranged (composed), molded, layered or frozen; whether simple or sophisticated, give a salad a starring role in your next meal!

# GOAT CHEESE AND GREENS

▼

*Goat cheese encircled with roasted red pepper and served warm atop a combination of torn arugula, radicchio and romaine lettuce provides an enticing blend of colors and flavors.*

1 head radicchio, torn
1 (½-ounce) package arugula, stems removed, leaves torn
3 cups torn romaine lettuce
½ cup olive oil
¼ cup lemon juice
3 tablespoons minced green onion
2 tablespoons snipped fresh basil

¼ teaspoon salt
⅛ teaspoon pepper
2 (4-ounce) packages chèvre cheese
1 (14-ounce) jar roasted red pepper, drained
24 drained calamata olives
2 tablespoons olive oil
– freshly ground pepper

Combine radicchio, arugula and romaine; refrigerate, covered. In small bowl, combine ½ cup oil, lemon juice, green onion, basil, salt and pepper; whisk to blend. Cut cheese into 16 equal pieces; shape into balls. Cut pepper into 16 equal strips; wrap one strip around each cheese ball. Arrange seam side down in glass baking dish. Scatter with olives; drizzle with 2 tablespoons olive oil and sprinkle with freshly ground pepper. Marinate, covered, at room temperature 1 hour.

To Serve: Arrange greens on 8 individual salad plates. Microwave cheese and olives (HIGH) until warm (40 to 50 seconds), or bake in preheated 400° oven until cheese softens slightly (6 to 7 minutes). Arrange 2 cheese balls and 3 olives on each plate of greens. Drizzle with salad dressing. Serve immediately.

*8 servings.*

**Variation:** Substitute 1 (6-ounce) log Wisconsin goat cheese for 2 (4-ounce) packages chèvre cheese. Heat oven to 400°. Slice cheese into 6 equal rounds. Dredge all sides of cheese slices in ¼ cup dry Italian bread crumbs; spray with no stick cooking spray. Bake until cheese softens slightly (about 7 minutes). Arrange on salad greens. (Omit red pepper, olives, 2 tablespoons olive oil and freshly ground pepper.) Serve immediately.

# GREEK SALAD

▼

*Olive oil, feta cheese, calamata olives and garlic — all scrumptious staples of Mediterranean countries — are showcased in a traditional Greek salad.*

8 cups torn romaine lettuce
1 small red onion, thinly sliced
1 medium tomato, diced
¼ cup olive oil
1 tablespoon red wine vinegar
2 teaspoons lemon juice

1 tablespoon finely snipped fresh oregano
½ teaspoon minced garlic
½ teaspoon salt
⅛ teaspoon coarsely ground pepper
½ cup drained calamata olives
1 (4-ounce) package crumbled feta cheese

In large salad bowl, combine romaine, onion and tomato; refrigerate. In small bowl, combine olive oil, vinegar, lemon juice, oregano, garlic, salt and pepper; whisk to blend.

To Serve: Drizzle dressing over greens; add olives and toss lightly. Sprinkle with feta cheese.

*8 servings.*

*Goat Cheese and Greens page 111*

# SUN-DRIED TOMATO 'N GREENS

▼

*This sophisticated salad is enhanced by the intense flavor of marinated sun-dried tomatoes and a dressing using their marinating oil.*

| | |
|---|---|
| 1 (8-ounce) jar marinated sun-dried tomatoes | ½ small red onion sliced, separated into rings |
| 4 cups torn romaine lettuce | 1 cup sliced fresh mushrooms |
| 2 cups torn Boston lettuce | 2 tablespoons salad vinegar |
| | ⅛ teaspoon salt |
| | ⅛ teaspoon pepper |

Drain tomatoes and reserve ¼ cup of the oil. Cut ⅓ cup marinated tomatoes into julienne strips. Combine tomatoes, lettuce, red onion and mushrooms in salad bowl. In small bowl, combine reserved oil, vinegar, salt and pepper; whisk to blend. Drizzle over salad mixture; toss lightly.

*6 servings.*

*Drying tomatoes in the sun without seasonings or salt results in an intensive, distinctive tomato flavor.*

Mushroom

# SPINACH AND BOSTON LETTUCE SALAD

▼

*Delicate Boston lettuce combined with spinach is the base for a light vinaigrette laced with walnut oil. Toasted walnuts add crunch.*

| | |
|---|---|
| 4 cups torn spinach | ¼ cup walnut oil |
| 3 cups torn Boston lettuce | 2 tablespoons sugar |
| ½ cup walnut halves | ½ teaspoon salt |
| 2 tablespoons raspberry vinegar | – dash pepper |
| | – fresh raspberries |

Refrigerate prepared greens to chill and crisp. Heat oven to 350°. In medium saucepan, bring water to a boil; add walnuts, simmer 3 minutes. Drain, rinse and pat dry on paper towels. Bake until toasted (5 to 7 minutes), stirring occasionally. Cool walnuts; chop. Combine greens in large bowl; sprinkle with walnuts. In small bowl, combine vinegar, oil, sugar, salt and pepper; whisk to blend. Drizzle over salad; toss to combine. Arrange on salad plates; garnish with raspberries.

*6 servings.*

*The small loosely packed heads of Boston lettuce have dark green outer leaves. Leaf color gradually lightens towards the center.*

*Waltnut oil has a rich nutty flavor that adds interest to salads.*

# CITRUS SALAD TOSS

▼

*Enliven tossed greens with sunny citrus sections and creamy avocado pieces. Delicate, aromatic red wine vinegar gives character to the pleasant vinaigrette dressing.*

½ cup canola oil
¼ cup red wine vinegar
¼ cup sugar
½ teaspoon salt
½ teaspoon poppy seed
½ teaspoon dry mustard
¼ cup finely chopped red onion

2 grapefruit, peeled, sectioned
2 avocados, peeled, cut into chunks
12 cups torn greens (red-tipped and green leaf lettuce or Boston lettuce)
1 carambola (star fruit), sliced crosswise

Combine oil, vinegar, sugar, salt, poppy seed, dry mustard and onion; refrigerate, covered. Toss grapefruit and avocados together; refrigerate, covered.

To Serve: Whisk dressing to blend. In large bowl, toss greens, grapefruit, avocodos and dressing. Spoon onto large serving platter. Garnish with carambola.

*12 servings.*

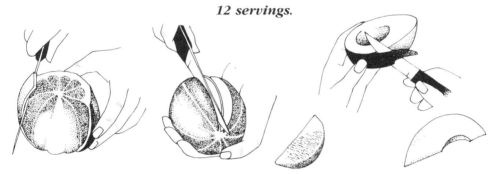

**Citrus Sections:**
Cut off each end of citrus. With sharp knife, cut from top to bottom, removing peel including white inner pith. Make a cut into the citrus, slicing close to dividing membranes and removing each wedge shaped slice as it is cut.

**To Peel and Seed Avocado:**
Cut in half lengthwise around seed. Twist halves apart. Remove seed by slipping tip of spoon under and lifting out carefully. Peel and slice halves with sharp knife.

# PIGNOLI AND PEAR SALAD

▼

*Succulent slices of fresh pear join pignoli nuts, onion and greens in a handsome salad for two.*

2 teaspoons sherry wine vinegar
1 teaspoon honey mustard
3 tablespoons olive oil
¼ teaspoon dried basil, crumbled
⅛ teaspoon salt
– dash pepper

1½ cups torn red-tipped leaf lettuce
2 tablespoons pignoli nuts, toasted
2 slices red onion, separated into rings
1 large ripe pear
1 tablespoon lemon juice

In small bowl, combine vinegar, mustard, oil, basil, salt and pepper; whisk to blend. In medium bowl, toss lettuce, pignoli nuts and onion rings. Cut pear into thin slices; toss with lemon juice. Toss pears and dressing with greens. Serve immediately.

*2 servings.*

*Aromatic red wine vinegars give character to vinaigrette dressings.*
*Sherry wine vinegar is made from sweet sherry and imparts a nutty flavor.*

113

# ARTICHOKE 'N ORANGE TOSSED SALAD

*A mimosa dressing of champagne and orange juice is the pleasing companion for orange pieces, artichoke hearts and greens. Add pignoli nuts and dressing just before serving.*

¼ cup dry champagne
¼ cup orange juice
¼ cup light olive oil
¼ cup white wine vinegar
2 tablespoons sugar
½ teaspoon grated orange peel
¼ teaspoon salt
– dash white pepper
1 orange, rind and membrane removed, finely chopped

1 (14-ounce) can quartered artichoke hearts, drained
1 orange, rind and membrane removed, cut into chunks
1 head Boston lettuce, torn (5 cups)
½ head romaine lettuce, torn (5 cups)
½ cup pignoli nuts, toasted

In medium bowl, combine champagne, orange juice, oil, vinegar, sugar, orange peel, salt and pepper; whisk to blend. Stir in finely chopped orange. Refrigerate, covered. In large salad bowl, layer artichoke hearts, orange chunks and greens. Refrigerate, covered.

To Serve: Sprinkle pignoli nuts over salad; drizzle with dressing. Toss to combine.

*10 servings.*

*Pignoli nuts, popular in Mediterranean cuisine, come from pine tree cones.*

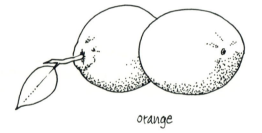

orange

# APPLES 'N GREENS

*With sugar and spice, the dressing does double duty for a festive do-ahead salad. Not only does it dress the greens, it keeps the apple pieces from darkening.*

½ cup apple juice
2 tablespoons lemon juice
2 tablespoons cider vinegar
2 tablespoons vegetable oil
1½ tablespoons brown sugar
1 teaspoon Dijon mustard
¼ teaspoon pepper

⅛ teaspoon salt
⅛ teaspoon ground cinnamon
– dash ground nutmeg
1 medium Red Delicious apple
1 medium Granny Smith apple
4 cups torn red-tipped leaf lettuce
4 cups torn romaine lettuce

In medium bowl, combine all ingredients except apples and lettuce; whisk to blend. Core and cut apples into bite-size pieces. Toss apples in dressing. Combine greens and gently layer over apples. Refrigerate, covered, several hours.

To Serve: Toss lightly; serve in bowl or on individual plates.

*8 servings.*

# ASPARAGUS 'N RASPBERRY SALAD

*It's the berries...tender, steamed asparagus spears dotted with ruby red raspberries and drizzled with a raspberry dressing.*

| | |
|---|---|
| 2 pounds asparagus | – Raspberry Salad Dressing, (page 126) |
| – leafy greens | ½ cup fresh raspberries |

Break off tough ends of asparagus as far down as stalks snap easily. Wash thoroughly. Remove scales if sandy or tough. Place steamer basket in Dutch oven or skillet; add small amount of water and bring to a boil. Arrange asparagus in steamer basket; simmer, covered, until tender (6 to 7 minutes). Rinse in cold water; drain. Spread on paper towels to dry. Refrigerate, covered.

To Serve: Arrange chilled asparagus on lettuce-lined serving platter or 8 individual salad plates. Drizzle dressing over spears. Garnish with raspberries.

*8 servings.*

# BROCCOLI SALAD

*Raisins and sunflower nuts are the surprise additions making this nutritional salad a taste sensation.*

| | |
|---|---|
| 2 pounds broccoli, cut into florets (5 cups) | ½ cup sunflower nuts |
| | ¼ cup chopped red onion |
| 10 slices crisply-cooked bacon, crumbled | 1 cup mayonnaise |
| | 2 tablespoons sugar |
| ½ cup golden raisins | 2 tablespoons white wine vinegar |

Combine broccoli, bacon, raisins, sunflower nuts and onion in large bowl. In small bowl, combine mayonnaise, sugar and vinegar; blend well. Toss dressing with broccoli mixture. Refrigerate, covered, several hours.

*Amount: 6 cups.*

**Variation:** Substitute 1 cup seedless red grapes, halved for raisins.

# BLACK BEAN EN SALADE

*Shiny, succulent black beans contrast with a colorful confetti of corn and red pepper for a fiesta salad. A sassy citrus dressing adds the final touch for casual entertaining.*

| | |
|---|---|
| 2 (15-ounce) cans black beans, rinsed, drained | ⅔ cup freshly squeezed lemon juice |
| 1 (10-ounce) package frozen whole kernel corn, thawed | ⅓ cup freshly squeezed lime juice |
| 1 (½-pound) jicama, peeled, cut into julienne strips | 3 tablespoons olive oil |
| | ¼ cup sugar |
| 1 red bell pepper, diced | 2 teaspoons minced garlic |
| 5 green onions, thinly sliced | ⅛ teaspoon Tabasco |
| | ¼ teaspoon salt |
| | – pepper |

Combine black beans, corn, jicama, red pepper and green onions in large bowl. In small bowl, combine remaining ingredients; stir until sugar is dissolved. Pour over bean mixture; toss to coat. Refrigerate, covered, several hours or overnight. Before serving, toss again and drain excess dressing.

*Amount: 6 cups.*

# SPAGHETTI SALAD

*Here's a stouthearted salad to serve as a side dish or light entrée. Beautifully suited for an outdoor barbecue or picnic, it can be made a day ahead of serving.*

1 (16-ounce) package dry spaghetti
1 bunch green onions with green tops, sliced (½ cup)
3 large tomatoes, chopped (3 cups)
1 large green bell pepper, chopped (1 cup)

1 large cucumber, seeded, chopped (1½ cups)
⅓ to ½ cup Salad Supreme Seasoning
1 tablespoon chopped hot jalapeño pepper
1 (8-ounce) bottle zesty Italian dressing

Break spaghetti into thirds. Cook according to package directions until almost tender; drain. Rinse with cold water; drain. In large bowl, toss cooked spaghetti with remaining ingredients until well combined. Refrigerate, covered, several hours or overnight. Toss before serving.

*Amount: 12 cups.*

**Tip:** Stir in additional Salad Supreme Seasoning as needed; its flavor becomes less intense on standing.

*Salad Supreme Seasoning, a combination of spices and other seasonings, can be found on the grocery shelf.*

# FUSILLI PASTA SALAD

*Spiral pasta strands team with fresh vegetables, roasted red pepper and pepperoni slices in a zesty salad.*

1 (16-ounce) package dry fusilli pasta
2 (6-ounce) jars marinated artichoke hearts
2 cups broccoli florets
2 cups cauliflower florets
1 cup shredded carrot (1 large)
1 (7-ounce) jar roasted red pepper, drained, cut into thin strips

1 (6-ounce) can pitted small ripe olives, drained
1 (3½-ounce) package sliced pepperoni, slices cut in half
1 (8-ounce) package mozzarella cheese, cut into ½-inch cubes
1 (16-ounce) bottle zesty Italian dressing, divided

Cook fusilli according to package directions, in boiling water with 2 teaspoons salt; drain. Rinse with cold water; drain. Drain artichokes, reserving marinade; chop coarsely. In large bowl, combine fusilli, artichokes, reserved marinade, broccoli, cauliflower, carrot, red pepper, olives, pepperoni and mozzarella. Pour 1 cup dressing over salad; toss to coat. Refrigerate, covered, several hours or overnight.

To Serve: Toss salad, adding reserved dressing as necessary.

*Amount: 10 cups.*

*Fusilli Pasta: A spiraled spaghetti that can be about one and one-half to twelve inches long.*

# POTATO SALAD VINAIGRETTE

*New potatoes are marinated in a zesty red wine vinaigrette for a robust European-style salad.*

2 pounds small new potatoes
¼ cup snipped fresh parsley
½ cup diced green bell pepper
½ cup thinly sliced green onions
½ cup vegetable oil
¼ cup red wine vinegar
1 tablespoon Dijon mustard
1 teaspoon sugar
1 teaspoon salt
½ teaspoon pepper
½ pound bacon, crisply cooked, crumbled (optional)

Place potatoes in large saucepan. Cover with cold water; add ½ teaspoon salt. Bring to a boil, covered, over high heat. Reduce heat; simmer until barely tender (15-20 min.). (Do not overcook.) Drain. Cut potatoes in halves or quarters; arrange in 7 × 11-inch glass baking dish. Sprinkle with parsley, green pepper and green onions. In small bowl, combine oil, vinegar, mustard, sugar, salt and pepper; whisk to blend. Pour dressing over vegetables while potatoes are still warm; toss gently. Marinate at room temperature 1 hour before serving.

To Serve: Spoon into serving bowl; sprinkle with bacon.

*Amount: 6 cups.*

**Tip:** Salad may be refrigerated, covered, several hours or overnight. Remove from refrigerator 1 hour before serving.

Parsley

# TORTELLINI 'N VEGGIE SALAD

*Chicken and prosciutto ham-filled rings of pasta called tortellini make a robust salad with an Italian accent.*

1 (9-ounce) package fresh tortellini with chicken and prosciutto
½ teaspoon minced garlic
½ cup olive oil and vinegar salad dressing
½ cup chopped parsley
½ cup sliced green onions
½ cup chopped red bell pepper
1 to 2 tablespoons snipped fresh basil
1 (6-ounce) jar marinated artichoke hearts, undrained, cut-up
1 cup broccoli florets
⅓ cup freshly grated Parmesan cheese
8 cherry tomatoes, halved

Cook tortellini according to package directions; drain. Combine garlic and salad dressing; toss with warm tortellini. Stir in parsley, green onions, red pepper, basil and artichoke hearts. Blanch broccoli in boiling water until bright green (about 1 minute); drain. Rinse with cold water; drain. Refrigerate salad and broccoli separately, covered, several hours or overnight.

To Serve: Toss Parmesan cheese and broccoli with salad. Spoon into serving bowl. Garnish with cherry tomatoes.

*Amount: 6 cups.*

# LENTIL 'N RICE SALAD

*Lentils are one of the most nutritious legumes. For this do-ahead salad they combine with rice, vegetables and seasonings for a unique menu addition.*

| | |
|---|---|
| 1 cup dried lentils | 1 (2¼-ounce) package sliced |
| 3 (10½-ounce) cans chicken | almonds |
| broth | ½ cup chopped red bell pepper |
| 1 (4.3-ounce) package long | ½ teaspoon dried thyme, |
| grain and wild rice mix with | crumbled |
| herbs | 1 teaspoon sugar |
| ½ cup sliced green onions | ½ cup red wine vinaigrette |
| ⅔ cup sliced celery | salad dressing |

Pick over and rinse lentils. In Dutch oven, bring chicken broth to a boil; stir in lentils. Simmer, covered, 20 minutes. Stir in rice and seasoning packet. Simmer, covered, until rice and lentils are tender (about 25 minutes). Drain; rinse. Drain well. Combine lentils and remaining ingredients in bowl; toss thoroughly. Refrigerate, covered, several hours or overnight. Toss gently; spoon into serving bowl.

*Amount: 5 cups.*

# FIESTA SALAD

*Red, white and green...the Mexican flag colors are showcased in this south-of-the-border medley. Cilantro, also known as coriander, is a popular addition to Mexican dishes.*

| | |
|---|---|
| 1 (1½-pound) jicama, peeled | ¼ cup lemon juice |
| 1 medium zucchini | ½ teaspoon dry mustard |
| 1 red apple, cored, quartered | 1 teaspoon salt |
| 2 green onions, cut into 2-inch | ¼ teaspoon pepper |
| pieces | ½ cup vegetable oil |
| 6 sprigs fresh parsley | ½ (2-ounce) bottle (¼ cup) |
| 1 (½-ounce) package fresh | pignoli nuts, toasted |
| cilantro | |

Cut jicama, zucchini and apple into 2 × ⅛-inch julienne strips; combine in bowl. With blender or food processor running, drop onion, parsley and cilantro through feed tube, processing until minced. Turn machine off; add lemon juice, mustard, salt and pepper. With machine running, slowly add oil through feed tube, processing until thick. Pour dressing over salad; toss to combine. Refrigerate, covered, 1 to 2 hours.

To Serve: Drain excess dressing; sprinkle with pignoli nuts.

*Amount: 8 cups.*

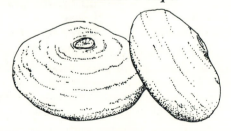

Jicama

*Jicama is sometimes referred to as a Mexican potato. Its inside is white, crisp and juicy, and it has a water chestnut flavor.*

# FRESH FRUIT SALAD

▼

*A honey-citrus dressing puts this picturesque summer salad in the warm weather winner's circle. Have it ready and waiting in the refrigerator.*

3 kiwi fruit, peeled, quartered
  lengthwise
1 medium cantaloupe, cut into
  balls
1 medium pineapple, peeled,
  cored, cubed
⅓ cup orange juice

2 tablespoons lemon juice
3 tablespoons honey
3 tablespoons snipped fresh
  mint leaves
1 pint fresh strawberries,
  quartered
– fresh mint leaves

Cut kiwi quarters in half crosswise; combine with melon and pineapple in 2½ to 3-quart serving bowl. In small bowl, combine orange juice, lemon juice, honey and snipped mint; whisk to blend. Drizzle over fruit; toss gently. Refrigerate, covered, 2 to 3 hours. Before serving, stir in strawberries. Garnish with mint leaves.

*Amount: 9 cups.*

strawberry

# APPLE FLUFF SALAD

▼

*All ages will love this airy concoction with the contrast of tart red apples and the crunch of Spanish peanuts. Prepare the cooked dressing ahead to allow for ample cooling time.*

1 (15¼-ounce) can chunk
  pineapple in its own juice
2 cups miniature marshmallows
½ cup sugar
1 tablespoon flour
5 teaspoons white vinegar
1 egg, slightly beaten

2 large tart red apples, cored,
  cut into ¾-inch cubes (about
  2½ cups)
1¼ cups Spanish peanuts (with
  skins) or salted peanuts
1 (8-ounce) container frozen
  non-dairy whipped topping,
  thawed
– stemmed maraschino
  cherries (optional)

Drain pineapple; reserve juice. Combine pineapple and marshmallows in large bowl. Refrigerate, covered, several hours or overnight. Combine sugar and flour in 1½-quart saucepan. Stir in vinegar, egg and reserved pineapple juice. Bring to a boil; cook 2 minutes, stirring constantly. Cool slightly; refrigerate, covered. About 1 hour before serving, combine pineapple-marshmallow mixture with dressing, apples and peanuts. Fold in whipped topping.

To Serve: Spoon into serving bowl. Garnish with maraschino cherries.

*Amount: 7 cups.*

*Cortland, Gala, Red Delicious or Winesap apples are excellent for salads.*

# FRUITED CHICKEN 'N GREENS SALAD

▼

*In this sensational summertime salad entrée, grilled chicken breasts nestle among artfully arranged greens and fruit. A quickly microwaved hot dressing adds the finishing touch.*

1 (4-ounce) package mixed
   salad greens (8 cups)
½ cantaloupe, cubed (1½ cups)
1 cup fresh raspberries
2 kiwi fruit, peeled, sliced
⅓ cup coarsely chopped
   pecans, toasted
¼ cup vegetable oil

2 tablespoons raspberry vinegar
1 tablespoon sugar
¾ teaspoon salt, divided
– dash Tabasco
4 skinless, boneless chicken
   breast halves
– vegetable oil
⅛ teaspoon pepper
2 tablespoons sliced green
   onions

Prepare grill. Arrange salad greens, fruits and pecans on 4 dinner plates. Combine oil, vinegar, sugar, ½ teaspoon of the salt and Tabasco in 1-cup glass measure; set aside. Brush both sides of chicken with oil; sprinkle with pepper and remaining ¼ teaspoon salt. Spray grill rack with no stick cooking spray. Using direct heat cooking method, arrange chicken breasts, rib side up, 4 to 5 inches over medium coals. Grill, covered, 5 minutes. Turn chicken, continue grilling until juices run clear (3 to 5 minutes). Place one chicken breast over greens on each plate. Microwave dressing (HIGH) until boiling (about 30 seconds). Drizzle hot dressing over salads; sprinkle with onions. Serve immediately.

*4 servings.*

# CHICKEN 'N WALNUT SALAD

▼

*Crème Fraîche, a nutty-flavored slightly soured cream, and snipped fresh tarragon added at the last minute enhance a classic chicken salad.*

1½ cups chopped walnuts
1 (10-ounce) carton Crème
   Fraîche
¾ cup mayonnaise
½ teaspoon salt

¼ teaspoon white pepper
7 cups cubed cooked chicken
2 cups diagonally sliced celery
2 tablespoons snipped fresh
   tarragon
– fresh tarragon sprigs

Heat oven to 350°. In small saucepan, bring water to a boil, add walnuts; simmer 3 minutes. Drain, rinse and pat dry on paper towels. Arrange on baking pan. Bake until toasted (5 to 7 minutes), stirring occasionally. Cool. Combine Crème Fraîche, mayonnaise, salt and pepper. Combine chicken, celery, walnuts and dressing; toss to coat. Refrigerate, covered, several hours or overnight.

To Serve: Gently toss in snipped tarragon; spoon into lettuce-lined bowl and garnish with fresh tarragon sprigs.

*9 servings.*

**Tips:** To cook chicken, see page 105. If substituting dried tarragon for fresh, stir 2 teaspoons dry crumbled tarragon into Crème Fraîche.

*Boiling walnuts, before toasting, removes excess oil and results in a crisp texture and delicate taste.*

# SMOKED TURKEY SALAD

*Savory smoked turkey ribbons and traditional Waldorf salad ingredients combine for a superb nut-topped main dish. Crusty rolls complete the menu.*

¾ pound (¼-inch thick) smoked turkey breast slices
1 large Granny Smith apple, cored, diced
1 cup red seedless grapes
¾ cup sliced celery

½ cup light mayonnaise
1 tablespoon lemon juice
1 tablespoon Dijon mustard
⅛ teaspoon white pepper
¼ teaspoon grated lemon peel
½ cup walnut halves
– grape clusters

Heat oven to 350°. Slice turkey into 2 × ½-inch julienne strips. Toss with apple, grapes and celery. Combine remaining ingredients except walnuts and grape clusters; stir into turkey mixture. Refrigerate, covered, up to 4 hours. In medium saucepan, bring water to a boil; add walnuts. Simmer 3 minutes; drain. Rinse and pat dry on paper towels. Arrange walnuts on baking pan; bake until toasted (5 to 7 minutes), stirring occasionally. Cool walnuts; chop.

To Serve: Stir ¼ cup nuts into salad; mound salad in large bowl and sprinkle with remaining walnuts. Garnish with grape clusters.

*Amount: 6 cups.*

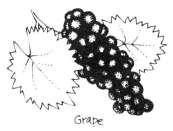

Grape

# TURKEY SALAD WITH RASPBERRY VINAIGRETTE

*Julienne strips of turkey breast marinate with colorful vegetables and olives in a raspberry vinaigrette. Serve from lettuce-lined bowl or on individual salad plates.*

½ cup raspberry vinegar
¼ cup olive oil
1½ teaspoons dried basil, crumbled
¼ teaspoon minced garlic
1½ teaspoons sugar
1 pound (½-inch thick) deli turkey breast slices

1 green bell pepper, cut into julienne strips
1 red bell pepper, cut into julienne strips
1 yellow bell pepper, cut into julienne strips
1 (2¼-ounce) can sliced ripe olives, drained
1 cup cherry tomato halves
– leaf lettuce

In small bowl, combine vinegar, oil, basil, garlic and sugar; whisk to blend. Cut turkey slices into julienne strips. In large bowl, combine turkey, peppers, olives and tomatoes. Add dressing; toss to coat. Refrigerate, covered, several hours or overnight.

To Serve: Line bowl with leaf lettuce; spoon in salad.

*Amount: 8 cups.*

*Berry vinegars are made by steeping berries in white vinegar. The fruit imparts its special color, flavor and aroma.*

# SEAFOOD FETTUCCINE SALAD

*Imitation crabmeat teamed with fettuccine makes this as easy as it is tasty. The Italian dressing, onion and lemon juice impart a delightful tartness.*

½ (16-ounce) package dry
  fettuccine
½ cup diced red onion
¾ cup diced celery
½ cup diced green bell pepper
1 pound frozen imitation
  crabmeat, thawed, flaked

1 cup mayonnaise
⅓ cup Italian dressing
1 tablespoon lemon juice
1 teaspoon celery seed
¼ teaspoon dried oregano,
  crumbled
½ teaspoon salt
⅛ teaspoon pepper

Cook fettuccine according to package directions; drain. Rinse with cold water; drain. In large bowl, combine fettuccine, onion, celery, green pepper and crabmeat. In small bowl, combine remaining ingredients. Toss with pasta mixture until thoroughly combined. Refrigerate, covered, several hours or overnight.

*Amount: 8 cups.*

*Imitation crabmeat is sometimes called "surimi." It is made from a white fish and is generally low in fat and calories.*

# TUNA SALAD TOSS

*That shelf staple, tuna, is transformed into elegant eating with an herb-enhanced yogurt dressing.*

4 cups torn romaine lettuce
1 cup torn watercress
½ cup chopped fresh basil
½ cup thinly sliced English
  cucumber
1 (8-ounce) carton plain
  yogurt

1 tablespoon Dijon mustard
1 tablespoon snipped fresh dill
½ teaspoon salt
⅛ teaspoon pepper
1 stalk lemon grass
2 (6½-ounce) cans chunk white
  tuna in water, drained
1 cup seasoned croutons

In large bowl, combine romaine, watercress, basil and cucumber. Refrigerate, covered. In small bowl, combine yogurt, mustard, dill, salt and pepper. Peel off fibrous leaves of lemon grass; finely mince tender center section. Stir 1 tablespoon into yogurt mixture. Refrigerate, covered.

To Serve: Toss tuna, yogurt mixture and croutons with greens. Serve immediately.

*4 to 5 servings.*

**Tip:** Two teaspoons grated lemon peel can be substituted for lemon grass.

*Watercress is an aquatic plant with tiny green leaves often used as an herb or garnish or as a salad green mixed with other greens.*

# SALMON SALAD WITH CREAMY TARRAGON DRESSING

*A deluxe do-ahead with picture-perfect presentation. Ideal for an impressive pre-theatre or concert repast. The flavor of tarragon harmonizes beautifully with fish.*

¾ cup chopped fresh parsley
⅓ cup sliced green onions
½ teaspoon minced garlic
⅔ cup sour cream
1 tablespoon tarragon vinegar
1 teaspoon Dijon mustard
½ teaspoon dried tarragon, crumbled
⅛ teaspoon salt

2 salmon steaks (1-inch thick)
– olive oil
½ teaspoon salt
¼ teaspoon pepper
1 (4-ounce) package mixed salad greens (8 cups)
8 ounces asparagus, cooked, chilled, quartered
8 cherry tomatoes

Combine parsley, green onions, garlic, sour cream, vinegar, mustard, tarragon and ⅛ teaspoon salt in blender until puréed. Rinse salmon; pat dry with paper towels. Brush both sides with olive oil; sprinkle with ½ teaspoon salt and pepper. Heat broiler. Arrange steaks on lightly oiled broiler pan; broil 4 inches from heat until slightly opaque in center (about 10 minutes), turning once. Divide greens, asparagus and tomatoes among 4 dinner plates. Remove bone and skin from salmon; break salmon into pieces, dividing among plates. Spoon dressing over salmon.

*4 servings.*

**Tip:** Salmon can be broiled ahead, refrigerated and served cold over salad greens.

# CHALUPA

*A fiesta feast featuring well-seasoned pork, beans and a potpourri of colorful toppings.*

1 pound dry pinto beans
3 pounds pork roast
7 cups water
1 cup chopped onion
2 teaspoons minced garlic
2 to 3 tablespoons chili powder
1 tablespoon salt
1 tablespoon ground cumin
1 teaspoon dried oregano, crumbled
½ teaspoon cayenne pepper
1 (4-ounce) can chopped green chiles

Toppings:
2 large tomatoes, diced
3 (4-ounce) packages shredded sharp Cheddar cheese
8 green onions, including some tops, sliced
½ head iceberg lettuce, shredded
1 (6-ounce) carton frozen avocado dip, thawed
1 (2¼-ounce) can sliced ripe olives, drained
1 (8-ounce) carton sour cream
– taco or picante sauce
1 (16-ounce) package tortilla chips

Pick over and rinse pinto beans. Combine beans and all ingredients except toppings in Dutch oven. Bring to a boil, reduce heat. Simmer, covered, until roast falls apart and beans are tender (3½ to 4 hours). Uncover; simmer until of desired consistency (about 30 minutes). Skim off any excess fat. Remove roast and discard bones; cut meat into bite-size pieces. Return meat to beans. Prepare topping ingredients.

To Serve: Place tortilla chips on individual plates; spoon Chalupa over chips. Add toppings as desired.

*10 servings.*

**Tip:** Chalupa meat mixture can be baked in a preheated 350° oven until beans are tender and roast falls apart (about 3 hours).

# HAM 'N CHEESE SALAD

*All-American sandwich ingredients — ham and cheese — steal the show in a main dish, do-ahead salad. We like this served with dark rye rolls or chewy bagel sticks.*

1½ pounds new red potatoes
1½ teaspoons salt, divided
½ cup light olive oil
⅓ cup chopped fresh parsley
¼ cup white wine
3 tablespoons white wine vinegar
¼ cup minced green onions
½ teaspoon minced garlic

3 tablespoons Dijon mustard
1 teaspoon sugar
½ teaspoon white pepper
½ pound cooked ham, cut into julienne strips
4 ounces Jarlsburg cheese, cut into julienne strips
2 cups shredded red cabbage
⅓ cup chopped walnuts, toasted

Place potatoes in large saucepan. Cover with cold water; add ½ teaspoon of the salt. Bring to a boil, covered, over high heat. Reduce heat; simmer until barely tender (15 to 18 minutes). Drain; cool slightly. Cut into 1½-inch cubes. In small bowl, combine oil, parsley, wine, vinegar, green onions, garlic, mustard, remaining 1 teaspoon salt, sugar and white pepper; whisk to blend. Pour about ⅔ cup dressing over potatoes; toss lightly. Cool to room temperature. Gently stir in ham, cheese, cabbage and remaining dressing. Refrigerate, covered, several hours or overnight. Garnish with walnuts.

*Amount: 8 cups.*

# SHERRIED CRANBERRY MOLD

*Here's a shimmering, sherry-sparked stunner for your holiday table. Chill in your prettiest mold and garnish with complementary orange twists.*

1 (20-ounce) can crushed pineapple in its own juice
1 (6-ounce) package raspberry flavor gelatin
¾ cup cream sherry

1 medium Granny Smith apple, cored, diced
1 cup chopped celery
½ cup chopped pecans
1 (16-ounce) can whole-berry cranberry sauce
– leafy greens

Drain pineapple; reserve juice. Add enough water to juice to measure 1¾ cups. Bring to a boil, pour over gelatin in large bowl; stir to dissolve. Add sherry; refrigerate until slightly thickened. Stir in pineapple, apple, celery, pecans and cranberry sauce. Pour into 6-cup mold. Refrigerate, covered, until firm (several hours or overnight).

To Serve: Unmold onto platter lined with leafy greens.

*12 servings.*

Apple

# RASPBERRY SALAD SQUARES

▼

*The crunchy, creamy and fruit-flavored layers in this do-ahead salad adapt to almost any menu. We've updated this favorite for lightness and ease of preparation.*

1½ cups crushed pretzels
2 tablespoons sugar
½ cup margarine or butter, melted
1 (8-ounce) package lowered fat cream cheese, softened
½ cup sugar
1½ teaspoons grated lemon peel

1 (4-ounce) container frozen non-dairy whipped topping, thawed
3 (0.3-ounce) packages sugar free raspberry flavor gelatin
3½ cups boiling water
2 (12-ounce) packages frozen, slightly sweetened raspberries, thawed
– leafy greens

Heat oven to 350°. Combine pretzels, 2 tablespoons sugar and margarine; press on bottom of 9 × 13-inch glass baking dish. Bake until lightly browned (about 10 minutes); cool. In large bowl, beat cream cheese, ½ cup sugar and lemon peel; fold in whipped topping. Spread cheese mixture evenly over crust. Refrigerate, covered. Dissolve gelatin in boiling water; chill until slightly thickened. Fold in raspberries; pour over cheese mixture. Refrigerate, covered, until firm.

To Serve: Cut into squares; place on salad plates lined with leafy greens.

***15 servings.***

*It is easy to crush pretzels, crackers or cookies by putting them in a zipper closure food storage bag and rolling with a rolling pin.*

# FROSTY FRUIT CUP

▼

*This appetizing alternative to fresh fruit adapts to brunch, luncheon and supper menus. Slushy consistency is important, so be sure to remove from freezer in time.*

1 (3-ounce) package lemon flavor gelatin
1 cup boiling water
1 (6-ounce) can frozen orange juice concentrate
1 (20-ounce) can crushed pineapple in its own juice, undrained

1 (16-ounce) package frozen cantaloupe/honeydew melon balls, separated
2 to 3 teaspoons minced crystallized ginger
12 (5-ounce) stemmed clear plastic cups
6 strawberries, halved

In medium bowl, dissolve gelatin in boiling water. Stir in orange juice until dissolved. Stir in pineapple, melon balls and ginger. Divide evenly among plastic cups; freeze.

To Serve: Let cups stand at room temperature until slushy (1 to 1½ hours). Garnish each cup with strawberry half.

***12 servings.***

**Tip:** Defrosting time will vary with room temperature.

# RASPBERRY SALAD DRESSING

*A versatile raspberry-infused topping for crisp greens, vegetables or fresh fruit is quickly blended in food processor or blender.*

| | |
|---|---|
| 1 cup fresh raspberries, divided | 1 tablespoon sour cream |
| ⅓ cup raspberry vinegar | 1 tablespoon minced shallots |
| ¼ cup sugar | ½ teaspoon minced garlic |
| 2 tablespoons Dijon mustard | ⅛ teaspoon salt |
| | ⅛ teaspoon white pepper |
| | 1¼ cups vegetable oil |

Slightly crush ½ cup of the raspberries; stir in raspberry vinegar. Let stand about 10 minutes. Strain raspberries; discard seeds. In food processor combine raspberry liquid with remaining ingredients except oil and remaining ½ cup raspberries. With machine running, slowly pour in oil in a steady stream. Refrigerate, covered.

To Serve: Drizzle dressing over chilled asparagus, spinach, mixed greens or favorite fruit. Garnish with remaining ½ cup raspberries.

*Amount: 2 cups.*

# BALSAMIC VINAIGRETTE

*For peak flavor, combine ingredients several hours before serving.*

| | |
|---|---|
| 2 tablespoons light olive oil | 1½ teaspoons snipped fresh basil |
| 3 tablespoons chicken broth | 1 teaspoon Dijon mustard |
| 1 clove garlic, peeled, halved | 2 tablespoons balsamic vinegar |
| 1½ teaspoons snipped fresh tarragon | ½ teaspoon lemon juice |
| | ⅛ to ¼ teaspoon salt |
| | – dash freshly ground pepper |

Combine oil, broth, garlic, tarragon, basil and mustard in small bowl. Let stand at room temperature about 1 hour. Whisk in vinegar, lemon juice, salt and pepper. Refrigerate, covered, up to 3 days. Remove garlic before serving. Shake well before serving.

*Amount: ½ cup.*

*Balsamic vinegar is made from aged juice of the white grape.*

# FRESH HERB VINAIGRETTE

*Chef's choice of vinegar and fresh herbs combine for a versatile French-style dressing.*

| | |
|---|---|
| ½ cup light olive oil | 1 teaspoon minced garlic |
| ½ cup white wine vinegar or raspberry vinegar | ⅛ teaspoon salt |
| ¼ cup snipped fresh herbs | ½ to 1 teaspoon sugar |
| | – dash freshly ground pepper |

Combine all ingredients in small bowl; whisk to blend. Refrigerate, covered, 2 or more hours before serving.

*Amount: 1 cup.*

# ORANGE YOGURT DRESSING

▼

**This creamy orange-flavored dressing can be made in minutes.**

½ cup orange juice
   concentrate, thawed

2 to 3 tablespoons honey
1 (8-ounce) carton plain nonfat
   yogurt

In small bowl, combine orange juice concentrate and honey. Fold in yogurt until thoroughly combined. Refrigerate, covered, several hours or overnight.

*Amount: 1½ cups.*

**Variation:** Two packets low calorie sugar substitute can be substituted for honey.

# SWEETLY SOUR YOGURT DRESSING

▼

**Slightly sweet, this dressing is lower in calories than many other options.**

1 (8-ounce) carton plain nonfat
   yogurt
¼ cup reduced calorie
   mayonnaise

3 tablespoons white wine vinegar
2 tablespoons sugar
1 teaspoon minced onion
½ teaspoon paprika
¼ teaspoon dry mustard

Combine all ingredients in small bowl until blended. Refrigerate, covered, several hours or overnight.

*Amount: 1 cup.*

# SALADS IN A SNAP

▼

**Jazz up the tried and true with innovative seasonings or unexpected ingredients. Then take a few minutes to arrange attractively and garnish with an imaginative touch...it makes all the difference.**

**Beefy Salad:** Combine salad greens with thinly sliced red onion rings and thinly sliced, cooked roast beef. Toss with red wine vinegar and oil salad dressing.

**Beef 'n Fruit Platter:** Line serving platter with lettuce leaves. Arrange thinly sliced, cooked roast beef in center of platter; surround with cut-up fruits. Serve with sweet raspberry dressing.

**Chutney Chicken Salad:** Combine 1 pint deli chicken salad deluxe or fruited chicken salad, 3 tablespoons chutney and ¾ teaspoon curry powder. Top with ¼ cup toasted sliced almonds. Serve on cantaloupe slices.

**Potato Salad with Pizzazz:** To 1 pound deli potato salad, add 1 cup chopped apple, 1 tablespoon chutney and 1 to 2 teaspoons curry powder.

**Dilled Potato Salad:** To 1 pound deli potato salad, add 1 tablespoon snipped fresh dill and 2 teaspoons Dijon mustard.

Raspberries

# FRESH HERBS

▼

| Herb | Taste | Good With |
|------|-------|-----------|
| **Arugula*** | Pungent and peppery | Green salads, pasta, potatoes, citrus fruits, tomatoes, avocados |
| **Basil** | Sweet, subtle vegetable flavor; clove-like aroma | Tomato and pasta dishes, pesto, vegetable soups, eggs, poultry, fish, carrots, zucchini, eggplant, beans, peas |
| **Chives** | Delicate onion | Eggs, fish, vegetables, chicken, sauces, cottage cheese, potatoes, herb butters |
| **Cilantro** (Fresh Coriander, Chinese Parsley) | Distinctively peppery | Salsas, avocado, Mexican and Oriental dishes, peas, lentil or chicken soup, tomatoes, spinach, egg salad |
| **Dill** | Slightly sharp yet sweet flavor, with a hint of parsley; aromatic | Seafood, potatoes, eggs, chicken, lamb, pork, herb butters, peas, carrots, green beans, cabbage |
| **Marjoram** | Mild oregano flavor, but sweeter; slightly minty | Pork, lamb, poultry, fish, beef, veal, eggs, carrots, mushrooms, spinach, peas, broccoli, potatoes, asparagus |
| **Mint** | Sweet, spicy, aromatic | Fruit drinks, tea, frozen desserts, peas, lamb, Middle Eastern dishes |
| **Oregano** | Pungent and spicy; similar to but stronger than marjoram | Poultry, lamb, pork, pizza, pasta, bean soups, Italian and Greek dishes, eggplant, zucchini, broccoli, lentils |
| **Rosemary** | Bold, pine-like, fresh | Lamb, poultry, pork, fish, herb breads, potatoes, peas, green beans, spinach, mushrooms, cauliflower |
| **Sage** | Aromatic and woodsy with a hint of eucalyptus | Poultry, pork, veal, lamb, game, stuffings, cheese, potatoes, onions, tomatoes, eggplant |
| **Tarragon** | Sweet, savory flavor with a hint of licorice | Poultry, seafood, beef, eggs, veal, herb butters, mayonnaise-based salad dressings, carrots, potatoes |
| **Thyme** | Spicy, slightly pungent-sweet | Braised meats, soups, stews, seafood, poultry, game birds, egg dishes, corn, tomatoes, green beans, peas, carrots |
| **Watercress*** | Mild peppery flavor | Green salads, sandwiches, eggs, cottage cheese |

* Used as an herb or salad green

## HERB HINTS

▼

**Preparation:** Wash herbs before using; pat dry between paper towels. Cut herbs easily by placing leaves in a glass measuring cup and snipping with kitchen shears. When cutting more than ¼ cup, it's helpful to use a food processor.

**Storage:** Refrigerate fresh herbs, tightly covered, in the vegetable keeper for 2 to 3 days. For longer storage (5 to 7 days), place stems in glass of water; cover leaves loosely with plastic bag and secure with a rubber band. Refrigerate.

**Substitutions:** Dried herbs have a more concentrated flavor than fresh. A general formula is 1 teaspoon dried herbs = 1 tablespoon fresh herbs.

# VEGETABLES & SIDE DISHES

Today, we relish the vegetable and side dish portions of a meal, not only because they look and taste great, but because we value their exceedingly important nutritional contributions. The variety of available vegetables is appealingly endless. Speedy and careful shipping from field to market and progressive processing methods join to bring us the best of global markets at peak freshness.

Our assortment of vegetable recipes, plus inviting ideas for pasta, stuffing and rice, promise to bring this part of your menu planning to life like never before. A variety of cooking methods to suit your tastes and timetable, sensational seasonings and marvelous ingredient medleys are at your fingertips.

# BEAN 'N VEGGIE CASSEROLE

▼

*Hearty enough for a vegetarian main dish; congenial enough to accompany a variety of casual entrées. Canned vegetables undergo creative transformation with microwave quick speed.*

1 medium onion, chopped (¾ cup)
1 small green bell pepper, cut into julienne strips (1 cup)
1 rib celery, sliced (½ cup)
1½ teaspoons minced garlic
1 (12-ounce) can whole kernel corn with red and green sweet pepper, drained
1 (15-ounce) can kidney beans, drained

1 (15-ounce) can pinto beans, drained
1 (8¼-ounce) can peeled tomatoes, drained, diced
1 tablespoon Worcestershire
1 teaspoon dried basil, crumbled
1 teaspoon dried oregano, crumbled
½ teaspoon salt
¼ teaspoon pepper
1 (4-ounce) package shredded Cheddar cheese (1 cup)

In a 2-quart microwavable casserole, combine onion, pepper, celery and garlic; cover with plastic wrap. Microwave (HIGH) 2½ minutes; drain. Stir in corn, kidney beans, pinto beans, tomatoes, Worcestershire, basil, oregano, salt and pepper. Microwave (HIGH), covered, until heated through (7 to 9 minutes), stirring once. Sprinkle cheese evenly over top. Let stand, covered, 5 minutes; serve immediately.

*Amount: 6 cups.*

# BROCCOLI CORN CASSEROLE

▼

*When your oven is taken up by a large turkey, roast or ham, put your microwave to good use with this delightful do-ahead. A browned butter-crumb mixture makes ordinary vegetables taste very special.*

¼ cup butter or margarine
⅓ cup dry bread crumbs

2 (10-ounce) packages frozen chopped broccoli, thawed, drained, squeezed dry
2 (17-ounce) cans cream-style corn
2 eggs, slightly beaten

In small saucepan, over medium heat, heat butter until browned. Stir in bread crumbs. In 2-quart microwavable casserole, combine broccoli, corn, eggs and all but 2 tablespoons crumb mixture. Refrigerate casserole and reserved crumb mixture, covered, several hours or overnight.

To Serve: Let stand at room temperature 1 hour. Uncover broccoli. Microwave (MEDIUM-HIGH, 70% power) for 20 minutes, stirring every 5 minutes. Sprinkle remaining crumbs over top. Microwave (MEDIUM-HIGH, 70% power) until heated through and set in center (5 to 7 minutes). Let stand 5 minutes before serving.

*10 to 12 servings.*

**Tip:** Casserole can be baked in 350° oven, uncovered, until set in center (60 to 70 minutes).

*Sugar Snap Peas
'n Onions
page 138*

# BROCCOLI 'N CAULIFLOWER SAUTÉ

*Pleasantly accented with lemon zest, garlic and shallots, fresh vegetables are quickly sautéed to tender-crisp perfection for a flavorful and attractive presentation.*

| | |
|---|---|
| 2 pounds broccoli | ½ cup chicken broth |
| 2½ pounds cauliflower | ½ teaspoon salt |
| 5 to 6 tablespoons vegetable oil, divided | ⅛ teaspoon pepper |
| 2 teaspoons minced garlic | 2 teaspoons lemon zest (below) |
| ⅓ cup finely chopped shallots | |

Separate broccoli and cauliflower into 1-inch florets. Trim and discard stem ends from broccoli. Peel remaining stems and thinly slice. In 12-inch skillet, heat 5 tablespoons oil over medium heat. Sauté garlic and shallots until tender but not browned (1 to 2 minutes). Remove with slotted spoon; reserve. In same skillet, stir-fry broccoli and cauliflower over medium-high heat 2 minutes, adding 1 tablespoon more oil if needed. Stir in ½ cup chicken broth. Cook, covered, over medium-high heat until crisp-tender (2 to 3 minutes). Remove cover; continue cooking and stirring to reduce remaining liquid (about 2 minutes). Sprinkle with salt and pepper. Stir in reserved garlic and shallots along with lemon zest; toss gently. Spoon into heated serving bowl.

*10 servings.*

**Citrus Zest:** Using a citrus zester, place bent sharp edge against lemon, lime or orange. Firmly press down on citrus peel while pulling zester toward you. Thin fine strands of citrus zest will come through.

# BROCCOLI 'N PISTACHIO BUTTER

*Here's just the gourmet touch you are looking for to dress up microwaved broccoli and other vegetables. It's delicious over fish and poultry, as well, adding special flavor and texture.*

| | |
|---|---|
| 1 to 1½ pounds broccoli | ½ cup water |
| | – Pistachio Butter (below) |

Divide broccoli into spears. Remove 1 to 1½ inches from tough stem ends. Peel skin from lower 2 inches of stalks. Pour water into a microwavable 8 × 12-inch baking dish. Arrange broccoli with florets to center. Cover with plastic wrap; vent one corner. Microwave (HIGH) until crisp-tender (8 to 12 minutes), rotating dish ½ turn halfway through cooking time. Let stand, covered, 2 to 3 minutes. Arrange on serving platter; drizzle with Pistachio Butter.

*3 to 4 servings.*

**Pistachio Butter:** Combine ¼ cup chopped green onions, 2 tablespoons water, 1 tablespoon white wine vinegar and ⅛ teaspoon pepper in small saucepan. Bring to a boil; boil gently until volume is reduced by half (30 to 60 seconds). Stir in ¼ cup cold butter; whisk vigorously over medium heat. Do not boil. Whisk in an additional ½ cup cold butter, cut into cubes, 1 cube at a time. Beat until just melted. Stir in ⅓ cup coarsely chopped pistachio nuts, 1 tablespoon snipped fresh parsley and 1 tablespoon lime juice.

*Amount: 1 cup.*

# CARROTS 'N AMARETTO

*A festive and colorful side dish with an amaretto-laced butter sauce. Prepare and cook the carrots ahead so there's little left to do when guests arrive.*

Peel and cut 3 pounds carrots into julienne strips. Fill Dutch oven half full of water; stir in ½ teaspoon salt. Bring water to a boil; stir in carrots. Cook until almost tender (about 5 minutes); drain. Plunge into ice water until chilled; drain. Refrigerate, covered.

To Reheat: Remove carrots from refrigerator; let stand at room temperature 1 hour. Melt ⅓ cup margarine or butter in large skillet or wok. Stir in carrots and ⅓ to ½ cup almond-flavored liqueur. Cook over medium heat, stirring and tossing gently until heated through (5 to 6 minutes). Spoon into heated serving bowl; serve immediately.

*12 servings.*

# CINNAMON-SPICED CARROTS

*Subtly spiced, frozen carrots are microwaved with no need for thawing step. A great source of Vitamin A and potassium, carrots also are noteworthy for their fiber and beta-carotene content.*

**2 (14-ounce) packages frozen tiny whole carrots**

**⅓ cup cinnamon schnapps**
**2 tablespoons margarine or butter**

Arrange carrots in 2-quart microwavable casserole; stir in schnapps. Microwave (HIGH), covered, until heated through (18 to 20 minutes), stirring 3 times. Stir in margarine.

*8 servings.*

# CORN ON THE COB

*Three ways to cook fresh corn on the cob offer convenient choices. Boiling and microwaving work well anytime and grilling is particularly appropriate for an outdoor barbecue.*

**Boiled:** Remove husks and silk from corn. Drop into enough boiling water to cover. When water returns to a boil, cover and cook until tender (3 to 7 minutes, depending on size and age of ears of corn).

**Grilled:** Prepare grill. Remove husks and silk from corn; rinse corn. Arrange individual ears on a double thickness of heavy-duty aluminum foil; drizzle with 1 to 2 tablespoons water or add 1 to 2 ice cubes. Bring sides of foil together above corn; fold down loosely, allowing for heat circulation. Fold short ends up and over; crimp to seal. Using direct heat cooking method, arrange corn on grill rack 4 to 5 inches over heat. Grill, covered, over medium heat until corn is tender (30 to 40 minutes), turning several times.

**Microwaved:** Remove husks and silk from medium-size ears of corn; rinse corn. Arrange in microwavable dish; add ¼ cup water. Cover with plastic wrap; vent one corner. Microwave (HIGH) until kernels are almost tender, turning corn over and rearranging halfway through cooking time. Cook 2 ears for 3½ to 4½ minutes; cook 4 ears for 6½ to 8 minutes. Let stand, covered, 3 minutes.

# PICKLED CUCUMBERS

▼

*These zesty sweet-sour slices of dill-sparked cucumber promise to enliven any meal. Thorough draining and do-ahead preparation are important for optimum flavor.*

4 medium cucumbers,
   unpeeled (about 2¼ pounds)
1 tablespoon salt
¼ cup coarsely snipped fresh
   dill or 2 tablespoons dried
   dill weed

1 cup white wine vinegar
1 cup sugar
½ cup water
1 teaspoon salt
– fresh dill sprigs (optional)

Cut cucumbers into paper-thin slices. Arrange on large platter; sprinkle with 1 tablespoon salt. Cover cucumbers with another platter; weigh down with heavy object to press out excess liquid. Let stand at room temperature 1 hour. Pour off liquid; drain cucumbers on paper towels. In medium non-metal bowl, layer cucumbers and dill. Combine vinegar, sugar, water and 1 teaspoon salt; pour over cucumbers. Refrigerate, covered, several hours or overnight.

To Serve: Spoon cucumbers into serving bowl. Garnish with fresh dill sprigs.

*Amount: 4 cups.*

# GREEN BEANS 'N RED PEPPER

▼

*If you wish, trim and cook fresh beans hours or a day ahead. The speedy sautéing step comes just before serving this elegant crowd-sized combination.*

3 pounds fresh green beans
1 teaspoon salt (optional)
½ cup margarine or butter
1 (6-ounce) red bell pepper,
   cut into julienne strips

2 teaspoons lemon juice
1 cup salted cashews
¼ teaspoon salt
⅛ teaspoon pepper

Trim ends from beans. In large kettle, bring 3 quarts water and salt to a boil. Add beans; bring water back to boiling. Cook beans, uncovered, until crisp-tender (8 to 10 minutes). Plunge into cold water until beans are cold (3 to 4 minutes). Drain. Refrigerate, covered, several hours or overnight.

To Reheat: Remove beans from refrigerator; let stand at room temperature 1 hour. Melt margarine in Dutch oven or wok. Sauté bell pepper over medium heat 2 minutes. Stir in beans, lemon juice, cashews, salt and pepper. Cook over medium-high heat, stirring and tossing gently, until heated through (6 to 8 minutes). Transfer to large heated serving bowl or platter. Serve immediately.

*12 servings.*

**Tip:** Three (16-ounce) packages frozen cut green beans can be substituted for fresh. Cook according to package directions; chill and continue as in recipe above.

**Variation:**

**Green Beans 'n Sesame Seeds:** Omit red bell pepper, cashews and ¼ teaspoon salt. Stir ¼ teaspoon garlic salt into melted margarine along with beans, lemon juice and pepper; sprinkle with 2 tablespoons sesame seeds just before serving.

# CREAMY KOHLRABI

▼

*A member of the cabbage family but closer in looks to the turnip, kohlrabi's mild flavor is enhanced by a creamy, dill-seasoned sauce. Choose small bulbs for best taste and texture.*

| | |
|---|---|
| 6 small kohlrabi (1½ to 2 pounds), peeled | – dash Tabasco |
| ½ teaspoon salt | 3 tablespoons chopped fresh dill |
| 2 tablespoons margarine or butter | ¾ teaspoon salt |
| 1 cup whipping cream | ⅛ teaspoon pepper |
| 1 tablespoon lemon juice | 2 tablespoons freshly grated Parmesan cheese |
| | ⅓ cup shredded Swiss cheese |

In large saucepan, cook kohlrabi in boiling salted water 5 minutes. Drain; cool 5 to 10 minutes. Cut into ⅛-inch-thick slices. In large skillet, melt margarine; toss kohlrabi slices in margarine until coated. Stir in cream; bring to a boil. Reduce heat; simmer until kohlrabi is tender and cream is thickened (about 10 minutes). Stir in lemon juice, Tabasco, dill, ¾ teaspoon salt and pepper. Spoon into serving bowl; sprinkle with cheeses.

*4 to 6 servings.*

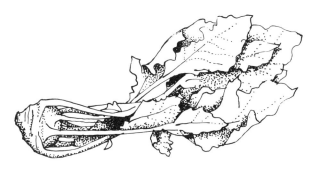

Kohlrabi

# SPRING PEAS

▼

*A last-minute, mint-refreshed medley is made easily in the microwave. We particularly like this with lamb and fish entrées.*

| | |
|---|---|
| 3 (10-ounce) packages frozen tiny peas | ⅔ cup water |
| 1 (8-ounce) can sliced water chestnuts, drained | ¼ cup orange-flavored liqueur |
| 2 tablespoons fresh mint, finely snipped | 2 tablespoons margarine or butter |
| | ½ teaspoon salt |

In 3-quart microwavable casserole, combine peas, water chestnuts, mint and water. Microwave (HIGH), covered, until crisp-tender (15 to 17 minutes), stirring twice. Remove from microwave; let stand covered, 3 minutes. Drain; stir in liqueur, margarine and salt.

*10 servings.*

# DUCHESS DO-AHEAD POTATOES

▼

*As lovely as you will find in any fine restaurant, these do-ahead and freeze potato "puffs" are surprisingly easy to make. A zipper closure freezer storage bag makes an ideal substitute for a pastry bag – just follow our simple directions.*

| | |
|---|---|
| 6 to 9 medium red potatoes (about 2 pounds) | 2 eggs |
| 1 teaspoon salt | 2 tablespoons snipped chives |
| ¼ cup milk | 2 large zipper closure freezer storage bags |
| ¼ cup margarine or butter, softened | – parchment paper |
| | – melted butter |
| | – paprika |

Peel potatoes; cut into 1½-inch cubes. In large saucepan, cover potatoes with water; add salt. Heat to boiling, covered; reduce heat and simmer until tender (20 to 25 minutes). Drain potatoes; mash until no lumps remain. Beat in milk, margarine and eggs; stir in chives. Spoon potatoes into one of the freezer storage bags; snip off one corner of bag, making small opening in corner of bag. Line baking sheet with parchment paper. Pipe potatoes onto parchment-lined baking sheet in circular mounds. Place in freezer to firm. Transfer to second food storage bag and freeze until needed.

To Serve: Heat oven to 425°. Arrange potatoes on parchment-lined baking sheet. Brush with melted butter. Bake until potatoes are light brown (15 to 20 minutes). Sprinkle with paprika.

*8 servings.*

**Tip:** If you do not like the looks of some of your mounds of potatoes, scrape them off parchment, add back to bag and re-pipe.

# CREAMY MASHED POTATOES

▼

*Just like made-at-the-last-minute mashed potatoes but far more convenient, this creamy concoction takes the "lumps" out of preparation panic. Be sure to allow time for the potatoes to come to room temperature before baking them.*

| | |
|---|---|
| 6 medium red potatoes (about 2 pounds) | ⅓ cup half-and-half, whipping cream or milk |
| 1 teaspoon salt | 3 tablespoons butter or margarine |
| ½ cup milk | – paprika |

Peel potatoes; cut into 1½-inch cubes. Place potatoes in large saucepan. Cover with water; add salt. Bring to a boil, covered, over high heat. Reduce heat and simmer until tender (25 to 30 minutes). Heat milk, half-and-half and butter until butter is melted; reserve and refrigerate ¼ cup. Drain potatoes quickly and thoroughly. Wipe excess moisture from pan. Return hot potatoes to hot pan; quickly mash with hand potato masher. Beat hot milk mixture into potatoes until desired consistency (not all liquid may be needed). Spoon into buttered 1½-quart casserole; smooth top. Cover and refrigerate. To Bake: Remove from refrigerator; pour on reserved ¼ cup milk mixture. Bring to room temperature (about 2 hours). Heat oven to 350°. Bake, uncovered, until hot (about 25 minutes). Remove from oven; stir. Garnish with paprika.

*6 to 8 servings.*

**Tips:** A hand potato masher produces the best results. An electric mixer can cause the potatoes to become "gummy" or "sticky". If an electric mixer is used, use on the lowest mixer speed and do not overmix.

Potatoes can be reheated in the microwave. Microwave (HIGH), covered, until heated through (about 10 minutes), rotating twice; stir.

# JO JO POTATOES

▼

*Choose baking potatoes or frozen wedges for this savory selection. Wedges should be of like size for even cooking, and turning is essential for perfect browning. All ages love potatoes fixed this way!*

| | |
|---|---|
| 4 medium baking potatoes, unpeeled | ½ teaspoon garlic powder |
| ¼ cup flour | ½ teaspoon salt |
| ¼ cup freshly grated Parmesan cheese | ¼ teaspoon white pepper |
| | 1 large zipper closure food storage bag |
| | ½ cup butter or margarine |

Heat oven to 450°. Cut each potato into 4 lengthwise wedges; place in cold water. Combine flour, cheese, garlic powder, salt and white pepper in food storage bag; drain potatoes. Shake potatoes in bag a few at a time until coated. Melt butter in oven in jelly roll pan. Arrange potato wedges, cut side down, on pan; sprinkle with remaining coating mixture. Bake 10 minutes. Turn other cut side of potatoes down; bake 10 minutes. Turn skin side down and continue baking until browned and tender (about 5 minutes).

*4 servings.*

**Variation:** One (24-ounce) package frozen home-style hearty-cut potato wedges, thawed, can be substituted for raw potatoes.

# ROSEMARY NEW POTATOES

▼

*The use of fresh rosemary is essential here for two reasons – potatoes take on its marvelous pine like flavor, and the fresh sprigs remain intact for easy removal before serving. A member of the mint family, it is used for flavoring only, not for eating.*

| | |
|---|---|
| 6 new red potatoes | 2 tablespoons minced shallots |
| ¼ cup olive oil | 1 (1½-ounce) package fresh rosemary |
| 1 teaspoon lemon juice | ¼ teaspoon salt |

Heat oven to 375°. Scrub potatoes; arrange in small casserole. Combine olive oil and lemon juice; pour over potatoes. Rotate potatoes to coat evenly with oil. Sprinkle minced shallots over potatoes; arrange fresh rosemary in oil around potatoes. Bake until tender (40 to 50 minutes), turning potatoes after 20 minutes. Drain potatoes; remove rosemary. Arrange potatoes in serving dish. Sprinkle with salt.

*2 servings.*

# NEW POTATOES

▼

*Garden-fresh potatoes simply seasoned and oven-baked Scandinavian-style. The addition of sugar brings out the full flavor of this spring and summer staple.*

| | |
|---|---|
| 1 pound new potatoes | 2 teaspoons sugar |
| 2 tablespoons margarine or butter, melted | 1 teaspoon salt |
| | ½ teaspoon coarsely ground pepper |

Heat oven to 375°. Coat potatoes with margarine; arrange in baking pan. Combine sugar, salt and pepper; sprinkle over potatoes. Bake until tender (40 to 45 minutes).

*4 to 5 servings.*

# POTATOES...OVEN BROWNED

*For carefree convenience, prepare potatoes ahead and bake them right along with the entrée. The cheese-crumb topping ensures a golden brown exterior for this impressive side dish.*

| | |
|---|---|
| 10 medium baking potatoes, peeled, halved lengthwise | ¾ teaspoon salt |
| ½ cup margarine or butter, softened | ¼ teaspoon white pepper |
| ¾ teaspoon garlic powder | 3 tablespoons freshly grated Parmesan cheese |
| | 3 tablespoons dry bread crumbs |

Heat oven to 325°. Cut deep slits in rounded side of potatoes at ¼-inch intervals, being careful not to cut all the way through potatoes. Arrange potatoes, flat side down, on 10 × 15-inch jelly roll pan. Combine margarine, garlic powder, salt and white pepper; spread evenly over potatoes. Place potatoes on lowest oven rack. Bake 45 minutes. Remove potatoes from oven; baste with pan drippings. Combine Parmesan cheese and bread crumbs; sprinkle evenly over potatoes. Continue baking until topping is nicely browned and potatoes are fork-tender (about 15 minutes).

### 10 to 15 servings.

**Tip:** Potatoes can be peeled and sliced ahead. Cover with cold water. Refrigerate, covered, several hours or overnight. Drain potatoes; pat dry.

Potato

# POTATO 'N VEGGIE KABOBS

*The key to success with these handsome kabobs is careful monitoring of the potatoes during the boiling step. They must remain firm to avoid breaking apart when skewered. Grill them alongside an entrée for a perfect patio supper.*

| | |
|---|---|
| ½ cup margarine or butter, softened | ⅛ teaspoon pepper |
| 2 tablespoons snipped fresh rosemary | 12 small new potatoes |
| 2 tablespoons snipped fresh chives | ½ teaspoon salt |
| 2 teaspoons lemon juice | – water |
| ½ teaspoon white wine Worcestershire sauce | 2 medium yellow squash, cut into 1-inch slices |
| | 2 medium zucchini, cut into 1-inch slices |
| | – vegetable oil |

Combine margarine, rosemary, chives, lemon juice, Worcestershire and pepper; spoon herb butter into serving bowl. Let stand at room temperature until serving time. Prepare grill. Cook new potatoes in boiling salted water to cover until just tender (18 to 20 minutes); drain. Alternate potatoes and squash on metal skewers, leaving ½ inch space between each. Spray grill rack with no stick cooking spray. Using direct heat cooking method, arrange skewers on grill rack 4 to 5 inches from medium-hot coals. Grill, uncovered, until squash is crisp-tender (15 to 20 minutes), turning and basting with vegetable oil. Serve with herb butter.

### 4 servings.

# SPAGHETTI SQUASH WITH FRESH TOMATOES

▼

*"When in Rome" or even if you're not, you can enjoy an authentic Italian vegetable treat. The recipe uses Roma or "plum" tomatoes because with their small egg shape and full flavor, they are ideal for sauces. Italian parsley is distinctively dark green and highly flavored.*

1 (3 to 3½-pound) spaghetti
    squash
2 tablespoons olive oil
2 green onions, including
    some tops, thinly sliced
1 teaspoon minced garlic
1½ pounds ripe Roma tomatoes,
    seeded, coarsely chopped
    (3 cups)

½ teaspoon salt
⅛ teaspoon pepper
2 tablespoons margarine or
    butter
½ cup freshly shredded
    Parmesan cheese, divided
2 tablespoons snipped fresh
    Italian parsley
– fresh Italian parsley sprigs
    (optional)

Pierce squash several times with long-tined fork; place on paper towel in microwave. Microwave (HIGH), turning over once, until shell "gives" slightly when pressed (10 to 14 minutes). Let stand 5 minutes. Meanwhile, combine oil, green onions and garlic in 1½-quart microwavable dish. Microwave (HIGH) 1 minute; stir in tomatoes, salt and pepper. Microwave (HIGH) until tomatoes are just heated through (4 to 5 minutes), stirring once. Cut squash in half lengthwise; scoop out seeds. "Rake" through squash with fork, forming spaghetti-like strands. In large bowl, toss together squash, margarine, ¼ cup of the Parmesan cheese and 2 tablespoons Italian parsley. Arrange squash on serving platter; spoon hot tomato mixture on top. Sprinkle with remaining ¼ cup Parmesan cheese. Garnish with Italian parsley sprigs.

*6 to 8 servings.*

# SUGAR SNAP PEAS 'N CARROTS

▼

*In just minutes, you have a quickly sautéed vegetable combo to add color and crunch to any entrée. So called for their high sugar content, sugar snap peas are cooked, served and eaten whole in their pods.*

¼ cup margarine or butter
4 teaspoons minced shallots
1 (14-ounce) package frozen
    baby carrots

1 (14-ounce) package frozen
    sugar snap peas
¼ cup water
½ teaspoon salt
¼ teaspoon white pepper
– zest of 1 lemon (page 130)

In large skillet, melt margarine; sauté shallots over medium-high heat until tender (1 to 2 minutes). Stir in carrots, peas, water, salt and pepper. Cook, covered, over medium-high heat, stirring occasionally, until vegetables are just tender (4 to 6 minutes). Spoon into serving dish. Garnish with lemon zest.

*8 servings.*

Sugar Snap Pea

# SUGAR SNAP PEAS 'N ONIONS

▼

*Combining the best qualities of ordinary green peas and Asian snow peas, the sugar snap variety blends beautifully with bright pepper strips, tiny onions and delicately-flavored pistachio nuts.*

| | |
|---|---|
| 1 (16-ounce) bag frozen sugar snap peas | 2 tablespoons water |
| 1½ cups frozen pearl onions, thawed | 2 tablespoons margarine or butter, melted |
| 1 roasted sweet red pepper, cut into ¼ × 1-inch strips | ½ cup roasted, shelled pistachio nuts, chopped |

In 2-quart microwavable casserole, combine sugar snap peas, onions, red pepper and water; cover. Microwave (HIGH) until crisp-tender (7 to 8 minutes), stirring once; drain. Toss with margarine and pistachio nuts.

*8 servings.*

# SWEET 'N SOUR RED CABBAGE

▼

*An integral part of Scandinavian and German cuisine, red cabbage is enhanced by the addition of vinegar. Choose a firm, heavy head with fresh looking leaves and store in a cool place until ready to prepare.*

| | |
|---|---|
| 1 (2¼-pound) head red cabbage | 2 tablespoons flour |
| 2 tablespoons margarine or butter | 2 tablespoons sugar |
| | 1 teaspoon salt |
| 1 tablespoon caraway seed | 1 cup water |
| | ¼ cup cider vinegar |

Remove outer leaves and core from cabbage; cut cabbage into thin slices. Melt margarine in large Dutch oven. Combine caraway seed, flour, sugar and salt. Layer half of the cabbage in pan; sprinkle with half of the flour mixture. Repeat layers. Pour water over cabbage. Bring to a boil; reduce heat. Simmer, covered, until crisp-tender (about 15 minutes). Remove from heat; stir in vinegar.

*8 servings.*

# YAMS 'N ESCALLOPED APPLES

▼

*Maple syrup adds a sumptuous sweet glaze to this favorite autumnal accompaniment. Layer ingredients ahead, if you wish, and microwave just before serving. Very tasty with ham and other pork entrées.*

| | |
|---|---|
| 2½ pounds yams (5 medium) | 1 (12-ounce) package frozen escalloped apples, thawed |
| | ½ cup maple syrup |

Place unpeeled yams in large saucepan; cover with water. Bring to a boil; reduce heat and simmer covered, until tender (25 to 30 minutes). Drain, cool and peel. Cut crosswise into ½-inch slices. In 2-quart microwavable casserole, layer half of yams, all of escalloped apples and remaining yams. Pour maple syrup over yams. Microwave (HIGH), covered, until heated through (8 to 10 minutes), rotating ¼ turn twice. Let stand 3 minutes. Spoon syrup over yams; serve with slotted spoon.

*6 servings.*

# STUFFED SWEET POTATOES

▼

*This elegant escort for pork, poultry or wild game entrées brings a medley of marvelous flavors and a dash of bright color to dinner plates.*

6 medium sweet potatoes or yams
– vegetable oil
3 tablespoons margarine or butter, softened

1 (8¼-ounce) can crushed pineapple in its own juice, drained
1 (6-ounce) can frozen orange juice concentrate, thawed
¼ teaspoon salt
½ cup chopped walnuts (optional)
1 cup miniature marshmallows

Heat oven to 400°. Scrub potatoes; rub well with oil. Pierce with fork. Bake until soft to pressure (about 1 hour). Let cool slightly. Slice potatoes in half lengthwise, carefully scoop out potato, leaving skin intact. Mash potato until smooth; blend in margarine, pineapple, orange juice concentrate and salt. Stir in walnuts. Stuff potato shells with potato mixture. Refrigerate, covered, several hours or overnight.

Heat oven to 400°. Bake, uncovered, 30 minutes; sprinkle with marshmallows. Continue baking until marshmallows are melted (5 to 7 minutes).

*12 servings.*

# VEGETABLE PLATTER

▼

*This artistic platter will assure there's a favorite vegetable for everyone at the table. The microwave seems just made for cooking vegetables, retaining texture, color and nutrients to perfection.*

1 (2½-pound) head cauliflower
1 (1¾-pound) bunch broccoli
1 pound carrots
½ cup mayonnaise
1 teaspoon prepared mustard

½ teaspoon dried dill weed, crumbled
½ cup (2 ounces) shredded mild Cheddar cheese
3 tablespoons margarine or butter, melted

Remove cauliflower leaves; cut 1-inch hole out of core. Wrap cauliflower in plastic wrap. Separate broccoli into florets with 3 inch stems. Arrange in 9 × 11-inch glass dish with stems to outside; cover. Cut carrots into ¼-inch slices; arrange in microwavable dish. Add ¼ cup water; cover dish. Microwave cauliflower (HIGH) until crisp-tender (5 to 8 minutes); cover with a bowl. Microwave carrots (HIGH) until crisp-tender (6 to 8 minutes), rotating once; cover with towel. Microwave broccoli (HIGH), until crisp-tender (6 to 7 minutes), rotating once. Combine mayonnaise, mustard and dill. Arrange cauliflower in center of 12-inch microwavable platter. Surround with sections of carrots and broccoli. Spread sauce over cauliflower; sprinkle with cheese. Drizzle margarine over carrots and broccoli. Microwave (HIGH), uncovered, until cheese is melted (2 to 4 minutes), rotating once. Serve immediately.

*10 to 12 servings.*

# VEGGIE-CHEESE PIE

▼

*A cheese-dusted crust is heaped with garden-fresh veggies and topped with crumbly, salty Greek feta cheese. This main or side dish pie is an inspired way to salute the fruits of your gardening labors.*

1 (9-inch) refrigerated pie crust
1 cup freshly shredded Parmesan cheese, divided
1 to 2 tablespoons olive oil
1 cup coarsely chopped red onion
1 teaspoon minced garlic
¼ teaspoon salt
⅛ teaspoon pepper

1 yellow summer squash, cut into ¼-inch slices (about 1 cup)
1 zucchini, cut into ¼-inch slices
2 tomatoes, seeded, thinly sliced
1 (4-ounce) package crumbled feta cheese with basil and tomato

Heat oven to 425°. Prepare and bake pie crust according to package directions for 9-inch one-crust pie. Sprinkle crust with ½ cup of the Parmesan cheese; set aside. In small skillet, heat olive oil; sauté onion and garlic until soft (10 to 12 minutes). Stir in salt and pepper. Layer pie crust with onion mixture, yellow squash, zucchini and tomato slices. Sprinkle evenly with remaining ½ cup Parmesan cheese. Sprinkle with feta cheese. Cover with foil ring (see tip). Bake until cheese is melted and veggies are crisp-tender (about 25 minutes). Remove foil ring; let stand 10 minutes; cut into wedges.

*6 servings.*

**Tip:** To prevent excessive browning of crust, cut piece of foil slightly larger than pie pan; fold into quarters. Round off outer edge; cut curve in center 3 inches from outer edge. Unfold and center over top of pie.

# SPANISH RICE ESPECIAL

▼

*We've updated an old favorite with contemporary touches like zesty seasonings, nuggets of bacon and a crown of Cheddar.*

8 slices bacon
1 cup chopped onion
¼ cup chopped green bell pepper
1 (14½-ounce) can stewed tomatoes
1¼ cups water
¾ cup uncooked long grain rice

½ cup chili sauce
½ teaspoon salt
½ teaspoon celery salt
1 teaspoon brown sugar
½ teaspoon Worcestershire
1 teaspoon paprika
– dash pepper
½ cup (2 ounces) shredded sharp Cheddar cheese

Cook bacon until crisp; drain and crumble. Reserve 2 tablespoons bacon drippings; sauté onion and green pepper in drippings until tender. Stir in bacon and remaining ingredients except cheese. Simmer, covered, until moisture is absorbed (about 40 minutes). *Sprinkle with cheese; cover until cheese is melted (about 2 minutes).

*Amount: 8 cups.*

**Tip:** *For do-ahead convenience, recipe can be prepared to this point, covered and refrigerated. To complete, place in microwavable baking dish; cover. Microwave (HIGH) 5 minutes; stir. Microwave (HIGH) until heated through (2 to 3 minutes). Sprinkle with cheese; let stand, covered, 2 minutes.

# RICE 'N LEMON

▼

*When you want a congenial, mildly flavored accompaniment to conform to almost any menu, here's the answer. Just a spark of lemon zest and minced garlic combine with rosemary for subtle seasonings.*

| | |
|---|---|
| 2 (14½-ounce) cans ⅓-less-salt chicken broth | 4 teaspoons grated lemon peel |
| ½ teaspoon minced garlic | 1½ teaspoons dried rosemary, crumbled |
| 1¾ cups uncooked long-grain rice | 3 tablespoons margarine or butter |

In heavy 3-quart saucepan, bring broth and garlic to a boil; stir in rice. Simmer, covered, until liquid is absorbed (about 20 minutes). Stir in lemon peel, rosemary and margarine.

*10 servings.*

# PECAN RICE

▼

*A splash of sherry adds sophistication; toasted pecans add crunch. This side dish is particularly pleasing when playing a supporting role to Cornish game hens and other poultry and game entrées.*

| | |
|---|---|
| 1 (14½-ounce) can chicken broth | 1 cup sliced fresh mushrooms |
| 1 tablespoon dry sherry | ½ cup sliced green onions, including some tops |
| – water | 1 teaspoon minced garlic |
| 1 cup uncooked long-grain rice, rinsed | ½ cup coarsely chopped pecans, toasted |
| 2 tablespoons margarine or butter | 1 tablespoon grated orange zest (page 130) |

In medium saucepan, combine chicken broth, sherry and enough water to equal 2 cups total liquid; bring to a boil. Stir in rice; reduce heat to simmer. Cook, covered, until tender (15 to 20 minutes). Drain any remaining liquid. In small skillet, melt margarine; sauté mushrooms, green onions and garlic until tender (about 3 minutes). Combine with rice. Place in microwavable casserole. Refrigerate, covered.

To Serve: Microwave (HIGH) until heated through (6 to 7 minutes), stirring twice. Stir in pecans and orange peel.

*Amount: 8 (½-cup) servings.*

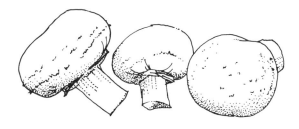

Mushroom

# GARLIC 'N LEMON PASTA ACCOMPANIMENT

▼

*The light touch of lemon eliminates the possibility of any bitter taste from the garlic. Although this must be prepared just before serving, it goes together quickly and is an ideal companion for favorite veal, fish and poultry dishes.*

| | |
|---|---|
| ½ pound dry angel hair pasta | 1 tablespoon lemon juice |
| ¼ cup olive oil | 1 teaspoon dried marjoram, |
| 2 tablespoons margarine or | crumbled |
| butter | ½ teaspoon salt |
| 1 teaspoon minced garlic | ¼ teaspoon pepper |
| 1 teaspoon grated lemon peel | ¼ cup chopped fresh parsley |

Cook angel hair pasta according to package directions in boiling water with 1 teaspoon salt; drain. In small saucepan, heat oil and margarine; stir in garlic, lemon peel, lemon juice, marjoram, salt and pepper; simmer 2 minutes. Transfer pasta to heated serving bowl. Toss with oil mixture and parsley. Serve immediately.

*Amount: 6 cups.*

# GORGONZOLA 'N FETTUCCINE

▼

*For a distinctive meatless main dish or sumptuous side dish, this recipe always wins raves from blue cheese aficionados. Gorgonzola's flavor is less bold than many other blue cheeses, making it a popular culinary choice.*

| | |
|---|---|
| 3 cups broccoli florets | ¾ pound dry or 1 pound fresh |
| 1 cup whipping cream | egg fettuccine |
| 6 ounces Gorgonzola cheese, | 1 (8-ounce) carton four cheese |
| rind removed, crumbled | gourmet blend |

Blanch broccoli in boiling water to cover, over medium heat, 2 minutes; drain. Plunge into ice water until cold; drain. Dry florets on paper towels. In small saucepan, heat cream and Gorgonzola, stirring frequently until cheese is melted. Cook pasta according to package directions in boiling water with 2 teaspoons salt until almost tender (7 to 9 minutes for dry, 30 to 120 seconds for fresh); drain. Spoon pasta onto heated serving platter; pour sauce over pasta. Sprinkle with broccoli florets and four cheese blend. Toss gently until evenly coated. Serve immediately.

*4 main course servings or*
*6 accompaniment servings.*

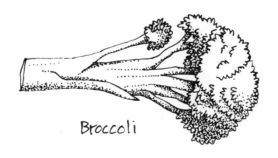

Broccoli

# PASTA AND ARTICHOKE HEARTS

▼

*Have the rest of your menu in final heating stages before preparing this
high-style fish or chicken accompaniment. Do use freshly grated
Parmesan—it makes a great difference. A truly terrific pasta pleaser!*

| | |
|---|---|
| 1 (6-ounce) jar marinated artichoke hearts | ½ cup cottage cheese |
| 1 tablespoon olive oil | 1 (8-ounce) carton sour cream |
| 1 tablespoon margarine or butter | ½ teaspoon salt |
| ½ cup diced onion | ⅛ teaspoon white pepper |
| ¾ teaspoon minced garlic | ⅜ pound (6 ounces) dry or ½ pound fresh egg fettuccine |
| 2 teaspoons dried basil, crumbled | ⅓ cup freshly grated Parmesan cheese |
| | – snipped fresh parsley |

Drain liquid from artichoke hearts into large skillet. Stir in olive oil and
margarine; heat until margarine is melted. Sauté onion and garlic until onion is
soft (8 to 10 minutes). Cut artichokes into bite-size pieces. Stir artichokes and
basil into skillet; heat through (about 5 minutes). Remove from heat; stir in
cottage cheese, sour cream, salt and white pepper. Cover; keep warm. Cook
pasta according to package directions in boiling water with 1 teaspoon salt
until almost tender (7 to 9 minutes for dry, 30 to 120 seconds for fresh); drain.
Stir Parmesan cheese into sauce. Pour fettuccine over sauce; toss gently until
evenly coated. Garnish with parsley. Serve immediately.

***3 to 4 accompaniment servings.***

# PASTA PERFECTO

▼

*"Perfecto" is right! This salmon-hued, delicately seasoned pasta is
grandly gourmet in appearance and flavor. Although the pasta is cooked
just before serving, portions of the preparation can be done ahead for
streamlined last-minute tossing.*

| | |
|---|---|
| ¼ cup margarine or butter | 1 (1-ounce) bottle pignoli nuts (¼ cup) |
| 1 (28-ounce) can pear-shaped tomatoes, undrained | 1 cup whipping cream |
| ¼ cup shredded carrot | ½ teaspoon salt |
| ¼ cup finely chopped celery | ⅛ to ¼ teaspoon white pepper |
| ¼ cup finely chopped onion | ¾ pound dry or 1 pound fresh egg linguini |
| 1 teaspoon minced garlic | 2 tablespoons margarine or butter |
| 1 tablespoon dried basil, crumbled | 2 tablespoons snipped fresh parsley |
| 1 teaspoon dried marjoram, crumbled | |

Heat oven to 350°. In large skillet, melt margarine. Purée tomatoes with juice in
blender or food processor; pour into skillet. Stir in carrot, celery, onion, garlic,
basil and marjoram. Bring to a boil; reduce heat to simmer. Cook, uncovered,
until slightly thickened (about 30 minutes), stirring occasionally. Toast pignoli
nuts in oven until lightly browned (5 to 8 minutes). Divide nuts equally; chop
half the nuts coarsely; set both aside. Stir cream, chopped pignoli nuts, salt and
pepper into tomato mixture. Cook over low heat just until heated through
(5 to 8 minutes). Cook pasta according to package directions in boiling water
with 2 teaspoons salt until almost tender (7 to 9 minutes for dry, 30 to
120 seconds for fresh); drain. Pour into heated serving bowl; toss with
margarine. Pour sauce over pasta. Toss gently to coat evenly. Sprinkle with
reserved whole pignoli nuts and snipped parsley. Serve immediately.

***6 to 8 accompaniment servings.***

# STUFFING BALLS

▼

*This gets high marks for seasoning and for convenience when the corn bread is readied ahead. It's a dandy do-ahead when you want to serve stuffing but don't want the fuss of conventional methods. The stuffing balls look very attractive surrounding the entrée on a large heated platter.*

¾ cup margarine or butter
1 cup chopped onion
1½ cups chopped celery
¼ cup chopped fresh parsley
½ cup crumbled fresh sage or
   1 tablespoon dried sage
1½ teaspoons salt
½ teaspoon pepper

1 teaspoon dried thyme,
   crumbled
½ teaspoon dried marjoram,
   crumbled
½ teaspoon ground nutmeg
6 cups dry bread cubes
6 cups crumbled corn bread
1¾ cups chicken broth

In large skillet, melt margarine; add onion, celery, parsley, sage, salt, pepper, thyme, marjoram and nutmeg. Cook, stirring occasionally until onion and celery are tender. Combine bread cubes and corn bread with onion mixture. Add broth and mix lightly. Shape into 12 balls, using ½ cup packed mixture per ball. Place in buttered 9 × 13-inch baking pan. Refrigerate, covered, several hours or overnight.

To Bake: Heat oven to 325°. Bake, covered, 30 minutes; uncover and bake 15 to 20 minutes longer. Remove from pan with wide spatula.

***Amount: 12 stuffing balls.***

# WILD RICE

For sophisticated serving, simple preparation and significant wholesomeness, the answer is wild rice. This aquatic grain-like seed possesses so many attributes, we enthusiastically dedicate an entire chapter to utilizing and enjoying its rich, nutty flavor to the fullest.

This North Country native makes an appealing addition to breakfast, lunch and dinner menus...even dessert, as you will find when you sample the unique rice-enriched custard. The flavor of wild rice is as robust as it is congenial, making it a prize ingredient in a wide range of recipes, from breads and soups to hearty main and side dishes, salads and casseroles. Enjoy the nutty flavor and chewy texture of this prestigious Minnesota favorite.

# WILD RICE

▼

***Basic cooking method.***

**1 cup uncooked wild rice**        **4 cups water**
                                    **1 teaspoon salt**

Rinse wild rice in a strainer under running water or in a bowl of water; drain. In heavy saucepan, bring wild rice, water and salt to a boil; reduce heat and simmer, covered, until kernels open and are tender but not mushy (45 to 55 minutes). Drain.

### *Amount: 3 to 4 cups.*

Chicken or beef broth can be substituted for water in cooking wild rice; omit salt.

**Variations:**

Stir one of the following into cooked wild rice:

- ¼ cup melted margarine or butter
- ½ cup chopped onion and 2 cups sliced fresh mushrooms sautéed in ¼ cup margarine or butter until tender (2 to 3 minutes)
- ½ cup sliced almonds, sautéed in ¼ cup margarine or butter (2 to 3 minutes)
- ½ cup chopped green onions, sautéed in ¼ cup margarine or butter until tender (2 to 3 minutes), ¼ cup snipped fresh parsley and 2 tablespoons dry sherry

# WILD RICE SOUP

▼

***This is Byerly's #1 most popular recipe! It's elegant, rich and a meal in a bowl – Minnesota style. Serve it with fresh fruit and crusty rolls or crackers.***

**6 tablespoons margarine or butter**        **3 tablespoons chopped slivered almonds**
**1 tablespoon minced onion**                **½ teaspoon salt**
**½ cup flour**                              **1 cup half-and-half**
**3 cups chicken broth**                     **2 tablespoons dry sherry (optional)**
**2 cups cooked wild rice**                  **– snipped fresh parsley or chives**
**⅓ cup diced ham**
**½ cup finely shredded carrots**

Melt margarine in saucepan; sauté onion until tender. Blend in flour; gradually stir in broth. Cook over medium heat, stirring constantly, until mixture comes to a boil; boil and stir 1 minute. Stir in wild rice, ham, carrots, almonds and salt; simmer about 5 minutes. Blend in half-and-half and sherry; heat to serving temperature. Garnish with parsley.

### *Amount: 6 cups.*

**Variation:**

**Chicken Wild Rice Soup:** Reduce chicken broth to 2½ cups. Substitute 2 cups cubed, cooked chicken for ham. Omit salt. Substitute 1 (12-ounce) can evaporated skimmed milk for the half-and-half. Prepare as directed.

### *Amount: 7 cups.*

*Oriental Chicken 'n*
*Wild Rice Soup*
*page 146*

# PORK CHOPS & WILD RICE FAMILY STYLE

▼

*This marvelous main dish medley is easy to prepare when the wild rice has been precooked. Brighten the plate with crimson spiced apple rings and spears of cooked fresh broccoli.*

- 2 cups cooked wild rice
- 4 lean (1 to 1½-inch-thick) boneless pork chops
- 2 tablespoons vegetable oil
- ½ teaspoon salt
- ¼ teaspoon pepper

- ½ cup minced onion
- 1 (10¾-ounce) can cream of mushroom soup with ⅓ less salt
- ½ cup water
- 2 tablespoon dry sherry or sauterne

Heat oven to 325°. Spoon wild rice into lightly greased 7 × 11-inch baking pan. In heavy skillet, brown chops in oil; season with salt and pepper. Arrange browned chops on top of rice. In same skillet, sauté onion until golden; drain. Stir in soup, water and sherry. Bring to a boil, stirring up browned portions for extra flavor; pour over chops and rice. Bake, covered, 30 minutes. Uncover and bake until meat reaches an internal temperature of 150° (10 to 15 minutes longer).

*4 servings.*

# ORIENTAL CHICKEN 'N WILD RICE SOUP

▼

*A few minutes of stir-frying and simmering will create steaming bowls of this light but satisfying soup for a first course or main dish. The exotic flavors of fresh ginger, soy sauce and Oriental vegetables make this soup exceptional.*

- 1½ pounds skinless, boneless chicken breasts
- 1 tablespoon vegetable oil
- 1 teaspoon minced garlic
- 2 to 3 teaspoons minced gingerroot
- 2 tablespoons soy sauce

- 1 (46-ounce) can chicken broth
- 2 cups cooked wild rice
- ½ cup diagonally sliced green onions
- ½ pound snow peas, strings removed, sliced diagonally

Slice chicken into julienne strips. Heat oil in large kettle or Dutch oven. Stir-fry chicken 2 minutes over medium-high heat. Stir in garlic and gingerroot, stir-fry 1 minute. Stir in soy sauce, chicken broth and wild rice. Bring to a boil; reduce heat. Simmer, covered, 10 minutes. Stir in green onions and snow peas; heat through (about 1 minute).

*Amount: 8 cups.*

### WILD RICE FOOD VALUE
*Wild rice is high in protein, low in fat and contains potassium, phosphorus and B vitamins. A ½ cup serving provides 70 to 95 calories.*

### WILD RICE ARITHMETIC
*1 lb. wild rice measures 2⅔ to 2¾ cups.*
*1 cup uncooked wild rice = 3 to 4 cups cooked.*
*1 lb. wild rice cooked = 20 to 24 (½ cup) servings.*

# ROAST PHEASANT WITH WILD RICE STUFFING

*First class flavor and presentation for VIP dining. Wild rice mingles with other savory ingredients to stuff the hunter's bounty. A rich cream sauce is served on the side to be spooned over pheasant and stuffing.*

2 (2 to 2½-pound) pheasants
¼ cup margarine or butter
⅓ cup chopped onion
⅓ cup diced celery
3 cups cooked wild rice
2 cups dry bread cubes
1 tablespoon snipped fresh
   parsley
¾ teaspoon poultry seasoning
½ teaspoon salt
– dash pepper
1 cup chicken broth
1 egg, beaten
1 (8-ounce) package bacon
   (8 slices)
– Cream Sauce (below)

Heat oven to 350°. Rinse pheasants; drain and pat dry. Melt margarine in skillet; sauté onion and celery until tender. Stir in wild rice, bread cubes, parsley and seasonings. Gently stir in broth and egg. Stuff each body cavity with ½ of dressing. Arrange pheasants, breast side up, on rack in shallow roasting pan. Place 4 slices bacon on top of each pheasant, covering surface area. Roast until meat thermometer reaches 170 to 175° (1½ to 2 hours). Remove stuffing; crumble bacon into stuffing.

To Serve: Cut pheasants in half. Serve with wild rice stuffing and Cream Sauce.

*4 servings.*

Cream Sauce:
1 cup chopped carrots
1 cup sliced onions
1½ cups chicken broth
2 tablespoons margarine or
   butter
3 tablespoons flour
½ cup whipping cream
⅛ teaspoon dried thyme,
   crumbled
⅛ teaspoon white pepper
1 tablespoon dry sherry

Simmer carrots and onions in chicken broth about 15 minutes. Strain, reserving broth. In small saucepan, melt margarine; blend in flour. Gradually stir in reserved broth and remaining ingredients, stirring constantly until mixture comes to a boil; boil and stir 1 minute.

*Amount: 2 cups.*

# FAR EAST WILD RICE BAKE

*A meat and wild rice casserole with an Asian accent of favorite Oriental seasonings. Wonderful for after-work entertaining on chilly evenings.*

1½ pounds meat loaf mixture
   (ground beef, pork, veal)
3 cups cooked wild rice
2 tablespoons margarine or
   butter
½ cup chopped onion
½ cup chopped green bell
   pepper
⅓ cup soy sauce
2 (10¾-ounce) cans cream of
   chicken soup with ⅓ less salt
2 teaspoons grated gingerroot
1 (8-ounce) can sliced water
   chestnuts, drained
1 (14½-ounce) can bean
   sprouts, drained, rinsed
1 (6-ounce) package wide-style
   chow mein noodles

Brown meat loaf mixture in skillet; drain. Add to wild rice. In same skillet, melt margarine; sauté onion and green pepper until tender (about 5 minutes). Combine soy sauce, soup, ginger, water chestnuts and bean sprouts. Stir in meat mixture, onion and green pepper. Pour into greased 3-quart casserole. Refrigerate, covered, up to 24 hours.

Heat oven to 350°. Bake, covered, 45 minutes. Uncover; sprinkle with noodles. Bake until heated through (15 to 20 minutes longer).

*6 to 8 servings.*

# CHICKEN AMANDINE CASSEROLE

▼

*No precooking of chicken is necessary for this delicately-flavored luncheon or supper dish.*

1 cup uncooked wild rice
4 cups water
½ teaspoon salt
1¾ pounds boneless chicken breasts, skin removed, cubed (3 cups)
½ cup sliced green onions
½ cup chopped fresh parsley

1 (4-ounce) can sliced mushrooms, drained
½ cup freshly grated Parmesan cheese
1 (10½-ounce) can chicken broth
1 (10¾-ounce) can cream of chicken soup with ⅓ less salt
¼ teaspoon pepper
⅓ cup slivered almonds, toasted

Rinse wild rice in a strainer under running water or in bowl of water; drain. In heavy saucepan, bring wild rice, water and salt to a boil; reduce heat. Simmer, covered, 40 minutes. Drain.

Heat oven to 350°. Combine chicken, green onions, parsley, mushrooms, cheese and wild rice. Combine chicken broth, soup and pepper until smooth; stir into rice mixture. Spoon into 3-quart casserole. Bake, covered, 35 minutes; uncover, stir. Bake, uncovered, until bubbly in center (about 20 minutes longer). Let stand, covered, about 10 minutes. Sprinkle almonds on top.

*6 servings.*

# WILD RICE HAMBURGERS

▼

*That all-American grilled favorite is enriched with wild rice and chopped onion.*

1 pound lean ground beef
1 cup cooked wild rice
½ cup chopped onion

1 teaspoon salt
¼ teaspoon pepper
6 hamburger buns

Prepare grill. In large bowl, combine all ingredients except buns until well blended. Shape into 6 hamburger patties. Using direct heat cooking method, arrange patties on grill 4 to 5 inches from medium-hot coals. Grill, covered, to desired doneness (4 to 6 minutes per side). Serve immediately on buns.

*6 servings.*

# BEEFY WILD RICE MEATBALLS

▼

*These stouthearted meatballs are oven-browned for convenience and then baked in a sherry-laced cream sauce. Serve them over rice or mashed potatoes along with glazed carrots or a favorite green vegetable.*

¾ cup cooked wild rice
1½ pounds lean ground beef
⅓ cup minced onion
½ teaspoon minced garlic
1½ teaspoons seasoned salt
⅓ cup milk
1 (10¾-ounce) can cream of chicken soup with ⅓ less salt

⅓ cup water
¼ cup dry sherry
¼ teaspoon pepper
¼ teaspoon poultry seasoning
1 teaspoon browning and seasoning sauce
– hot cooked rice or mashed potatoes

Heat oven to 375°. Combine wild rice, ground beef, onion, garlic, salt and milk; shape into 1-inch balls. Arrange in 10 × 15-inch jelly roll pan. Bake until lightly browned (about 15 minutes). Combine remaining ingredients except rice in 2-quart casserole; stir in meatballs. Bake, covered, until bubbly in center (about 40 minutes). Serve over rice.

*6 to 8 servings.*

# LUMBERJACK OMELET

▼

*The versatility of wild rice extends to hearty egg dishes like this Paul Bunyan special.*

| | |
|---|---|
| 1 (0.9-ounce) package hollandaise sauce mix | ⅛ teaspoon pepper |
| 3 eggs, slightly beaten | ⅓ cup fancy shredded Swiss cheese |
| 1 tablespoon cold water | ½ cup hot cooked wild rice |
| ¼ teaspoon salt | 2 slices bacon, crisply fried, crumbled |

Prepare hollandaise sauce according to package directions; keep warm. Beat eggs, water, salt and pepper together. Heat buttered 8-inch omelet pan over medium heat. Pour egg mixture into pan. Cook until mixture thickens, lifting cooked portions around edges to allow uncooked portion to flow underneath. Combine cheese, wild rice and bacon; sprinkle over half of omelet. Fold omelet in half; slide onto warmed plate. Pour ½ cup hollandaise sauce over omelet (refrigerate remaining sauce). Serve immediately.

*1 serving.*

# NORTH COUNTRY BRUNCH PIE

▼

*Beyond ordinary quiche, this dish is ideal for a brunch, luncheon or light supper.*

| | |
|---|---|
| 1 (9-inch) pie crust | ¼ teaspoon pepper |
| 2 teaspoons Dijon mustard | 1½ cups cooked wild rice |
| 4 eggs, slightly beaten | 6 slices bacon, crisply fried, crumbled |
| 1 cup half-and-half | ¼ cup minced green onions |
| 1 teaspoon Worcestershire | 1 cup shredded Swiss cheese (4 ounces) |
| ½ teaspoon salt | |

Heat oven to 425°. Line 9-inch pie pan with crust; flute edge. Pierce with fork in many places. Bake on bottom oven rack until golden (about 12 minutes). Pierce again with fork, not going through crust. Brush pie crust with mustard. Beat eggs, half-and-half, Worcestershire, salt and pepper together. Fold in remaining ingredients; pour into crust. Bake on bottom oven rack 10 minutes. Reduce oven temperature to 325°; bake until knife inserted near center comes out clean (about 30 minutes longer). Let stand 5 to 10 minutes before cutting.

*6 servings.*

**Tip:** Baked pie may be frozen. Thaw in refrigerator overnight. Reheat, uncovered, in preheated 350° oven until heated through (30 to 35 minutes). Serve immediately.

# WILD RICE WALDORF SALAD

▼

*Add wild rice to usual Waldorf Salad ingredients and you create a robust rendition to serve as both salad and side dish.*

| | |
|---|---|
| 1 (8-ounce) can pineapple tidbits in own juice | ½ cup diced celery |
| 2 cups cooked wild rice | ½ cup chopped walnuts, toasted |
| 2 Granny Smith apples, diced (2 cups) | ½ cup sour lean |
| 2 red Delicious apples, diced (2 cups) | ½ cup mayonnaise |
| | 1 tablespoon lemon juice |
| | ¼ cup sugar |

Drain pineapple, reserving 1 tablespoon juice. Combine pineapple, wild rice, apples, celery and walnuts in large bowl. Stir reserved pineapple juice and remaining ingredients together until sugar is dissolved. Fold dressing into salad. Refrigerate, covered, several hours.

*Amount: 8 cups.*

# PORK AND WILD RICE SALAD

▼

*Tender morsels of pork tenderloin marry well with colorful fresh fruits and mushrooms.*

2 pork tenderloins (about
  1½ pounds total)
– vegetable oil
4 cups cooked wild rice
2 cups red seedless grapes
  (¾ pound)
1 cup green seedless grapes
  (½ pound)
1¼ cups cubed fresh pineapple

4 ounces fresh mushrooms,
  sliced
⅓ cup chopped red onion
⅓ cup balsamic vinegar
⅓ cup olive oil
2 tablespoons honey
1 teaspoon salt
¼ teaspoon pepper
1 cup coarsely chopped
  walnuts, toasted
– red-tipped leaf lettuce

Heat oven to 425°. Arrange tenderloins on broiler pan or on rack in shallow pan, tucking tails under to make uniform thickness, if necessary. Brush with oil. Roast until instant-read meat thermometer reaches 160° (25 to 28 minutes). Remove from oven; refrigerate until cold. Cut into about ¾-inch cubes. In large bowl, combine pork and rice. Stir in grapes, pineapple, mushrooms and onion. Combine vinegar, oil, honey, salt and pepper; whisk to blend. Pour over salad, tossing to coat. Refrigerate, covered, several hours or overnight.

To Serve: Fold in walnuts; spoon onto serving platter lined with leaf lettuce.

*10 (1-cup) servings.*

# TURKEY CRANBERRY 'N WILD RICE SALAD

▼

*This is a great way to use leftover turkey during the holidays. Purchase and freeze extra cranberries when they are readily available and substitute deli turkey to make this colorful salad year-round.*

1½ pounds cooked turkey,
  cubed (4 cups)
3 cups cooked wild rice
1½ cups raw cranberries,
  coarsely chopped
1 cup chopped celery
⅓ cup chopped green onions
½ cup chopped fresh parsley
¼ cup orange juice

¼ cup cholesterol-free liquid
  egg substitute, thawed
1½ tablespoons wild rice vinegar
  with chives
1 tablespoon sugar
1½ teaspoons Dijon mustard
½ teaspoon salt
⅓ cup vegetable oil
1 cup slivered almonds,
  toasted
– lettuce leaves

In large bowl, combine turkey, wild rice, cranberries, celery and green onions. In a small bowl, combine parsley, orange juice, egg substitute, vinegar, sugar, mustard and salt. Slowly whisk in oil until smooth and slightly thickened. Add dressing to turkey mixture; cover and refrigerate several hours or overnight.

To Serve: Stir in almonds. Serve on lettuce leaves on individual salad plates.

*8 (1-cup) servings.*

**Tip:** Cider vinegar may be substituted for wild rice vinegar with chives.

Wild Rice

# WILD AND BROWN RICE ACCOMPANIMENT

▼

*The warm nutty flavors of wild and brown rice blend into a delectable side dish. It can be prepared ahead of time, refrigerated and popped into the microwave for reheating just before serving.*

| | |
|---|---|
| 1½ cups uncooked wild rice | 3 (14½-ounce) cans chicken broth |
| 3 cups boiling water | ½ teaspoon dried thyme, crumbled |
| 1 cup uncooked brown rice | ¼ teaspoon dried marjoram, crumbled |
| 1 cup chopped onion | ½ teaspoon salt |
| 1 cup diagonally sliced carrots | ¼ teaspoon pepper |
| ¾ cup chopped celery | |

In heavy saucepan, soak wild rice in boiling water 30 minutes. Drain; rinse thoroughly. In Dutch oven or large skillet, combine all ingredients. Bring to a boil; reduce heat, simmer covered, until rice is tender and liquid is absorbed (50 to 60 minutes). Spoon into 3-quart microwavable bowl. Serve immediately or refrigerate, covered. To Reheat: Microwave (HIGH), covered, until heated through (9 to 11 minutes), stirring twice.

*12 (⅔-cup) servings.*

# WILD RICE BROCCOLI BAKE

▼

*Frozen broccoli and cooked wild rice combine to create a vegetable dish which is sure to become a traditional family favorite.*

| | |
|---|---|
| 2 tablespoons margarine | 1 (10¾-ounce) can cream of chicken soup |
| ½ cup chopped onion | ¼ teaspoon salt |
| 1 (4.5-ounce) can sliced mushrooms, drained | 1 (8-ounce) package shredded Colby and Monterey Jack cheese, divided (2 cups) |
| 2 (10-ounce) packages frozen chopped broccoli, thawed | 1 cup homestyle croutons |
| 2 cups cooked wild rice | 2 tablespoons margarine, melted |

Heat oven to 350°. In large skillet, melt margarine over medium heat; sauté onion until tender (5 to 7 minutes). Remove from heat and stir in mushrooms, broccoli, wild rice, soup, salt and 1½ cups of the cheese. Spoon into buttered 1½-quart glass baking dish. Sprinkle with remaining cheese. Combine croutons and margarine; layer over cheese. Bake, uncovered, until heated through (25 to 30 minutes).

*6 to 8 servings.*

**Tip:** Vegetable dish may be assembled and refrigerated several hours or overnight. To Heat: Bake, uncovered, in a preheated 350° oven until heated through (45 to 50 minutes).

**STORAGE OF WILD RICE**

*Store uncooked wild rice tightly covered in a cool, dry place. It keeps almost indefinitely. Refrigerate cooked wild rice up to one week, tightly covered. Freeze cooked wild rice in a vapor-resistant and moisture-resistant container for up to two months.*

*Wild Rice is the "caviar" of gourmet grains. Its delicious year-round and adds elegance to any dish.*

# BLUEBERRY 'N WILD RICE MUFFINS

▼

*Two Minnesota favorites – wild rice and blueberries – team up for invitingly innovative muffins.*

1½ cups flour
½ cup sugar
2 teaspoons baking powder
1 teaspoon grated lemon peel
1 teaspoon ground coriander
½ teaspoon salt

¼ cup vegetable oil
2 eggs, slightly beaten
½ cup milk
1 cup unsweetened frozen
   blueberries
1 cup cooked wild rice
– Topping (below)

Heat oven to 400°. Grease 12-cup (2½ to 2¾-inch) muffin pan or line with paper baking cups. Combine flour, sugar, baking powder, lemon peel, coriander and salt in large bowl. In small bowl, whisk oil, eggs and milk together. Coat blueberries with 1 tablespoon dry ingredients. Stir liquid ingredients into dry ingredients just until blended. Fold in blueberries and wild rice. Spoon into greased muffin cups; sprinkle each muffin with ¼ teaspoon topping. Bake until wooden pick inserted in muffin comes out clean (20 to 25 minutes). Let stand on wire rack 5 minutes; remove muffins from pan. Serve warm.

### Amount: 12 muffins.

**Topping:** Combine 1 tablespoon sugar, ¼ teaspoon ground coriander and 1 teaspoon grated lemon peel.

# WILD RICE CUSTARD

▼

*This tempting and unusual variation of old-fashioned baked custard has a superb spicy flavor with a hint of almond.*

2 cups half-and-half
4 eggs
¼ cup sugar
¼ teaspoon ground nutmeg
⅛ teaspoon ground cinnamon
⅛ teaspoon salt

1 teaspoon vanilla
½ teaspoon almond extract
½ cup cooked wild rice
¼ cup golden raisins
– Cinnamon Whipped Cream
   (below)

Heat oven to 325°. Scald half-and-half. Meanwhile, beat eggs and sugar until frothy. Stir in half-and-half and remaining ingredients except Cinnamon Whipped Cream. Divide mixture evenly among 6 (6-ounce) custard cups. Arrange custard cups in 9 × 13-inch baking pan. Place on oven rack; add very hot water to within 1-inch of top of custard cups. Bake until knife inserted near center comes out clean (30 to 40 minutes). Remove custard cups from pan; cool on wire rack 30 minutes. Serve warm or refrigerate, uncovered, until cool; cover.

To Serve: Top each custard with a dollop of Cinnamon Whipped Cream.

### 6 servings.

**Cinnamon Whipped Cream:** Beat ½ cup whipping cream with 4 teaspoons powdered sugar and ⅛ teaspoon cinnamon until soft peaks form.

# BREADS & COFFEE CAKES

**B**read baking just isn't what it used to be. It's better! Thanks to the popularity of quick breads, innovations in yeast products, and a helping hand from the food processor and other appliances, everyone can enjoy the incomparable flavor and unmatched aroma of freshly baked breads.

On a tight timetable but looking for a recipe to impress? Try our mouthwatering Caramel Apple Brunch Rolls, Garlic 'n Herb Biscuits which begin with refrigerated dough, or trendy Focaccia fashioned from convenient frozen dough.

With just a little more time, you can turn out a batch of mouthwatering muffins to fill the bread basket. We have special selections for any and every meal, not to mention snacks. Quick breads, most of them one-bowl beauties, are flavored with bits of fruit, nuts, almond flavoring and other readily available ingredients. Mini or regular-sized loaves make great gifts and great eating.

We round out this incomparable collection with coffee and brunch cakes, Texas Garlic Toast, a colorful Fruity Yogurt Breakfast Tart, a lovely Holiday Tea Ring and even pizza crusts for good measure.

# FOCACCIA

▼

*The rage of trendy restaurant bread baskets can be a compliment catcher on your own dinner table. Frozen bread dough makes it ultra-easy and the creative variations enhance any number of menus. Especially tasty with Italian dishes.*

| | |
|---|---|
| 1 (1-pound) loaf frozen bread dough, thawed | ½ cup freshly grated Parmesan cheese |
| 1 teaspoon minced garlic | ½ teaspoon dried rosemary, crumbled |
| 2 tablespoons olive oil | |

Grease baking sheet. Shape thawed bread dough into a ball. Press into 10-inch circle on greased baking sheet. With finger, poke deep holes at 1-inch intervals. Place small amount of garlic in each hole. Drizzle olive oil over dough; brush lightly to distribute evenly. Combine cheese and rosemary; sprinkle evenly over surface. Let rise in warm place until doubled in size (about 20 minutes). Heat oven to 400°. Bake until lightly browned (14 to 16 minutes). Cut into wedges.

*Amount: 12 slices.*

**Variations:**

**Gorgonzola 'n Pignoli Nuts:**  Substitute ½ cup crumbled Gorgonzola cheese and 2 tablespoons lightly toasted pignoli nuts for Parmesan cheese and rosemary.

**Sun-dried Tomatoes 'n Basil:**  Coarsely chop 3 to 4 marinated sun-dried tomatoes; place small amount in each hole with garlic. Thinly slice 1 shallot, separating into rings; arrange over oiled surface of dough. Substitute ½ teaspoon dried basil, crumbled, for rosemary.

# LEMON POPOVERS

▼

*Lemon peel adds a fresh taste to this simple popover batter. Team these with your favorite entrée or salad for a final touch that's sure to impress.*

| | |
|---|---|
| 2 cups flour | ¼ teaspoon salt |
| 2 cups milk | 1 tablespoon grated lemon peel |
| 4 eggs | |

Generously grease 10 to 12 (6-ounce) custard cups or popover pans. Heat oven to 425°. Combine all ingredients in blender or food processor; process until thoroughly blended. Fill greased custard cups ⅔ full. (Can stand at room temperature 1 hour). Bake popovers 20 minutes; reduce oven temperature to 350° and bake 25 to 30 minutes longer. With a bamboo skewer, poke hole in side of each popover; bake 5 to 10 minutes longer.

*Amount: 10 to 12 large popovers.*

**Variation:**  One teaspoon ground cardamom can be added to batter.

*Focaccia*
*page 153*

# CHEESE 'N HERB FRENCH BREAD

▼

*If you thought good French bread couldn't be improved upon, wait until you try this combination. Fragrant herb butter mingles with melted cheese for fabulous results. Be sure to allow an hour of standing time for flavors to permeate the spread.*

½ cup margarine or butter, softened
1 tablespoon dried parsley flakes
½ teaspoon dried oregano, crumbled

½ teaspoon dried dill weed, crumbled
½ teaspoon minced garlic
½ (1-pound) package twin French bread
1 (8-ounce) package sliced mozzarella cheese

Combine margarine, herbs and garlic; let stand 1 hour to blend flavors. Heat oven to 350°. With sharp knife, cut French bread into 20 slices about ¾ inch wide, cutting not quite through loaf. Spread herbed butter between slices. Cut each slice of cheese into quarters; insert between bread slices, folding to fit. Place bread on large sheet of foil; wrap loosely around sides and ends of bread, leaving foil open at top. Bake until heated through and cheese is melted (20 to 25 minutes). Serve immediately.

*Amount: 20 slices.*

# TEXAS GARLIC TOAST

▼

*Have this on hand in your freezer for impromptu entertaining. It can go from freezer to grill or broiler. Watch carefully while cooking for golden brown results.*

1 cup margarine or butter
1 to 2 tablespoons minced garlic

1 (24-ounce) loaf Texas Toast bread
1 zipper closure freezer storage bag

Melt margarine with garlic; let stand 10 minutes. Arrange bread in single layer on 2 baking sheets. Generously brush garlic mixture on both sides of bread. Freeze, uncovered, until firm (about 30 minutes). Using wide spatula, loosen slices from pan. Place slices in freezer storage bag; seal. Freeze until needed.

To Grill: Prepare grill. Arrange frozen slices around outer edge of grill. Grill, turning frequently, until golden brown. Watch closely to prevent burning. Serve immediately.

To Broil: Heat broiler. Arrange frozen slices on baking sheet. Broil 5 inches from heat until golden brown (2 to 2½ minutes); turn. Continue broiling until second side is golden brown (45 to 60 seconds). Serve immediately.

*Amount: 16 slices.*

# GARLIC 'N HERB BISCUITS

▼

*You will want to keep the ingredients for these on hand to brighten everyday meals in a jiffy. Better have "seconds" ready to serve because these dressed up refrigerator biscuits go down real easy!*

¼ cup margarine or butter
2 tablespoons snipped fresh parsley
2 tablespoons freshly grated Parmesan cheese
1 tablespoon sesame seed, toasted

2 teaspoons minced garlic
1 teaspoon dried basil, crumbled
½ teaspoon dried thyme, crumbled
1 (10-ounce) package refrigerated flaky buttermilk biscuits

Heat oven to 400°. Melt margarine in 9-inch round cake pan. Stir in parsley, cheese, sesame seed, garlic, basil and thyme; smooth to cover bottom of pan. Cut each biscuit in half. Arrange halves, cut side down, in circular pattern over butter mixture, covering entire surface of pan. Bake until golden brown (15 to 17 minutes). Invert onto serving plate. Serve warm.

*Amount: 10 biscuits.*

# ENGLISH TEA SCONES

▼

*Have a heart – a cranberry sparked scone heart. Scones are somewhat like a biscuit in texture and are an enticing addition to any tea table, reception buffet or shower menu. We offer an Americanized version of Devonshire Cream, fluffier and sweeter.*

| | |
|---|---|
| 2 cups flour | 1 egg, slightly beaten |
| ¼ cup sugar | – milk |
| 2½ teaspoons baking powder | 1 egg white, slightly beaten |
| ½ teaspoon salt | 2 tablespoons sugar |
| 6 teaspoons margarine or butter | 1 tablespoon grated orange peel |
| ⅓ cup dried cranberries, coarsely chopped | – Mock Devonshire Cream (below) |

Heat oven to 425°. Combine flour, ¼ cup sugar, baking powder and salt. With pastry blender, cut in margarine until mixture resembles coarse crumbs. Stir in dried cranberries. Combine egg with enough milk to measure ⅔ cup; stir into flour mixture with fork just until mixture holds together. Gently form into a ball with fingers; turn onto lightly floured surface. Knead gently 10 to 12 strokes. With floured rolling pin, lightly roll dough on floured surface to ½-inch thickness. Cut with floured 2¼-inch heart-shaped cutter, re-rolling dough as necessary. Arrange scones on ungreased baking sheet about 2 inches apart. Brush with egg white. Combine 2 tablespoons sugar and orange peel; sprinkle over tops of scones. Bake until lightly browned (8 to 10 minutes). Serve warm with Mock Devonshire Cream.

*Amount: 16 scones.*

**Mock Devonshire Cream:**  Beat 1 (3-ounce) package softened cream cheese until light and fluffy. Gradually beat in ½ cup heavy whipping cream until smooth. Beat in 2 teaspoons powdered sugar and ¼ teaspoon vanilla. Refrigerate, covered, 3 to 4 hours.

*Amount: 1 cup.*

# PUMPKIN SCONES

▼

*Often cooked on a griddle in Great Britain, our version is baked like biscuits after a quick and easy blending of ingredients. These are fabulous with whipped cream cheese or Maple Butter (page 157).*

| | |
|---|---|
| 2 cups flour | ¼ cup margarine or butter |
| ½ cup firmly packed brown sugar | ½ cup golden raisins or currants |
| 2 teaspoons baking powder | 1 egg, slightly beaten |
| 2 teaspoons pumpkin pie spice | ¾ cup pumpkin |
| ¼ teaspoon salt | 2 tablespoons milk |
| | – granulated sugar (optional) |

Heat oven to 400°. Combine flour, brown sugar, baking powder, pumpkin pie spice and salt. With pastry blender, cut in margarine until mixture is crumbly. Stir in raisins. Combine egg, pumpkin and milk; stir into dry ingredients until liquid is absorbed and mixture is well blended. Gather dough into a ball; pat into a circle about ¾ inch thick on lightly floured surface. Using a 2¼-inch round cutter, cut into scones. Arrange on ungreased baking sheet; sprinkle tops with sugar. Bake until wooden pick inserted in center comes out clean (10 to 12 minutes). Remove from baking sheet; cool on wire rack.

*Amount: 10 to 12 scones.*

# BUTTERMILK APPLE MUFFINS

▼

*There's no need to purchase buttermilk...just make your own for these apple and pecan-flecked gems. The vinegar-milk mixture below equals ½ cup buttermilk.*

| | |
|---|---|
| 1½ teaspoons distilled vinegar<br>  – whole milk | 1½ cups flour |
| ¾ cup firmly packed brown<br>  sugar | ½ teaspoon baking soda |
| | ¼ teaspoon salt |
| 1 egg, slightly beaten | ¼ teaspoon ground cinnamon |
| ⅓ cup vegetable oil | ¼ teaspoon ground nutmeg |
| 1 teaspoon vanilla | 1 cup chopped Granny Smith<br>  apple (1 medium) |
| | ¼ cup chopped pecans |

Pour vinegar into 1-cup glass measuring cup. Add milk to reach ½-cup line. Let stand until slightly thickened (about 5 minutes). Line 12 (2½ to 2¾-inch) standard muffin cups with paper baking cups. Heat oven to 350°. In large bowl, combine brown sugar and egg; gradually beat in oil and vanilla. In small bowl, combine flour, baking soda, salt, cinnamon and nutmeg. Stir into brown sugar mixture. Fold in apples, pecans and soured milk just until blended. Spoon batter into lined muffin cups, filling ¾ full. Bake until wooden pick inserted in center of muffin comes out clean (25 to 30 minutes). Let stand on wire rack 5 minutes; remove muffins from pan. Serve warm.

*Amount: 12 muffins.*

Apple

# SUNSHINE MUFFINS

▼

*Bursting with flavorful, nutritious ingredients, these jumbo-sized muffins have a rich carrot cake-like texture. Like most quick breads, they are at their best served warm from the oven.*

| | |
|---|---|
| 2 cups flour | 1 Granny Smith apple, peeled,<br>  shredded (1 cup) |
| ¾ cup sugar | |
| 2 teaspoons baking soda | ½ cup golden raisins |
| ½ teaspoon salt | ½ cup chopped pecans |
| 1 teaspoon ground cinnamon | 3 eggs, slightly beaten |
| 1 teaspoon ground nutmeg | ½ cup vegetable oil |
| 2 cups shredded carrots | 2 teaspoons vanilla |

Grease 6 (3½-inch) jumbo muffin cups or line with paper baking cups. Heat oven to 350°. Combine flour, sugar, baking soda, salt, cinnamon and nutmeg. Stir in carrots, apple, raisins and pecans. Combine eggs, oil and vanilla until blended; stir into flour mixture just until blended. Spoon batter into greased muffin cups. Bake until wooden pick inserted in center of muffin comes out clean (28 to 32 minutes). Let stand on wire rack 5 minutes; remove muffins from pan. Serve warm.

*Amount: 6 jumbo muffins.*

**Variation:** Substitute ⅓ cup chopped dried apricots for shredded apple.

# CORN MUFFINS WITH MAPLE BUTTER

▼

*There's no need to settle for one size...make into mini muffins, standard or jumbo muffins, depending on personal preference. Fluffy maple butter adds a Minnesota touch to this and other breads.*

| | |
|---|---|
| 1 cup cornmeal | 1 cup buttermilk |
| 1 cup flour | 2 eggs |
| 2 teaspoons baking powder | ¼ cup honey |
| ¾ teaspoon salt | ¼ cup vegetable oil |
| ½ teaspoon baking soda | – Maple Butter (below) |

Grease 12 (2½ to 2¾-inch) standard muffin cups or line with paper baking cups. Heat oven to 425°. In large bowl, combine cornmeal, flour, baking powder, salt and baking soda. In small bowl, whisk buttermilk, egg, honey and oil together until well blended. Stir into dry ingredients just until all ingredients are moistened. Spoon batter into greased muffin cups. Bake until light golden brown (12 to 18 minutes). Let stand on wire rack 5 minutes; remove muffins from pan. Serve warm.

*Amount: 12 muffins.*

**Tip:** For mini-muffins, prepare 36 mini-muffin cups; bake 8 to 10 minutes. For jumbo muffins, prepare 6 jumbo muffin cups; bake 15 to 20 minutes.

**Maple Butter:** With electric mixer, whip ½ cup soft butter. Thoroughly blend in ¼ cup maple syrup. Serve with warm corn muffins.

*Amount: ¾ cup*

# CONFETTI MUFFINS

▼

*This change of pace from sweeter batters showcases savory bits of red and green pepper, sprinklings of herbs and piquant Dijon mustard. Team them with barbecued entrées, hearty soups and main dish salads.*

| | |
|---|---|
| ½ cup margarine or butter | 1½ cups flour |
| ⅓ cup chopped green onions | 2 tablespoons sugar |
| ⅓ cup minced red bell pepper | 2 teaspoons baking powder |
| ¼ cup minced green bell pepper | ½ teaspoon salt |
| ¼ cup snipped fresh parsley | ½ teaspoon baking soda |
| ⅔ cup sour cream | ½ teaspoon dried basil, crumbled |
| 2 eggs, slightly beaten | ¼ teaspoon dried tarragon, crumbled |
| 1 tablespoon Dijon mustard | |

Grease 10 (2½ to 2¾-inch) standard muffin cups or line with paper baking cups. Heat oven to 400°. Melt margarine in heavy skillet over medium heat. Sauté green onions and peppers until tender and beginning to brown (5 to 7 minutes), stirring frequently. Stir in parsley; cool to lukewarm. Whisk sour cream, eggs and mustard together in medium bowl; stir in onion mixture. Combine flour, sugar, baking powder, salt, baking soda and herbs in large bowl. Stir sour cream mixture into flour mixture just until blended. Spoon into greased muffin cups. Bake until wooden pick inserted in center of muffin comes out clean (20 to 23 minutes). Let stand on wire rack 5 minutes; remove muffins from pan. Serve warm or at room temperature.

*Amount: 10 muffins.*

# DOUBLE CHOCOLATE CHIP MUFFINS

▼

*Double your chocolate-eating pleasure with these rich chip and nut-studded muffins. Super as a sweet snack and a tea table tantalizer.*

| | |
|---|---|
| 2 cups flour | ⅔ cup milk |
| ⅓ cup firmly packed brown sugar | ½ cup margarine or butter, melted, cooled |
| ⅓ cup granulated sugar | 1½ teaspoons vanilla |
| 2 teaspoons baking powder | ½ cup vanilla milk chips |
| ½ teaspoon salt | ½ cup semisweet chocolate chips |
| 2 eggs, slightly beaten | ½ cup chopped pecans, toasted |

Grease 12 (2½ to 2¾-inch) standard muffin cups and edges surrounding cups. Heat oven to 400°. Combine flour, sugars, baking powder and salt in large bowl. In small bowl, whisk together eggs, milk, margarine and vanilla; stir into flour mixture just until blended. Stir in chips and pecans. Spoon into greased muffin cups. Bake until wooden pick inserted in center of muffin comes out clean (17 to 20 minutes). Let stand on wire rack 5 minutes; remove muffins from pan. Serve warm or at room temperature.

*Amount: 12 muffins.*

**Variation:** Substitute buttermilk for milk; add ½ teaspoon soda to flour mixture.

**Tip:** Foil or paper-lined muffin cups can be used in place of greased muffin cups. Grease edges surrounding cups, since these are large muffins.

# ORANGE POPPY SEED MUFFINS

▼

*Morsels of fresh orange zest and poppy seed create a delicately flavored muffin perfect for pairing with main dish salads.*

| | |
|---|---|
| ½ cup vanilla yogurt | 3 tablespoons orange juice |
| ⅓ cup margarine or butter, softened | 1⅓ cups flour |
| 1 egg | 1¼ cups sugar, divided |
| 1 tablespoon grated orange zest (page 130) | 1 tablespoon poppy seed |
| | ½ teaspoon salt |
| | ½ teaspoon baking soda |
| | ¼ cup margarine, melted |

Grease 12 (2½ to 2¾-inch) standard muffin cups or line with paper baking cups. Heat oven to 400°. Combine yogurt, ⅓ cup margarine, egg, orange zest and juice in mixer bowl; beat until smooth. Combine flour, 1 cup of the sugar, poppy seed, salt and baking soda; blend into yogurt mixture just until all ingredients are moistened (about 1 minute). Spoon into greased muffin cups. Bake until wooden pick inserted in center of muffin comes out clean (17 to 20 minutes). Let stand on wire rack 5 minutes; remove muffins from pan. Brush tops with melted margarine; dip into remaining sugar. Serve warm.

*Amount: 12 muffins.*

*For that just baked flavor and texture, re-heat stored, but not frozen, muffins in the microwave. Wrap an average-sized muffin in a paper towel or napkin. Microwave (HIGH) one muffin 10 to 15 seconds; 20 to 25 seconds for two.*

# PEAR BREAD

▼

*Fresh pears are the focal point of these delicately-spiced loaves. Fruit breads like this one are easier to slice after a stand time.*

| | |
|---|---|
| ¾ cup firmly packed brown sugar | 2 cups flour |
| ½ cup margarine or butter, softened | 1½ teaspoons ground ginger |
| 2 eggs | 1 teaspoon mace |
| 2⅓ cups coarsely chopped peeled pears (about 4), divided | 1 teaspoon baking soda |
| | 1 teaspoon salt |
| | ½ teaspoon ground cinnamon |
| 2 tablespoons lemon juice | ½ cup chopped nuts |
| 1 teaspoon vanilla | ¼ cup granulated sugar |
| | 1½ teaspoons margarine or butter, softened |

Grease and flour 2 (8½ × 4½-inch) loaf pans. Heat oven to 350°. Beat brown sugar and margarine; beat in eggs, ⅓ cup of the chopped pears, lemon juice and vanilla until smooth. Combine flour, ginger, mace, baking soda, salt and cinnamon; stir into brown sugar mixture. Fold in remaining pears and nuts. Spoon mixture into greased and floured pans. Combine ¼ cup sugar and 1½ teaspoons margarine to make crumbly mixture. Sprinkle loaves with mixture. Bake until wooden pick inserted in center of loaf comes out clean (55 to 60 minutes). Cool in pans 5 minutes; remove to wire rack to cool completely. Wrap in plastic wrap; refrigerate up to 4 days.

*Amount: 2 loaves.*

Pear

# APPLE PECAN BREAD

▼

*This handsome harvest-time loaf with a surprise ingredient – sharp Cheddar. You will love the full-bodied flavor and muted sweetness.*

| | |
|---|---|
| ½ cup margarine or butter, softened | ½ teaspoon salt |
| ¾ cup sugar | ¼ teaspoon ground cinnamon |
| 2 eggs | ⅛ teaspoon ground nutmeg |
| 1¾ cups flour | 1 large Granny Smith apple, peeled, shredded (1 cup) |
| 1 teaspoon baking powder | ½ cup shredded sharp Cheddar cheese (2 ounces) |
| ½ teaspoon baking soda | ⅓ cup chopped pecans |

Grease an (8½ × 4½-inch) loaf pan. Heat oven to 350°. Beat margarine and sugar until fluffy; beat in eggs. Combine flour, baking powder, baking soda, salt, cinnamon and nutmeg; blend into margarine mixture alternately with apple. Fold in cheese and pecans. Spoon batter into greased pan. Bake until wooden pick inserted in center of loaf comes out clean (60 to 65 minutes). Cool in pan 10 minutes; remove loaf to wire rack to cool completely. Wrap in plastic wrap; refrigerate up to 4 days.

*Amount: 1 loaf.*

# POLKA DOT BANANA BREAD

▼

*Dotted with chocolate chips and pecans, these loaves have the added nutrition of whole wheat flour and bananas. The crack that appears along the top of most baked quick breads is to be expected.*

1 cup whole wheat flour
1 cup all-purpose or
  unbleached flour
1 teaspoon baking soda
⅛ teaspoon salt
½ cup mini chocolate chips
½ cup chopped pecans
2 eggs

½ cup firmly packed brown
  sugar
¼ cup margarine or butter,
  melted
1 teaspoon vanilla
3 ripe medium bananas,
  mashed (about 1½ cups)
¼ cup plain yogurt

Grease 2 (7½ × 3½-inch) loaf pans. Heat oven to 350°. In large bowl, combine flours, baking soda, salt, chocolate chips and pecans. Beat eggs, sugar, margarine, vanilla, bananas and yogurt together until well blended; stir into dry ingredients just until all ingredients are moistened. Spoon batter into greased pans, filling ⅔ full. Bake until deep golden brown and wooden pick inserted in center of loaf comes out clean (50 to 60 minutes). Cool in pan 10 minutes; remove loaves to wire rack to cool completely. Wrap in plastic wrap; refrigerate up to 4 days.

*Amount: 2 loaves.*

Banana

# POPPY SEED ALMOND TEA BREAD

▼

*Gifts from the kitchen are priceless! This recipe is designed to make five mini loaves without the confusion of having to double or triple the recipe.*

5 foil baby (5¾ × 3¼ × 2-inch)
  loaf pans
2 cups granulated sugar
3 eggs
1 cup margarine or butter,
  softened
1½ tablespoons poppy seed
2 teaspoons almond extract,
  divided

2 teaspoons vanilla, divided
3 cups flour
1½ teaspoons baking powder
1 teaspoon salt
1½ cups milk
½ cup powdered sugar
2 tablespoons orange juice
½ teaspoon butter flavoring

Thoroughly grease pans. Heat oven to 350°. Beat granulated sugar, eggs and margarine until light and fluffy. Beat in poppy seed, 1½ teaspoons of the almond extract and 1½ teaspoons of the vanilla. Combine dry ingredients; add alternately with milk to sugar mixture, mixing just until thoroughly combined. Pour into greased pans. Bake until wooden pick inserted in center of loaf comes out clean (40 to 45 minutes). Combine powdered sugar and orange juice in glass measuring cup; microwave (HIGH) until sugar is dissolved (about 30 seconds). Stir in butter flavoring and remaining almond extract and vanilla. Brush warm topping on warm loaves. Cool on wire rack. Wrap in plastic wrap; refrigerate up to 4 days.

*Amount: 5 loaves.*

# APPLE NUT COFFEE CAKE

▼

*It's easy to achieve just-baked flavor, even with do-ahead preparation. This coffee cake can be assembled and refrigerated several hours or overnight before being baked.*

| | |
|---|---|
| 2 cups flour | 2 eggs, beaten |
| ¾ cup granulated sugar | 1 cup buttermilk |
| 1 cup firmly packed brown sugar, divided | 1 cup chopped Granny Smith apple |
| 1 teaspoon baking powder | ½ cup chopped pecans |
| 1 teaspoon baking soda | 1 teaspoon ground cinnamon |
| ½ teaspoon salt | ¼ teaspoon ground nutmeg |
| ⅔ cup margarine or butter, melted | – Glaze (below) |

Grease 8 × 12-inch glass baking dish. In large bowl, combine flour, granulated sugar, ½ cup of the brown sugar, baking powder, baking soda and salt. In small bowl, combine margarine, eggs and buttermilk; stir into dry ingredients just until combined. Fold in apples. Spoon batter into greased dish. Combine remaining ½ cup brown sugar, pecans, cinnamon and nutmeg; sprinkle over batter. Refrigerate, covered, several hours or overnight.

To Bake: Heat oven to 350°. Bake until wooden pick inserted in center comes out clean (35 to 40 minutes). Cool slightly; drizzle with Glaze.

*12 servings.*

**Glaze:** In small bowl, combine ½ cup powdered sugar, 1½ teaspoons soft margarine or butter, ¼ teaspoon vanilla and 1 to 2 tablespoons milk or cream until smooth and of drizzling consistency.

# TRIPLE BERRY BRUNCH CAKE

▼

*A triple treat of fresh Minnesota berries is folded into a creamy vanilla batter, resulting in a red, white and blue coffee cake just made for a party. It's especially fetching for summer's patriotic holidays.*

| | |
|---|---|
| ¾ cup sugar | ½ teaspoon salt |
| ¼ cup shortening | ¾ cup blueberries |
| 1 egg | ¾ cup raspberries |
| ¾ cup milk | ¾ cup cut-up strawberries |
| 1 teaspoon vanilla | ⅓ cup sugar |
| 2 cups flour | 1 teaspoon margarine or butter, melted |
| 2 teaspoons baking powder | |

Grease and flour 9 × 9-inch baking pan. Heat oven to 375°. Combine ¾ cup sugar, shortening and egg in large bowl; beat until light and fluffy (about 3 minutes). Beat in milk and vanilla. Blend in flour, baking powder and salt; fold in berries. Pour into greased and floured pan. Combine ⅓ cup sugar and melted margarine; sprinkle evenly over batter. Bake until wooden pick inserted in center comes out clean (45 to 50 minutes). Cool on wire rack. Serve slightly warm or at room temperature.

*9 to 12 servings.*

**Tip:** If using frozen berries, do not thaw.

# CARAMEL APPLE BRUNCH ROLLS

▼

*And you thought caramel apples only came on a stick! Usher in autumn with these luscious warm-from-the-oven treats. We guarantee they will become a year-round family favorite.*

| | |
|---|---|
| 1 cup firmly packed brown sugar | 1 (1-pound) loaf frozen sweet roll baking dough, thawed |
| ½ cup butter or margarine | 2 tablespoons butter or margarine, melted |
| 1 tablespoon light corn syrup | 1 cup chopped, peeled apple |
| ½ cup chopped pecans | ¼ cup granulated sugar |
| | 1 teaspoon apple pie spice |

In small saucepan, combine brown sugar, butter and corn syrup; cook and stir over low heat until blended. Pour evenly into 9 × 13-inch baking pan. Sprinkle pecans evenly over caramel; set aside. On lightly floured pastry cloth, roll dough into a 10 × 15-inch rectangle. Brush with melted butter. In small bowl, combine remaining ingredients; spread evenly over butter. Starting with 15-inch side, roll up tightly, pressing edge to seal. Cut dough into 12 equal pieces; place cut side down on caramel in pan. Cover loosely with plastic wrap and cloth towel. Let rise in warm place (on wire rack placed over large pan of hot water) until doubled in size (45 to 60 minutes).

Heat oven to 375°. Bake, uncovered, until golden brown (25 to 30 minutes). Cool in pan 5 minutes; invert onto serving platter or foil.

*Amount: 12 rolls.*

# FRUITY YOGURT BREAKFAST TART

▼

*It's almost like having dessert for breakfast! A kaleidoscope of colorful fresh fruits top a creamy yogurt filling. Heated preserves are drizzled over the top for a festive finishing touch.*

| | |
|---|---|
| 3½ cups cracklin' oat bran cereal | 2 (8-ounce) containers peach lowfat yogurt |
| 2 tablespoons firmly packed brown sugar | ¾ teaspoon fresh lemon juice |
| ½ teaspoon ground cinnamon | 2 kiwi fruit, peeled, sliced |
| 6 tablespoons margarine or butter, melted | ½ cup seedless red grape halves |
| 1 envelope unflavored gelatin | 1 banana, sliced |
| ¼ cup water | 1 cup fresh strawberry halves |
| | ¼ cup peach preserves |

Heat oven to 375°. In food processor, process cereal until coarse crumbs form (about 2 cups). Blend in brown sugar and cinnamon. Pour in melted margarine; continue processing until well blended. Press into 10½-inch tart pan with removable bottom. Bake until set (7 to 9 minutes). Cool completely. In small saucepan, sprinkle gelatin over water; let stand 5 minutes to soften. Stir over low heat until completely dissolved (1 to 2 minutes); cool. In medium bowl, combine yogurt and lemon juice. Stir in gelatin; chill until slightly thickened. Spread yogurt filling evenly in tart shell; chill until firm (about 30 minutes). Arrange fresh fruit in desired pattern. In small saucepan, heat preserves until melted; strain. Drizzle over fruit to glaze. Refrigerate until served.

*10 servings.*

**Variation:** Substitute fresh fruits in season.

# HOLIDAY TEA RING

▼

*Serious bake-from-scratch cooks will rave about this tea ring, and only you will know that a convenience mix streamlined preparation. A bonus is the make-ahead option so you can serve it right from the oven. Try our selection of festive fillings, all of which are congenial with the simple almond-flavored frosting.*

| | |
|---|---|
| 1 (16-ounce) package hot roll mix | – one of the fillings (below) |
| | – frosting (below) |
| 1 tablespoon margarine or butter, softened | – red and green candied cherries |

Thoroughly grease baking sheet or line with parchment. Mix and knead hot roll mix according to package directions. Cover dough with large bowl; let rise 5 minutes. Roll out dough on floured surface with floured stockinette-covered rolling pin to a 12 × 15-inch rectangle. Brush with margarine; spread with filling. Starting with 12-inch side, roll up tightly. Place, seam side down, on greased baking sheet. Form into a ring, sealing ends together. Make cuts 1½ inches apart, slicing almost to center of ring. Twist slices onto their sides. Cover with greased plastic wrap. Refrigerate until double in size or until ready to bake (4 hours or overnight).

To Bake: Remove tea ring (on baking sheet) from refrigerator. Fill 9 × 13-inch pan half full of hot water. Set baking sheet over hot water for 30 minutes. Heat oven to 375°. Uncover tea ring; bake until golden brown (18 to 22 minutes). Remove to wire rack to cool. Drizzle with frosting while warm. Decorate with candied cherries. Best served shortly after baking.

### 8 to 10 servings.

**Apricot Filling:** Combine 1 (6-ounce) package dried apricots, finely chopped, ¼ cup sugar and ⅔ cup orange juice in small saucepan. Cook over medium-low heat until thick (about 10 minutes), stirring occasionally. Stir in ¼ cup chopped almonds (optional). Cool to room temperature.

**Date Filling:** Combine 1 cup finely chopped dates, 2 tablespoons sugar, 1 tablespoon lemon juice and ¼ cup water in small saucepan. Cook over medium-low heat, until thick (about 10 minutes), stirring occasionally. Cool to room temperature.

**Cinnamon-Sugar Filling:** Combine ⅓ cup sugar, ¼ cup chopped nuts, ¼ cup raisins or coconut and 1 teaspoon ground cinnamon.

**Frosting:** Combine 1 cup sifted powdered sugar, 1 tablespoon soft butter, ⅛ teaspoon almond extract and 1½ tablespoons half-and-half until smooth and of spreading consistency.

# BASIC PIZZA CRUST

▼

*With an assist from the food processor, it is simple to make homemade pizza crust. Rising and standing times are brief and preparation is uncomplicated. The basic crust produces a crisp base for your favorite toppings.*

| | |
|---|---|
| 1 (¼-ounce) package active dry yeast | 2½ cups bread or all purpose flour |
| 1 teaspoon sugar | 1½ tablespoons olive oil |
| ¾ cup warm water (110 to 115°) | ¾ teaspoon salt |
| | – cornmeal |

In medium bowl, sprinkle yeast and sugar over warm water; stir to dissolve. Let stand until foamy (about 5 minutes). Combine flour, oil and salt in food processor bowl. With machine running, pour yeast mixture through feed tube; process until dough cleans side of bowl (about 2 minutes). If dough sticks to bowl, add more flour through feed tube 1 tablespoon at a time, incorporating each addition before adding more. If dough is too dry, add more water through feed tube 1 teaspoon at a time, incorporating each addition before adding more. Process until smooth and elastic (30 to 60 seconds). Transfer dough to oiled bowl; turn oiled side up. Cover with plastic wrap and cloth towel. Let rise in warm place until doubled in size (about 20 minutes).

Grease 2 pizza pans, pizza screens or baking sheets; sprinkle pans with cornmeal. Heat oven to 425°. Divide dough in half, shape into balls; let stand 5 to 10 minutes. On lightly floured surface, roll each ball of dough into a 12-inch circle. Transfer rolled dough to pizza pan. Add your choice of toppings. Bake on lowest oven rack until crust is golden brown (15 to 25 minutes).

*Amount: 2 (12-inch) crusts or 6 (6-inch) crusts.*

**Kneading Method:** Follow method for Whole Wheat Pizza Crust. Let rise and shape as above.

# WHOLE WHEAT PIZZA CRUST

▼

*For a soft, chewy-texture, give this whole wheat rendition a try.*

| | |
|---|---|
| 2 (¼-ounce) packages active dry yeast | 2 cups bread or all purpose flour |
| 1 teaspoon sugar | 1½ cups whole wheat flour |
| 1¼ cups warm water (110 to 115°) | 1 tablespoon olive oil |
| | 1 teaspoon salt |
| | – cornmeal |

In glass measuring cup, sprinkle yeast and sugar over warm water; stir to dissolve. Let stand until foamy (about 5 minutes). Combine flours, oil and salt in large bowl. Add yeast mixture; stir until dough cleans side of bowl. If dough is too dry, add more water, 1 teaspoon at a time. Knead dough on floured surface until smooth and elastic (8 to 10 minutes). Transfer dough to oiled bowl; turn oiled side up. Cover with plastic wrap and cloth towel. Let rise in warm place until doubled in size (about 25 minutes).

Grease 3 pizza pans, pizza screens or baking sheets; sprinkle pans with cornmeal. Divide dough into thirds; shape into balls. Let stand 5 to 10 minutes. Heat oven to 425°. On lightly floured surface, roll each ball of dough into a 12-inch circle. Transfer rolled dough to pans. Add your choice of toppings. Bake on lowest oven rack until crust is golden brown (15 to 25 minutes).

*Amount: 3 (12-inch) crusts or 8 (6-inch) crusts.*

**Food Processor Method:** Follow method for Basic Pizza Crust. Let rise and shape as above.

**Tips:** Both pizza crust recipes can be refrigerated for up to 2 days. Allow dough to stand at room temperature, covered, for 2 hours before shaping.

To pre-bake either type of crust, bake in preheated 425° oven until set and golden brown (6 to 10 minutes). Baked crusts can then be refrigerated or frozen for later use.

# DESSERTS

Think of these recipes as "designer desserts." They are just that — designed to "sweeten" any entertaining occasion or family gathering. There is something to satisfy every sweet tooth, from the fan of old-fashioned favorites like Triple Berry Shortcake to the adventuresome globe-trotter who thrives on foreign finales like Chocolate Tortoni Cups and Cranberry Clafoutis.

Chocolate lovers, get ready to set indulgence records. Double Dutch Mocha Mousse, Chocolate Fondue, Double Chocolate Cookie Roll, Chocolate Decadence and Mousse à la White Chocolate await you.

Our party presentations include the showy Flaming Carambola Sundae, rainbow-hued Ice Cream Bombe and Apricot 'n Meringue Dessert, to name a few. Styled for casual crowd-sized serving, you can't miss with a Make Your Own Sundae Bar or the young-at-heart Banana Split Dessert. For those of you who enjoy making food gifts, wrap a festive package of Swedish Nuts or Chocolate Mocha Dusted Almonds — tasteful thank yous for a hostess, teacher or special neighbor.

# WHITE CHOCOLATE RASPBERRY CRÈME

▼

*Savor summer's bounty in this masterpiece, which combines liqueur-flavored berries with a delicate white chocolate mixture.*

1 (5.5-ounce) carton fresh
  raspberries (1 cup), divided
1 tablespoon raspberry-
  flavored liqueur
½ cup sugar, divided
5 egg yolks, slightly beaten

1¾ cups whipping cream
1 (3-ounce) Swiss white
  confectionery bar (white
  chocolate), finely chopped
¼ cup Crème Fraîche
¼ teaspoon vanilla
– Crème Fraîche

Reserve 6 raspberries for garnish. Sprinkle liqueur over remaining berries. Whisk ¼ cup of the sugar into egg yolks until sugar is dissolved. In medium saucepan, bring remaining ¼ cup sugar and whipping cream to simmer over medium heat, stirring constantly. Remove cream mixture from heat; stir in confectionery bar until melted. Slowly whisk hot cream mixture into yolks; stir in ¼ cup Crème Fraîche and vanilla.

Heat oven to 300°. Arrange 6 (6-ounce) custard cups in 9 × 13-inch baking pan. Divide raspberries evenly among cups; pour cream mixture over berries. Pour boiling water into pan to a depth of 1 inch. Bake until knife inserted near center of a custard cup comes out clean (about 1 hour). Remove custard cups from water; cool about 30 minutes. Refrigerate, covered, 4 hours or overnight. Garnish with dollop of Crème Fraîche and a reserved berry.

*6 servings.*

# POTS DE CRÈME

▼

*A creamy, dreamy dessert with a divine hint of black raspberry.*

5 ounces semisweet baking
  chocolate
¼ cup black raspberry-flavored
  liqueur

¾ cup reduced cholesterol
  liquid whole eggs
⅔ cup sugar
½ pint heavy whipping cream
– whipped cream
10 fresh raspberries

In small saucepan over low heat, melt chocolate with liqueur; cool. In food processor, process eggs and sugar. With machine running, gradually add chocolate mixture. Continue processing while slowly pouring in cream until thoroughly combined. Pour into 10 pots de crème, demitasse cups or ⅓-cup ramekins. Refrigerate, covered, several hours or overnight.

To Serve: Garnish each serving with whipped cream and a raspberry.

*10 servings.*

*Triple Berry Shortcake*
*page 172*

# CRANBERRY CLAFOUTIS

▼

*An intriguing interpretation of the custard-like pancake which originated in France.*

| | |
|---|---|
| 2 cups fresh or frozen cranberries | 1 cup sugar |
| ¾ cup cranberry juice cocktail | ¼ cup flour |
| ¼ cup Campari liqueur | ⅓ cup Crème Fraîche |
| 4 eggs | 1 cup milk |
| | 1 tablespoon sugar |
| | – Crème Fraîche |

In medium saucepan over medium heat, simmer cranberries with cranberry juice cocktail and liqueur 5 minutes. Remove cranberries with slotted spoon; bring remaining liquid to a boil. Boil and stir until liquid is reduced to ¼ cup. Cool.

Heat oven to 375°. Grease 1½-quart casserole. Beat eggs, 1 cup sugar, flour, ⅓ cup Crème Fraîche and milk until smooth; stir in cranberry liquid. Arrange cranberries in greased casserole. Pour egg mixture over cranberries; sprinkle 1 tablespoon sugar over top. Bake until golden brown and custard is set (45 to 55 minutes). Serve warm with a dollop of Crème Fraîche.

*8 servings.*

# FRUIT 'N CRÈME FRAÎCHE

▼

*Salute the summer season with this simple but sophisticated dessert.*

| | |
|---|---|
| 2 cups seedless green grapes | 1 (10-ounce) carton Crème Fraîche (1¼ cups) |
| 2 cups fresh blueberries | 3 tablespoons brown sugar |
| 2 cups fresh raspberries or sliced strawberries | |

Layer fruit in order given in glass serving bowl. Spread Crème Fraîche over fruit. Sprinkle brown sugar evenly over top. Refrigerate, covered, several hours or overnight.

*Amount: 6 cups.*

# CRÈME FRAÎCHE

▼

*Very French and very festive for topping any dessert enhanced by a creamy accompaniment.*

| | |
|---|---|
| ½ pint whipping cream (1 cup) | 1 (8-ounce) carton sour cream |

Combine cream and sour cream in glass bowl; cover with plastic wrap. Let stand at room temperature until thickened, about 8 hours in warm weather and up to 24 hours in cold weather. Refrigerate, covered.

*Amount: 2 cups.*

**Tip:** The flavor of Crème Fraîche becomes more tart the longer it is refrigerated. It will keep up to 2 weeks in the refrigerator.

# DOUBLE DUTCH MOCHA MOUSSE

▼

*This showy company dessert is sure to receive rave reviews.*

1 (6-ounce) package semisweet chocolate chips, melted
1 (14-ounce) can sweetened condensed milk

2 tablespoons double Dutch chocolate instant coffee powder
¼ cup coffee-flavored liqueur
1 pint heavy whipping cream, whipped
– Lacy Dessert Cups (below)
– Chocolate Cutouts (below)

In medium bowl, combine chocolate chips, sweetened condensed milk, instant coffee and liqueur. Fold in whipped cream. Freeze, covered, until firm (about 4 hours).

To Serve: Divide mousse evenly between Lacy Dessert Cups. Garnish with small chocolate cutouts.

*Amount: 6 cups mousse.*

# LACY DESSERT CUPS

▼

*Nutty, lacy cups for Double Dutch Mocha Mousse or your favorite ice cream.*

1 cup flour
1 cup finely chopped pecans
½ cup light corn syrup

½ cup firmly packed brown sugar
½ cup butter
1 teaspoon vanilla

Grease dark baking sheets. Heat oven to 300°. Mix flour and pecans; set aside. Combine corn syrup, brown sugar and butter in heavy saucepan. Bring to a boil over medium heat, stirring constantly. Remove from heat; blend in flour mixture and vanilla. Drop by heaping tablespoonfuls onto greased baking sheets, spreading to form thin circles. Make and bake only 4 cookies at a time. Bake until lightly browned (8 to 10 minutes). Cool on baking sheet until cookies can be lifted without wrinkling but are still flexible (1 to 2 minutes). Using a spatula, carefully lift cookies from sheet and shape over small inverted custard cups. Cool completely; remove from custard cups. Store in airtight container at room temperature several hours or overnight. Fill with Double Dutch Mocha Mousse or your favorite ice cream. Garnish with chocolate cutouts.

*Amount: 14 dessert cups.*

# CHOCOLATE CUTOUTS

▼

Unwrap a 1½ ounce plain milk chocolate candy bar. Place, smooth side up, on microwavable plate. Microwave (MEDIUM-LOW, 30% power) 30 seconds. Using a small metal cookie cutter of desired shape, press evenly and firmly into chocolate. Transfer cutout to dessert or refrigerate until ready to use.

# TIRAMISU

▼

*Generously flavored with coffee, this Italian confection showcases mascarpone cheese.*

2 (8-ounce) cartons
   mascarpone cheese
½ cup sugar
1 cup whipping cream
2 tablespoons light rum
½ teaspoon vanilla
3 (3-ounce) packages
   ladyfingers

1 cup brewed espresso coffee,
   cooled
1 (2¼-ounce) package sliced
   almonds, toasted (½ cup)
1½ teaspoons unsweetened
   cocoa
– stemmed maraschino
   cherries

Combine cheese, sugar, whipping cream, rum and vanilla in large mixer bowl; beat until smooth and creamy. Arrange 1½ packages ladyfingers, cut side down, in bottom of 7 × 11-inch glass baking dish. Pour half of coffee over ladyfingers. Spread half of cheese mixture over ladyfingers. Sprinkle half of nuts and half of cocoa over cheese. Arrange remaining ladyfingers over cocoa; sprinkle with remaining coffee and layer with remaining cheese, nuts and cocoa. Refrigerate, covered, several hours or overnight.

To Serve: Garnish with maraschino cherries. Carefully scoop down through all layers; serve in sherbet dishes or on dessert plates.

*12 to 15 servings.*

**Tips:** To substitute for brewed espresso coffee, use 3 rounded teaspoons instant espresso and 1 cup boiling water.

To substitute for 2 (8-ounce) cartons mascarpone cheese, use 1 (8-ounce) package softened cream cheese, 1 (15-ounce) carton ricotta cheese and 1 teaspoon lemon juice. Increase sugar to 1 cup; reduce whipping cream to ½ cup.

# MOUSSE À LA WHITE CHOCOLATE

▼

*This heavenly white chocolate composition melts in your mouth.*

1 (6-ounce) package premier
   white baking bars, coarsely
   chopped
1½ cups heavy whipping cream,
   divided
¼ cup sugar
¼ cup boiling water

2 tablespoons meringue
   powder
4 kiwi fruit, peeled, halved
¼ cup honey
2 tablespoons orange-flavored
   liqueur
1 kiwi fruit, peeled, sliced
3 fresh strawberries, halved

Combine baking bars and ¼ cup of the cream in large microwavable bowl. Microwave (MEDIUM-LOW, 30% power), stirring once until baking bars are almost melted (about 2½ minutes); stir until smooth. Refrigerate 10 minutes, stirring occasionally. Dissolve sugar in boiling water; cool. In small mixer bowl, combine meringue powder and sugar water (mixture will appear lumpy); beat until stiff and glossy. In chilled bowl, whip remaining 1¼ cups cream until stiff peaks form. Gently fold whipped cream and meringue into white chocolate mixture. Refrigerate, covered, several hours or overnight.

Combine 4 kiwi fruit, honey and liqueur in blender; purée just until smooth. Strain sauce to remove seeds. Refrigerate, covered.

To Serve: Divide sauce among 6 footed sherbet dishes; top with mousse. Garnish with kiwi fruit slice and strawberry half.

*6 servings.*

# CHOCOLATE DECADENCE

▼

*A chocolate-lover's dream dessert.*

- 2 (8-ounce) packages semisweet chocolate
- ½ cup butter
- 1½ teaspoons granulated sugar

- 1 teaspoon hot water
- 4 eggs, separated
- – Raspberry Sauce (below)
- 1 cup whipping cream
- 2 tablespoons powdered sugar

Generously butter bottom of 8½-inch springform pan. Heat oven to 425°. In heavy saucepan, melt chocolate and butter. Stir in granulated sugar and water until well blended. Beat in egg yolks, one at a time. Beat egg whites until stiff but not dry. When chocolate mixture has cooled slightly, gently fold ¼ of mixture into egg whites. Fold in remaining chocolate. Pour into buttered pan. Bake 15 minutes. (Cake will look underbaked.) Cool on wire rack. Refrigerate or freeze. Prepare Raspberry Sauce.

To Serve: Thaw cake if frozen. Whip cream until stiff peaks form; beat in powdered sugar. Remove side from springform pan. Frost top of cake with whipped cream. Cut into wedges while cold. Let stand at room temperature 15 minutes before serving. Top with Raspberry Sauce.

*12 servings.*

**Raspberry Sauce:** Thaw 2 (10-ounce) packages frozen raspberries. In heavy saucepan, bring berries to a boil. Combine 2 tablespoons cornstarch with ¼ cup water; stir into berries. Cook over medium heat until thickened, stirring constantly. Boil and stir 1 minute. Remove from heat; stir in 2 tablespoons sugar. Press plastic wrap onto surface of sauce; cool and refrigerate.

*Amount: 2 cups.*

# LEMON CURD PAVLOVA

▼

*An inviting variation of the national dessert of Australia.*

- – parchment paper
- 4 egg whites
- ¼ teaspoon cream of tartar
- 1¾ cups sugar, divided
- 1½ teaspoons grated lemon peel
- ¼ cup lemon juice

- ½ cup margarine or butter
- 2 eggs plus 1 egg yolk, well-beaten
- – real whipped heavy cream in aerosol can
- – candied lemon slices (optional)

Draw a 9-inch circle on parchment paper; place paper on large baking sheet. Heat oven to 300°. In small mixer bowl, beat egg whites and cream of tartar until frothy. Gradually beat in ¾ cup of the sugar until stiff and glossy. Spread meringue on circle. Bake until lightly browned (about 75 minutes). Cool thoroughly away from drafts.

Combine lemon peel, lemon juice, remaining 1 cup sugar and margarine in heavy saucepan. Heat over medium-low heat until margarine is melted. Stir in eggs; cook over medium-low heat until mixture thickens slightly (about 10 minutes). Cool. Carefully remove meringue from parchment paper; place meringue on serving platter. Spread lemon curd on top of meringue to within 1 inch of edge. Refrigerate up to 4 hours.

To Serve: Cut into wedges; garnish each wedge with a swirl of whipped cream and a candied lemon slice.

*10 servings.*

**Variation:** For fluffy lemon filling, fold ½ cup whipping cream, whipped, into lemon curd.

# CHOCOLATE HAZELNUT CHEESECAKE

*Cheesecake like this, redolent with rich liqueur-laced ingredients, is festive enough for any occasion.*

1½ cups finely ground vanilla
    wafer crumbs
¾ cup hazelnuts (filberts),
    toasted, ground
2 tablespoons sugar
2 tablespoons butter or
    margarine, melted
3 (8-ounce) packages cream
    cheese, softened
1 cup sugar

2 tablespoons flour
⅛ teaspoon salt
4 eggs
4 ounces semisweet chocolate,
    melted
¼ cup dark chocolate-flavored
    liqueur
1 teaspoon vanilla
⅛ teaspoon almond extract
– Chocolate Curls (below)

Butter bottom and about 1½ inch up side of 10-inch springform pan. Combine crumbs, hazelnuts, 2 tablespoons sugar and butter; pat crumb mixture onto bottom and up side of pan. Refrigerate until firm (about 30 minutes). Heat oven to 300°. Bake crust 15 minutes; remove from oven. Cool completely.

Heat oven to 325°. In large mixer bowl, beat cream cheese until creamy; beat in 1 cup sugar, flour and salt. Beat in eggs just until blended. Stir in chocolate, liqueur, vanilla and almond extract; pour into crust. Bake until center appears nearly set (45 to 50 minutes). Remove cheesecake to wire rack. Cool 10 minutes. Using thin spatula, carefully loosen side of cheesecake from pan. Cool 30 minutes longer; remove side of pan. Refrigerate, covered.

To Serve: Cut into thin wedges; garnish with Chocolate Curls.

***12 to 16 servings.***

## CHOCOLATE CURLS

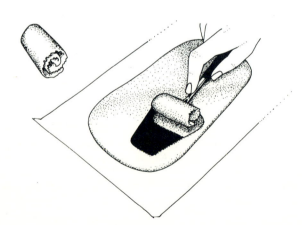

Melt semisweet chocolate chips or squares or vanilla flavored candy coating; pour onto baking sheet. With spatula, spread into ⅛ to ¼ inch thick layer. Refrigerate until just firm, but still pliable (10 to 15 minutes). Pull a cheese plane across chocolate to form curls of desired size. Transfer curls with wooden pick to dessert or refrigerate up to 24 hours.

# DOUBLE CHOCOLATE COOKIE ROLL

▼

*Double your chocolate-eating pleasure with this delectable do-ahead.*

1 (3.9-ounce) package instant
  chocolate fudge pudding and
  pie filling
1 cup milk
1¼ teaspoons almond extract,
  divided

1 (12-ounce) carton non-dairy
  whipped topping, thawed,
  divided
1 (9-ounce) package chocolate
  wafers
– stemmed maraschino
  cherries, well-drained
– sliced almonds, toasted

In small mixer bowl, combine pudding mix, milk and ½ teaspoon of the
almond extract. Beat on low speed until smooth and thickened. Blend in
½ carton whipped topping. Spread tops of all wafers (except 1 for 1 dessert
roll or 2 for 2 dessert rolls) with a rounded tablespoon pudding mixture. Place
on large tray; place tray in freezer until pudding is slightly set but not frozen
(15 to 25 minutes). On large piece of foil, arrange wafers on edge to form
1 long roll. (Roll will be long; make 2 rolls if serving platter will not
accommodate length of 1 roll.) End rolls with unfrosted wafer(s). Wrap tightly;
refrigerate at least 8 hours or overnight.

One to two hours before serving, combine remaining whipped topping with
remaining ¾ teaspoon of almond extract. Arrange roll(s) on serving platter.
Frost with whipped topping. Garnish with cherries and almonds. Refrigerate
until serving time.

To Serve: Cut diagonally into slices.

*16 servings.*

# STRAWBERRY RHUBARB CHEESECAKE SQUARES

▼

*This delicious duo blends into a crimson cheesecake topping.*

¾ cup margarine or butter,
  softened
⅓ cup firmly packed brown
  sugar
1½ cups flour
½ cup coarsely chopped pecans
2 (8-ounce) packages reduced-
  fat cream cheese, softened
2 eggs

1¾ cups sugar, divided
2 teaspoons vanilla
¾ pound fresh or frozen
  rhubarb, coarsely chopped
  (3 cups)
1 cup sliced fresh strawberries
  (8 medium)
4 teaspoons cornstarch
¼ cup water
½ cup finely chopped pecans

Grease 9 × 13-inch baking pan. Heat oven to 375°. Combine margarine, brown
sugar, flour and coarsely chopped pecans; press on bottom of greased pan.
Bake until browned (10 to 12 minutes). Combine cream cheese, eggs, ¾ cup of
the sugar and vanilla in bowl; beat until smooth. Pour over crust; return to
oven and bake until cheesecake is set (about 20 minutes). In large saucepan,
combine rhubarb, remaining 1 cup sugar and strawberries. Dissolve cornstarch
in water; stir into fruit mixture. Bring to a boil; reduce heat to medium and
cook, stirring constantly, until rhubarb is tender and mixture is thickened (8 to
10 minutes). Cool slightly; spread fruit mixture over cheesecake. Sprinkle top
with finely chopped pecans; refrigerate 8 hours or overnight. Cut into squares.

*12 to 16 servings.*

# TROPICAL TORTE

▼

*A luscious cake with baked-on meringue is topped with tropical fruit and sweetened whipped cream.*

½ cup shortening
¾ cup powdered sugar
4 eggs, separated
1 cup flour
1 teaspoon baking powder
¼ teaspoon salt
3 tablespoons milk
1 cup granulated sugar

5 tablespoons granulated sugar, divided
3 tablespoons sliced almonds, divided
½ pint carton heavy whipping cream (1 cup)
1 papaya, peeled, diced
2 kiwi fruit, peeled, sliced
1 cup sliced fresh strawberries
– fresh strawberries (optional)

Grease and flour 2 (9-inch) round pans. Heat oven to 325°. Beat shortening and powdered sugar; beat in egg yolks, one at a time. Combine flour, baking powder and salt; add to sugar mixture alternately with milk. Spread batter in greased and floured pans. Beat egg whites until frothy; gradually add 1 cup granulated sugar, beating until stiff and glossy. Spread over cake batter. Sprinkle each meringue-covered layer with 1 tablespoon of the granulated sugar and 1 tablespoon of the almonds. Bake 30 minutes. Remove from pans; cool on wire rack.

To Assemble: Place 1 cake layer on serving plate, meringue side down. Whip cream until stiff peaks form; beat in 1 tablespoon of the remaining granulated sugar. Spoon about half of whipped cream over cake. Combine cut-up fruit with remaining 2 tablespoons granulated sugar; spread over whipped cream. Place second cake layer over fruit, meringue side up. Spread remaining whipped cream in center of meringue. Refrigerate, covered, 2 to 4 hours before serving.

To Serve: Garnish with remaining 1 tablespoon sliced almonds and strawberries.

*8 to 10 servings.*

# TRIPLE BERRY SHORTCAKE

▼

*Old-fashioned flavors are updated with a baking mix, but of course fresh berries are the sumptuous stars.*

2 cups buttermilk baking mix
2 tablespoons granulated sugar
1 egg
¼ cup margarine or butter, melted
⅔ cup half-and-half

1½ teaspoons vanilla, divided
1 pint heavy whipping cream
3 tablespoons powdered sugar
1 cup fresh blueberries
1 cup fresh raspberries
2 cups sliced fresh strawberries

Grease 9-inch round pan. Heat oven to 450°. Combine baking mix, granulated sugar, egg, margarine, half and half and ½ teaspoon of the vanilla; beat about 30 seconds. Spread dough in greased pan, pushing up edge slightly. Bake until wooden pick inserted in center comes out clean (12 to 15 minutes). Remove shortcake from pan; cool on wire rack. Whip cream until stiff peaks form; beat in powdered sugar and remaining 1 teaspoon vanilla. Cut shortcake into 2 horizontal layers. Spread half of whipped cream on bottom layer. Combine berries; spoon half over whipped cream. Top with second layer and spoon on remaining whipped cream and berries.

*8 servings.*

# THREE FRUIT STRUDEL

▼

*Dried and fresh fruits are tucked into flaky phyllo dough to make individually shaped strudels.*

⅓ cup coarsely chopped dried
   apricots
1 large tart apple, peeled,
   cored, thinly sliced
⅓ cup raisins
⅓ cup chopped pecans
1 teaspoon grated lemon peel
1 tablespoon lemon juice

⅓ cup firmly packed brown
   sugar
¼ teaspoon ground cinnamon
¼ teaspoon ground nutmeg
8 phyllo sheets, thawed
   according to package
   directions
⅓ to ½ cup butter, melted
– powdered sugar or Butter
   Icing (below)

Heat oven to 400°. Combine apricots, apple, raisins, pecans, lemon peel, lemon juice, brown sugar and spices. Place unfolded phyllo sheets between slightly dampened towels to keep from drying out. Arrange large sheet of waxed paper on work surface. Place 1 phyllo sheet on waxed paper; brush with butter. Cover with second phyllo sheet; brush with butter. Repeat with 2 more phyllo sheets and butter. Cut phyllo layers in half lengthwise to make 2 (6 × 18-inch) rectangles. Repeat with 4 remaining sheets. Spoon ¼ of apple mixture on center of each rectangle. Fold long sides of phyllo over filling. Fold opposite ends of phyllo up and over filling. Brush with butter. Place, seam side down, on ungreased baking sheet. Bake until puffed and golden brown (18 to 20 minutes). Cool slightly. Serve warm, sprinkled with powdered sugar or cool completely and drizzle with Butter Icing.

*4 servings.*

**Butter Icing:** Combine 1 cup sifted powdered sugar, 1 tablespoon soft butter, ⅛ teaspoon almond extract and 1 to 2 tablespoons milk; mix until smooth.

# EASY BERRY TRIFLE

▼

*This showy sensation features raspberries, blueberries and strawberries.*

3 cups fresh raspberries,
   divided
3 cups fresh blueberries or
   blackberries, divided
1 cup sliced fresh strawberries
⅓ cup superfine sugar

4 tablespoons orange or
   raspberry-flavored liqueur,
   divided
1 (5.1-ounce) package vanilla
   instant pudding and pie
   filling
4 cups milk
½ teaspoon almond extract
1 (22-ounce) angel food cake

Combine 2 cups each of the raspberries and blueberries and 1 cup strawberries. Lightly crush berries; toss with sugar and 1 tablespoon of the liqueur; set aside. Prepare pudding mix with milk and almond extract according to package directions. Divide angel food cake into 3 equal sections; tear into 2-inch pieces. Arrange ⅓ of cake pieces in trifle bowl; sprinkle with 1 tablespoon of remaining liqueur. Spoon ⅓ of berry mixture (about 1⅓ cups) over cake; cover with ⅓ of pudding (about 1⅓ cups). Repeat layers twice. Spoon remaining 1 cup each raspberries and blueberries on top of trifle. Refrigerate, covered, several hours.

*10 to 12 servings.*

**Tip:** A 4-quart casserole can be substituted for trifle bowl.

# APRICOT 'N MERINGUE DESSERT

*This dreamy do-ahead dessert cuts into attractive squares for simple serving.*

2 cups crushed round butter-flavored crackers
⅓ cup margarine or butter, melted
4 egg whites
1 cup sugar

3½ ounces sweetened flake coconut (1⅓ cups)
1 (21-ounce) can apricot pie filling
½ teaspoon almond extract
1 (8-ounce) carton frozen whipped topping, thawed

Heat oven to 300°. Combine crumbs and margarine; spread evenly in 9 × 13-inch baking pan. Beat egg whites until soft peaks form; gradually add sugar. Beat until stiff and glossy (about 10 minutes). Spread meringue evenly over crumb layer. Bake until golden (about 40 minutes); cool. Increase oven temperature to 325°. Spread coconut evenly in shallow baking pan. Bake until golden brown (about 10 minutes), stirring frequently. Cool. Combine pie filling and almond extract; spread over meringue. Carefully spread whipped topping over pie filling; sprinkle with toasted coconut. Refrigerate, covered, several hours. Cut into squares.

*15 to 18 servings.*

# CHOCOLATE FONDUE

*Dessert becomes a participatory pleasure with everyone choosing favorite dippers to coat with the rich brandy-laced sauce.*

12 ounces imported Swiss chocolate, milk chocolate or semisweet chocolate chips
½ cup half-and-half or whipping cream
1 teaspoon vanilla

2 tablespoons cherry-flavored brandy or orange-flavored liqueur (optional)
– bite-size pieces of angel food, sponge or pound cake, ladyfingers, unfrosted brownies, fresh fruit or well-drained canned fruit

Combine chocolate, half-and-half, vanilla and brandy in chafing dish, fondue pot, double boiler or electric skillet over very low heat. Stir until chocolate is melted and very smooth. Keep warm over very low heat. (Do not overheat; chocolate breaks down.) Arrange pieces of cake and other dippers attractively on platter. Spear with fondue forks or bamboo skewers and dunk into chocolate mixture.

*Amount: 2 cups sauce (6 to 8 servings).*

strawberry

# SPICED POACHED PEARS

▼

*Bosc, Anjou and Comice pears are perfect for this light and spicy fresh fruit treat.*

| | |
|---|---|
| 1½ **cups orange juice** | ½ **teaspoon whole cloves** |
| 2 **(1-inch) cinnamon sticks** | 4 **medium pears** |
| 1 **whole nutmeg, crushed** | – **fresh mint sprigs** |

Combine orange juice, cinnamon sticks, nutmeg and cloves in medium saucepan. Bring to a boil; reduce heat and simmer, covered, 10 minutes. Remove core from pears at bottom end, leaving stem end intact. Add pears to juice; simmer, covered, just until tender (about 20 minutes). Remove cinnamon sticks, nutmeg and cloves. Serve pears whole in individual dessert dishes with juice spooned over them. Garnish with mint.

*4 servings.*

Pear

# APPLES...GLAZED

▼

*This saucy autumnal apple and spice combination is surprisingly simple to prepare in the microwave.*

| | |
|---|---|
| 4 **Golden Delicious apples,** **peeled, cored** | 1½ **cups hot water** |
| ½ **cup sugar** | ¼ **cup light rum** |
| ½ **teaspoon ground cinnamon** | – **Coffee Cream Topping** **(below)** |
| 1 **tablespoon lemon juice** | 1 **tablespoon sliced almonds,** **toasted** |

Arrange apples in deep 2½-quart microwavable casserole. Combine sugar, cinnamon, lemon juice and water; pour over apples. Cover; microwave (HIGH), rearranging apples and basting with syrup twice, until apples are tender (14 to 15 minutes). Remove apples from syrup. Pour syrup into 4-cup glass measure; return apples to casserole. Microwave (HIGH) syrup until reduced to ¾ cup (15 to 17 minutes). Stir in rum; pour over apples. Refrigerate, basting occasionally.

To Serve: Spoon apples and syrup into individual serving dishes. Top with Coffee Cream Topping; sprinkle with almonds.

*4 servings.*

**Coffee Cream Topping:**  Pour ½ cup whipping cream into chilled bowl; stir in ½ teaspoon instant coffee crystals. Let stand 1 minute. Stir in ¼ cup sifted powdered sugar and ½ teaspoon vanilla. Beat until stiff peaks form. Fold in 1 tablespoon syrup from apples.

# ICE CREAM BOMBE

▼

*All the assembling of this colorful, liqueur-laced beauty is done ahead and you have the option of making one mold or individual servings.*

1 quart chocolate ice cream
2 tablespoons chocolate-flavored liqueur
1 teaspoon brandy
2 quarts vanilla ice cream, divided
⅓ cup finely chopped pistachio nuts, divided
1 tablespoon almond extract
– green food color

2 tablespoons light rum
¼ cup chopped pecans
¼ cup chopped well-drained maraschino cherries
¼ cup finely-chopped candied pineapple
– red food color
1 pint whipping cream
¼ cup powdered sugar
1 tablespoon brandy

Oil and line 12-cup Bundt® pan with plastic wrap. Soften chocolate ice cream; beat in chocolate-flavored liqueur and 1 teaspoon brandy until smooth and well blended. Pack into lined pan; freeze until firm. For second layer, soften 1 quart of the vanilla ice cream; beat in 3 tablespoons pistachios, almond extract and green food color until well blended. Pack into pan over first layer; freeze until firm. For third layer, soften remaining 1 quart vanilla ice cream; beat in rum, pecans, cherries, pineapple and red food color until well blended. Pack into pan over second layer; freeze until firm.

When solidly frozen, whip cream until stiff peaks form; beat in powdered sugar and 1 tablespoon brandy. Unmold ice cream onto chilled serving platter; remove plastic wrap. Quickly frost with whipped cream mixture; freeze.

To Serve: Sprinkle with remaining pistachios; cut into wedges.

### *16 to 20 servings.*

**Variation:**  For individual molds or servings, cut recipe amounts in half; pack each layer into 15 paper baking cups placed in muffin pans or into individual gelatin molds.

# BANANA SPLIT DESSERT

▼

*Remember this frozen dessert for birthday parties and group entertaining.*

1 (10¾-ounce) frozen pound cake, thawed
1 quart vanilla ice cream, softened
3 bananas, thinly sliced
1 (18.5-ounce) jar chocolate fudge topping, divided

1 quart strawberry ice cream, softened
1 (8¼-ounce) can crushed pineapple in heavy syrup, well-drained
– sweetened whipped cream
– chopped pecans
12 stemmed maraschino cherries, well-drained

Cut pound cake into 16 even slices; arrange on bottom of 9 × 13-inch pan. Spread with vanilla ice cream; arrange bananas over ice cream in single layer. Drizzle with 1 cup of the fudge topping. Freeze until firm (8 hours or overnight). Spread strawberry ice cream over topping; sprinkle with pineapple. Drizzle with remaining fudge topping. Freeze, covered, until firm.

To Serve: Cut into 12 servings; arrange on individual dessert plates. Top each serving with a dollop of whipped cream; garnish with pecans and a cherry.

### *12 servings.*

# MAKE YOUR OWN SUNDAE BAR

▼

*Step right up to a sumptuous sundae bar and concoct your own creation from a tantalizing array of ice cream and toppings.*

| INGREDIENTS | 12 SERVINGS | 24 SERVINGS | 48 SERVINGS |
|---|---|---|---|
| ICE CREAM<br>½ cup or 1 large scoop per serving | 2 quarts | 1 gallon | 2 gallons |
| FUDGE OR BUTTERSCOTCH SAUCE<br>1 ounce per serving<br>(2 tablespoons) | 12 ounces | 24 ounces | 48 ounces |
| STRAWBERRY, PINEAPPLE OR MARSHMALLOW SAUCE<br>1½ ounces per serving<br>(3 tablespoons) | 18 ounces | 36 ounces | 72 ounces |
| WHIPPING CREAM, WHIPPED<br>2 tablespoons per serving | ½ pint | 1 pint | 2 pints |
| CHOPPED NUTS<br>2 teaspoons per serving | ½ cup | 1 cup | 2 cups |

**Do-Ahead Ice Cream Balls:** Line 10 × 15-inch jelly roll pans with waxed paper. Scoop ice cream into balls; arrange on pans. Freeze until solid. Transfer to covered freezer containers, separating layers with waxed paper. Store up to one week.

# CHOCOLATE TORTONI CUPS

▼

*This chocolate and whipped cream frozen treat is studded with cookie bits and pecans.*

20 (2½-inch) foil baking cups
2 (4-ounce) bars German's sweet chocolate
⅔ cup light corn syrup
2 cups heavy whipping cream, divided

½ teaspoon vanilla
1½ cups broken pecan sandies cookies (about 12)
2 (2-ounce) packages chopped pecans (1 cup)
– chocolate-flavored decors

Place foil cups in muffin pans. In 2-quart microwavable bowl, combine chocolate and corn syrup. Microwave (HIGH) 1 minute; stir. Microwave (HIGH) until almost melted (1 to 1½ minutes); stir until smooth. Stir in ½ cup of the cream and vanilla until well blended. Refrigerate until cool (about 15 minutes). In chilled bowl, whip remaining 1½ cups cream until soft peaks form. Gradually fold chocolate mixture into whipped cream. Fold in cookies and pecans. Spoon into foil cups; sprinkle with decors. Freeze until firm. Overwrap with heavy duty foil; return to freezer until ready to serve.

*Amount: 20 tortoni cups.*

Maraschino Cherry

# FLAMING CARAMBOLA SUNDAE

▼

*Carambola or "star fruit" adds an exotic touch to this brandy-sparked ice cream topping.*

| | |
|---|---|
| 1 carambola (star fruit) or pear, sliced | 2 tablespoons brown sugar |
| 1 tablespoon lemon juice | ⅛ teaspoon ground cinnamon |
| 2 tablespoons margarine or butter | 2 tablespoons brandy, warmed |
| | – vanilla ice cream |

In small bowl, combine carambola slices and lemon juice. Melt margarine in skillet over medium heat; sauté carambola until crisp tender (7 to 10 minutes), turning once. Stir in brown sugar and cinnamon. Add warm brandy and ignite immediately, shaking skillet gently until flame subsides. Serve warm over ice cream.

*2 servings.*

**Tip:** To warm brandy, measure 2 tablespoons into glass measure; microwave (HIGH) 15 seconds.

# PIÑA COLADA SHERBET

▼

*We've transformed a favorite sipper into a fantastic light dessert.*

| | |
|---|---|
| 1 (15-ounce) can cream of coconut | ¼ cup light rum |
| 1 (20-ounce) can crushed pineapple in its own juice | 1 cup orange juice |
| | – whole fresh strawberries |

Combine all ingredients except strawberries; pour into 8 × 8-inch baking pan. Freeze until solid. When frozen, scoop half of mixture into food processor. Pulse mixture until finely chopped, then run continuously until smooth. Spoon into freezer container or dessert dishes. Repeat with remaining mixture. Garnish with whole berry before serving.

*Amount: 1 quart.*

# PINEAPPLE-MANGO SHERBET

▼

*A Caribbean cooler laced with orange-flavored liqueur.*

| | |
|---|---|
| 1 large orange | ½ cup plain yogurt |
| 2 mangoes, peeled, pitted, cut into 1-inch pieces | 1 teaspoon orange-flavored liqueur |
| 1 cup pineapple cubes | – fresh mint sprigs and orange twists |
| ⅓ cup sugar | |

Line baking sheet with waxed paper. Using zester or vegetable peeler, remove 1 tablespoon peel from orange; set aside. Remove and discard remaining peel; cut orange into segments, removing any white pith. Arrange orange, mango and pineapple cubes on waxed paper-lined baking sheet. Freeze until firm (30 to 45 minutes). In food processor, process orange, mango, pineapple, reserved peel and sugar until combined. With machine running, add yogurt and liqueur; process until smooth and fluffy (about 3 minutes). Pour into 8 × 8-inch baking pan. Freeze, covered, until firm, several hours or overnight. Let stand at room temperature 10-15 minutes before serving. Scoop into footed sherbet dishes. Garnish with mint and orange twists.

*Amount: 6 cups.*

# KIWI ICE

*Choose fully ripe kiwi for peak flavor and add food color with care so green hue is elegantly subtle.*

5 kiwi fruit (1 pound), peeled,
  cut up
½ cup sugar

3 tablespoons lime juice
¾ cup water
1 drop green food color

Combine kiwi, sugar and lime juice in small saucepan. Bring to a boil; reduce heat and simmer until fruit is softened. Strain through cheesecloth to remove seeds. Stir in water and food color. Pour into shallow pan. Freeze, covered, until almost firm (3 to 4 hours). Scoop into food processor; blend until smooth and slushy. Return to pan; freeze, covered, until almost firm (1 to 1½ hours). Scoop into chilled sherbet dishes.

*4 (½-cup) servings.*

# CAMPARI ICE

*Spiked with Campari, an Italian aperitif wine, this rosy-hued ice is a breeze to prepare for a refreshing finale.*

3 cups cranberry juice cocktail
1 cup Campari liqueur

⅓ cup orange juice
1 cup sugar

Combine all ingredients in medium saucepan. Bring to a boil; reduce heat to medium and simmer, stirring constantly, over medium heat until sugar is dissolved. Pour into shallow baking pan. Cool. Freeze, stirring occasionally, until set, several hours or overnight.

To Serve: Scoop into chilled sherbet dishes or serve with a variety of colored ices.

*8 (½-cup) servings.*

# GRAPEFRUIT ICE

*Use dainty scoops for palate cleansers between courses or larger portions for a tartly refreshing dessert.*

6 cups unsweetened grapefruit
  juice

¾ to 1 cup sugar
– fresh mint sprigs

In large bowl, stir juice and sugar together until sugar is dissolved. Pour into 9 × 13-inch baking pan. Freeze, covered, until almost firm (about 4 hours). Scoop into food processor; process until smooth and slushy. Return to pan; freeze, covered, until firm (about 1 hour). Remove from freezer 5 minutes before serving. Scoop into chilled sherbet dishes.

*20 (½-cup) servings.*

**Tip:** Best if made with freshly squeezed grapefruit juice (8 medium grapefruit yield 6 cups juice).

*Sorbet is a blend of fruit and sweetener with gelatin or egg white added. Sherbets main ingredients are fruit, juices, sweetener and milk solids. Ices are made with one or more pureed fruits or fruit juices and a sweetener.*

# SWEDISH NUTS

▼

*A great addition to a tea table or dessert buffet.*

1 egg white
1½ tablespoons water

1 (12-ounce) can mixed nuts
¾ cup sugar
½ teaspoon ground cinnamon

Butter 9 × 13-inch baking pan. Heat oven to 350°. Beat egg white and water until frothy; fold in nuts. Combine sugar and cinnamon; stir into nuts until well coated. Spread nuts in buttered pan. Bake until golden brown (20 to 25 minutes), stirring every 10 minutes. Stir; let nuts cool in pan. Store in airtight container.

*Amount: 3 cups.*

# CHOCOLATE MOCHA DUSTED ALMONDS

▼

*A luxurious chocolate-covered snack to serve with after-dinner coffee.*

½ cup powdered sugar
1 tablespoon unsweetened
    cocoa

1 tablespoon instant coffee
    crystals
⅔ cup milk chocolate chips
2 cups natural whole almonds

Line baking sheet with waxed paper. In large bowl, combine powdered sugar, cocoa and instant coffee; set aside. Pour chocolate chips into 1-quart glass measuring cup. Microwave (MEDIUM, 50% power) until most chips appear soft and shiny (3 to 3½ minutes); stir until smooth. Stir almonds into chocolate until completely coated. Spoon chocolate-covered almonds into powdered sugar mixture. Toss with fork until almonds are separated and evenly coated. Spread on waxed paper-lined baking sheet. Refrigerate 1 hour to set chocolate. Spoon into airtight container and store in refrigerator.

*Amount: 2 cups.*

# CAKES, PIES & TARTS

Simply divine or divinely simple — the choice is yours when it comes to our cake selections. The lofty Lemony Lemon Cake is dressed to impress, but has stiff competition from European tortes like German Chocolate Mocha Torte. Looking for something tasty and totable for your next potluck? Try the compliment-catching Amaretto Cake. When there's a birthday or other special occasion, choose a dark dazzler like our luscious Chocolate Sour Cream Cake.

It's been said that "the true test of a good cook is a good pie." Whether that's true or not, we all certainly remember with fondness our last piece of perfect pastry. We ease into this bountiful blue ribbon collection with a recipe for Chocolate Pecan Pie. You will find a creative abundance of pies and tarts that will inspire you to put your rolling pin in motion.

# CHOCOLATE SOUR CREAM CAKE

*Go ahead and indulge yourself. This dark chocolate-sour cream sensation with rich, fudgy frosting is irresistible.*

| | |
|---|---|
| – parchment paper | 3 eggs |
| 2¼ cups cake flour | 1½ teaspoons vanilla |
| 2 teaspoons baking soda | 3 ounces unsweetened |
| ½ teaspoon salt | chocolate, melted, cooled |
| ½ cup butter, softened | 1 (8-ounce) carton sour cream |
| 2¼ cups firmly packed brown | 1 cup boiling water |
| sugar | – Fudgy Chocolate Frosting |
| | (below) |

Lightly grease bottoms and sides of 2 (9-inch) round cake pans. Line bottoms of pans with circles of parchment or waxed paper. Sprinkle sides of pans with flour; tap out excess. Heat oven to 350°. In medium bowl, combine flour, baking soda and salt. In large mixer bowl, beat butter, brown sugar, eggs and vanilla until light and fluffy. Beat in chocolate, then sour cream. With mixer at low speed, beat in flour mixture, alternating with boiling water, until batter is smooth. Divide and spread batter evenly in greased and lined pans. Bake on center oven rack until wooden pick inserted in center of cake comes out clean (30 to 35 minutes). Cool in pans on wire racks 10 minutes. Run a knife around edges of layers; invert onto racks. Carefully peel off paper; invert layers again so they are right side up. Cool completely. Frost with Fudgy Chocolate Frosting.

### *10 to 12 servings.*

**Fudgy Chocolate Frosting:** With electric mixer, beat 6 tablespoons soft butter until light and fluffy. Beat in ¾ cup unsweetened cocoa, 3½ cups powdered sugar, 7 tablespoons milk and 1 teaspoon vanilla. Continue beating until thick, fluffy and of spreading consistency, adding more milk if necessary.

**Variations:**

**Black Forest Cake:** Soak 1 (16-ounce) can drained tart cherries in cherry-flavored liqueur for 2 hours. Drain; spoon half of cherries over bottom cake layer. Beat ½ pint whipping cream with 1 (⅓-ounce) package Whip it and 1 tablespoon powdered sugar. Cover cherries with whipped cream. Top with second cake layer and spoon on remaining whipped cream and cherries. Garnish with grated chocolate.

**Mexican Chocolate Cake:** Add 2½ teaspoons ground cinnamon to dry cake ingredients. Add ¼ teaspoon ground cinnamon to Fudgy Chocolate Frosting.

**Turtle Cake:** Frost bottom cake layer with Fudgy Chocolate Frosting. Spread ½ cup butterscotch caramel fudge topping over frosting; top with ¼ cup chopped pecans. Place second cake layer over pecans; frost top of cake. Sprinkle with chopped pecans and drizzle with caramel topping.

*German Chocolate Mocha Torte page 186*

*Nutcracker Sweet page 188*

*Fresh Raspberry Pie page 192*

# APPLE HARVEST CAKE WITH CARAMEL SAUCE

▼

*A rich, warm caramel sauce gilds wedges of moist applesauce cake.*

| | |
|---|---|
| 1 (8-ounce) package chopped dates | 2 eggs |
| ½ cup apple juice | 3 cups flour |
| 1½ cups firmly packed brown sugar | 1 tablespoon baking soda |
| | 2 teaspoons ground cinnamon |
| ¾ cup butter or margarine | 1 teaspoon ground nutmeg |
| 2½ cups unsweetened applesauce | ½ teaspoon ground cloves |
| | 1 cup chopped walnuts |
| | – Caramel Sauce (below) |

In small saucepan, combine dates and apple juice; bring to a boil. Cool. Heat oven to 350°. In large mixer bowl, beat brown sugar and butter until light and fluffy. Beat in applesauce and eggs. Combine flour, baking soda, cinnamon, nutmeg and cloves; gradually stir into applesauce mixture. Stir in date mixture and walnuts until well blended. Pour batter into greased and floured 12-cup Bundt® pan. Bake until wooden pick inserted in center of cake comes out clean (50 to 60 minutes). Cool cake in pan on wire rack 30 minutes. Invert onto wire rack; cool completely.

To Serve: Spoon warm Caramel Sauce over each piece.

### 18 to 24 servings.

**Caramel Sauce:** Combine 1⅓ cups firmly packed brown sugar, ⅓ cup half-and-half, ¼ cup light corn syrup and ¼ cup butter in heavy saucepan. Bring to a boil over low heat, stirring constantly; boil 1 minute. Stir in 1 teaspoon vanilla. Serve warm.

### Amount: 1½ cups.

# PINEAPPLE 'N COCONUT CAKE

▼

*Add a taste of Hawaii to your next party with this golden layered cake. It's filled with a pineapple-cream cheese mixture and garnished with toasted coconut.*

| | |
|---|---|
| 1 (18.25-ounce) package yellow cake mix without pudding | 1¾ cups milk |
| | 1 (20-ounce) can crushed pineapple, well drained |
| 1 (8-ounce) package cream cheese, softened | 1 pint whipping cream |
| 1 (3.4-ounce) package instant coconut cream pudding and pie filling | 2 (⅓-ounce) packages Whip it |
| | ⅓ cup powdered sugar |
| | ½ teaspoon vanilla |
| | 1 cup sweetened shred coconut, toasted |

Grease 2 (9 × 13-inch) baking pans; line with waxed paper. Lightly grease waxed paper. Heat oven to 350°. Prepare cake mix according to package directions. Spread batter evenly in greased and lined pans. Bake until wooden pick inserted in center comes out clean (20 to 25 minutes). Cool in pans on wire racks 10 minutes; invert cakes onto cooling racks. Carefully peel off paper. Cool completely.

Place 1 cake layer on large serving platter. Beat cream cheese, instant pudding mix and milk in small mixer bowl until blended. Beat 2 minutes at medium speed; blend in pineapple. Spread over cake layer; top with second layer. Beat whipping cream about 30 seconds. Add Whip it and powdered sugar; beat until stiff peaks form. Blend in vanilla. Spread whipped cream over sides and top of cake. Garnish with toasted coconut. Refrigerate until serving time.

### 12 to 16 servings.

**Tip:** To toast coconut, spread in 9 × 13-inch baking pan. Bake at 350° until golden brown, stirring twice (5 to 7 minutes).

# AMARETTO CAKE

*Gloriously golden, ravishingly rich and fabulously flavored with almond liqueur.*

1 cup butter, softened
2¾ cups sugar, divided
6 eggs
1 (8-ounce) carton sour cream
2 teaspoons almond extract
1 teaspoon vanilla extract
¼ teaspoon lemon extract
¼ teaspoon orange extract

½ teaspoon salt
¼ teaspoon baking soda
3 cups cake flour
½ cup Amaretto
2 tablespoons butter
1 tablespoon water
2 tablespoons Amaretto
¾ cup chopped or sliced almonds, toasted

Grease and flour 10-inch tube pan. Heat oven to 325°. Beat 1 cup butter and 2½ cups of the sugar until light and fluffy. Add eggs, one at a time, beating 1 minute after each addition. Beat in sour cream and extracts. Stir salt and baking soda into cake flour. Add flour mixture and ½ cup Amaretto alternately to creamed mixture, stirring until well blended. Pour into greased and floured pan. Bake until wooden pick inserted in center of cake comes out clean (75 to 85 minutes). Cool cake in pan on wire rack 25 minutes. Invert onto plate; cool completely.

Melt 2 tablespoons butter in small saucepan. Stir in water and remaining ¼ cup sugar. Bring to a boil; boil 2 minutes. Stir in 2 tablespoons Amaretto and almonds. Spoon over cake.

*18 to 24 servings.*

*Amaretto is an Italian liqueur made from apricot stones with a sweet, nutty flavor.*

# CREAM CAKE

*Whatever your nationality, you will appreciate this variation of Norwegian Bløtkake.*

– parchment paper
4 eggs, separated
2 cups granulated sugar
1½ teaspoons vanilla
2 cups flour
2 teaspoons baking powder
1 teaspoon salt

1 cup cold water
1 cup seedless raspberry jam or sweetened lingonberries
1 pint heavy whipping cream
1 tablespoon powdered sugar
½ teaspoon vanilla
½ pint fresh raspberries

Line bottom of 10-inch springform pan with parchment paper. Heat oven to 350°. Beat egg yolks, granulated sugar and 1½ teaspoons vanilla in large mixer bowl until well blended. Combine flour, baking powder and salt; add alternately with water to sugar mixture. Beat egg whites until stiff peaks form; fold into batter until well blended. Pour into lined pan. Bake until wooden pick inserted in center of cake comes out clean (50 to 60 minutes). Cool in pan on wire rack 10 minutes. Run knife around side of pan. Remove side and bottom of pan. Peel off paper. Cool completely. Slice cake horizontally into 2 equal layers. Spread top of bottom layer with jam. Whip cream until stiff peaks form; beat in 1 tablespoon powdered sugar and ½ teaspoon vanilla. Spread half of whipped cream over bottom layer. Top with second cake layer. Spread remaining whipped cream over top of cake. Refrigerate several hours or overnight. Garnish with raspberries.

*10 to 12 servings.*

# SHERRY BUNDT POUND CAKE

▼

*This buttery pound cake has whispers of rum and almond and makes a "beautiful base" for fresh fruit and a Sherry Cream Sauce.*

| | |
|---|---|
| 1 cup butter or margarine, softened | 5 eggs |
| ½ cup shortening | 3½ cups flour |
| 3 cups sugar | ½ teaspoon baking powder |
| 1 teaspoon rum extract | 1 cup milk |
| 1 teaspoon almond extract | – Sherry Cream Sauce (below) |
| | 2 pounds fresh strawberries, sliced |

Generously grease and flour 12-cup Bundt® or 10-inch tube pan. Heat oven to 300°. In large mixer bowl, beat butter, shortening and sugar until light and fluffy. Beat in extracts and eggs. Combine flour and baking powder. Blend dry ingredients and milk alternately into butter mixture until well blended, beginning and ending with flour. Pour batter into greased and floured pan. Bake until wooden pick inserted in center of cake comes out clean (about 1½ hours). Cool cake in pan on wire rack 15 minutes. Invert onto rack to cool completely. Slice and serve cake with Sherry Cream Sauce and strawberries.

### 18 to 24 servings.

**Sherry Cream Sauce:** Combine ⅔ cup sugar, ¼ cup cornstarch and ¼ teaspoon salt in 3-quart saucepan. Gradually stir in 4 cups milk and ¼ cup cream sherry. Bring to a boil over medium heat, stirring constantly. Boil and stir 1 minute. Stir some hot sauce into 4 slightly beaten egg yolks; return mixture to pan. Cook, stirring constantly, ½ minute. Blend in ¼ cup butter. Refrigerate, covered, until serving.

### Amount: 3 cups.

# BUNDT CAKE À L'ORANGE

▼

*A zesty orange glaze is poured over a delicately flavored orange cake for a creative crowd-sized dessert.*

| | |
|---|---|
| 1 cup butter or margarine, softened | ¼ cup orange juice |
| 1 cup sugar | 2 cups flour |
| 3 eggs, separated | 1 teaspoon baking powder |
| 2 tablespoon orange-flavored liqueur | 1 teaspoon baking soda |
| – grated peel of 1 orange | 1¼ cups sour cream |
| | – Glaze (below) |
| | – sweetened strawberries (optional) |

Grease generously and flour 12-cup Bundt® pan. Heat oven to 350°. In large mixer bowl, beat butter and sugar until fluffy. Beat in egg yolks one at a time. Blend in liqueur, orange peel and juice. Combine dry ingredients; with mixer at low speed, blend dry ingredients into butter mixture alternately with sour cream. Beat egg whites until stiff peaks form; fold into cake batter until well blended. Pour batter into greased and floured pan. Bake until wooden pick inserted in center of cake comes out clean (45 to 50 minutes).

Prepare Glaze. Let cake cool in pan on wire rack 10 to 15 minutes. Invert onto rack or plate. Poke holes in cake with tines of fork; slowly pour Glaze over cake. Cool completely. Serve with sweetened strawberries.

### 18 to 24 servings.

**Glaze:** Combine ½ cup unsifted powdered sugar, 3 tablespoons orange juice and 1 tablespoon orange-flavored liqueur; blend until smooth.

# FUDGY RUM BUNDT CAKE

*We offer a choice of two glazes. If you can't decide between them, why not artistically drizzle both over the cake for contrasting elegance?*

1½ cups cake flour
3 tablespoons unsweetened
  cocoa
1½ teaspoons baking powder
¾ teaspoon baking soda
¾ teaspoon salt
1 cup butter or margarine,
  softened
1¾ cups sugar, divided

4 ounces unsweetened
  chocolate, melted, cooled
3 egg yolks
¾ cup whipping cream
½ cup water
2 tablespoons rum
½ cup chopped pecans
5 egg whites
⅛ teaspoon cream of tartar
– White Chocolate Glaze or
  Chocolate Glaze (below)

Generously grease 12-cup Bundt® pan with shortening. Sprinkle shortening with cocoa; tap out excess. Heat oven to 350°. Combine flour, cocoa, baking powder, soda and salt; set aside. In large mixer bowl, beat butter and 1½ cups of the sugar until light and fluffy. Blend in cooled chocolate. Beat in egg yolks until fluffy. Blend in whipping cream, water, rum and pecans. Fold in dry ingredients. Beat egg whites and cream of tartar until mixture begins to hold shape. Add remaining ¼ cup sugar, 1 tablespoon at a time; beat until whites hold soft peaks. Fold ¼ of whites into batter; gently fold in remaining whites until well blended. Pour into greased and cocoa-covered pan. Bake until wooden pick inserted in center of cake comes out clean (about 45 minutes).

Cool in pan on wire rack 10 minutes. (Cake will fall slightly.) Invert cake onto rack; cool completely. Place rack holding cake over large baking sheet. Spoon Glaze over top, allowing some to drip down side. Transfer cake to serving plate.

### 16 to 24 servings.

**White Chocolate Glaze:** Melt 1 (3-ounce) Swiss white confectionery bar (white chocolate); cool slightly. Beat in 1 cup sifted powdered sugar, ¼ cup sour cream, 1 tablespoon softened butter and 2 to 3 tablespoons whipping cream until glaze is smooth and of medium thin consistency.

**Chocolate Glaze:** Melt 3 tablespoons butter or margarine and 2 ounces unsweetened chocolate over low heat. Remove from heat; stir in 1 cup sifted powdered sugar and ½ teaspoon vanilla. Blend in 2 to 3 tablespoons hot water until glaze is of medium thin consistency.

Nuts

# ALMOND 'N COFFEE TORTE

▼

*The flourless batter is like an almond meringue in texture and is divine layered with a mocha-flavored filling and sweetened whipped cream.*

- parchment paper
6 eggs
2 cups sugar
6 (3½-ounce) packages whole natural almonds, finely ground (5½ cups)
2 tablespoons coffee-flavored liqueur, divided

3 tablespoons double-strength cold coffee, divided
1 (4-ounce) bittersweet chocolate bar
½ pint heavy whipping cream
1 tablespoon powdered sugar
½ teaspoon vanilla
- Chocolate Curls (page 170) or chocolate coffee beans

Line 2 (9½-inch) springform pan bottoms with parchment paper. Heat oven to 350°. Beat eggs and sugar until light and fluffy. Fold in ground almonds. Spread batter evenly in paper-lined pans. Bake until wooden pick inserted in center of cake comes out clean (30 to 40 minutes). (Cake will be golden brown and cracked on surface.) Cool in pans on wire racks 15 minutes. Run knife around side of each pan. Remove side and bottom of each pan; peel off parchment paper.

Place 1 layer upside down on serving plate. Combine 1 tablespoon liqueur and 1 tablespoon coffee; sprinkle on bottom layer. Melt chocolate in remaining 2 tablespoons coffee; stir in remaining 1 tablespoon liqueur. Cool. Whip cream until stiff peaks form; beat in powdered sugar and vanilla. Spread chocolate mixture over bottom cake layer; place remaining layer right side up over chocolate mixture. Spread whipped cream over top of cake. Refrigerate several hours or overnight. Garnish with Chocolate Curls.

*10 to 12 servings.*

**Tip:** To make double-strength coffee, use 2 tablespoons coffee granules for each 6-ounce cup brewed.

# GERMAN CHOCOLATE MOCHA TORTE

▼

*A majestic mocha layering of cake, frosting and chopped pecans.*

1 (18.25-ounce) package German chocolate cake mix
1¼ cups double-strength cold coffee
⅓ cup vegetable oil
3 eggs
½ cup butter or margarine, softened

3 cups powdered sugar
3 tablespoons unsweetened cocoa
2 teaspoons vanilla
5 tablespoons double-strength cold coffee
1 (6-ounce) package chopped pecans, divided

Grease and flour 3 (9-inch) round cake pans. Heat oven to 350°. In large mixer bowl, combine cake mix, 1¼ cups coffee, oil and eggs. Mix according to package directions. Pour batter into greased and floured pans. Bake until wooden pick inserted in center comes out clean (15 to 20 minutes). Cool 10 minutes in pans on wire racks; remove from pans. Cool completely on wire racks. In large mixer bowl, beat butter, powdered sugar, cocoa, vanilla and 5 tablespoons coffee. Measure 1 cup frosting; set aside. Stir 1 cup of the pecans into remaining frosting. Place first cake layer upside down on serving plate; frost top only with half of pecan frosting. Add second layer right side up; frost top only with remaining pecan frosting. Add third layer right side up; frost top only with plain frosting. Sprinkle remaining pecans over top of cake.

*12 to 16 servings.*

**Tip:** If you do not have three (9-inch) round cake pans, refrigerate the extra batter while the first 2 layers bake, then bake the third layer.

# LEMONY LEMON CAKE

▼

*You will find the tart lemon curd filling complements the sweeter flavor of cake and whipped cream.*

- parchment paper
2¾ cups cake flour
1½ cups granulated sugar
1½ teaspoons baking soda
¾ teaspoon salt
1⅓ cups buttermilk
½ cup butter or margarine, softened
¼ cup shortening

3 eggs
1½ teaspoons vanilla
1½ tablespoons grated lemon peel
2½ tablespoons lemon juice
1 cup whipping cream
2 tablespoons powdered sugar
– Lemon Curd Filling (below)
– candied lemon slices

Lightly grease bottom of 2 (8-inch) round cake pans. Line bottoms of pans with circles of parchment paper. Heat oven to 350°. In large mixer bowl, beat flour, granulated sugar, baking soda, salt, buttermilk, butter, shortening, eggs, vanilla, lemon peel and juice on low speed, scraping bowl constantly until moistened (about 30 seconds). Beat on high speed, scraping bowl occasionally until well blended (about 3 minutes). Spread batter evenly in greased and lined pans. Bake on center oven rack until wooden pick inserted in center of cake comes out clean (35 to 40 minutes). Meanwhile, prepare Lemon Curd Filling. Cool layers in pans on wire racks 10 minutes. Run a knife around edges of layers; invert onto racks. Carefully peel off paper; invert layers again so they are right side up. Cool completely.

Cut each cake layer horizontally into 2 layers. Whip cream until stiff peaks form; beat in powdered sugar. Spread bottom layer with ½ cup lemon curd; top with cake layer. Fold ⅓ cup lemon curd into ⅓ cup whipped cream; spread on second layer. Top with another cake layer; spread cake with ½ cup lemon curd. Top with final cake layer; spread cake with ⅓ cup lemon curd and spread remaining whipped cream over top. Garnish with candied lemon slices.

### *10 to 12 servings.*

**Lemon Curd Filling:**  Combine ½ tablespoon grated lemon peel, ¼ cup lemon juice, 1 cup sugar and ½ cup butter or margarine in heavy 1-quart saucepan. Heat over medium-low heat until butter is melted. Beat 2 eggs plus 1 egg yolk. Stir some hot sauce into beaten eggs. Stir into lemon mixture; continue cooking until mixture thickens (about 5 minutes), stirring constantly. Cool slightly; refrigerate, covered.

### *Amount: 1⅔ cups.*

Lemon

# NUTCRACKER SWEET

▼

*Double your dessert-eating pleasure with two kinds of nuts in a sensational spice-sparked crust.*

1¼ cups flour
3 tablespoons granulated sugar
⅛ teaspoon ground cinnamon
⅛ teaspoon ground nutmeg
½ cup butter or margarine
1 egg, slightly beaten
2 tablespoons butter or
  margarine
¾ cup light corn syrup
1 teaspoon vanilla

½ cup firmly packed brown
  sugar
1 tablespoon flour
⅛ teaspoon salt
3 eggs, slightly beaten
1 (2-ounce) package pecan
  halves
1 (3½-ounce) jar macadamia
  nuts
– sweetened whipped cream

Heat oven to 350°. In medium bowl, combine flour, granulated sugar, cinnamon and nutmeg. With pastry blender or 2 knives, cut in ½ cup butter until mixture resembles coarse crumbs. Lightly mix in 1 egg with fork until pastry just holds together. Press evenly into bottom and up side of 9-inch tart pan with removable bottom. In 2-quart saucepan, melt 2 tablespoons butter; remove from heat. Beat in corn syrup, vanilla, brown sugar, flour, salt and 3 eggs just until blended. Arrange pecans and macadamia nuts on bottom of crust; carefully pour egg mixture over nuts. Bake until knife inserted 1 inch from edge of pan comes out clean (35 to 40 minutes). Cool on wire rack. Refrigerate, covered.

To Serve: Remove rim from pan. Cut into wedges; top with sweetened whipped cream.

*12 servings.*

# APPLE TORTE

▼

*Simple, but sublime when you're hungry for a fruit dessert that's equally satisfying served warm or chilled.*

1½ cups chopped, peeled apples
¾ cup granulated sugar,
  divided
½ teaspoon ground cinnamon,
  divided
½ cup chopped pecans

1 egg
1 teaspoon baking powder
½ cup flour
6 tablespoons butter, melted
½ pint whipping cream
2 tablespoons powdered sugar

Generously grease 8 or 9-inch pie pan. Heat oven to 325°. Spread apples over bottom of pie pan. Combine ¼ cup of the granulated sugar, ¼ teaspoon of the cinnamon and pecans; sprinkle over apples. Beat egg, remaining ½ cup sugar, baking powder, flour and butter until thoroughly combined. Spread batter over apples. Bake until crust is golden brown (35 to 45 minutes). Whip cream until stiff peaks form; beat in powdered sugar and remaining ¼ teaspoon cinnamon.

To Serve: Cut torte into wedges; top each with a dollop of whipped cream.

*6 servings.*

**Variation:**

**Peach Torte:** Substitute chopped, peeled peaches for apples. Omit cinnamon. Substitute almonds for pecans. Add ¼ teaspoon almond extract to whipped cream.

# CHOCOLATE PECAN PIE

*Pecan pie becomes even more decadent when chocolate chips are added to the luscious, rich filling.*

1 cup light corn syrup
3 eggs
⅓ cup sugar
¼ cup butter, melted
½ teaspoon salt
1 (6-ounce) package semisweet chocolate chips, melted
1 cup coarsely chopped pecans

1 (9-inch) unbaked pie shell
¼ cup semisweet chocolate chips
1 small zipper closure food storage bag
– Whipped Cream Mounds (below)
– Chocolate Decorations (below)

Heat oven to 375°. In large mixing bowl, combine corn syrup, eggs, sugar, butter and salt; beat until blended. Gradually beat in melted chocolate; stir in pecans. Pour into unbaked pie shell. Bake on lowest oven rack until filling is completely puffed across top and crusted over (55 to 60 minutes). Cool.

Pour ¼ cup chocolate chips into food storage bag; seal. Submerge bag in very hot water until chips are melted. Snip off corner of bag, making a tiny hole; drizzle melted chocolate evenly over pie and up onto edge of crust. Refrigerate at least 4 hours.

To Serve: Garnish each pie slice with Whipped Cream Mound and Chocolate Decorations.

### 8 to 10 servings.

**Tip:** To prevent excessive browning on top of pie, cut piece of foil 10 inches long; fold into quarters. Round off outer edge; cut curve in center 3 inches from outer edge. Unfold foil ring and center over edge of pie crust before baking. Remove foil 10 to 15 minutes before end of baking.

**Whipped Cream Mounds:** In small chilled bowl, whip 1 cup whipping cream until soft peaks form; beat in 1 teaspoon vanilla and 2 teaspoons butter brickle schnapps. Gradually beat in ¼ cup powdered sugar until stiff peaks form. Spoon into small zipper closure food storage bag; seal. Snip off corner of bag; pipe into mounds on waxed paper-lined baking sheet. Freeze. Remove mounds; place in freezer storage bag or container. Freeze until needed. Remove from freezer 10 minutes before serving.

## CHOCOLATE DECORATIONS

In small zipper closure freezer storage bag, melt 1 ounce semisweet chocolate and 1 teaspoon shortening. Trace desired design on white paper; place under waxed paper. Snip a tiny hole in corner of bag; trace design with melted chocolate making ⅛ inch wide lines. Refrigerate until firm (at least 30 minutes). Carefully peel waxed paper off design; arrange on dessert.

# CHOCOLATE SATIN PIE

▼

*Enchantingly elegant and invitingly indulgent, this recipe is a winner with rich flavor and creamy texture.*

| | |
|---|---|
| 3 ounces unsweetened chocolate | 1 (9-inch) baked pie shell, cooled |
| ¾ cup butter, softened | ½ pint heavy whipping cream (1 cup) |
| 1 cup sugar | |
| 1½ teaspoons vanilla | 1 tablespoon sugar |
| ¾ cup reduced cholesterol liquid whole eggs | – chocolate curls or chopped nuts |

Melt and cool chocolate. Beat butter and 1 cup sugar until fluffy; blend in chocolate and vanilla. Beat in liquid eggs 5 minutes. Spoon mixture into pie shell. Beat whipping cream until soft peaks form; beat in 1 tablespoon sugar until stiff peaks form. Spread over chocolate; garnish with chocolate curls. Refrigerate at least 4 hours before serving.

*8 servings.*

**Variation:** One (4-ounce) bar bittersweet chocolate can be substituted for unsweetened chocolate.

*Reduced cholesterol liquid whole eggs contain 80% less cholesterol but the same amount of fat as fresh whole eggs.*

# WHITE CHOCOLATE PIE

▼

*A buttery toasted-almond crust is topped with a creative liqueur-laced white chocolate filling.*

| | |
|---|---|
| 3 (2¾-ounce) packages slivered blanched almonds, toasted | 3 tablespoons white chocolate-flavored liqueur |
| 3 tablespoons butter, melted | 1½ teaspoons vanilla |
| 2 tablespoons light corn syrup | ¼ teaspoon almond extract |
| 3⅓ (3-ounce) Swiss white confectionery bars (white chocolate) (10 ounces), broken | 2 tablespoons sugar |
| | ¼ cup hot water |
| | 2 tablespoons meringue powder |
| 3 tablespoons butter | 1¾ cup whipping cream |
| ⅓ cup milk | – sliced toasted almonds or kiwi slices |

Finely chop almonds; stir in butter and corn syrup. Press evenly into well greased 10-inch pie pan. In heavy saucepan over low heat, melt white confectionery bars and butter in milk. Cool thoroughly; stir in liqueur, vanilla and almond extract. Pour into large bowl. Dissolve sugar in water; cool. In small mixer bowl, combine meringue powder and sugar mixture (mixture will appear lumpy); beat until stiff and glossy. Whip cream until stiff peaks form. Gently fold whipped cream and meringue into white chocolate mixture until thoroughly combined. Pour into nut crust. Freeze until firm (about 5 hours).

To Serve: Allow to stand at room temperature 10 to 15 minutes before slicing. Garnish each piece with almonds or kiwi.

*10 servings.*

# TRIPLE CHOCOLATE 'N TOFFEE PIE

*Begin with the convenience of prepared chocolate crumb crust and add layer upon layer of luscious ingredients.*

1 pint chocolate chocolate chip ice cream, softened
1 (8-inch) chocolate crumb pie crust
½ cup chocolate fudge topping
4 (1.4-ounce) original English toffee candy bars, crushed (1 cup), divided
1 pint butter pecan ice cream, softened
– whipped cream (optional)

Spoon softened chocolate ice cream evenly into crust. Spread chocolate topping evenly over ice cream. Sprinkle with ¾ cup of the crushed candy. Spoon softened butter pecan ice cream over candy. Sprinkle with remaining ¼ cup crushed candy. Freeze until firm (3 to 4 hours). Remove from freezer 5 to 10 minutes before serving. Top with whipped cream.

*6 to 8 servings.*

# SOUR CREAM RAISIN PIE

*The popularity of this pie is traced to colonial days when soured cream was common due to lack of refrigeration.*

1½ cups raisins
1 cup water
⅔ cup sugar
2 tablespoons cornstarch
3 tablespoons cold water
3 egg yolks
1 tablespoon margarine or butter
2 teaspoons vanilla
1 (16-ounce) carton sour cream, divided
1 (9-inch) baked pie shell, cooled
1 cup chopped pecans

In heavy saucepan, cook raisins in 1 cup water until plumped. Stir in sugar, cornstarch, 3 tablespoons water, egg yolks, margarine and vanilla. Cook over medium heat, stirring constantly, until mixture comes to a boil; boil and stir 1 minute. Cool 10 minutes. Fold in 1 cup of the sour cream. Pour into pie shell. Carefully spread remaining sour cream over surface of pie; sprinkle with pecans. Refrigerate.

*6 to 8 servings.*

# MEXICAN FIESTA PIE

*Margaritas in unique dessert form provide a creative way to cool-down after a hearty meal or on warm summer evenings. The pretzel crust harmonizes beautifully with the easy-do frozen filling.*

6 tablespoons margarine or butter, melted
3 tablespoons sugar
1¼ cups finely ground pretzels
1 quart vanilla ice milk, softened
½ (10-ounce) can frozen margarita concentrate, thawed
– Lime Twists (page 62)

Heat oven to 350°. Combine margarine, sugar and pretzels; pat into 9-inch glass pie pan, reserving 2 tablespoons of mixture for topping. Bake 10 minutes. Cool. Blend ice milk and 5 ounces of concentrate until thoroughly combined. (Save remaining concentrate for another use.) Spoon into crust; sprinkle with remaining crumbs. Freeze. Garnish with lime slices.

*6 to 8 servings.*

# IRISH CREAM PIE

▼

*This do-ahead features a lighter-than-air marshmallow filling in a chocolate wafer crust.*

¼ cup margarine or butter, melted
2 tablespoons instant Irish cream coffee powder
1 cup chocolate wafer crumbs
3¼ cups miniature marshmallows

¼ cup milk
¼ cup sugar, divided
2 tablespoons whiskey
2 cups whipping cream, divided
– green food color
– Mocha Fudge Sauce (below)

Heat oven to 350°. In small bowl, combine margarine and coffee powder; stir in wafer crumbs. Press in bottom and up side of 9-inch pie pan. Bake until set (8 to 10 minutes); cool.

In 2-quart saucepan, combine marshmallows, milk and 2 tablespoons sugar. Cook over medium-low heat, stirring constantly, until marshmallows are melted. Pour into large bowl; cool completely. Stir in whiskey. In chilled bowl, whip 1½ cups whipping cream until stiff peaks form; fold into marshmallow mixture. Gently fold in food color, a drop at a time until desired color is reached. Pour into cooled crust. In chilled bowl, whip remaining ½ cup whipping cream until stiff peaks form; beat in remaining 2 tablespoons sugar. Spread over marshmallow filling. Refrigerate 4 hours or overnight.

To Serve: Drizzle Mocha Fudge Sauce over pie; pass remaining sauce.

*8 servings.*

# MOCHA FUDGE SAUCE

▼

*This sauce was developed to drizzle over Irish Cream Pie, but it is also delicious over ice cream.*

1 cup firmly packed brown sugar
½ cup light corn syrup
2 tablespoons instant espresso powder

3 ounces unsweetened chocolate, coarsely chopped
½ cup half-and-half
3 tablespoons white chocolate-flavored liqueur

In small heavy saucepan, combine brown sugar, corn syrup and espresso powder. Bring to a boil over medium heat, stirring constantly until sugar is dissolved and mixture is thickened (1 to 2 minutes). Remove from heat; stir in chocolate until melted. Slowly stir in half-and-half; add liqueur. Serve warm or chilled over Irish Cream Pie or ice cream. Store, covered, in refrigerator.

*Amount: 2 cups.*

# FRESH RASPBERRY PIE

▼

*A mid-summer night's dream of a dessert featuring velvety garnet red raspberries.*

4 cups fresh raspberries, divided
⅔ cup water
1 cup sugar
3 tablespoons cornstarch

¼ cup water
2 teaspoons lemon juice
½ cup Crème Fraîche
1 (9-inch) baked pie shell, cooled
– Crème Fraîche

Place 1 cup of the berries and ⅔ cup water in small saucepan. Bring to a boil; reduce heat, simmer 5 minutes. Strain to remove seeds. Combine sugar, cornstarch and ¼ cup water in saucepan; stir in strained raspberry liquid. Cook over low heat, stirring constantly, until mixture boils. Cook and stir 1 minute. Remove from heat, stir in lemon juice. Cool. Spread ½ cup Crème Fraîche evenly in bottom of baked pie shell. Arrange remaining 3 cups berries over Crème Fraîche. Spread raspberry glaze over berries. Refrigerate until firm. Garnish with additional Crème Fraîche.

*6 to 8 servings.*

# PUMPKIN PIE

*Sumptuous when crowned with one of the luscious Pumpkin Pie Toppers.*

| | |
|---|---|
| 3 eggs | ½ teaspoon ground nutmeg |
| 1 (15 to 16-ounce) can pumpkin (1¾ cup) | ¼ teaspoon ground cloves |
| 1 cup firmly packed brown sugar | ¼ teaspoon ground ginger |
| 1 teaspoon ground cinnamon | 1 (12-ounce) can evaporated milk |
| ½ teaspoon salt | 1 (9-inch) unbaked deep dish pastry shell |

Heat oven to 450°. Beat eggs slightly in mixing bowl; blend in pumpkin, brown sugar, cinnamon, salt, nutmeg, cloves, ginger and milk; pour into pastry shell. Bake on lowest oven rack 10 minutes; reduce oven temperature to 350° and continue baking until knife inserted near center comes out clean (about 50 minutes longer). Cool.

*6 servings.*

**Tip:** One and one-quarter cups non-dairy creamer may be substituted for the evaporated milk.

# PUMPKIN PIE TOPPERS

*Nothing plain or ordinary about pumpkin pie when you choose your favorite finishing touch for party perfect presentation.*

**Maple Whipped Cream Topping:** Whip ½ pint heavy whipping cream until stiff peaks form; beat in ¼ cup pure maple syrup. Refrigerate. Spread over cooled pie.

**Sour Cream Topping:** Combine 1 cup sour cream, 2 tablespoons sugar, ½ teaspoon vanilla and ½ teaspoon grated orange peel. Spread evenly over hot baked pie. Refrigerate. Just before serving, sprinkle ⅓ cup toasted sliced almonds in circle around outer edge of pie.

**Spiced Whipped Cream Topping:** Whip ½ pint heavy whipping cream until stiff peaks form; beat in 2 tablespoons powdered sugar, ¼ teaspoon ground cinnamon and ⅛ teaspoon ground nutmeg. Refrigerate. Spread over cooled pie.

**Streusel Topping:** Combine ¼ cup flour, ¼ cup sugar, ½ teaspoon ground cinnamon and ¼ teaspoon ground ginger. Blend in ¼ cup softened margarine or butter. Stir in ⅔ cup chopped pecans. Sprinkle over pie during last 20 to 25 minutes of baking time.

# PECAN CRANBERRY PIE

*Tart cranberries marry well with the sweet pecan filling for a unique fusion of flavors.*

| | |
|---|---|
| 4 eggs, slightly beaten | 1 cup dark corn syrup |
| ⅔ cup sugar | 1 cup coarsely chopped cranberries |
| 2 tablespoons margarine or butter, melted | 1 cup chopped pecans |
| | 1 (9-inch) unbaked pastry shell |

Heat oven to 350°. Beat eggs, sugar, margarine and corn syrup until blended. Stir in cranberries and pecans. Pour into unbaked pastry shell. Cover edge of pie crust with 2-inch strip of foil to prevent excess browning. Bake on lowest oven rack until knife inserted halfway between outer edge and center comes out clean (60 to 70 minutes). Remove foil after baking 45 minutes. Serve warm or refrigerate.

*8 servings.*

# STRAWBERRY RHUBARB TART

▼

*Just a whisper of orange embellishes the popular pairing of garden fresh rhubarb and strawberries for an elegant tart.*

| | |
|---|---|
| 1½ cups flour | 1 tablespoon grated orange peel |
| 1¾ cups granulated sugar, divided | 1 (.25 ounce) envelope unflavored gelatin |
| ¼ cup butter or margarine | 2 tablespoons orange-flavored |
| ¼ cup vegetable oil | liqueur |
| 6 tablespoons cold water, divided | 1 pound fresh strawberries, sliced (2 cups) |
| 1¼ pounds rhubarb, cut into ½-inch pieces (4 cups) | ½ pint heavy whipping cream |
| | 2 tablespoons powdered sugar |

Heat oven to 400°. Combine flour and ¼ cup of the granulated sugar. Cut in butter with pastry blender or 2 knives until mixture resembles coarse crumbs. Stir in oil with a fork until all ingredients are moistened. Stir in 3 tablespoons of the water, 1 at a time, until dough leaves side of bowl and forms a ball. On lightly floured surface, roll out dough to 14-inch circle. Fit into 11-inch tart pan with removable bottom, pressing dough against side of pan without stretching dough; trim dough. Pierce bottom of crust with fork. Line crust with 18-inch piece of foil; fill to rim with dried beans. Bake on lowest oven rack 15 minutes. Remove foil and beans. Bake until crust is golden (8 to 10 minutes longer). Cool.

Combine rhubarb, remaining 1½ cups granulated sugar and orange peel in 2-quart saucepan; cook, stirring occasionally, until rhubarb softens (8 to 10 minutes). Soften gelatin in 3 tablespoons water for 5 minutes. Stir into hot rhubarb mixture until gelatin is dissolved. Stir in liqueur. Refrigerate mixture until chilled (30 to 45 minutes). Pour into baked crust. Arrange strawberries attractively on top of rhubarb. Refrigerate up to 5 hours.

Beat whipping cream until stiff peaks form; beat in powdered sugar. Spoon into pastry bag with star tip. Pipe around edge of tart, leaving center filling exposed. Refrigerate until serving time.

To Serve: Remove rim from pan, leaving tart on bottom of pan. Cut into wedges.

*8 to 10 servings.*

# ALMOND MINI-TARTS

▼

*Golden goodies for an elegant tea table or cookie tray.*

| | |
|---|---|
| ½ (15-ounce) package refrigerated all ready pie crusts | 2 tablespoons whipping cream |
| | ½ cup ground almonds |
| 1 egg | ½ cup sugar |
| | ½ teaspoon almond extract |
| | 1 tablespoon flour |

Let pie crusts stand according to package directions. Unfold onto lightly floured surface. Heat oven to 375°. Cut pastry into 20 circles using 2½-inch fluted cookie cutter, re-rolling as necessary. Gently press circles of dough into 1⅞-inch mini muffin tins, shaping to fit. In mixer bowl, combine remaining ingredients. Spoon 2 teaspoons mixture into each tart shell. Bake until puffed and golden brown (15 to 18 minutes). Cool in pan 5 minutes; remove to wire rack. Cool completely.

*Amount: 20 mini-tarts.*

# FRESH PEACH AND STRAWBERRY TART

▼

*Into a rich crumb-nut tart crust goes a satiny no-bake cream cheese layer—the perfect base for a luscious glazed-fruit topping.*

1 (5¼-ounce) package orange-flavored thin gingersnaps
2 (2.25-ounce) packages natural whole almonds, ground (about 1 cup)
¼ cup margarine or butter, melted
½ cup whipping cream
1 (8-ounce) package cream cheese, softened
½ cup sugar
1 teaspoon vanilla
1 teaspoon grated orange peel
2 peaches, peeled, thinly sliced
2 tablespoons orange juice
½ cup sliced strawberries
⅓ cup peach preserves
1 tablespoon light corn syrup
– Orange Twists (page 62) (optional)

Heat oven to 350°. Crush gingersnaps into fine crumbs; combine with ground almonds and melted margarine. Press mixture into bottom and up side of 11-inch tart pan. Place tart pan on baking sheet; bake until golden brown (about 15 minutes); cool. Beat whipping cream until soft peaks form. In large mixer bowl, beat cream cheese and sugar at medium speed until fluffy; stir in vanilla and orange peel. Fold in whipped cream. Spread evenly into cooled crust. Refrigerate, covered, 2 to 4 hours. Combine peaches and orange juice; drain well. Arrange peaches and strawberries over filling. In small saucepan, combine preserves and corn syrup; heat until melted. Strain. Brush over fresh fruit. Garnish with orange curls. Serve immediately or refrigerate several hours.

*10 to 12 servings.*

strawberry

# LEMON CURD MINI-TARTS

▼

*We've streamlined these tiny tangy morsels using frozen pie crust dough.*

1½ teaspoons grated lemon peel
¼ cup lemon juice
1 cup sugar
½ cup butter or margarine
2 eggs plus 1 egg yolk, well beaten
2 (9-inch) frozen pie crust dough, thawed
– sweetened whipped cream (optional)

Combine lemon peel, lemon juice, sugar and butter in heavy saucepan. Heat over medium-low heat until butter is melted. Stir in eggs, cook over medium-low heat until mixture thickens slightly (10 to 15 minutes). Cool slightly. Refrigerate, covered.

Heat oven to 425°. Roll each pastry round on lightly floured surface to ¼-inch thickness. Cut each round into 8 (2¾-inch) circles. Gently press circles of dough into 1⅞-inch mini-muffin cups, shaping to fit; prick thoroughly. Bake until lightly browned (8 to 10 minutes). Cool 3 to 4 minutes; gently remove from pan. Cool completely.

To Serve: Fill each tart shell with lemon curd; top with a dollop of sweetened whipped cream.

*Amount: 16 mini-tarts.*

# FRUIT TARTS

▼

*Several convenience products make these jewel-tone treats unbelievably easy to prepare.*

1 (15-ounce) package refrigerated all ready pie crusts

1 (8-ounce) package cream cheese, softened

½ cup powdered sugar

2 tablespoons orange-flavored liqueur

1½ pounds fresh strawberries, sliced (3 cups)

½ (⅓-ounce) package clear glaze for fresh fruit tarts or cakes

Heat oven to 425°. Cut each pie crust into 5 circles with 4-inch cookie cutter. Invert muffin pan. Fit each circle over back of muffin cup; press against muffin cup. Prick thoroughly. Bake until golden brown (8 to 10 minutes). Cool; remove from muffin pans. Beat cream cheese, powdered sugar and liqueur until smooth; spoon into tart shells. Arrange berries over filling. Prepare glaze according to package directions. Spoon over tarts. Refrigerate up to 6 hours.

*Amount: 10 tarts.*

**Variations:**

- Substitute 1 (10-ounce) carton Crème Fraîche and ¼ cup powdered sugar for cream cheese and powdered sugar in filling above.
- Substitute 1 (8-ounce) package strawberry, peach, blueberry or raspberry flavored cream cheese, ½ teaspoon almond extract and 2 tablespoons milk for filling. Use corresponding fresh fruit.

# COOKIES, BARS & CONFECTIONS

Cookies and bars just can't be beat for desserts, snacking, lunch boxes, holiday sweet trays and gift-giving. Why? Because everyone loves them! The variety is endless, the preparation simple and speedy, and the eating — well, just wait and see.

Our best bar bonanza includes colorful ribbon selections, mouthwatering fruit and nut-studded squares. Scottish shortbread renditions and major league chocolate-flavored winners. The cookie treasury offers a wealth of all-American and European-inspired recipes.

We encourage you to read through each recipe completely before you begin so you are aware of any steps in the process that may require a little extra time. Sometimes we call for chilling the dough for easier handling, baking in a certain sequence, or allowing time for cooling before continuing. Most of the recipes, however, go from bowl to oven to enjoyment with streamlined efficiency.

We think you will find plenty of inspiration for a forever full cookie jar.

Dear Judy,
Thought you'd
enjoy some of
your favorite
cookies.
Love,
Grandma

# CARAMEL CHOCOLATE THUMBPRINTS

▼

*This sweet-tooth special features streamlined preparation right down to the fuss-free method for drizzling on the melted chocolate chips. A delightful blend of chocolate and caramel makes these a good choice for a special occasion.*

| | |
|---|---|
| ⅔ cup sugar | ¼ teaspoon salt |
| ½ cup butter, softened | ⅔ cup chopped pecans |
| 1 egg, separated | 16 caramels, unwrapped |
| 2 tablespoons milk | 1 tablespoon water |
| 1 teaspoon vanilla | ½ cup semisweet chocolate |
| 1 cup flour | chips |
| ⅓ cup unsweetened cocoa | 1 small zipper closure food |
| | storage bag |

In medium bowl, beat sugar and butter. Beat in egg yolk, milk and vanilla until well combined. Combine flour, cocoa and salt; blend into butter mixture. Divide dough in half. Place each portion of dough on sheet of plastic wrap; shape into a 1 × 8-inch log. Beat egg white until frothy. Brush each log with egg white; roll in pecans to coat evenly. Refrigerate, covered, until firm enough to slice (about 1 hour).

Heat oven to 350°. Slice each log into 16 (½-inch) slices. Arrange slices on ungreased baking sheet about 2 inches apart. Bake until set (10 to 12 minutes). While cookies are baking, place caramels and water in microwavable bowl. Microwave (HIGH) until caramels are melted (1 minute). Stir until completely melted. After removing cookies from oven, immediately press center of each cookie with thumb to make indentation. Immediately spoon ½ teaspoon caramel in center of each cookie.

Carefully remove to wire rack to cool completely. When cookies are cooled, pour ½ cup chocolate chips into food bag; seal. Submerge bag into very hot water until chips are melted. Cut a tiny hole in corner of bag; drizzle melted chocolate evenly over cookies. Store in airtight container. These cookies do not freeze well.

*Amount: 32 cookies.*

# MINNESOTA SNOWBALLS

▼

*Now you can make "snowballs" year-round! Pistachio-sparked cookie balls are rolled in powdered sugar coating.*

| | |
|---|---|
| 1 cup butter, softened | 2½ cups flour |
| ½ cup powdered sugar | ¾ cup lightly salted, shelled |
| ½ teaspoon vanilla | pistachio nuts, finely chopped |
| ¼ teaspoon almond extract | – powdered sugar |

In mixer bowl, beat butter, ½ cup powdered sugar and extracts until fluffy. Stir in flour and nuts. Refrigerate, covered, until firm enough to handle (1 to 2 hours).

Heat oven to 375°. Shape dough into 1-inch balls; place on ungreased baking sheets. Bake until set but not brown (10 to 15 minutes). Cool cookies on wire rack 2 minutes, then carefully roll in powdered sugar. Cool on wire racks. When cool, roll in powdered sugar again. Store in airtight container. These cookies may be frozen.

*Amount: 4 dozen.*

*Caramel Chocolate Thumbprints*
*page 197*

*Hazelnut White Chocolate Chip Cookies*
*page 198*

*Corn Flake Date Cookies*
*page 199*

*Shortbread Heart Cookies*
*page 201*

# HAZELNUT WHITE CHOCOLATE CHIP COOKIES

▼

*Hazelnuts, dates and white chocolate combine to make these distinctively different. In some areas of the country hazelnuts are known as filberts.*

1¾ cups flour
¾ teaspoon baking powder
1 cup firmly packed brown sugar
1 (6.5-ounce) jar chocolaty creamy hazelnut spread (Nutella)
½ cup butter, softened
1 egg

1 teaspoon vanilla
1 (3-ounce) Swiss white confectionery bar (white chocolate), coarsely chopped (about ½ cup)
1 (3-ounce) package coarsely chopped hazelnuts (filberts), roasted, skins removed (about ¾ cup)
½ cup chopped pitted dates

In medium bowl, combine flour and baking powder. In large mixer bowl, beat brown sugar, hazelnut spread and butter until blended. Stir in egg and vanilla. Gradually beat in flour mixture until just blended. Stir in remaining ingredients. Refrigerate, covered, until dough is firm enough to handle (about 30 minutes).

Lightly grease baking sheets. Heat oven to 350°. Using 1⅝-inch diameter cookie dipper, drop dough by tablespoonfuls onto greased baking sheets, leaving 2 inches between cookies. Bake until bottoms of cookies are lightly browned and cookies are set (about 10 minutes). Cool on baking sheets 3 minutes; remove to wire racks to cool. Store in airtight container. These cookies may be frozen.

*Amount: about 3 dozen.*

**Variation:** Substitute semisweet chocolate for white chocolate and omit dates.

**Tip:** To roast hazelnuts (filberts), heat oven to 275°. Spread nuts in single layer in shallow pan. Roast until skins crack (20 to 30 minutes). To remove skins, rub hazelnuts while warm with a rough cloth (some of the skins will remain).

# CHERRY 'N WHITE CHOCOLATE DROPS

▼

*A delicious duo of white chocolate and dried cherries gives these simply made drop cookies blue ribbon status. The chilling step is important for nice shaping and minimal spreading.*

⅔ cup firmly packed brown sugar
⅓ cup butter, softened
1 egg
½ teaspoon cherry extract
1 cup flour

½ teaspoon baking powder
1 (2-ounce) package dried cherries (about ½ cup)
1 (3-ounce) Swiss white confectionery bar (white chocolate), coarsely chopped (about ½ cup)
¼ cup chopped pecans

In large mixer bowl, beat brown sugar and butter. Beat in egg and cherry extract. Combine flour and baking powder; blend into butter mixture. Stir in cherries, white confectionery bar and pecans. Refrigerate dough, covered, until firm enough to dip (about 1 hour).

Grease baking sheets. Heat oven to 375°. Using 1⅝-inch diameter cookie dipper, drop dough by tablespoonfuls onto greased baking sheets, leaving 2 inches between cookies. Bake until cookies are lightly browned and just set (10 to 12 minutes). Let stand on baking sheets 3 minutes; remove to wire racks to cool. Store in airtight container. These cookies may be frozen.

*Amount: about 2 dozen.*

# CHOCOLATE DIPPED BISCOTTI 'N ALMONDS

*With an Italian accent and a crisp rusk-like texture, these almond-infused treats are twice-baked. Rotating baking sheets assures even "toasting" and perfect golden color.*

1¾ cups flour
1 teaspoon baking powder
¼ teaspoon baking soda
¼ teaspoon salt
2 cups sliced almonds, finely chopped
⅔ cup sugar

2 eggs
½ cup vegetable oil
1 teaspoon almond extract
1 teaspoon orange extract
¼ cup flour
½ cup semisweet chocolate chips, melted
1 tablespoon shortening

Grease baking sheet. Heat oven to 350°. In medium bowl, combine 1¾ cups flour, baking powder, baking soda, salt and almonds. In large mixer bowl, beat sugar and eggs at medium speed until thick and pale in color; beat in oil and extracts. At low speed gradually beat in flour mixture. Turn dough out onto lightly floured surface; knead, adding ¼ cup flour to form a soft dough. Shape into two 7½ × 2-inch rolls. Place rolls several inches apart on greased baking sheet. Bake on upper rack of oven until lightly browned and very firm (about 30 minutes).

Remove from oven; cool on baking sheet until just warm (15 minutes). With serrated knife, cut diagonal ½-inch slices by holding roll near the end being sliced and pressing gently on top. Place slices close together on lightly buttered baking sheets. Place oven racks in upper and lower thirds of oven. Toast slices 8 minutes; turn slices. Rotate baking sheets from top to bottom and front to back of oven. Bake until golden brown (6 to 8 minutes). Transfer to wire racks to cool. In small saucepan, melt chocolate chips and shortening over low heat. Dip top only of each biscotti into chocolate; place on wire racks until set. Store in loosely covered container.

*Amount: about 24 slices.*

# CORN FLAKE DATE COOKIES

*Breakfast cereal is transformed into a delightful drop cookie. We don't recommend freezing, but don't worry, they will disappear before you know it.*

1 cup margarine or butter, softened
¾ cup firmly packed brown sugar
¼ cup granulated sugar
2 eggs
2 tablespoons milk

1 teaspoon vanilla
2 cups flour
1 teaspoon baking soda
½ teaspoon salt
1 cup chopped walnuts
1 cup chopped dates
2⅔ cups corn flakes

Grease baking sheets. Heat oven to 350°. In mixer bowl, beat margarine and sugars until fluffy. Beat in eggs, milk and vanilla. Combine flour, baking soda and salt; stir into sugar mixture. Stir in walnuts, dates and corn flakes. Drop by level tablespoonfuls 2 inches apart onto greased baking sheets. Bake until lightly browned (8 to 10 minutes). Cool cookies on baking sheets 2 minutes. Remove to wire racks to cool. Store in loosely covered container. These cookies do not freeze well.

*Amount: about 5 dozen.*

# CHOCOLATE 'N CRANBERRY COOKIES

*The use of dried rather than fresh cranberries makes these a year-round cookie jar favorite. They flatten a bit during baking and develop an appealing glossy top.*

2 (4-ounce) semisweet chocolate bars, coarsely chopped
2 tablespoons butter
½ cup flour
¼ teaspoon baking powder
¾ cup firmly packed brown sugar
2 eggs
¼ teaspoon almond extract
1 (2½-ounce) package dried cranberries, coarsely chopped (about ¾ cup)
⅓ cup vanilla milk chips

Melt chocolate and butter together; stir until smooth. Set aside until cool. In medium bowl, combine flour and baking powder; set aside. In large mixer bowl, beat sugar and eggs until fluffy. Gradually beat in chocolate mixture. Stir in almond extract and flour mixture. Fold in cranberries and vanilla milk chips. Refrigerate, covered, until firm enough to shape into balls (about 1 hour).

Lightly grease baking sheets. Heat oven to 350°. Using small (1¼-inch diameter) cookie dipper, scoop dough and roll into 1-inch balls. Arrange on greased baking sheets. Bake until cookies are just set (about 10 minutes). Let stand on baking sheets 3 minutes; remove to wire racks to cool. Store in airtight container. These cookies may be frozen.

*Amount: about 4 dozen.*

# BANANA OATMEAL COOKIES

*This is the kind of soft banana-flavored drop cookie you remember from Grandmother's fragrant kitchen. Its moist texture keeps it from crumbling in the lunch box.*

¾ cup margarine or butter, softened
¾ cup granulated sugar
¼ cup firmly packed brown sugar
1 egg
1 cup ripe mashed banana (about 3 bananas)
2 cups uncooked quick-cooking rolled oats
1½ cups flour
1 teaspoon ground cinnamon
½ teaspoon baking soda
½ teaspoon salt
¼ teaspoon ground nutmeg
½ cup milk chocolate chips or raisins

Grease baking sheets. Heat oven to 375°. In mixer bowl, beat margarine and sugars until fluffy. Beat in egg and banana. Combine dry ingredients; blend in. Fold in chocolate chips. Drop by teaspoonfuls onto greased baking sheets. Bake until lightly browned and no imprint remains when touched (10 to 12 minutes). Remove to wire racks to cool. These cookies may be frozen.

*Amount: 5 dozen.*

Banana

# SHORTBREAD HEART COOKIES

▼

*Decorative pearl sugar doesn't melt during baking and offers an attractive pearly white, opaque topping. A perfect cookie for Valentine's Day, showers, weddings, teas or even the holidays.*

| | |
|---|---|
| 1½ cups butter, softened | 1 teaspoon vanilla |
| 1 cup firmly packed brown sugar | 3 cups flour |
| | ½ teaspoon salt |
| | – pearl sugar |

In mixer bowl, beat butter, brown sugar and vanilla until light and fluffy. Stir in flour and salt just until blended. Form dough into 4 balls; refrigerate, covered, 1 to 2 hours.

Heat oven to 325°. On lightly floured surface, roll one ball of dough at a time to ⅜-inch thickness. Cut with 2-inch heart-shaped cookie cutter. Arrange on ungreased baking sheets. Sprinkle tops with pearl sugar. Bake until cookies are set and lightly browned (15 to 19 minutes). Remove to wire rack to cool. Store in loosely covered container. These cookies may be frozen.

*Amount: 4 dozen.*

# CHERRY JEWELS

▼

*Old-fashioned refrigerator cookies sparkle with red and green cherry "jewels" for party-perfect presentation. Ideal with a refreshing fruit sorbet after a hearty holiday meal.*

| | |
|---|---|
| 1 cup butter, softened | ¼ teaspoon cream of tartar |
| 1 cup powdered sugar | ½ cup chopped pecans |
| 1 egg | ¾ cup red candied cherries |
| 2¼ cups flour | ¾ cup green candied cherries |

In mixer bowl, beat butter, sugar and egg until fluffy. Combine flour and cream of tartar. Stir flour mixture and pecans into sugar mixture. Divide dough in half; stir red cherries into one half and green cherries into other half. Refrigerate dough until firm enough to shape (about 1 hour). Shape each half into a roll 1½ inches in diameter; wrap in plastic wrap. Refrigerate until firm enough to slice (4 or more hours).

Heat oven to 375°. Cut rolls into ¼-inch slices. Arrange 1 inch apart on ungreased baking sheets. Bake until set but not brown (6 to 7 minutes). Remove immediately to wire racks to cool. Store in loosely covered container. These cookies may be frozen.

*Amount: 7½ dozen.*

# ITALIAN ALMOND DROPS

▼

*These porous, almond-laced cookies require a two-hour standing time before baking. This gives them their traditional consistency...a crisp exterior and a chewy interior. American-style macaroons usually contain coconut, whereas European versions like this one feature ground almonds.*

| | |
|---|---|
| 2 egg whites | ¼ teaspoon salt |
| 1 cup ground blanched almonds | ½ teaspoon almond extract |
| | – powdered sugar |
| 1 cup granulated sugar | – pearl sugar |

Grease well and flour baking sheets. In mixer bowl, beat egg whites until stiff peaks form. Combine almonds, granulated sugar and salt; fold into egg whites. Fold in extract. Drop by teaspoonfuls onto greased and floured baking sheets. Sprinkle with powdered sugar and pearl sugar. Let stand 2 hours before baking.

Heat oven to 300°. Bake until lightly browned (15 to 20 minutes). Remove immediately to wire racks to cool. Store in a loosely covered container. These cookies may be frozen.

*Amount: 3 dozen.*

# FRENCH NEAPOLITANS

▼

*Preparation begins a day ahead of baking with the chilling of colorful dough ribbons. Each layer has its own delicious flavoring in the finest French tradition. A stellar addition to your most festive cookie tray.*

| | |
|---|---|
| 1 cup margarine or butter, softened | ¼ teaspoon salt |
| 1½ cups sugar | 2 tablespoons poppy seed |
| 1 egg | ¼ cup chopped nuts |
| 1 teaspoon vanilla | 1 ounce unsweetened |
| 2½ cups flour | chocolate, melted |
| 1½ teaspoons baking powder | ¼ cup chopped maraschino cherries, drained |
| | 2-3 drops red food color |

In mixer bowl, beat margarine, sugar, egg and vanilla until fluffy. Stir in flour, baking powder and salt. Divide dough into 3 equal parts. Add poppy seed to 1 part, nuts and melted chocolate to 1 part, and cherries and a few drops of food color to 1 part. Refrigerate parts separately until firm enough to roll out. Roll each part into 5 × 9-inch rectangle on lightly floured surface. On large piece of foil, stack dough in layers with chocolate in middle. Wrap and refrigerate 8 hours or overnight.

Heat oven to 375°. Cut dough lengthwise into 3 strips. Cut strips crosswise into ⅛-inch slices; place on ungreased baking sheets. Bake until lightly browned (8 to 10 minutes). Remove to wire racks to cool. Store in loosely covered container. These cookies may be frozen.

*Amount: 8 to 9 dozen.*

## Short-Term Cookie Storage

- Cool completely.

- Store soft cookies in a tightly-covered container. If they lose their softness, wrap a wedge of raw apple or a slice of bread in waxed paper and store it with the cookies. Remove after twenty-four hours.

- Store crisp cookies in a container with a loose-fitting lid. If cookies soften, recrisp by heating them in a preheated 300° oven for 3-5 minutes.

- Bar cookies can be stored in their baking pan covered lightly with aluminum foil or plastic wrap.

- It is best to store each flavor of cookie separately.

- Cookies with cream cheese or yogurt frosting must be covered and refrigerated.

- Most types of cookies can be stored at room temperature 3 to 7 days, depending on the type of cookie.

## Long-Term Cookie Storage

- Cool completely.

- Place in freezer container, freezer-weight plastic storage bags or heavy-duty aluminum foil. Separate cookie layers with foil or plastic wrap.

- Freeze for up to 6 months.

- Cookies are best stored unfrosted. To freeze frosted cookies, arrange on tray. Freeze, uncovered, until firm. Wrap, label and freeze. They may be stored for up to 3 months.

- Thaw frozen cookies, loosely covered, 10-20 minutes at room temperature.

# PUFF PASTRY TWISTS

*Here's a deluxe do-ahead where gourmet ingredients give gourmet results. If you plan to freeze these twists, do so before baking them. Otherwise, serve them the same day they are baked for optimum enjoyment.*

½ (7-ounce) roll almond paste
¼ cup sugar
1 egg
1½ teaspoons almond extract

1 (17½-ounce) package frozen puff pastry, thawed according to package directions
– Icing (below)
1 (2¼-ounce) package sliced almonds (¾ cup) toasted, coarsely chopped

In small mixer bowl, beat almond paste and sugar until blended. Beat in egg and almond extract; refrigerate, covered.

Heat oven to 375°. Unfold 1 sheet of pastry on floured pastry cloth; roll into 14-inch square. Repeat with second sheet. Spread almond paste mixture evenly over 1 sheet. Carefully arrange second sheet over filling. (Can be done easily by rolling top sheet around a rolling pin and unrolling over filling.) Using fluted pastry wheel or pizza cutter, cut dough into 14 (1-inch) strips; cut each strip crosswise into quarters. Twist each piece twice; arrange on ungreased baking sheets.* Bake until golden brown (10 to 12 minutes). Remove to wire rack placed over waxed paper. Prepare Icing and drizzle over twists; sprinkle with toasted almonds. Serve slightly warm or at room temperature on same day baked.

*Amount: 56 twists.*

**Icing:** In small bowl, combine 1 cup sifted powdered sugar, ⅛ teaspoon almond extract and 1 to 2 tablespoons milk to make icing of drizzling consistency.

**Tip:** *At this point, twists can be frozen. When frozen, carefully transfer to moisture and vaporproof freezer container. Seal, label, and freeze up to 3 months. When ready to bake, heat oven to 375°. Arrange frozen twists on ungreased baking sheets; bake until golden brown (11 to 14 minutes). Top with icing and almonds.

## Cookie Baking Tips:

- Use a shiny, heavy-gauge aluminum cookie sheet that is flat, and has only one edge.

- Cookie sheets should be 2 inches narrower and shorter than the oven cavity for good heat circulation.

- Cookies should be of the same size and thickness for uniform baking. Space them evenly on the sheet.

- Check cookies for doneness at the minimum baking time given.

- For evenly browned cookies, bake one sheet at a time in the center of the oven. If baking two sheets at a time, place one above the other. Halfway through baking time, rotate sheets top to bottom and front to back.

- Remove cookies from the baking sheet immediately upon removal from the oven, unless the recipe says to cool them on the baking sheet for a specified length of time.

- Remove cookies with wide spatula to prevent breakage.

- When trying a new recipe, it is helpful to experiment by baking one test cookie.

- Always bake cookies on cool baking sheets.

# CHUNKY CHOCOLATE 'N NUT BARS

▼

*This double chocolate delight is a moist, dense and chewy bar that travels well.*

¾ cup margarine or butter,
   softened
2⅓ cups firmly packed brown
   sugar
3 eggs
1 teaspoon vanilla
2¾ cups flour
2½ teaspoons baking powder

½ teaspoon salt
1 (3-ounce) Swiss white
   confectionery bar (white
   chocolate), coarsely chopped
1 (3-ounce) Swiss bittersweet
   chocolate bar, coarsely
   chopped
1 cup chopped pecans

Grease 9 × 13-inch baking pan. Heat oven to 350°. Beat margarine, brown sugar, eggs and vanilla until fluffy. Stir in dry ingredients, chocolate pieces and nuts. Spread in greased pan. Bake until edges are browned and center is set (30 to 35 minutes.) Cool. Cut into bars.

*Amount: 4 dozen (1 × 2-inch) bars.*

# NUTTY CHOCOLATE AND COCONUT SQUARES

▼

*A busy-day bar with on-the-double microwave preparation. Avoid over-cooked corners by shielding them with small pieces of foil, as directed.*

½ cup firmly packed brown
   sugar
½ cup margarine or butter,
   softened
1 cup flour
¼ teaspoon ground cinnamon
2 eggs

2 (2-ounce) packages chopped
   pecans (1 cup)
1 (6-ounce) package semisweet
   chocolate chips
1 cup shredded coconut
½ cup firmly packed brown
   sugar
2 tablespoons flour
1 teaspoon vanilla

In medium bowl, beat ½ cup brown sugar and margarine. Stir in 1 cup flour and cinnamon. Press mixture evenly in 8 × 8-inch glass baking dish. Shield top corners of dish with small triangles of foil. Microwave (HIGH) 2 minutes; rotate dish ¼ turn. Microwave (HIGH) until crust browns and looks mostly dry (1 to 2 minutes). Beat eggs; stir in remaining ingredients. Spread egg mixture evenly over crust. Reshield corners. Microwave (HIGH) 3 minutes. Remove foil; rotate dish ¼ turn. Microwave (HIGH) until topping is set and looks mostly dry (about 2 minutes). Cool completely on flat heatproof surface. Cut into squares.

*Amount: 3 dozen (1½-inch) squares.*

**Chocolate Choices**

- **Unsweetened Chocolate:** This chocolate is pure chocolate liquor with no sugar added. Chocolate liquor contains no alcohol; it is the liquid remaining after the cocoa beans have been roasted, shelled and ground. Unsweetened chocolate is sometimes called baking or bitter chocolate.

- **Semisweet or Bittersweet:** These contain chocolate liquor and varying amounts of cocoa butter, sugar and vanilla. These chocolates can often be interchanged in recipes.

- **Milk Chocolate:** This is semisweet chocolate with dried or condensed milk added.

- **White Chocolate:** This chocolate does not contain chocolate liquor and, therefore, is not really chocolate. It is a mixture of cocoa butter, sugar, milk solids and vanilla.

- **Cocoa Powder:** This is chocolate liquor which has had most of the cocoa butter removed and which has been ground into a powder. Dutch process cocoa has a stronger flavor and color because it has been treated with an alkali, which helps neutralize the natural acidity of cocoa.

# CHOCOLATE CHEESECAKE BARS

*When you're cooking for a crowd, choose these easy, elegant marbled bars. Watch the baking time carefully to keep the texture marvelously moist. Refrigerate leftovers.*

| | |
|---|---|
| 1½ ounces unsweetened chocolate | 2 eggs |
| ½ cup margarine or butter | ½ cup reduced fat sour cream |
| ¾ cup water | 1 (8-ounce) package reduced-fat cream cheese, softened |
| 2 cups flour | ⅓ cup granulated sugar |
| 1½ cups firmly packed brown sugar | 1 egg, slightly beaten |
| 1 teaspoon baking soda | 1 tablespoon vanilla |
| ½ teaspoon salt | 1 (6-ounce) package semisweet chocolate chips |

In small saucepan, combine unsweetened chocolate, margarine and water; bring to a boil. Remove from heat, stir until chocolate is melted; cool.

Grease and flour 10 × 15-inch jelly roll pan. Heat oven to 375°. In mixer bowl, combine flour, brown sugar, baking soda and salt; blend in 2 eggs and sour cream. Blend in chocolate mixture until smooth. Combine cream cheese, granulated sugar, 1 egg and vanilla until smooth. Spread chocolate batter evenly in prepared pan. Drop cream cheese mixture by tablespoonfuls randomly over chocolate batter. With knife, cut through batter in wide zigzag pattern to create a marbled effect. Sprinkle with chocolate chips. Bake until wooden pick inserted in center comes out clean (about 25 minutes). Cool on wire rack. Store, covered, in refrigerator. These bars may be frozen.

*Amount: 50 (1½ × 2-inch) bars.*

# ROCKY ROAD BROWNIES

*Kids of all ages find these double-chocolate brownies irresistible. Big-batch results make them a hit for potlucks, large parties, teen gatherings and as a totable treat to reward the winning team.*

| | |
|---|---|
| 1 (12-ounce) package semisweet chocolate chips | ½ teaspoon salt |
| 1 cup margarine or butter | 1 teaspoon vanilla |
| 4 eggs | 3 cups miniature marshmallows |
| 2 cups sugar | 1 (6-ounce) package chopped pecans (1½ cups) |
| 3 cups flour | 1 (6-ounce) package semisweet chocolate chips |
| 1 teaspoon baking powder | |

Grease 9 × 13-inch baking pan. Melt 12-ounce package chocolate chips and margarine in medium saucepan over medium-low heat, stirring occasionally; cool.

Heat oven to 375°. In mixer bowl, beat chocolate mixture, eggs and sugar. Blend in flour, baking powder, salt and vanilla. Spoon evenly into greased pan. Bake 25 minutes. Remove from oven; sprinkle with marshmallows, pecans and 6-ounce package chocolate chips. Bake until golden brown (15 to 25 minutes longer). Cool. Cut with knife dipped in warm water. These bars do not freeze well.

*Amount: 4 dozen (1½-inch) squares.*

# DOUBLE CHOCOLATE BARS

*A beauty of a bar with a lush, marbled interior, nuggets of pistachios and a white chocolate glaze. For picture-perfect presentation, wait until the glaze has set before cutting.*

¾ cup butter, softened
1¼ cups sugar
4 eggs
1½ teaspoons vanilla
½ teaspoon salt
1 cup flour
½ (4-ounce) semisweet
    chocolate bar, melted,
    cooled

2 tablespoons chocolate-
    flavored liqueur
1 (3-ounce) Swiss white
    confectionery bar (white
    chocolate), melted, cooled
¾ cup chopped pistachio nuts
⅓ cup chopped pistachio nuts
– White Chocolate Glaze (below)

Grease 9 × 13-inch baking pan. Heat oven to 350°. In mixer bowl, beat butter and sugar until fluffy. Beat in eggs, one at a time, beating well after each addition. Stir in vanilla, salt and flour until just blended. Remove 1 cup batter to medium bowl; stir in semisweet chocolate and liqueur. Set aside. Stir white confectionery bar and ¾ cup pistachios into remaining batter; spoon evenly into greased pan and smooth surface. Drop heaping tablespoonfuls of dark batter onto light batter in 9 to 12 random places. With knife, cut through batter in wide zigzag pattern to create a marbled effect; smooth top. Sprinkle with ⅓ cup pistachios. Bake on lowest oven rack until wooden pick inserted in center comes out clean (about 20 minutes). Cool completely. Prepare glaze. Immediately drizzle over bars. Refrigerate until glaze is set (about 30 minutes). Cut into bars. These bars do not freeze well.

### Amount: 32 (1⅝ × 2¼-inch) bars.

**White Chocolate Glaze:** Combine 1 (3-ounce) Swiss white confectionery bar (white chocolate) and 1 teaspoon vegetable oil; melt over low heat until smooth, stirring often.

## Cookies To Go:

- Select good travelers like unfrosted drop cookies, fruit cookies and bars. We do not recommend shipping frosted or very tender, fragile cookies.

- Wrap soft and crisp cookies separately.

- Place the heaviest cookies in the bottom of the container.

- Choose a sturdy unbreakable container with a tight-fitting lid. Line it with foil, waxed paper, or plastic wrap. Cookie tins or coffee cans with tight-fitting lids are excellent for mailing. Create a thick cushion on the bottom, using crumpled wax paper, foil or paper toweling.

- Wrap cookies individually, in pairs or in groups of four, using plastic wrap or foil. Arrange cookies back to back with wax paper between each. Pack into container as tightly as possible without crushing. Fill spaces with crumpled wax paper, foil or paper toweling. Seal with tape. Do not use popcorn as "filler."

- Place cookie container inside a sturdy packing box. Surround with bubble wrap, foam packing pieces, crumpled newspaper or shredded paper. Seal box with strapping tape.

- Label box clearly. Cover address with transparent tape to protect it from moisture. Mark package "Perishable." Consult the post office for the best method of mailing.

# APRICOT OATMEAL BARS

▼

*Showcase your favorite preserves in these versatile bars. For variety, substitute equal amounts of other compatible nuts and preserves like cherry and almonds or raspberry and walnuts.*

| | |
|---|---|
| 1¼ cups flour | ½ teaspoon baking soda |
| 1¼ cups uncooked rolled oats | ¼ teaspoon salt |
| ¾ cup margarine or butter, melted | 1 (10-ounce) jar apricot preserves |
| ½ cup sugar | ½ cup shredded coconut |
| 2 teaspoons brandy extract | ¼ cup chopped pecans |

Grease 9 × 13-inch baking pan. Heat oven to 350°. In large bowl, combine flour, oats, margarine, sugar, brandy extract, baking soda and salt; mix until crumbly. Reserve about ¾ cup mixture; press remaining mixture in greased pan. Spread preserves evenly over crust, leaving ½-inch around edges; sprinkle with coconut, pecans and reserved crumbs. Bake until edges are lightly browned (20 to 25 minutes). Cool completely. Cut into bars. These bars may be frozen.

*Amount: 3 dozen (1½ × 2-inch) bars.*

**Variation:** One cup of your favorite preserves and/or ¼ cup any nuts may be substituted for apricots and pecans.

# CRANBERRY-DATE CRUMB BARS

▼

*No water addition is necessary during cranberry cooking step. You'll still get a rich, thick filling to layer with the oat mixture. A complementary fresh orange glaze is the final festive touch for these unique two-tone bars.*

| | |
|---|---|
| 1 (12-ounce) package cranberries | 1¼ cups firmly packed brown sugar |
| 1 (8-ounce) package chopped dates | ½ teaspoon baking soda |
| 1 teaspoon vanilla | ¼ teaspoon salt |
| 2 cups flour | 1 cup margarine or butter, melted |
| 1½ cups uncooked rolled oats | 1½ cups sifted powdered sugar |
| ½ cup uncooked oat bran cereal or wheat germ | ½ teaspoon vanilla |
| | ½ teaspoon grated orange peel |
| | 1 to 2 tablespoons orange juice |

In 2-quart saucepan, combine cranberries and dates. Cook, covered, over low heat until cranberries pop (10 to 15 minutes), stirring frequently. Stir in vanilla.

Heat oven to 350°. In large bowl, combine flour, oats, bran, brown sugar, baking soda and salt. Stir in margarine until blended. Pat a generous half of oat mixture in ungreased 9 × 13-inch baking pan. Bake 8 minutes. Remove from oven. Spread cranberry mixture evenly over baked mixture. Sprinkle remaining oat mixture over filling; pat gently. Bake until golden brown (20 to 22 minutes longer). Cool. Combine powdered sugar, vanilla, orange peel and enough orange juice for desired drizzling consistency. Drizzle over topping. Cut into bars. Store in airtight container. These bars do not freeze well.

*Amount: 4 dozen (1 × 2-inch) bars.*

• Twelve ounces of fresh cranberries equal three cups.

• Cranberries can be stored for up to one month in the refrigerator.

• Cranberries can be frozen. Do not prewash the cranberries. Freeze them in the original, unopened package and wrap that package in foil or place it in a freezer food storage bag. They can be frozen up to nine months. When using frozen cranberries, do not thaw them.

# SHORTBREAD...TRADITIONAL

▼

*Of all the shortbread recipes we tested, this was the favorite and most like the superior-quality imported variety. Butter is essential for the classic rich flavor. Rice flour contributes to the traditional texture of this shortbread.*

| | |
|---|---|
| 1 cup butter, softened | ¼ cup granulated sugar |
| ¼ cup firmly packed brown sugar | 1 teaspoon vanilla |
| | ⅓ cup white rice flour |
| | 1⅔ cups flour |

Butter 9 × 9-inch baking pan. Heat oven to 325°. In large bowl, beat butter, sugars and vanilla until light and fluffy. Combine rice flour and flour; stir into butter mixture just until smooth and no longer crumbly. Press dough evenly into buttered pan. Bake until golden brown and somewhat springy to the touch (45 to 50 minutes). Cool in pan on wire rack until slightly warm. Cut into bars. Remove from pan when completely cool. These bars may be frozen.

*Amount: 2 dozen (1 × 3-inch) bars.*

# THREE LAYER RIBBON SQUARES

▼

*Decidedly special-occasion fare, these rich, ribbon bars are glazed with chocolate after a two-step baking process. A homemade almond paste assures peak flavor and a luscious layer of preserves promotes moistness.*

| | |
|---|---|
| ⅓ cup margarine or butter, softened | ⅔ cup blanched almonds, ground |
| ½ cup sugar | ⅔ cup sugar |
| 1 egg, separated | ¼ teaspoon salt |
| 1 tablespoon milk | 1 egg |
| 1 cup flour | ½ teaspoon almond extract |
| ½ teaspoon baking powder | 2 to 3 drops green food color |
| ¼ cup apricot or peach preserves | – Chocolate Glaze (below) |

Grease 8 × 8-inch baking pan. Heat oven to 375°. In mixer bowl, beat margarine, ½ cup sugar, egg yolk and milk until fluffy. Combine flour and baking powder; stir into sugar mixture. Spread dough evenly in greased pan; press firmly with floured fingers. Bake until lightly browned (12 to 15 minutes). Remove from oven; spread preserves over hot crust. Combine ground almonds, ⅔ cup sugar, salt, egg, reserved egg white, almond extract and green food color. Pour filling over preserve layer; spread evenly. Bake until golden brown and top springs back slightly when pressed with fingertips (about 25 minutes longer). Cool.

Prepare Chocolate Glaze; spread over squares. Let stand at least 1 hour before cutting into squares. These squares do not freeze well.

*Amount: 3 dozen (1¼-inch) squares.*

**Chocolate Glaze:** Melt ½ ounce unsweetened chocolate and 1 tablespoon margarine or butter in small heavy saucepan. Stir in ½ cup powdered sugar, ½ teaspoon almond extract and 1½ tablespoons boiling water until smooth.

# WALNUT-BERRY SQUARES

▼

*Reminiscent of old-world delicacies, these rich squares feature a very generous addition of ground walnuts, a layer of strawberry preserves and a walnut-accented glaze.*

| | |
|---|---|
| 2 cups flour | 5 cups ground walnuts |
| ½ cup sugar | 1½ cups sugar |
| ⅛ teaspoon salt | 2 eggs |
| 1 cup margarine or butter | 1 tablespoon vanilla |
| 1 cup strawberry jam | 1 teaspoon salt |
| | – Glaze (below) |

Heat oven to 350°. In medium bowl, combine flour, ½ cup sugar and salt. Cut in margarine with pastry blender until mixture resembles coarse crumbs. Press dough evenly in ungreased 10 × 15-inch jelly roll pan. Bake until lightly browned (about 15 minutes). Remove from oven; cool slightly. Spread jam evenly over crust to within ½ inch of edges. In medium bowl, combine remaining ingredients except Glaze; spread evenly over jam. Bake until lightly browned and center is set (about 25 minutes longer). Cool. Prepare Glaze; drizzle over topping. Cut into squares. These squares do not freeze well.

*Amount: 8 dozen (1¼-inch) squares.*

**Glaze:** In small bowl, combine ½ cup sifted powdered sugar, 1 tablespoon melted butter, 1 tablespoon milk and ½ teaspoon black walnut extract. Beat until smooth.

# ALMOND BUTTER BARS

▼

*A shortbread-like layer is enhanced with a scene-stealing brown sugar-almond topping. A superb, delicately-flavored bar for all occasions.*

| | |
|---|---|
| ½ cup butter or margarine, softened | ½ cup firmly packed brown sugar |
| ½ cup powdered sugar | ¾ teaspoon lemon juice |
| 1 cup flour | 1 tablespoon water |
| 3 tablespoons butter or margarine | ¾ cup sliced almonds |
| | ½ teaspoon almond extract |

Heat oven to 350°. Beat ½ cup butter and powdered sugar until fluffy; beat in flour. Press evenly in ungreased 9 × 9-inch baking pan. Bake until lightly browned (12 to 15 minutes); remove from oven. In small saucepan, melt 3 tablespoons butter; stir in brown sugar, lemon juice and water. Bring to a boil, stirring constantly. Remove from heat; stir in almonds and almond extract. Spread evenly over crust. Bake until bubbly in center (10 to 15 minutes longer). Cool slightly; cut into bars. Cool completely. These bars may be frozen.

*Amount: 2 dozen (1½ × 2¼-inch) bars.*

**Almond Selection:**

**Natural almonds,** which can be purchased whole or sliced, have their shells removed but retain their paper-thin brown skins. Some brands refer to the sliced natural almonds as "almond slices" and others refer to them as "sliced almonds." They are the same, each with a thin band of skin which many chefs find more attractive than their skinless counterparts.

**Blanched almonds,** available whole, sliced, slivered, ground, in paste and roasted, have both shells and skins removed. They are appropriate when the flavor and texture of almonds is desired without the brown-colored skin.

# CHERRY BARS

▼

*A favorite flavor combo...chocolate and cherry...team with popular peanut butter for a bountiful batch of sweet treats. Take care to spread each layer evenly for a pretty presentation.*

¾ cup margarine or butter,
  softened
¾ cup powdered sugar
1 tablespoon milk
1½ cups flour
½ teaspoon baking powder
2 cups granulated sugar
⅔ cup evaporated milk
⅛ teaspoon salt
12 large marshmallows

½ cup margarine or butter
½ (12-ounce) package cherry
  chips (1 cup)
¼ teaspoon almond extract
1 (12-ounce) package
  semisweet chocolate chips
¾ cup peanut butter
1 (3½-ounce) package
  blanched salted peanuts,
  finely chopped

Heat oven to 325°. Combine ¾ cup margarine, powdered sugar, milk, flour and baking powder; press evenly in ungreased 9 × 13-inch baking pan. Bake until lightly browned (25 to 30 minutes); cool. In heavy saucepan, combine granulated sugar, evaporated milk, salt, marshmallows and ½ cup margarine. Bring to a boil; cook 5 minutes over low heat, stirring constantly. Remove from heat; add cherry chips and almond extract; stir until chips are melted. Pour mixture evenly over crust. In heavy saucepan, melt chocolate chips and peanut butter over low heat, stirring constantly. Spread evenly over cherry layer. Sprinkle with peanuts. Refrigerate, covered, until firm. Cut into squares. Store, covered, in refrigerator.

*Amount: about 9 dozen (1-inch) squares.*

# FRUITCAKE BARS

▼

*Jewel-toned candied fruits, brandy and oodles of pecans add up to a moist, company-best bar for holiday enjoyment. These are good "keepers" when properly stored in an airtight container.*

½ pound red candied cherries,
  halved (1½ cups)
½ pound green candied
  cherries, halved (1½ cups)
¼ cup brandy or rum
1 (8-ounce) package chopped
  dates

2½ cups pecan halves
1 cup flour
1 cup powdered sugar
1 teaspoon baking powder
¼ teaspoon salt
4 eggs, well-beaten
– Glaze (below)

Combine red and green cherries and brandy in large bowl; let stand 30 minutes. Add dates and pecans.

Thoroughly grease 10 × 15-inch jelly roll pan or two 9 × 9-inch baking pans. Heat oven to 350°. Combine flour, powdered sugar, baking powder, and salt; stir into fruit. Blend in eggs. Press batter evenly in well-greased pan. Bake until wooden pick inserted in center comes out clean (about 30 minutes in jelly roll pan; about 40 minutes in 9 × 9-inch pans). Prepare Glaze; spread evenly over bars while still warm. Cut into bars; remove to wire racks to cool thoroughly. Store in airtight container.

*Amount: 50 (1½ × 2-inch) bars.*

**Glaze:** Heat ¼ cup light corn syrup and 1 tablespoon water to a rolling boil; remove from heat and stir in 1 tablespoon brandy or rum. Cool slightly.

# CHOCOLATE TRUFFLES

▼

*A little extra attention produces spectacular results. Chilling the chocolate mixture makes it easy to handle, and the sophisticated variations offer high style. These make an enchanting hostess gift.*

| | |
|---|---|
| ½ cup whipping cream | – chopped pecans |
| ¼ cup unsalted butter | – semisweet chocolate or Swiss |
| 2 (4-ounce) semisweet | white confectionery bar |
| chocolate bars, broken into | (white chocolate) |
| small pieces | 30-36 petit four cases |

In heavy saucepan, bring cream and butter just to a boil over medium heat. Remove from heat; stir in chocolate until smooth. Refrigerate, uncovered, until fairly firm (1½ to 2 hours), stirring 2 to 3 times. While chocolate mixture is chilling, process pecans and/or chocolate in food processor or blender until finely chopped. Pour into saucers, set aside. To make truffles, scoop chocolate out of pan with small melon baller or measuring teaspoon; shape quickly into round ball. Shape 3 or 4 truffles, then roll in pecans or chocolate. Place on waxed paper-lined baking sheet. Refrigerate until firm. Place in airtight container; store, covered, in refrigerator. To Serve: Place truffles in petit four cases.

*Amount: 2½ to 3 dozen candies.*

**Variations:**

**Chocolate Coffee Truffles:** Omit chopped pecans and semisweet chocolate or Swiss white confectionery bar (white chocolate) for rolling. After stirring in chocolate until smooth; stir in ½ cup ground pecans. Refrigerate as above. Combine ¼ cup powdered sugar, 2 tablespoons unsweetened cocoa and 1 tablespoon instant coffee granules. Sift through fine mesh sieve. Shape truffles as above; roll in powdered sugar mixture. Store as above.

**Liqueur Truffles:** Omit unsalted butter. After stirring chocolate mixture until smooth, stir in ¼ cup liqueur of your choice. Refrigerate until fairly firm (45 to 60 minutes), stirring 2 or 3 times. Continue as directed above.

# CHOCO PEANUT BONBONS

▼

*We dare you to resist this mouth-watering flavor combination. In a word – yummy!*

| | |
|---|---|
| 1 cup powdered sugar | 2 tablespoons dark corn syrup |
| 2 tablespoons margarine or | 1 teaspoon vanilla |
| butter, softened | 1 (4-ounce) package German's |
| 1 cup finely chopped dates | chocolate |
| 1 cup chunky peanut butter | 1 (6-ounce) package semisweet |
| 1 cup chopped pecans | chocolate chips |
| | 2 tablespoons vegetable oil |

In large bowl, combine powdered sugar, margarine, dates, peanut butter, pecans, corn syrup and vanilla; knead with hands until thoroughly combined. Shape into 1-inch balls; refrigerate until firm. Heat chocolates and oil until chocolates are melted. Roll candies in warm chocolate mixture with fork or spoon. Arrange on waxed paper-lined pan. Refrigerate, covered, until firm.

*Amount: 4 dozen candies.*

# COOKIE BONBONS

▼

*These divine double-dipped confections require no baking. They're almost too pretty to eat.*

2 cups creme-filled chocolate cookie crumbs (20 to 22 cookies)
½ cup powdered sugar
2 tablespoons unsweetened cocoa
2 tablespoons light corn syrup
¼ cup clear mint-flavored liqueur

1 cup finely chopped pecans
¼ cup granulated sugar
1 (3 to 4-ounce) Swiss white confectionery bar (white chocolate)
1 (4-ounce) semisweet chocolate bar
36 petit four cases

In medium bowl, combine cookie crumbs, powdered sugar, cocoa, corn syrup, liqueur and pecans. Shape dough into 36 balls (about 1 heaping teaspoonful each). Roll in granulated sugar. Press on flat surface to flatten bottoms slightly. Melt white confectionery bar over low heat or in microwave. Insert wooden pick in bottom of bonbon; dip into white confectionery bar. Remove wooden pick; place bonbon on waxed paper-lined tray. Repeat with 17 more bonbons. Melt semisweet chocolate; repeat dipping process with remaining bonbons. With fork, drizzle contrasting chocolate over tops of bonbons. Refrigerate until chocolate is set. Place in petit four cases. Arrange in storage container. Refrigerate, covered, overnight or up to 2 weeks. Remove from refrigerator 30 minutes before serving. These candies do not freeze well.

***Amount: 3 dozen bonbons.***

## FROSTED DRIED APRICOTS 'N ALMONDS

▼

Dip dried apricot halves and whole skin-on almonds halfway into melted vanilla-flavored candy coating. Set on waxed paper until coating hardens. Arrange apricots and almonds on a plate to serve as part of a dessert buffet or add to a cookie or candy tray.

## CHOCOLATE-DIPPED STRAWBERRIES

▼

Rinse strawberries; dry completely with paper towels. In a small microwavable bowl, combine ½ cup semisweet chocolate chips and 1 tablespoon shortening. Microwave (MEDIUM, 50% power) 2½ minutes; stir until smooth. Dip lower ⅔ of berry into chocolate; arrange, stem side down, on cooling racks to harden. If desired, once the chocolate layer has hardened, make a "double dipped" berry by dipping just the tip of the berry into melted vanilla-flavored candy coating. Do not refrigerate.

# BEVERAGES

▼

——————————————————————————————————

       **B**everages do much more than warm, cool and accompany. They are a true symbol of hospitality, usually the first offering to a guest by a gracious host. They definitely set the scene and convey a "glad you're here" ambiance.

       Beverages should be suitable to the season and the occasion. Can you imagine a gala reception without the traditional punch bowl? What's a patio party without frosty slushes or Frozen Margaritas? Peppar Bloody Marys and Mimosas à la Asti Spumante brighten any brunch, and the conviviality of a holiday open house is heightened by a merry mixture served in festive glasses.

       This collection includes both hot and chilled sippers for year-round enjoyment. You may choose from alcoholic or non-alcoholic beverage selections. All are simply prepared and most can be partially or totally combined ahead of time. Last-minute additions, like carbonated beverages and alcohol, are gently stirred in just until blended to retain effervescence. For a touch of class serve with a colorful fruit twister.

# PEPPAR BLOODY MARYS

▼

*Forsake commercially-prepared mixes for a homemade blend par excellence. Prepare it as your guests like it – mild or spicy by adjusting the amount of pepper and Tabasco. Promises to get any brunch off to a zesty start!*

1 (46-ounce) can tomato juice, chilled
1 cup peppar vodka
3 tablespoons fresh lemon juice
1 tablespoon Worcestershire
1 tablespoon prepared horseradish

½ teaspoon seasoned salt
– ice cubes
– coarsely ground pepper (optional)
– Tabasco (optional)
8 pickled asparagus spears or green beans

In 2-quart container, combine tomato juice, vodka, lemon juice, Worcestershire, horseradish and seasoned salt. Divide mixture equally among 8 ice-filled glasses, rimmed with seasoned salt, if desired. Season with pepper and Tabasco. Garnish each glass with a pickled asparagus spear.

*8 servings.*

# FROZEN MARGARITAS

▼

*A fiesta drink if there ever was one, this south-of-the-border sipper is especially enchanting with Tex-Mex menus and patio suppers. Be adventuresome and try our tasty variations – they're as easy as pressing the button on your blender!*

1 (6-ounce) can frozen limeade concentrate, slightly thawed
½ cup tequila
⅓ cup Triple Sec
2 teaspoons meringue powder

2 tablespoons powdered sugar
– ice cubes
– lime juice
– margarita salt
– lime slices

In blender, combine limeade concentrate, tequila, Triple Sec, meringue powder and powdered sugar; add enough ice cubes to measure 5 cups. Blend until ice is finely ground. (Mixture will be opaque and frothy.) Dip rims of margarita glasses in lime juice, then in salt. Pour mixture into rimmed glasses. Garnish with lime slices.

*4 (1-cup) servings.*

**Tip:** For a large group, prepare 1 recipe at a time; pour into plastic container. Freeze, covered, up to one week. Stir before serving.

**Variations:**

**Caribbean Blue Margarita:** Substitute ⅓ cup Curacao for Triple Sec; garnish with mint sprig.

**Strawberry Margarita:** Add 1 cup sliced fresh strawberries to blender. Dip rims of glasses in superfine sugar; garnish with whole strawberry with stem.

*Peppar Bloody Marys*
*page 213*

# MIMOSAS À LA ASTI SPUMANTE

▼

*A deluxe drink with a new look: We've substituted Asti Spumante for the usual champagne to give it a bit more body. This sensational sparkler makes for elegant mid-morning through afternoon entertaining.*

½ gallon orange juice, chilled
¼ cup orange-flavored liqueur
1 (750-milliliter) bottle Asti Spumante, chilled

– ice cubes
– orange slices
– fresh mint sprigs

Combine orange juice, liqueur and Asti Spumante. Serve over ice cubes. Garnish with orange slice and mint sprigs.

*22 (½-cup) servings.*

# RASPBERRY OR STRAWBERRY SLUSH

▼

*Whether you use strawberries or raspberries, this party pink slush is perfect for child and adult get-togethers.*

2 (10-ounce) packages frozen raspberries or strawberries, in syrup, slightly thawed
1 (12-ounce) can frozen pink lemonade concentrate, partially thawed

1½ cups water
1½ cups ice cubes
32 ounces lemon-lime carbonated beverage, chilled
– fresh raspberries or strawberries

In blender, combine 1 package raspberries, ½ can lemonade concentrate, ¾ cup water and ¾ cup ice cubes; process until smooth. Pour into 4-quart plastic container. Repeat with remaining raspberries, lemonade concentrate, water and ice cubes. Freeze overnight.

To Serve: Let mixture stand at room temperature until it is a slushy consistency (about 2 hours). Pour into punch bowl; gently stir in carbonated beverage. Garnish with fresh berries.

*22 (½-cup) servings.*

# PEACH SLUSH

▼

*Peach-flavored schnapps is the secret ingredient in this go-down-easy slush sipper. Make ahead, freeze and serve it with brightly-colored straws.*

1 (12-ounce) can frozen pine-orange-guava juice concentrate, thawed
1 (10-ounce) can frozen peach daiquiri concentrate, thawed

5 cups water
2½ cups peach-flavored schnapps
⅓ cup lemon juice
6 (10-ounce) bottles club soda, chilled

In 4-quart plastic container, combine concentrates, water, schnapps and lemon juice. Freeze, covered, overnight. Before serving, let stand at room temperature 15 minutes to slightly thaw.

To Serve: Stir slightly; spoon ½ cup slush mixture into each serving glass. Stir in ¼ cup club soda.

*22 (¾-cup) servings.*

# RHUBARB PUNCH OR SLUSH

▼

*What's the mystery ingredient? Rhubarb – and it's just as luscious combined with strawberries in punch as it is in pie. This mixture can be used for punch or individual servings.*

8 cups (½-inch) sliced rhubarb (about 3 pounds)
2 cups sugar
8 cups water
½ cup lemon juice

1 (3-ounce) package strawberry flavor gelatin
1 liter vodka
1 (2-liter) bottle lemon-lime carbonated beverage, chilled
– fresh strawberries

In large saucepan, combine rhubarb, sugar, water, and lemon juice. Slowly bring mixture to a boil; boil 10 minutes, stirring occasionally, until rhubarb is thoroughly cooked. Remove from heat and stir in gelatin until dissolved. Cool; stir in vodka. Pour into 5-quart plastic container; freeze overnight. Remove from freezer 15 to 20 minutes before serving.

To Serve Punch: Just before serving, stir slush; pour into punch bowl. Gently stir in carbonated beverage. Garnish with fresh strawberries.

To Serve Slush: Combine ¾ cup slush with ¼ cup carbonated beverage. Serve with strawberry garnish.

*Punch: 48 (½-cup) servings.*

*Slush: 24 (1-cup) servings.*

# FRUIT TWISTERS

▼

*Fruits, olives and citrus strips, speared on long plastic picks, make colorful garnishes for beverages and pretty skewers for thick sandwiches.*

Lemon, orange, lime or pineapple wedge with stemmed maraschino cherry in center.

Ripe or green pitted olives and lemon or lime strip (below).

Strawberry and Citrus Strip (below).

Carambola (star fruit) slice and strawberry.

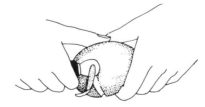

**Citrus Strip**

Hold bent "U-shaped" edge of citrus stripper against orange, lemon or lime. Firmly press down on citrus peel while pulling stripper toward you. A thin strip of peel will come through.

# CRAN-ORANGE PUNCH

▼

*A non-alcoholic sparkler, rosy-hued for a festive look. Just three ingredients combine for an inviting blend of fruit juices and ginger ale.*

1 (1-quart) bottle cranberry
   juice cocktail, chilled
4 cups orange juice, chilled

1 (2-liter) bottle ginger ale,
   chilled
– Ice Ring (page 217)

Combine liquid ingredients in punch bowl just before serving. Add ice ring.

*32 (½-cup) servings.*

# FRUITY TROPICAL PUNCH

▼

*A thirst-quenching non-alcoholic fruit-flavored punch for all ages – not too sweet and pleasantly effervescent.*

1 (64-ounce) carton pine-
   passion-banana juice or pine-
   orange-guava juice, chilled

1 (2-liter) bottle lemon-lime
   carbonated beverage, chilled
– Ice Ring (page 217)
– tropical fruit (optional)

Combine liquid ingredients in punch bowl just before serving. Add ice ring. Garnish with tropical fruit.

*33 (½-cup) servings.*

# GOLDEN FRUIT PUNCH

▼

*Toast the tropics and any special occasion with this non-alcoholic combo showcasing guava passion flavor. It's supurb for breakfasts, brunches, afternoon teas and receptions.*

2 (48-ounce) bottles guava
   passion fruit drink, chilled
1 (12-ounce) can frozen orange
   juice concentrate, thawed

1 (12-ounce) can frozen
   lemonade concentrate,
   thawed
1 (2-liter) bottle ginger ale,
   chilled
– Ice Ring (page 217)

Combine liquid ingredients in punch bowl just before serving. Add ice ring.

*46 (½-cup) servings.*

Pineapple

# SHERBET PUNCHES

▼

*There's lots of latitude here for combining favorite fruit juices for color-coordinated punches to enhance party themes and seasonal gatherings.*

**Pink Punch:**  Pour 1 (32-ounce) bottle chilled raspberry cranberry drink into punch bowl. Add 1 quart raspberry sherbet, shaped into balls. Pour in 1 (750-milliliter) bottle chilled white champagne. Serve immediately.

### 24 (½-cup) servings.

**Tip:**  Line jelly roll pans with sheets of waxed paper. Scoop sherbet into balls. Arrange on pans. Freeze until solid. Transfer to covered freezer containers, separating layers with waxed paper. Freeze, covered, up to one week.

**Variations:**

**Green Punch:**  Substitute 1 quart prepared chilled limeade and lime sherbet for the raspberry flavors.

**Yellow Punch:**  Substitute 1 quart chilled pineapple juice and pineapple sherbet for the raspberry flavors.

# CITRUS SAUTERNE PUNCH

▼

*This punch is just tart enough to provide a lovely accompaniment to savory or sweet nibblers. The elegant golden color makes it particularly attractive for spring through fall occasions – showers, receptions, adult birthdays, and Oktoberfest celebrations.*

1 (12-ounce) can frozen orange juice concentrate, thawed
1 (12-ounce) can frozen lemonade concentrate, thawed
2 (750-milliliter) bottles sauterne, chilled
2 (1-liter) bottles club soda, chilled
– carambola (star fruit) slices
– Ice Ring (below)

Combine liquid ingredients in punch bowl just before serving. Add ice ring. Garnish punch cups with carambola slices.

### 39 (½-cup) servings.

# ICE RING

▼

*For clearest ice, do not prepare more than 24 hours ahead.*

Pour ½ inch chilled distilled water into decorative metal ring mold. Freeze in coldest section of freezer until thin coating of ice forms on surface. Prepare fresh fruit such as slices of lemon, orange or lime, small clusters of grapes, stemmed cherries or strawberries, sprigs of mint or other fresh herbs. Crack ice crust with sharp object to expose water beneath. Working quickly, arrange prepared garnishes in water, making sure each piece is partially submerged. Return mold to freezer until water is frozen solid. Add 1 inch chilled distilled water; freeze solid. Fill mold to top with more chilled distilled water; freeze. When frozen solid, move mold to less cold section of freezer to prevent over-freezing. To remove ice ring from mold, dip very quickly into warm water or wrap hot wet towel around mold. Invert onto plate. Place in plastic bag; keep in freezer until serving time. Float in punch bowl.

# MERRY BERRY PUNCH

▼

*Rich claret color, refreshing berry flavor and a luxurious champagne addition give this punch a holiday glow. Have ingredients thoroughly chilled to combine minutes before serving.*

1 (32-ounce) bottle raspberry-
   cranberry drink, chilled
½ cup black-raspberry liqueur

2 (750-milliliter) bottles
   champagne, chilled
– fresh raspberries

Combine liquid ingredients in punch bowl just before serving. Garnish with raspberries.

*25 (½-cup) servings.*

# SPARKLING FALL CIDER

▼

*An autumn gathering can only be enhanced with this seasonal sparkler. Kids love it too, making it ideal for after-school gatherings, Halloween parties, Thanksgiving and other fall frolics.*

1 (2-quart) bottle apple juice,
   chilled
1 (1-liter) bottle ginger ale,
   chilled
– ice cubes

1 red apple, cut into 9 wedges
1 Granny Smith apple, cut into
   9 wedges
9 (4 to 5-inch) cinnamon sticks
9 star anise (optional)

In large pitcher, combine apple juice and ginger ale; stir to blend. Pour mixture into 9 glasses filled with ice. Garnish each glass with red and green apple wedge, cinnamon stick and star anise.

*9 (1-cup) servings.*

# BERRY HOT CIDER

▼

*A large electric coffee maker makes heating and flavor-blending ultra-convenient. When cold weather calls for a warm drink, this cider is appropriate for all ages and occasions.*

2 (48-ounce) bottles raspberry-
   cranberry drink
1 (32-ounce) bottle apple juice

1 (10-ounce) package frozen
   raspberries, thawed
2 cinnamon sticks
1 tablespoon whole cloves

Combine raspberry-cranberry drink and apple juice in coffee maker. Place raspberries, cinnamon sticks and cloves in percolator basket. Perk through cycle; remove basket before serving.

*21 (¾-cup) servings.*

Raspberries

# ICED PEACH MINT TEA

▼

*Cool shade and this gently-flavored iced tea make comfortable companions on the warmest of days. Only a brief steeping time is necessary to infuse the tea with fresh mint taste.*

| | |
|---|---|
| ¾ cup fresh mint leaves | 2 quarts boiling water |
| 10 to 12 peach-flavored tea bags | 1 quart cold water |
| ½ cup sugar | – ice cubes |
| | – fresh mint sprigs |

Pack mint leaves in tea ball or tie in cheesecloth bag. Add mint, tea bags and sugar to 2 quarts boiling water. Cover and steep 8 to 10 minutes. Remove tea bags and mint ball. Add cold water. Pour into tall pitcher and refrigerate until cold.

To Serve: Pour tea over ice cubes in tall glasses. Garnish with mint sprigs.

*12 (1-cup) servings.*

# ICED COFFEES

▼

*Summer days inspire summer ways of preparing old standbys. For coffee lovers, here are divine drinks spiced and iced to keep you cool as you savor your favorite brew.*

**Spiced and Iced Coffee:**

| | |
|---|---|
| 4 cups double strength hot coffee | 10 whole cloves |
| | 4 small cinnamon sticks |
| ¼ cup sugar | ½ cup coffee-flavored liqueur |
| 10 whole allspice | – Coffee Ice Cubes (below) |

In large pitcher, combine coffee, sugar and spices. Cover with plastic wrap; let stand at room temperature 1 hour. Stir in liqueur. Refrigerate until well chilled. Remove allspice, cloves and cinnamon sticks. Fill 4 glasses with coffee ice cubes. Pour spiced coffee over coffee ice cubes.

*4 servings.*

**Creamy Iced Coffee:**  In large glass, combine 1 tablespoon sweetened condensed milk and 1 cup cold double strength coffee. Add coffee ice cubes.

*1 serving.*

**Orange Iced Coffee:**  Combine ½ cup double strength cold coffee, ½ cup milk, ½ cup orange juice and 1 tablespoon sugar in blender; process until thoroughly combined. Pour into glasses, add coffee ice cubes and garnish with orange slices.

*2 servings.*

**Tip:**  To make double strength coffee, use two tablespoons coffee for each 6 ounce cup brewed.

**Coffee Ice Cubes:**  Freeze double strength coffee in ice cube trays. Remove cubes; store in plastic bags in freezer. Add to iced coffee drinks.

Coffee

# ICE CREAM COFFEES

*Cool and creative coffee drinks are welcome for between-meal or after-dinner enjoyment. We've included one wonderful warm drink to chase winter chills and reap raves from guests.*

**Coffee Malt:**

1 cup double strength cold
   coffee
3 tablespoons chocolate syrup

2 tablespoons malt powder
2 cups vanilla or coffee-
   flavored ice cream

Combine coffee, chocolate syrup and malt powder in blender; add 2 cups ice cream. Process until thick and creamy. Pour into 2 tall glasses.

*2 (1½-cup) servings.*

**Coffee Shake:**

1 cup vanilla or coffee-flavored
   ice cream

½ cup double strength cold
   coffee
½ cup crushed ice
¼ cup liqueur of choice

Process ice cream, coffee, crushed ice and liqueur in blender until smooth. Pour into tall glass.

*1 (1½-cup) serving.*

**Citrus Sherbet Coffee:**

1 cup double strength cold
   coffee
1 tablespoon sugar

1½ teaspoons grated orange peel
1½ teaspoons orange juice
½ cup rainbow sherbet
   – orange slice

Combine coffee, sugar, orange peel and juice in blender. Add rainbow sherbet; process until smooth. Pour into tall glass; garnish with orange slice.

*1 (1½-cup) serving.*

**Brandy 'n Chocolate Warmer:**

1 quart coffee-flavored ice
   cream, softened
½ cup brandy
1 tablespoon chocolate-
   flavored liqueur

1 tablespoon coffee-flavored
   liqueur
– freshly brewed double
   strength hot coffee
8 cinnamon sticks

Process ice cream, brandy, and liqueurs in blender until smooth; freeze in airtight container until firm (about 2 hours).

To Serve: Scoop ½ cup frozen mixture into each of eight coffee mugs; pour in coffee. Stir with cinnamon stick.

*8 servings.*

# ENLIGHTENED

▼

Enlightened means different things to different people. Here, it means "seeing the light" when it comes to eating wisely and in harmony with current guidelines for lower-fat cooking. It does not mean sacrificing flavor or appearance. The recipes in this collection are tasty and attractive proof of that!

Under the umbrella of "moderation," they represent appealing balance and variety. We have modified some of your favorite traditional recipes with adaptations that are quite simple and exceedingly satisfying. And we offer exciting new ideas, all of which use readily available, everyday ingredients. These recipes contain minimal fat and cholesterol and, when feasible, reduced sodium. They have been developed to approximate the guideline of three grams or less of fat per one ounce of cooked meat, fish or poultry. Each recipe in this chapter specifies the amount of calories, fat, cholesterol and sodium it contains per serving.

Included are entrees for all occasions, plus breads, side dishes and some truly delightful desserts. This superb collection is designed to promote "enlightened" eating with enthusiam!

# FRITTATA

▼

*A breakfast, brunch and supper dish par excellence, this versatile Italian creation is traditionally cut into wedges for serving.*

1 tablespoon margarine
1 medium new red potato, peeled, chopped (½ cup)
⅓ cup chopped green bell pepper
⅓ cup sliced onion, separated into rings
4 ounces cubed cooked chicken or turkey breast (½ cup)
½ teaspoon dried basil, crumbled

½ teaspoon dried dill weed, crumbled
⅛ teaspoon pepper
1 (8-ounce) carton cholesterol-free liquid egg substitute, thawed
1 roma tomato, thinly sliced
5 green bell pepper strips, ¼ inch wide
2 tablespoons freshly grated Parmesan cheese

Coat 9-inch skillet with no stick cooking spray; melt margarine in skillet. Stir in remaining ingredients except egg substitute and cheese. Cook, covered, over low heat until potato is almost tender (about 6 minutes), stirring occasionally. Pour egg substitute evenly over vegetables. Cook, covered, over low heat (4 to 5 minutes), gently lifting cooked portion around edge to allow uncooked portion to flow underneath. Arrange tomato slices and bell pepper strips over vegetable-egg mixture; sprinkle with cheese. Cook, covered, until set (2 to 3 minutes). Cut into wedges, serve immediately from skillet.

*4 servings.*

**Serving Size: ¼ of recipe**

| Calories | Fat | Cholesterol | Sodium |
|---|---|---|---|
| 130 | 5 Gm. | 25 Mg. | 190 Mg. |

# SLIMLINED HAM AND CHEESE STRATA

▼

*Enjoy an updated version of this brunch favorite using lower-fat ingredients.*

12 slices bread, crusts removed, cubed
1 (10-ounce) package frozen chopped broccoli, thawed, drained
1 cup diced cooked 96% fat-free ham (optional)
1 (4-ounce) package shredded part skim mozzarella cheese (1 cup)

1½ cups cholesterol-free liquid egg substitute, thawed
3½ cups skim milk
½ cup minced onion
1 teaspoon dry mustard
⅛ teaspoon pepper
4 ounces shredded reduced fat sharp Cheddar cheese (1 cup)

Coat 9 × 13-inch glass baking dish with no stick cooking spray. Layer bread, broccoli, ham and mozzarella in sprayed dish. Combine egg substitute, milk, onion, mustard and pepper until blended; pour over layers. Refrigerate, covered, several hours or overnight.

Heat oven to 325°. Bake, uncovered, 35 minutes. Top with Cheddar cheese; bake until knife inserted in center comes out clean (25 to 30 minutes longer). Let stand, covered, 10 minutes. Cut into squares.

*10 servings.*

**Serving Size: ¹⁄₁₀ of recipe With ham:**

| Calories | Fat | Cholesterol | Sodium |
|---|---|---|---|
| 190 | 5 Gm. | 25 Mg. | 600 Mg. |

**Serving Size: ¹⁄₁₀ of recipe Without ham:**

| 170 | 5 Gm. | 15 Mg. | 320 Mg. |

*Frittata*
*page 221*

# CHICKEN BREASTS 'N SPINACH ROLLS

*A piquant chutney sauce tops these delightfully flavored stuffed chicken breasts for a perfect party presentation.*

1 tablespoon olive oil
1 cup chopped fresh
  mushrooms
½ cup chopped onion
1 teaspoon minced garlic
2 cups chopped fresh spinach
4 (4-ounce) boneless skinless
  chicken breast halves

¼ teaspoon salt (optional)
½ cup low sodium chicken
  broth
¼ cup colonial chutney
  (Chut-nut)
1 tablespoon salad vinegar
¼ teaspoon dried thyme,
  crumbled
¼ teaspoon pepper

In medium skillet, heat oil over medium heat. Sauté mushrooms, onion and garlic, stirring occasionally, until onion is slightly soft (about 3 minutes). Stir in spinach; cook 2 to 3 minutes longer. Refrigerate until cool.

Flatten chicken breast halves to about ¼ inch thickness. Arrange equal portions of spinach mixture in center of each chicken breast half. Roll meat around filling to enclose; fasten with wooden picks. Refrigerate, covered, up to 24 hours.

Arrange chicken in skillet. Sprinkle with salt. Combine chicken broth, chutney, vinegar, thyme and pepper; pour over chicken. Bring to a boil over medium heat; reduce heat and simmer, covered, until chicken is no longer pink and filling is hot in center (10 to 11 minutes). Remove chicken to heated platter; remove wooden picks. Keep chicken warm. Bring chutney mixture to a boil. Cook, stirring occasionally, until reduced to ½ cup (about 5 minutes). Spoon over chicken.

*4 servings.*

**Serving Size: ¼ of recipe**

| Calories | Fat | Cholesterol | Sodium |
|----------|-----|-------------|--------|
| 230 | 6 Gm. | 65 Mg. | 240 Mg. |

# TURKEY VEGETABLE SAUTÉ

*This speedily sautéed entrée combines turkey and a pretty assortment of veggies. Dill adds a delightful flavor to this nutritious medley.*

⅓ cup flour
1½ teaspoons lemon and pepper
  seasoning
1 pound turkey breast slices
2 tablespoons olive oil
1 red bell pepper, cut into
  1-inch squares

4 ounces fresh mushrooms,
  sliced
½ pound asparagus, tough ends
  removed, cut into thirds
½ cup chicken broth
1 teaspoon dried dill weed,
  crumbled

Combine flour and seasoning; coat turkey in mixture. In 10-inch skillet, heat oil over medium heat. Sauté turkey slices until lightly browned on both sides. Stir in remaining ingredients. Bring to a boil; reduce heat and simmer, covered, until turkey juices run clear and vegetables are crisp-tender (about 10 minutes). Serve immediately.

*4 servings.*

**Serving Size: ¼ of recipe**

| Calories | Fat | Cholesterol | Sodium |
|----------|-----|-------------|--------|
| 250 | 8 Gm. | 70 Mg. | 380 Mg. |

# CHICKEN LASAGNA

▼

*Longing for lasagna, but uncertain of fat content? Here ground chicken teams with other lower-fat ingredients with no sacrifice in flavor, because traditional seasonings offer expected taste treat.*

1 pound ground skinless chicken, Italian-style
2 teaspoons olive oil
1 teaspoon minced garlic
5 tablespoons snipped fresh parsley, divided
1 teaspoon dried basil, crumbled
1 teaspoon dried oregano, crumbled
2 (14½-ounce) cans no-salt-added tomatoes, chopped
2 (8-ounce) cans no-salt-added tomato sauce

1 (6-ounce) can no-salt-added tomato paste
1 (15-ounce) carton lite ricotta
1 (8-ounce) package shredded part skim mozzarella cheese (2 cups)
½ cup cholesterol-free liquid egg substitute, thawed
¼ teaspoon salt
½ teaspoon pepper
1 (13-ounce) package frozen pre-boiled lasagna sheets
¼ cup freshly grated Parmesan cheese

Brown chicken in oil over medium heat, stirring occasionally. Drain any accumulated fat. Stir in garlic, 2 tablespoons of the parsley, basil, oregano, tomatoes, tomato sauce and tomato paste. Bring to a boil; reduce heat and simmer 20 minutes, stirring occasionally.

Heat oven to 375°. Combine ricotta, mozzarella cheese, egg substitute, salt, pepper and 2 tablespoons of the parsley. Spread about ½ cup of chicken mixture in 9 × 13-inch baking pan. Cover with single layer of 2 lasagna sheets. Spread ⅓ of cheese mixture and ⅓ of remaining chicken mixture over lasagna; repeat twice. Sprinkle with Parmesan cheese and remaining 1 tablespoon parsley. Bake uncovered until bubbly and lightly browned (40 to 50 minutes). Or, refrigerate covered up to 24 hours; bake 60 to 70 minutes. Let stand 10 minutes before cutting into squares.

*12 servings.*

**Tip:** One pound ground chicken combined with 1 teaspoon fennel seed, 1 teaspoon paprika, ¼ teaspoon black pepper and ¼ teaspoon crushed red pepper can be substituted for ground chicken Italian-style.

### Serving Size: ¹⁄₁₂ of recipe

| Calories | Fat | Cholesterol | Sodium |
|----------|------|-------------|---------|
| 260 | 9 Gm. | 40 Mg. | 280 Mg. |

*Suggested Dietary Guidelines for Americans from the U.S. Department of Agriculture and U.S. Department of Health and Human Services:*

*1. Eat a variety of foods.*

*2. Maintain a healthy weight.*

*3. Choose a diet low in fat, saturated fat, and cholesterol.*

*4. Choose a diet with plenty of vegetables, fruits and grain products.*

*5. Use sugars only in moderation.*

*6. Use salt and sodium only in moderation.*

*7. If you drink alcoholic beverages, do so in moderation.*

# TURKEY 'N BEEF LOAF

▼

*We give this appealing alternative to the usual meat loaf high marks for flavor as well as healthful eating. Shredded carrots add color, and you will enjoy the zest provided by horseradish and dry mustard.*

½ pound ground turkey
½ pound diet lean ground beef
½ cup quick-cooking oats
¼ cup skim milk
½ cup finely chopped onion
½ cup shredded carrot
1 egg white
1 tablespoon Worcestershire
1 teaspoon prepared
    horseradish

1 teaspoon minced garlic
1½ teaspoons dry mustard,
    divided
½ teaspoon salt
¼ teaspoon pepper
¼ cup reduced-calorie, low-
    sodium ketchup
2 tablespoons firmly packed
    brown sugar

Spray 8 × 4-inch loaf pan with no stick cooking spray. Heat oven to 350°. Combine ground turkey, ground beef, oats and milk. Gently mix in onion, carrot, egg white, Worcestershire, horseradish, garlic, ½ teaspoon of the dry mustard, salt and pepper. Pat meat mixture into sprayed pan. Bake 60 minutes. Combine ketchup, brown sugar and remaining 1 teaspoon dry mustard; spread over meat loaf. Continue to bake until meat thermometer registers 170° (15 to 20 minutes longer). Let stand 10 minutes before slicing.

*6 servings.*

**Serving Size: ⅙ of recipe**

| Calories | Fat | Cholesterol | Sodium |
|----------|-----|-------------|--------|
| 190 | 8 Gm. | 50 Mg. | 290 Mg. |

**Tip:** Fat is reduced to 6 Gm. and cholesterol is reduced to 45 Mg. if ground turkey breast is used.

# FISH 'N VEGGIES IN FOIL

▼

*Please pass the packets! Then fold away the foil to reveal succulent fish fillets, a bouquet of fresh vegetables and the surprise spark of ginger aroma and flavor.*

2 cups ⅛-inch sliced carrots
2 unpeeled tomatoes, cut into
    ¼-inch slices
1 small leek, cut into 1½-inch-
    long julienne strips (1 cup)
1 pound orange ruffie fillets,
    cut into 4 portions

1 teaspoon minced gingerroot
½ teaspoon paprika
¼ teaspoon pepper
4 teaspoons lemon juice
8 fresh basil leaves or
    2 teaspoons dried basil,
    crumbled

Heat oven to 450°. Cut 4 (12 × 16-inch) pieces of foil. Arrange ¼ of the carrots, tomatoes and leeks in center of each piece of foil; top with fillets. Sprinkle fillets with gingerroot, paprika, pepper and lemon juice. Top with basil. Fold foil edges together to form packet; place on baking sheet. Bake until fillets are opaque and flake with a fork and vegetables are crisp-tender (18 to 20 minutes).

To Serve: Place 1 packet on each dinner plate. Cut an "X" to open packet; pull back foil to reveal fillets.

*4 servings*

**Tip:** Packets may be made ahead and refrigerated up to 8 hours. Bake 23 to 25 minutes.

**Serving Size: ¼ of recipe**

| Calories | Fat | Cholesterol | Sodium |
|----------|-----|-------------|--------|
| 210 | 8 Gm. | 25 Mg. | 105 Mg. |

*Ground turkey is an excellent substitute for a higher-fat ground meat. Use it within two days of purchase.*

# TEMPTING TOPPERS FOR FISH

▼

*Terrific toppers take the ho-hum from plain fish fillets. Flavor bursts of herbs, spices, vinegars and lemon zest provide taste-tempting transformations in just a few minutes.*

Heat oven to 400°. Rinse 2 pounds cod; pat dry with paper towels. Arrange cod in baking dish. Spread evenly with one of the toppings below. Bake, uncovered, until cod just flakes with fork (10 to 15 minutes). Cut into 8 servings.

*8 servings.*

**Dilly Onion:** Combine ⅓ cup chopped green onions, ⅓ cup white wine vinegar, 1 tablespoon olive oil, 4 teaspoons snipped fresh dill and 2 teaspoons grated lemon peel.

### Serving size: ⅛ of recipe (including fish)

| Calories | Fat | Cholesterol | Sodium |
|----------|-----|-------------|--------|
| 110 | 2 Gm. | 50 Mg. | 65 Mg. |

**Dijon:** Combine ⅓ cup plain lowfat yogurt, 3 tablespoons Dijon mustard, 1 teaspoon dried dill weed, crumbled, and ¼ teaspoon ground pepper melange.

### Serving Size: ⅛ of recipe (including fish)

| Calories | Fat | Cholesterol | Sodium |
|----------|-----|-------------|--------|
| 100 | 1 Gm. | 50 Mg. | 140 Mg. |

**Red Pepper:** Place 1 large red bell pepper (seeded and quartered) on microwavable plate. Cover with plastic wrap; vent one corner. Microwave (HIGH) until tender (1½ to 2 minutes); cool slightly. In food processor, combine steamed pepper, ¼ cup sliced green onions, 3 tablespoons snipped fresh cilantro, 1 teaspoon minced garlic and ⅛ teaspoon salt; process until smooth.

### Serving Size: ⅛ of recipe (including fish)

| Calories | Fat | Cholesterol | Sodium |
|----------|-----|-------------|--------|
| 100 | 1 Gm. | 50 Mg. | 95 Mg. |

# OVEN-FRIED ORANGE RUFFIE

▼

*Just a few simple herbed coating ingredients and brief oven baking provide a crispy exterior for a favorite fish.*

- ⅔ **cup corn flake crumbs**
- 2 **tablespoons dried parsley, crumbled**
- 1 **teaspoon dried lemon peel**
- ¼ **teaspoon dried oregano, crumbled**
- ¼ **teaspoon dry mustard**
- ¼ **teaspoon salt**
- ¼ **teaspoon pepper**
- 1½ **pounds orange ruffie fillets**
  - **– lemon or lime wedges**

Spray 10 × 15-inch jelly roll pan with no stick cooking spray. Heat oven to 450°. Combine crumbs, parsley, lemon peel, oregano, dry mustard, salt and pepper. Cut fillets into 6 serving-size pieces. Coat both sides of fillets with crumb mixture. Arrange on sprayed pan. Bake until fillets just flake with fork (about 10 minutes). Garnish with lemon wedges; serve immediately.

*6 servings.*

### Serving Size: ⅙ of recipe

| Calories | Fat | Cholesterol | Sodium |
|----------|-----|-------------|--------|
| 180 | 8 Gm. | 25 Mg. | 260 Mg. |

# HERBED PORK TENDERLOIN WITH APRICOT GLAZE

▼

*Naturally-sweetened pourable fruit provides a complementary glaze for lean and tender pork tenderloins which have been seasoned with garlic and rosemary.*

| | |
|---|---|
| 2 (1-pound) pork tenderloins | ½ teaspoon pepper |
| 4 to 6 garlic cloves, cut into thin slivers | 2 teaspoons dried rosemary, crumbled |
| 2 teaspoons canola oil | ⅔ cup apricot pourable all fruit |
| ½ teaspoon salt | – fresh rosemary sprigs |

Heat oven to 425°. Cut ½-inch deep slits on surface of pork tenderloins; insert garlic. Combine oil, salt, pepper and rosemary. Place tenderloins on rack in roasting pan, tucking tails under to make uniform in thickness, if necessary. Rub with oil-seasoning mixture. Brush with apricot pourable fruit. Roast until instant read thermometer reaches 155° (20 to 25 minutes). Remove from oven; cover with foil and allow to stand 5 minutes before slicing. Garnish with rosemary.

*6 servings.*

**Serving Size: ⅙ of recipe**

| Calories | Fat | Cholesterol | Sodium |
|---|---|---|---|
| 290 | 7 Gm. | 110 Mg. | 280 Mg. |

# PEPPERED BEEF TOP SIRLOIN STEAK

▼

*Hold the bottled steak sauce, because you have your own robust rendition to serve with this grilled steak.*

| | |
|---|---|
| 1 pound boneless beef top sirloin steak | ¼ cup reduced-fat sour cream |
| 2 tablespoons cracked pepper | 1 tablespoon prepared horseradish |
| 1 teaspoon margarine | ½ teaspoon grated lemon peel |
| 2 tablespoons thinly sliced green onions | ¼ teaspoon garlic salt |

Trim any fat from steak. Press in 1 tablespoon pepper on each side of steak. Refrigerate, covered, 30 to 60 minutes. Heat broiler or grill. Melt margarine in small skillet. Sauté onions until tender. Stir in remaining ingredients; keep warm. Broil or grill steak 4 to 5 inches from heat until medium-rare to medium (10 to 12 minutes), turning once.

To Serve: Cut steak into 4 servings; spread with sauce. Serve immediately.

*4 servings.*

**Serving Size: ¼ of recipe**

| Calories | Fat | Cholesterol | Sodium |
|---|---|---|---|
| 180 | 7 Gm. | 70 Mg. | 190 Mg. |

- *Use minimal fat when cooking meat, poultry or fish. Excellent methods for cooking include baking, roasting, poaching, broiling, stir-frying, grilling and microwaving.*

- *Beef offers a wide variety of delicious choices. Lean cuts include round tip, top round steak, top loin, eye of round, tenderloin and sirloin.*

# BEEFY MEXICAN STEW

▼

*Olé for this snappy stew, featuring lean beef round steak with accents of green chiles and zesty red pepper. Serve it over nutrient-and-fiber-rich brown rice.*

1 pound bottom beef round
   steak, cut into ½-inch cubes
1 teaspoon corn oil
1 teaspoon minced garlic
1½ teaspoons dried oregano,
   crumbled
1 teaspoon ground cumin
½ teaspoon crushed red pepper
¼ teaspoon salt

½ cup coarsely chopped onion
4 medium tomatoes, chopped
   (4 cups), divided
½ cup water
1 (4-ounce) can whole green
   chiles
1 tablespoon cornstarch
2 cups cooked brown rice,
   cooked without salt

Brown beef in oil in 3 to 4-quart saucepan. Stir in garlic, oregano, cumin, red pepper and salt. Stir in onion, 3 cups of the tomatoes and water. Bring to a boil; reduce heat and simmer, covered, until beef is tender (about 1 hour). Drain chiles, reserving liquid. Cut chiles into ½-inch strips; add to beef mixture. Combine cornstarch and reserved chili liquid; gradually stir into stew. Cook until thickened. Stir in remaining 1 cup tomatoes; cook 1 minute longer. Serve over brown rice.

*4 servings.*

**Serving Size: ¼ of recipe**

| Calories | Fat | Cholesterol | Sodium |
|---|---|---|---|
| 320 | 8 Gm. | 60 Mg. | 520 Mg. |

# TURKEY CHILI

▼

*This choice chili recipe is high in flavor and low in fat. It's important to add seasonings to ground turkey during sautéeing so flavors thoroughly permeate.*

1½ cups chopped onions
1 cup chopped green bell
   pepper
1 (4-ounce) can diced green
   chiles
1 tablespoon minced garlic
1 pound ground turkey
1 to 2 tablespoons chili
   powder
½ teaspoon dried oregano,
   crumbled

½ teaspoon dried thyme,
   crumbled
¼ teaspoon cayenne pepper
¼ teaspoon ground cumin
¼ teaspoon salt
2 (14½-ounce) cans no-salt-
   added whole tomatoes,
   undrained, chopped
1 (15-ounce) can no-salt-added
   tomato puree
1 (15-ounce) can pinto beans,
   undrained

Spray skillet with no stick cooking spray. Add onions, green pepper, chiles and garlic; sauté over medium heat until tender (3 to 5 minutes). Stir in ground turkey, chili powder, oregano, thyme, cayenne pepper, cumin and salt; cook until turk is browned (about 5 minutes), stirring frequently. Stir in remaining ingredients. Bring to a boil; reduce heat and simmer, uncovered, until flavors are blended (45 to 60 minutes).

*6 servings.*

**Serving Size: ⅙ of recipe**

| Calories | Fat | Cholesterol | Sodium |
|---|---|---|---|
| 250 | 6 Gm. | 50 Mg. | 700 Mg |

**Tips:** To reduce sodium by 50%, drain chiles and beans. Measure liquid, substitute equal amount of water. Discard chili-bean liquid. Thoroughly rinse chiles and beans. Fat is reduced to 1 Gm. and cholesterol is reduced to 45 Mg. if ground turkey breast is used.

# WILD RICE MUSHROOM BAKE

▼

*Serve with fish, poultry, beef and the hunter's bounty.*

1 cup uncooked wild rice
1 (8-ounce) package fresh
  mushrooms, sliced (3 cups)
½ cup minced onion
1 (8-ounce) can sliced water
  chestnuts, drained

1 (10½-ounce) can condensed
  chicken broth
1 (10½-ounce) can low-sodium
  chicken broth
2 teaspoons minced garlic
½ teaspoon Italian seasoning,
  crumbled

Heat oven to 350°. Rinse rice in a strainer under running water or in a bowl of water; drain. Combine all ingredients in 2-quart casserole. Bake, covered, 75 minutes. Remove cover; stir. Continue baking until rice is tender (about 15 minutes longer). Let stand 5 to 10 minutes for rice to absorb all liquid.

*10 (½-cup) servings.*

**Tip:** To prepare ahead, bake in microwavable casserole and refrigerate, covered. Microwave (HIGH), covered, until casserole is hot (7 to 8 minutes), stirring once.

**Serving Size: ¹⁄₁₀ of recipe**

| Calories | Fat | Cholesterol | Sodium |
|----------|-----|-------------|--------|
| 100 | 1 Gm. | 0 Mg. | 200 Mg. |

# HERBED SUMMER SQUASH

▼

*The delicate flavor of summr squash blends well with savory herbs and a hint of yogurt. Take care not to overcook so squash holds its shape.*

1¼ pounds yellow summer
  squash
1 teaspoon margarine
2 tablespoons snipped fresh
  basil

2 tablespoons snipped fresh
  marjoram
½ teaspoon cornstarch
¼ cup plain nonfat yogurt,
  room temperature
⅛ teaspoon salt
– dash white pepper

Cut ends off squash; cut squash in half horizontally. Slice into 3 × ¼-inch strips. Coat 10-inch skillet with no stick cooking spray; heat margarine in skillet. Cook squash, basil and marjoram over medium heat, stirring constantly, until squash begins to soften (3 to 4 minutes). Remove from heat. Blend cornstarch into yogurt; stir into squash. Cook over low heat, stirring often until heated through (1 to 2 minutes). Sprinkle with salt and white pepper.

*6 servings.*

**Serving Size: ⅙ of recipe**

| Calories | Fat | Cholesterol | Sodium |
|----------|-----|-------------|--------|
| 30 | 1 Gm. | 0 Mg. | 60 Mg. |

*Keep your kitchen supplied with ingredients that add flavor without adding calories such as flavored vinegars, wine and a variety of mustards.*

# EASY ENLIGHTENED POTATO SALAD

▼

*You won't know the difference! A few simple substitutions and this hearty favorite is transformed into a fat-modified treat.*

| | |
|---|---|
| 3 pounds (7 to 8 large) uncooked red potatoes or 8 cups cubed cooked potatoes | 1 cup drained sweet pickle relish |
| ⅓ cup oil-free reduced-calorie Italian dressing | ½ cup thinly sliced radishes |
| ½ teaspoon salt | 1 cup thinly sliced celery |
| 2 (8-ounce) cartons cholesterol-free liquid egg substitute, thawed | 1 cup chopped onions |
| | – Dressing (below) |
| | – leaf lettuce |
| | – Tomato Crowns (below) |

Boil potatoes in skins in water just until tender. Drain; cool to lukewarm. Peel; cut into ½-inch cubes. Pour Italian dressing over potatoes, sprinkle with salt; toss to coat potatoes. Refrigerate, covered, several hours or overnight. Prepare egg product according to package directions for scrambled eggs, cooking thoroughly until no longer moist, but not brown. Chop scrambled eggs into small chunks; add to potatoes with remaining ingredients except leaf lettuce and Tomato Crowns. Stir in enough Dressing to coat all ingredients. Refrigerate, covered, until serving time.

To Serve: Spoon onto large lettuce-lined platter. Garnish with Tomato Crowns.

### Amount: 24 (½ cup) servings.

**Dressing:** Combine 1¾ cups reduced-calorie mayonnaise, 1 (8-ounce) carton plain nonfat yogurt, 2 tablespoons prepared mustard, 2 teaspoons sugar, 1 teaspoon salt, 1 teaspoon celery seed and ¼ teaspoon pepper.

### Serving Size: ½ cup

| Calories | Fat | Cholesterol | Sodium |
|---|---|---|---|
| 140 | 6 Gm. | 5 Mg. | 420 Mg. |

## TOMATO CROWNS

▼

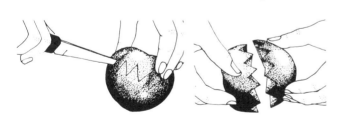 

| | | |
|---|---|---|
| Cut a zigzag pattern around the middle of a firm tomato, being sure to cut all the way into center. Adjust the last cut to meet evenly with the first cut. | Gently pull and twist the two cut halves apart. | Garnish center of tomato crowns with parsley or other fresh herbs. This method can also be used to make lemon, lime and orange crowns. |

# FRESH HERB VINAIGRETTE

▼

*Use your imagination in selecting compatible herb combinations for this basic recipe. The amount of oil is reduced by the addition of water.*

2 tablespoons light olive oil
⅓ cup white wine vinegar
2 tablespoons water
2 tablespoons snipped fresh herbs

1 teaspoon minced garlic
½ teaspoon sugar
⅛ teaspoon salt
– dash pepper

Combine all ingredients; whisk to blend or shake in bottle with tight-fitting cover. Refrigerate, covered, at least 1 hour before serving.

*Amount: ½ cup.*

**Serving Size: 1 Tablespoon**

| Calories | Fat | Cholesterol | Sodium |
|----------|-----|-------------|--------|
| 35 | 3 Gm. | 0 Mg. | 35 Mg. |

Tarragon          Thyme

# CREAMY GARLIC SALAD DRESSING

▼

*A delightfully creamy dressing with the zesty flavors of Dijon mustard, garlic and herbs. Drizzle it over cooked chilled vegetables or salad greens.*

1 cup reduced-calorie mayonnaise
½ cup nonfat plain yogurt

1 tablespoon Dijon mustard
2 teaspoons minced garlic
1 teaspoon fines herbes

Process all ingredients in blender or food processor until smooth. Refrigerate, covered, at least 1 hour before serving.

*Amount: 1½ cups.*

**Serving Size: 1 Tablespoon**

| Calories | Fat | Cholesterol | Sodium |
|----------|-----|-------------|--------|
| 35 | 3 Gm. | 5 Mg. | 75 Mg. |

- *Purchase fresh herbs from the produce department. Use dried and ground herbs when fresh are not available.*

- *A good rule of thumb for interchanging fresh and dried herbs is 1 teaspoon of dried herbs equals 1 tablespoon of fresh herbs.*

# PARTY-PERFECT POPOVERS

▼

*Crisp on the outside, airy on the inside, these popovers use only the white of the egg. Follow recipe directions and allow popovers to dry in a turned-off oven.*

3 egg whites
1½ tablespoons canola oil
½ tablespoon margarine, melted

1 cup skim milk
1 cup flour
⅛ teaspoon salt

Generously spray 6 (6-ounce) custard cups or popover pans with no stick cooking spray. Heat oven to 450°. Beat egg whites slightly; beat in oil, margarine and skim milk. Beat in flour and salt until almost smooth. Fill sprayed cups about half full. Place custard cups on baking sheet. Bake 20 minutes; reduce oven temperature to 350°. Continue baking until popovers are well browned (20 to 25 minutes longer). Remove from oven; loosen from cup, place at an angle in cup. Slit each popover with tip of paring knife to allow steam to escape. Turn oven off; return popovers to oven to let insides dry slightly (about 15 minutes). Serve hot.

*Amount: 6 popovers.*

**Serving Size: 1 popover**

| Calories | Fat | Cholesterol | Sodium |
|---|---|---|---|
| 140 | 5 Gm. | 0 Mg. | 105 Mg. |

# ZUCCHINI BREAD

▼

*This moist, spicy batter, ideal for loaf or muffins, has been revised to use less oil.*

1¾ cups flour
1 teaspoon baking soda
½ teaspoon ground cinnamon
½ teaspoon ground nutmeg
¼ teaspoon baking powder
¼ teaspoon salt

1 medium zucchini, shredded (1 cup)
⅔ cup sugar
½ cup buttermilk
¼ cup vegetable oil
2 egg whites
1 teaspoon vanilla

Spray 8½ × 4½-inch pan with no stick cooking spray. Heat oven to 350°. Combine flour, soda, cinnamon, nutmeg, baking powder and salt; set aside. Combine zucchini, sugar, buttermilk, oil, egg whites and vanilla in large bowl. Stir dry ingredients into zucchini mixture, stirring just until moistened. Pour batter into sprayed pan. Bake until golden brown and wooden pick inserted in center of loaf comes out clean (50 to 55 minutes). Cool in pan 15 minutes; remove to wire rack to cool completely.

*Amount: 1 loaf.*

**Muffin Variation:** Line 16 (2½-inch) muffin cups with paper baking cups. Heat oven to 375°. Prepare batter as above; fill muffin cups about half full. Bake until wooden pick inserted in center comes out clean (about 20 minutes). Let stand 5 minutes; remove muffins from pan to rack.

**Serving Size: ¹⁄₁₆ of recipe**

| Calories | Fat | Cholesterol | Sodium |
|---|---|---|---|
| 120 | 4 Gm. | 0 Mg. | 125 Mg. |

**Variation:** Stir in ½ cup chopped dried apricots with dry ingredients.

# OATMEAL DATE COOKIES

▼

*A low-fat oatmeal cookie, using egg whites and buttermilk, becomes a special treat. Store these in a tightly covered container.*

1 cup firmly packed brown
  sugar
¼ cup canola oil
½ cup lowfat buttermilk
3 egg whites
1 teaspoon vanilla

1¾ cups flour
1 teaspoon baking soda
½ teaspoon salt
½ teaspoon ground cinnamon
3 cups old-fashioned rolled oats
1 cup chopped dates

Heat oven to 375°. In large bowl, beat brown sugar and oil until fluffy. Beat in buttermilk, egg whites and vanilla until well combined. In small bowl, combine flour, baking soda, salt and cinnamon; gradually beat into sugar mixture. Stir in rolled oats and dates. Drop dough by level tablespoonfuls onto ungreased baking sheets. Bake until cookies are light golden brown (8 to 10 minutes). Remove to wire racks to cool.

*Amount: 3½ dozen.*

**Serving Size: 1 cookie**

| Calories | Fat | Cholesterol | Sodium |
|----------|-----|-------------|--------|
| 90 | 2 Gm. | 0 Mg. | 60 Mg. |

# LUSCIOUS COCOA CAKES

▼

*These tasty cakes with rich chocolate flavor are a good choice for occasional indulgences.*

18 (2½-inch) paper baking cups
1¼ cups flour
⅓ cup unsweetened cocoa
2 teaspoons baking powder
4 egg whites

½ cup margarine
¾ cup sugar
1 teaspoon vanilla
½ cup water
3 tablespoons powdered sugar

Line muffin pans with paper baking cups. Heat oven to 350°. Combine flour, cocoa and baking powder. Beat egg whites until stiff peaks form. Beat margarine, sugar and vanilla until fluffy. Blend in flour mixture alternately with water. Gently fold in egg whites. Spoon batter into muffin cups. Bake until wooden pick inserted in center comes out clean (20 to 25 minutes). Let stand 5 minutes. Remove muffins from pan to rack; cool completely. Lightly sprinkle tops with powdered sugar, about ½ teaspoon per cupcake.

*Amount: 18 cupcakes.*

**Serving Size: 1 cupcake**

| Calories | Fat | Cholesterol | Sodium |
|----------|-----|-------------|--------|
| 120 | 5 Gm. | 0 Mg. | 100 Mg. |

*For best results, when substituting margarine for butter or shortening in baking, use one labeled "margarine" not "spread."*

# LEMON-GO-LIGHTLY MERINGUE CAKE

▼

*This strawberry-crowned creation is streamlined and slim-lined with a lowfat-yellow cake mix.*

| | |
|---|---|
| 2 cups sliced fresh strawberries | 5 egg whites, divided |
| 1 tablespoon sugar | 1 tablespoon grated lemon peel |
| 1 (18.5-ounce) package lowfat yellow cake mix | ¼ teaspoon cream of tartar |
| | ¼ cup sugar |

Spray 2 (9-inch) round cake pans with no stick cooking spray. Heat oven to 350°. Combine strawberries and 1 tablespoon sugar; refrigerate, covered, until serving time. Prepare cake mix according to package directions, using 3 of the egg whites; fold in lemon peel. Bake until wooden pick inserted in center comes out clean (25 to 35 minutes). Cool in pans on wire rack 15 minutes; remove from pans onto wire racks; cool.

Place one layer on baking sheet. (Freeze second layer for a later use.) Increase oven temperature to 400°. In small mixing bowl, beat remaining 2 egg whites and cream of tartar until foamy. Gradually beat in ¼ cup sugar; continue beating until stiff and glossy. Spread meringue over top of cake layer. Bake until meringue is light brown (8 to 10 minutes). Cool completely. Transfer to serving platter. Just before serving, top with strawberries.

*8 servings.*

### Serving Size: ⅛ of recipe

| Calories | Fat | Cholesterol | Sodium |
|---|---|---|---|
| 180 | 2 Gm. | 0 Mg. | 260 Mg. |

# ANGEL-FRUIT TRIFLE

▼

*For a variation of an old English dessert, use convenience ingredients and a colorful palette of fresh fruits. Serve it from your prettiest bowl.*

| | |
|---|---|
| 1 (12-ounce) angel food loaf cake or ½ angel food cake | 2 cups frozen lite whipped topping, thawed, divided |
| 1 (0.9-ounce) package sugar-free vanilla instant pudding and pie filling | 1 pound fresh strawberries, sliced |
| 2 cups skim milk | 2 kiwi fruit, peeled, sliced |
| 1 tablespoon grated orange peel | 2 cups cubed pineapple |
| | 2 tablespoons sliced almonds, toasted |

Cut cake into about 1½-inch cubes. Prepare pudding according to package directions, using skim milk; fold in orange peel and 1 cup of the whipped topping. Arrange ⅓ of cake in 3-quart trifle or glass bowl. Layer ⅓ of strawberries, kiwi and pineapple over cake; spread ⅓ of pudding mixture over pineapple. Repeat layers twice more. Spread remaining 1 cup whipped topping over trifle. Refrigerate, covered, several hours or overnight. Just before serving, top with almonds.

*12 servings.*

### Serving Size: 1/12 of recipe

| Calories | Fat | Cholesterol | Sodium |
|---|---|---|---|
| 160 | 3 Gm. | 0 Mg. | 120 Mg. |

# STIR 'N ROLL PIE CRUST

▼

*Need a reliable, easy pastry recipe? We recommend this simple stirred version, which uses oil instead of solid shortening.*

| | |
|---|---|
| **1 cup flour** | **¼ cup canola oil** |
| **¼ teaspoon salt** | **3 tablespoons cold skim milk** |

Heat oven to 425°. In medium bowl, combine flour and salt; stir in oil and skim milk just until blended. Form dough into a smooth ball. Dampen counter top. Place one 12 × 15-inch sheet of waxed paper on dampened counter. Place pastry on paper; cover with another sheet of waxed paper. Roll dough into a 12-inch circle, turning dough and paper over once to roll evenly. Peel off top paper. Lift pastry and paper into 9-inch pie pan, paper side up; peel off remaining paper. Fit pastry into pan; trim edge even with rim. Press edge with tines of fork. Bake until golden brown (12 to 15 minutes). Remove to wire rack to cool.

*Amount: 1 (9-inch) pie shell.*

**Serving Size: ⅛ of recipe**

| Calories | Fat | Cholesterol | Sodium |
|---|---|---|---|
| 120 | 7 Gm. | 0 Mg. | 70 Mg. |

# FRESH STRAWBERRY PIE

▼

*Try it – you'll like it! Yogurt cheese that is. It replaces the usual cream cheese in this pie. Top with delicious fresh berries.*

| | |
|---|---|
| **– cheesecloth or coffee filters** | **½ teaspoon vanilla** |
| **1 (16-ounce) container nonfat plain yogurt (without gelatin)** | **1 (9-inch) Stir 'n Roll Pie Crust (above), baked** |
| **2 tablespoons powdered sugar** | **1 pound fresh strawberries (3 cups, halved)** |
| | **– strawberry pourable all fruit** |

To prepare yogurt cheese, arrange wire strainer lined with double thickness cheesecloth or coffee filters over large bowl. Spoon yogurt into lined strainer; cover with plastic wrap and refrigerate until liquid has drained from yogurt and yogurt is very thick (16 to 24 hours). Discard liquid. Combine powdered sugar, vanilla and yogurt cheese. Spoon into pie crust, spreading evenly. Arrange halved strawberries, upright, with hull end down pressing into cheese, in close even circles. Pour about 1 tablespoon pourable fruit through sieve to remove chunky pieces. Measure 1 tablespoon; brush tips of berries. Refrigerate up to 3 hours.

*8 servings.*

**Tip:** The sweetness of berries will vary; add extra sugar to yogurt cheese, if desired.

**Serving Size: ⅛ of recipe (including crust)**

| Calories | Fat | Cholesterol | Sodium |
|---|---|---|---|
| 180 | 7 Gm. | 0 Mg. | 100 Mg. |

# BERRY FILLED MERINGUES

▼

*Cloud-like meringue shells are topped with an exquisite berry filling. This absolutely elegant dessert is the perfect finale for a dinner party!*

- parchment paper
4 egg whites, at room temperature
½ teaspoon cream of tartar
1⅓ cups sugar, divided
¼ cup water
3 tablespoons cornstarch

1 (16-ounce) package no sugar added frozen raspberries, thawed, divided
¼ teaspoon grated lemon peel
1 tablespoon lemon juice
½ cup no-sugar-added frozen cranberry juice cocktail concentrate, thawed

Place sheet of parchment paper on large baking sheet. Outline 10 (3-inch) circles about 1 inch apart on paper; turn paper over on baking sheet. Heat oven to 250°. In large mixing bowl, beat egg whites and cream of tartar until frothy. Gradually beat in 1 cup of the sugar until stiff and glossy. Spoon about ⅓ cup meringue on each circle. With back of spoon, spread meringue over circle, hollowing out center and building up sides to about 1 inch high. Bake slightly below center of oven for 1 hour. Turn oven off; leave meringues in closed oven until dry when touched (2 to 3 hours). Cool on rack; peel off paper. Store meringues in container with loose-fitting lid. In 1-cup glass measure, combine water and cornstarch until cornstarch is dissolved. In medium saucepan, combine cornstarch mixture, ⅓ cup sugar, 1 cup of the raspberries and remaining ingredients. Cook over medium heat, stirring constantly, until mixture comes to a boil; boil and stir 1 minute. Stir in remaining raspberries. Refrigerate, covered.

To Serve: Fill meringue shells with ¼ cup filling.

*10 servings.*

**Serving Size: 1 meringue shell with filling**

| Calories | Fat | Cholesterol | Sodium |
|---|---|---|---|
| 150 | 0 Gm. | 0 Mg. | 25 Mg. |

**Serving Size: 1 meringue shell**

| | | | |
|---|---|---|---|
| 80 | 0 Gm. | 0 Mg. | 20 Mg |

# WHIPPED TOPPING

▼

*For best results, prepare this just before serving. The product, Whip it, is a stabilizer that keeps the topping firm enough to hold peaks.*

½ cup evaporated skimmed milk
½ teaspoon vanilla

1½ tablespoons sugar
1 (⅓-ounce) package Whip it

Chill milk, mixing bowl and beaters in freezer about 1 hour. Pour milk into mixing bowl. Add vanilla and sugar; whip ½ minute. Sprinkle with Whip it. Continue whipping until firm peaks form (about 5 minutes). Whipped topping maintains good consistency for about 15 minutes.

*Amount: 3 cups.*

**Serving Size: ¼ cup**

| Calories | Fat | Cholesterol | Sodium |
|---|---|---|---|
| 16 | 0 Gm. | 0 Mg. | 10 Mg. |

# BAKED CUSTARD

▼

*Our version of an old favorite has melt-in-your-mouth quality but is in tune with lowered fat recommendations. Topped with fresh fruit, it's perfect for breakfast!*

| | |
|---|---|
| 1 cup cholesterol-free liquid egg substitute, thawed | 1 teaspoon vanilla |
| 2 cups skim milk | ¼ teaspoon salt |
| ⅓ cup sugar | ¼ teaspoon ground cinnamon |
| | ¼ teaspoon ground nutmeg |
| | – boiling water |

Heat oven to 325°. Combine egg substitute, milk, sugar, vanilla and salt until blended. Arrange 6 (6-ounce) custard cups in 9 × 13-inch baking pan. Pour custard evenly into custard cups. Combine cinnamon and nutmeg; sprinkle over custard. Place pan on oven rack; pour boiling water into pan to a depth of 1 inch. Bake until knife inserted near center of cup comes out clean (65 to 75 minutes). Serve warm or chilled.

*6 servings.*

**Serving Size: ⅙ of recipe**

| Calories | Fat | Cholesterol | Sodium |
|---|---|---|---|
| 90 | 0 Gm. | 0 Mg. | 190 Mg. |

# COOKING FOR A CROWD

**D**on't panic — PLAN! Crowd-sized entertaining is not only manageable it's enjoyable. The main ingredient, to be added generously, is organization.

Begin with a plan which includes all the essentials — type of party, number of guests, time of day, budgetary and spatial restrictions and favored serving style. Select a menu that is well-balanced, creative, suitable for the occasion and can be prepared with ease. The foolproof, uncomplicated recipes were carefully developed for larger groups to assure complete confidence when preparing for festive occasions. In addition, we have provided guidelines to assist you in calculating the amounts needed to feed a crowd and tips for purchasing.

The recipes range from casual to elegant and will satisfy a variety of budgets, serving styles and skills. We think you will savor our choices and be able to greet your guests with genuine pleasure knowing that everyone is in store for a wonderful time!

# BEEF TENDERLOIN SUPREME

▼

*Hours before guests arrive complete the preparation of this superbly seasoned stuffed tenderloin. Close to serving time, slice, artfully arrange and garnish for a show-off presentation.*

- 2 (2½ to 3-pound) beef tenderloins
- 2 (10-ounce) packages frozen chopped spinach, thawed, squeezed dry
- 1 (8-ounce) package shredded sharp Cheddar cheese
- ¼ cup red wine
- ½ cup golden raisins, coarsely chopped
- 2 eggs, slightly beaten
- 1 teaspoon minced garlic
- ¼ cup finely chopped shallots
- 2 teaspoons salt
- ¼ teaspoon pepper
- – vegetable oil
- ½ teaspoon pepper melange
- – leafy greens

Heat oven to 425°. Make a lengthwise cut down center of each tenderloin, cutting to within ½ inch of other side. Pound meat with meat mallet to flatten into rough rectangles about 8 inches wide. Combine spinach, cheese, wine, raisins, eggs, garlic, shallots, salt and pepper. Spread half of mixture evenly over each piece of meat to ½ inch of lengthwise edges. Starting with long side, roll up meat jelly roll fashion; tie with string at 1-inch intervals. Brush entire surface of meat with oil. Sprinkle tops of roasts with pepper melange. Arrange roasts several inches apart on rack in shallow roasting or broiler pan. Roast to an internal temperature of 145 to 150° (40 to 45 minutes). Cool slightly; refrigerate, covered, several hours or overnight.

To Serve: Remove strings; carve crosswise into ⅜-inch slices. Arrange slices on lettuce-lined serving platter. Serve cold.

*Amount: 35 to 45 slices.*

# TANDOORI CHICKEN

▼

*Marinated, sumptuously seasoned and served chilled – a sensational centerpiece for a warm-weather menu.*

- 6 tablespoons Tandoori Barbecue Marinade
- 1 (16-ounce) carton plain yogurt
- ½ cup lemon juice
- 4 teaspoons salt
- 1 cup white wine vinegar
- ½ cup vegetable oil
- 20 boneless, skinless chicken breast halves
- – leaf lettuce
- – lemon slices

Combine Tandoori Marinade, yogurt, lemon juice, salt, vinegar and oil. Divide evenly between two 9 × 13-inch glass baking dishes. Cut slits 1 inch apart and about ½ inch deep on rib side of each chicken breast half; arrange 10 breast halves in each dish, turning to coat. Marinate, covered, in refrigerator several hours or overnight.

Heat broiler. Remove chicken from marinade; arrange 10 pieces, slit side up, on broiler pan. Spoon marinade over chicken to cover. Broil about 5 inches from heat for 6 minutes; turn and broil until chicken is no longer pink and juices run clear when cut at thickest part (5 to 7 minutes longer). Repeat with remaining chicken. Refrigerate, covered.

To Serve: Arrange chicken breasts on lettuce-lined platter. Garnish with lemon slices.

*20 servings.*

*Beef Tenderloin Supreme*
*page 237*

# AMOUNTS FOR 50

*Number of guests? Menu items? Time of day for serving? These are three key considerations when cooking for a crowd. Here we offer purchasing guidelines to ease you through the process.*

| Food | Serving Size | Amount for 50 |
|---|---|---|
| Coffee | one 6-ounce serving | 1 pound |
| Punch | one ½-cup serving | 6 quarts |
| Rolls | 1½ each | 6 dozen |
| Open Face Sandwiches | | 12 dozen |
| Ham (boneless-cooked) | | |
|     meal | 4-ounce serving | 12 pounds |
|     reception | 2 to 3 ounces | 7 to 9 pounds |
| Combination for reception | | |
|     ham/cold cuts | 2 ounces | 6 pounds |
|     cheese | 1 ounce | 3 pounds |
| Beef (boneless top round for roasting and slicing) | | |
|     meal | | 20 pounds |
|     reception | | 12 to 15 pounds |
| Chicken Salad | | |
|     luncheon | 1-cup serving | 3 gallons, 1 pint |
|     reception | ½-cup serving | 1½ to 2 gallons |
| Potato Salad | ½-cup serving | 1½ to 2 gallons |
| Cole Slaw | ½-cup serving | 1½ to 2 gallons |
| Baked Beans | ½-cup serving | 1½ to 2 gallons |
| Potato Chips | 1 ounce | 3 pounds |
| Olives or Pickles | | 2 quarts |
| Mixed Nuts | | 1½ pounds |
| Mints — pillows | | 1 pound |
|     — wafers | | 1½ pounds |
| Ice cream | ½-cup serving | 2 gallons |
| Butter | | 1 to 1½ pounds |

## PURCHASE POINTERS

1 (5-pound) chicken = 4 cups cooked and cubed

1 (10 to 12-pound) turkey = 14 cups cooked and cubed

1 (16 to 18-pound) turkey = 20 cups cooked and cubed

1 (18 to 20-pound) turkey = 23 cups cooked and cubed

1 (6¾-pound) turkey breast = 10 cups cooked and cubed

3 pounds whole boneless chicken breasts = 5 to 6 cups cooked and cubed

3 pounds chicken breasts with ribs, split = 4 to 4½ cups cooked and cubed

3 pounds boiling potatoes (7 to 8 large) = 8 cups cooked and cubed

# TACO SALAD FOR A CROWD

*A casual main dish salad for hosts who crave make-ahead preparation and the convenience of help-yourself serving.*

| Ingredients | 8 Servings | 25 Servings |
| --- | --- | --- |
| Ground beef | 2 pounds | 6 pounds |
| Minced garlic | 1 teaspoon | 1 tablespoon |
| Canned green chopped chiles, drained | 2 (4-ounce) cans | 6 (4-ounce) cans |
| Canned diced tomatoes, drained | 2 (14½-ounce) cans | 6 (14½-ounce) cans |
| Canned kidney beans, drained | 1 (16-ounce) can | 3 (16-ounce) cans |
| Salt | 1 teaspoon | 1 tablespoon |
| Pepper | ¼ teaspoon | ¾ teaspoon |
| Tomatoes, medium, chopped | 2 (2 cups) | 6 (6 cups) |
| Iceberg lettuce | ¾ of (25-ounce) head (8 cups) | 2 (25-ounce) heads (24 cups) |
| Shredded sharp Cheddar cheese | 1 (8-ounce) package | 3 (8-ounce) packages |
| Onion, medium, chopped | ⅓ pound (1 cup) | 1 pound (3 cups) |
| Sour cream | 1 (8-ounce) carton | 2 to 3 (8-ounce) cartons |
| Tortilla chips and/or | 8 ounces | 1½ to 2 pounds |
| Taco salad shells, baked | 2 (5.6-ounce) packages | |
| Taco sauce (optional) | | |

In large skillet, cook ground beef and garlic until meat is no longer pink. Drain off fat. Stir in chiles, tomatoes, kidney beans, salt and pepper. Simmer, uncovered, 30 minutes. Arrange tomatoes, lettuce, cheese, onion and sour cream in separate serving bowls.

To Serve 8: Arrange tortilla chips or salad shells on dinner plates. Spoon lettuce over chips; spoon meat mixture evenly over lettuce. Let guests complete salad with choice of toppings. Drizzle with taco sauce, if desired.

To Serve 25: Place tortilla chips, lettuce and meat mixture in serving dishes alongside toppings and allow guests to assemble their own salads.

### 8 or 25 servings.

*These recipes have been formulated for group serving. It is best to prepare one recipe several times, rather than doubling or tripling it, to assure that the seasonings, consistency, pan size and baking times will be accurate.*

# GINGERED CHICKEN SALAD

▼

*Ginger stems in syrup, not to be confused with the crystallized version, are the immature knobs of young ginger plants.*

1 pound pea pods, ends and
    strings removed
2 cups uncooked spiral
    macaroni
10 cups cubed cooked chicken
    or turkey
2 cups thinly sliced carrots
2 (8-ounce) cans sliced water
    chestnuts, drained

1 cup mayonnaise
¼ cup soy sauce
¼ cup dry sherry
¼ to ⅓ cup chopped ginger in
    syrup, drained
1 teaspoon minced garlic
½ teaspoon salt
¼ teaspoon pepper

Blanch pea pods in large kettle of boiling water for 30 seconds. Drain; rinse with cold water. Drain and pat dry. Cook macaroni in boiling salted water (3 quarts water, 1 teaspoon salt) until almost tender (7 to 10 minutes); drain. Rinse with cold water; drain thoroughly. Combine chicken, pea pods, macaroni, carrots and water chestnuts in large bowl. Combine remaining ingredients until well blended. Gently toss with chicken mixture. Refrigerate, covered, several hours or overnight.

*Amount: 19 cups.*

Edible-Podded Pea

# FRUITED CHICKEN SALAD

▼

*A perennial favorite for receptions, showers, luncheons and other festive gatherings; mound on a bed of purple kale for an eye-catching presentation.*

1½ cups uncooked rosamarina
9 cups cut-up cooked chicken
    or turkey
3 cups thinly sliced celery
¾ cup sliced green onions
1½ pounds whole green seedless
    grapes (3 cups)
½ pound whole red seedless
    grapes (1 cup)

1 pineapple, peeled, cored, cut
    up (2½ cups)
3 to 3½ cups mayonnaise
¼ cup lemon juice
½ teaspoon salt
½ teaspoon white pepper
– purple kale leaves
– cashews

Cook rosamarina in boiling salted water (2 quarts water, 1 teaspoon salt) until almost tender (5 to 8 minutes); drain. Rinse with cold water; drain. In large bowl, combine rosamarina, chicken, celery, green onions, grapes and pineapple. In small bowl, combine mayonnaise, lemon juice, salt and pepper; fold into chicken mixture. Refrigerate, covered.

To Serve: Line large serving platter with kale leaves; spoon salad onto greens. Sprinkle with cashews.

*Amount: 20 cups.*

# BEEF 'N SALSA BUNWICHES

▼

*A capital idea for casual entertaining and hearty appetites, salsa-sparked beef slices hit the spot.*

| | |
|---|---|
| 1 (5 to 6-pound) top round beef roast | 2 tablespoons chili powder |
| 1 (16-ounce) jar mild salsa | 2 teaspoons salt |
| 1 (16-ounce) jar medium salsa | 1½ teaspoons minced garlic |
| 3 beef bouillon cubes | 1 teaspoon ground cumin |
| 1 cup chopped onion | 1 tablespoon dried basil, crumbled |
| 3 tablespoons firmly packed brown sugar | 30 to 35 mini Kaiser or hard rolls, about 2 inches in diameter |

Heat oven to 350°. Place roast in large roaster or Dutch oven. Combine remaining ingredients except Kaiser rolls in saucepan. Bring to a boil; pour over roast. Bake, covered, until tender (about 2½ hours). Remove roast from pan; cool. Slice into thin bunwich-size servings (⅛ × 2½ × 2½ inches). Skim fat from salsa juices. Layer meat and salsa mixture in 3-quart casserole. Refrigerate, covered, several hours or overnight.

To Serve: Heat oven to 325°. Bake until heated through (40 to 50 minutes). Spoon meat and salsa onto rolls.

### *Amount: 30 to 35 mini bunwiches.*

**Variation:**  For a milder salsa mixture, substitute 1 (8-ounce) can tomato sauce and 1 cup water for 1 (16-ounce) jar medium salsa.

# BRISKET BUNWICHES

▼

*A gently spiced tomato sauce bastes and tenderizes the meat during cooking.*

| | |
|---|---|
| 1 (4 to 5-pound) trimmed beef brisket | ¼ cup firmly packed brown sugar |
| ¼ cup lemon juice | 1 teaspoon minced garlic |
| 1 tablespoon chili powder | 1 large onion, chopped (1½ cups) |
| ½ teaspoon salt | 1½ teaspoons prepared mustard |
| ¼ teaspoon pepper | 1 tablespoon Worcestershire |
| 1 (28-ounce) bottle ketchup | 1 teaspoon salt |
| 1 (28-ounce) can tomatoes, chopped | 24 to 30 mini Kaiser or hard rolls, about 2 inches in diameter |

Heat oven to 325°. Arrange meat in large roaster or Dutch oven; sprinkle with lemon juice, chili powder, salt and pepper. Bake, covered, for 2 hours. Remove meat from pan. Skim fat from meat juices; reserve remaining juice. In large bowl, combine ketchup and remaining ingredients except rolls. Stir in 1 cup reserved meat juice. Return meat to pan; cover with tomato mixture. Bake, covered, until tender (about 2 hours). Remove meat from liquid; cool slightly. Slice diagonally across grain into thin slices. Stir ¾ cup water into liquid. Return meat slices to liquid. Refrigerate, covered, several hours or overnight.

To Serve: Heat oven to 325°. Bake, covered, until heated through (about 50 minutes). Spoon meat mixture onto rolls.

### *Amount: 24 to 30 mini bunwiches.*

*Our beefy bunwich recipes have been customer favorites for years. We're happy to announce two newcomers to the "bunwich family," both sensational for Super Bowl Sunday, block parties, teen gatherings and family reunions— just make ahead, reheat, relax and enjoy.*

# SMOKED SALMON 'N CUCUMBER TEA SANDWICHES

▼

*Delicately-flavored with dill butter, these delectable tea table treats also make wonderful canapés. Combine butter ingredients ahead for peak flavor.*

½ cup unsalted butter, softened
2 tablespoons snipped fresh dill
2 teaspoons lemon juice
– dash white pepper

10 slices thin whole wheat sandwich bread
1 cup thinly-sliced English cucumber
¼ pound thinly-sliced smoked salmon

In small bowl, beat butter, dill, lemon juice and pepper. Trim crusts from bread slices. Spread 1 side of each slice with dill butter. On half of bread slices, arrange cucumber slices in 1 layer, overlapping slightly. Top with a thin layer of smoked salmon. Top each with one slice of bread, press slightly. Cut each sandwich into 4 triangles. Arrange on trays; cover with waxed paper, slightly dampened towel and plastic wrap. Refrigerate several hours or overnight.

*Amount: 20 tea sandwiches.*

**Tip:** The butter may be made a day in advance; refrigerate, covered. Soften before using.

# WATERCRESS 'N EGG SANDWICHES

▼

*Egg salad becomes elegant with the addition of watercress. Select watercress with good sized leaves and use promptly after purchasing or cutting.*

1 (1½-ounce) package watercress
5 eggs, hard-cooked, peeled
¼ cup salad dressing
2 tablespoons Dijon mustard

⅛ teaspoon paprika
– dash salt
– dash white pepper
22 slices thin white sandwich bread
– butter or margarine, softened

Strip leaves from watercress stems to equal ½ cup tightly packed; coarsely chop. Finely chop eggs. In medium bowl, combine salad dressing, mustard, paprika, salt and white pepper. Fold in watercress and eggs. Trim crusts from bread; spread lightly with butter. Spread about 2 tablespoons egg mixture evenly on each of 11 slices of bread. Top with remaining 11 slices of buttered bread. Cut sandwiches into squares, triangles or fingers. Arrange on large trays; cover with waxed paper, slightly dampened towel and plastic wrap. Refrigerate several hours or overnight.

*Amount: 44 tea sandwiches.*

*Prepare tea sandwiches ahead and carefully follow directions for covering and storing them.*

# SMOKED TURKEY AND BEEF ROLL-UPS

*Mustard gives a zippy accent to the savory spread gilding deli meats. For a menu that is table-ready double quick, add one or more salads and crusty rolls.*

¾ cup mayonnaise
⅓ cup Dijon mustard
⅓ cup freshly-grated Parmesan cheese
24 thin slices cooked deli smoked turkey breast (about 2 pounds)

24 thin slices cooked deli roast beef (about 2 pounds)
– leafy greens
– cherry tomatoes
– fresh parsley sprigs

Combine mayonnaise, mustard and cheese in small bowl. Spread 1 teaspoon mixture evenly over each turkey and beef slice. Roll up, jelly-roll fashion, starting at narrow end. Arrange on serving platter lined with leafy greens. Garnish with cherry tomatoes and parsley. Refrigerate, covered, until serving time.

*Amount: 48 roll-ups.*

# VEGETABLE CRUDITES

*Select firm, fresh unblemished vegetables and use baskets, platter or colorful pottery dishes for artistic, arresting arrangements.*

Wash and cut vegetables into desired shapes and sizes. Allow 4 to 8 pieces per person, depending on occasion and type of use (appetizer, salad, relish).

| Vegetable | Weight | Approximate Number of Prepared Pieces |
|---|---|---|
| asparagus* | 1 pound | 30 spears, ends and scales removed |
| broccoli* | 2¾ pounds | 45 (1¼-inch) florets |
| carrots | 1 pound | 65 (3 × ½-inch) sticks |
| cauliflower | 4¾ pounds | 75 (1¼-inch) florets |
| celery | 1¾ pounds | 100 (4 × ½-inch) sticks |
| cherry tomatoes | 1 pint (¾ pound) | 25 (1-inch) tomatoes |
| cucumber | 1¾ pounds | 45 (4 × ¾-inch) spears, unpeeled, seeded |
| green bell pepper | 7 ounces | 24 (3½ × ½-inch) sticks |
| jicama | 1¼ pounds | 40 (4 × ½-inch) sticks |
| mushrooms | 1 pound | 20 whole (1½ to 2-inch) caps |
| pea pods* | ¼ pound | 30 pods |
| Jerusalem artichokes** | 1 pound | 50 (¼-inch) slices, unpeeled |
| zucchini | 1¼ pounds (three 6-inch) | 35 (½-inch) slices, unpeeled |

*For a bright color, these vegetables may be blanched. Plunge into boiling water; start counting time immediately. Blanch 2 minutes; immediately plunge into ice water. Drain; pat dry with paper towels.

**Place sliced Jerusalem artichokes in solution of 1 tablespoon lemon juice and 1 quart water to prevent darkening. Drain; pat dry before serving.

Asparagus

# RICE 'N CHUTNEY SALAD

▼

*The fresh zest of ginger and chunky chutney adds flavor and personality to this excellent accompaniment salad.*

2 cups uncooked converted rice
2 tablespoons orange juice
1 large Granny Smith apple, chopped (2 cups)
¾ cup colonial chutney (Chut-nut)
½ cup safflower oil

1 teaspoon freshly grated gingerroot
½ teaspoon salt
⅛ teaspoon pepper
1 cup chopped celery
½ cup golden raisins
½ cup chopped red bell pepper
¼ cup minced green onions
¼ cup slivered almonds, toasted

Cook rice according to package directions; cool. Drizzle orange juice over apple; toss to coat. In small bowl, combine chutney, oil, gingerroot, salt and pepper. Stir in apple and orange juice. In large bowl, combine rice, celery, raisins, bell pepper and green onions. Add chutney mixture; toss to coat. Refrigerate, covered, several hours or overnight. Just before serving, stir in almonds.

*20 (½-cup) servings.*

# DILL POTATO SALAD

▼

*A do-ahead dilly of a salad with the delicious difference of cucumber dressing added to the standard mayonnaise. Serve year round with hot or cold meat and poultry entrées.*

5 pounds new red potatoes
2 teaspoons salt
2 cups sliced celery
2 bunches green onions, sliced (1 to 1¼ cups)

2 cups mayonnaise
1 (16-ounce) bottle creamy cucumber dressing
2 tablespoons dried dill weed, crumbled
– fresh dill sprigs

Scrub potatoes. Place in large Dutch oven; cover with cold water, add salt. Bring to a boil over high heat; reduce heat to medium. Boil gently until tender when pierced with a fork (20 to 25 minutes). Drain; cool. Cut potatoes into chunks. In large bowl, combine potatoes and remaining ingredients except fresh dill. Refrigerate, covered, several hours or overnight.

To Serve: Toss gently; spoon onto serving platter. Garnish with fresh dill.

*32 (½-cup) servings.*

Dill

# PENNE PASTA TOSS

▼

*The bold taste and chewy texture of sun-dried tomatoes and the rich tangy flavor of feta cheese combine well with tube-shaped penne pasta for a simple but trendy salad.*

1 (16-ounce) package
uncooked penne pasta
1 (8-ounce) bottle zesty Italian
dressing
2 large tomatoes, chopped
(2 cups)

1 (7-ounce) jar sun-dried
tomatoes in oil, drained,
chopped (½ cup)
2 (4-ounce) packages crumbled
feta cheese
½ cup chopped fresh parsley
¼ cup capers, drained

Cook pasta in boiling salted water (4 quarts water, 1 tablespoon salt) until almost tender (about 11 minutes); drain. Rinse with cold water; drain. In large bowl, combine pasta and dressing. Stir in remaining ingredients. Refrigerate, covered, several hours or overnight.

*28 (½-cup) servings.*

# COUSCOUS AND MARINATED VEGETABLES

▼

*Hold the pasta, potatoes and rice and pass the couscous instead. Here, we've combined it with colorful vegetables and a vinaigrette salad dressing.*

2 cups couscous
1 teaspoon salt
2 cups boiling water
2 (8-ounce) bottles Dijon
vinaigrette salad dressing
1 teaspoon sugar
¼ cup Dijon mustard
4 to 5 medium carrots, sliced
(2 cups)
2 medium zucchini, sliced
(2 cups)

2 medium yellow squash,
sliced (2 cups)
1 large red onion, coarsely
chopped
2 medium red bell peppers,
cut into 2¼-inch julienne
strips
2 (15-ounce) cans garbanzo
beans, drained
5 cups broccoli florets,
blanched, drained

In large bowl, combine couscous, salt and water; let stand, covered, 5 minutes. In medium bowl, combine salad dressing, sugar and mustard. In 6 to 8-quart container, combine remaining ingredients except broccoli; lightly toss with dressing and couscous. Refrigerate, covered, several hours or overnight. Refrigerate broccoli, covered, several hours or overnight.

To Serve: Gently toss broccoli into vegetable-couscous mixture.

*Amount: about 20 cups.*

*An important reminder in food preparation is to keep hot foods hot, above 150°, and cold foods cold, below 40°.*

*Never keep food at room temperature for more than two hours.*

# SPINACH SALAD

▼

*Your favorite creamy bacon dressing recipe has been expanded to dress a crowd-sized spinach salad. Keep greens looking fresh and perky by following the tip below.*

| | |
|---|---|
| ¼ cup cider vinegar | 2 (10-ounce) bags spinach |
| 1 cup mayonnaise | 4 eggs, hard-cooked, peeled, |
| 2 tablespoons light corn syrup | sliced |
| ¼ teaspoon salt | 2 cups fresh bean sprouts, |
| 1 (8-ounce) package bacon, | rinsed, well-drained |
| crisply fried, crumbled | 16 ounces fresh mushrooms, |
| ¼ cup finely chopped onion | sliced |
| 1 teaspoon minced garlic | 1 cup thinly sliced red onion |
| | rings |

In small bowl, gradually stir vinegar into mayonnaise; blend in corn syrup, salt, bacon, onion and garlic. Refrigerate, covered. Rinse and dry spinach. Remove stems; tear leaves into bite-sized pieces. Combine spinach with remaining ingredients in large bowl. Drizzle with dressing; toss to coat.

### 26 (1-cup) servings.

**Tip:** For easier mixing, prepare all ingredients ahead; store in separate containers in refrigerator. At serving time, toss half of ingredients with half of dressing. Repeat with remaining ingredients when needed.

Tomato

# TOSSED INSALATA

▼

*Toss together a savory selection of fresh greens and other colorful ingredients for an Italian theme menu or anytime you need a crowd-pleasing salad. Fennel, which resembles celery except for the bulb-like stalk, has a slightly licorice flavor.*

| | |
|---|---|
| 1 bulb fennel | 1 (6-ounce) can medium pitted |
| 4 medium ripe tomatoes | ripe olives, drained |
| 8 cups torn romaine lettuce | 2 cups shredded Parmesan |
| 8 cups torn iceberg lettuce | cheese |
| 6 cups torn red-tipped leaf | 1 large red onion, sliced, |
| lettuce | separated into rings |
| 1 large carrot, shredded | 1 (16-ounce) bottle zesty |
| (1 cup) | Italian dressing, divided |
| 1 (11½-ounce) jar | 1 (12-ounce) container |
| pepperoncini, drained | croutons (4½ cups) |

Rinse fennel; trim stalks and cut away base. Cut bulb lengthwise into quarters; cut into thin crosswise slices. Dice tomatoes, draining on paper towels. In 10-quart container, combine greens with carrot, pepperoncini, olives, cheese, onion rings, fennel and tomatoes; toss. Divide salad in half; lightly toss first half with ¼ cup dressing. When more salad is needed, repeat with remaining salad and ¼ cup dressing. Serve remaining dressing and croutons on the side.

### 32 (1-cup) servings.

# ORIENTAL COLE SLAW

▼

*Definitely a salad for all seasons with readily-available ingredients
creatively combined for an unusual and appealing offering. Marries
well with almost any entrée.*

| | |
|---|---|
| 1 (3-pound) head cabbage, finely shredded (about 12 cups) | 1 teaspoon salt |
| | ⅛ teaspoon pepper |
| ½ cup sliced green onions, including some tops | 2 (3-ounce) packages ramen noodles with chicken-flavor soup packet |
| ¼ cup sesame seed, toasted | |
| ⅓ cup sugar | 1 cup slivered almonds, toasted |
| ¾ cup vegetable oil | |
| ½ cup white wine vinegar | 2 (11-ounce) cans mandarin orange segments, drained |

Combine cabbage, green onion and sesame seed in large bowl. In small bowl,
combine sugar, oil, vinegar, salt, pepper and chicken flavoring from soup
packets. Beat with wire whisk until sugar is dissolved. Pour dressing over
cabbage mixture. Refrigerate, covered, 1 to 2 hours. Shortly before serving,
break up noodles; add with almonds and orange segments to salad; toss gently.

*24 (½-cup) servings.*

# GREEN PEA SALAD

▼

*An old-fashioned favorite is restyled for contemporary menus by using
crisp, juicy jicama strips.*

| | |
|---|---|
| 4 (10-ounce) packages frozen tender tiny peas, thawed | 1 cup thinly sliced celery |
| | ⅔ cup thinly sliced green onions |
| 8 ounces sharp Cheddar cheese, cut into ½-inch cubes | |
| | 1 cup mayonnaise |
| ¾ pound jicama, peeled, cut into julienne strips | ¼ cup Dijon mustard |
| | ½ teaspoon salt |
| 1 cup chopped red bell pepper | ¼ teaspoon white pepper |
| | – romaine lettuce |
| | – Red Pepper Tulip (below) |

Drain peas well. In large bowl, combine peas, cheese, jicama, bell pepper,
celery and green onions. In small bowl, combine mayonnaise, mustard, salt and
white pepper; gently stir dressing into vegetables. Refrigerate, covered, several
hours or overnight.

To Serve: Spoon into lettuce-lined bowl; garnish with red pepper tulip.

*24 (½-cup) servings.*

## PEPPER TULIP

▼

Wash a green, yellow or red bell pepper. Cut circular portion out of top,
removing stem. Remove seeds and membrane. Starting at cut edge, slice down
in a zigzag pattern around pepper to form petals. Adjust last cut to meet evenly
with first.

With tip of paring knife, make a small hole in center of bottom of pepper to
hold Onion Brush (page 93). Insert an Onion Brush, cut on only one end, into
hole.

247

# VEGETABLE MEDLEY

▼

*A marvelous mustard vinaigrette bathes garden-fresh vegetables. When marinating vegetables, rearrange occasionally to guarantee even distribution of flavor.*

½ cup red wine vinegar
3 tablespoons Dijon mustard
3 tablespoons finely minced shallots
3 tablespoons snipped fresh parsley
¼ cup vegetable oil
½ cup olive oil
1½ teaspoons salt

¼ teaspoon pepper
1½ pounds fresh green beans, ends removed (6 cups)
2 pounds fresh asparagus, tough ends removed
2 pounds carrots, cut into 2½ × ¼-inch julienne strips
3 (1-gallon) zipper closure food storage bags
– red-tipped leaf lettuce

Combine vinegar, mustard, shallots, parsley, oils, salt and pepper in medium bowl; whisk to blend. Blanch green beans, uncovered, in boiling salted water (3 quarts water, 1 teaspoon salt) until crisp-tender (4 to 5 minutes); drain. Plunge beans into ice water until cold (3 to 4 minutes); drain. In large skillet, blanch asparagus in ½ inch boiling water until crisp-tender (2 to 3 minutes); drain. Plunge into ice water until cold (2 minutes); drain. Blanch carrots in 1 quart boiling water until crisp-tender (3 to 4 minutes); drain. Plunge into ice water until cold (2 minutes); drain. Pat beans, asparagus and carrots dry with paper towels; place each vegetable in separate food storage bag. Add ½ cup dressing to each bag; refrigerate remaining dressing. Refrigerate vegetables up to 48 hours, turning occasionally for even marinating.

To Serve: Line a large serving platter with lettuce. Mound carrots in center and asparagus and green beans on either side. If desired, drizzle remaining dressing over vegetables.

*18 to 20 servings.*

# LAYERED VEGGIE SALAD

▼

*One of our all-time favorite mayonnaise-based dressings is infused with lemon, garlic and Dijon mustard for extra pizazz. Carefully toss salad just before serving.*

¾ pound pea pods, ends and strings removed
4 cups torn romaine lettuce
4 cups torn iceberg lettuce
½ cup thinly sliced green onions, including some tops
1 cup thinly sliced celery
1 (8-ounce) can sliced water chestnuts, drained
2 medium carrots, shredded (1½ cups)

1½ cups mayonnaise
1 tablespoon Dijon mustard
½ teaspoon minced garlic
¼ cup lemon juice
¼ teaspoon salt
¼ teaspoon white pepper
½ cup freshly grated Parmesan cheese
½ pound bacon, crisply fried, crumbled
15 cherry tomatoes, halved

Remove stems and strings from pea pods. Blanch pea pods in large kettle of boiling water 1 minute; drain. Plunge into ice water until cold (2 minutes); drain. Pat dry on paper towels; slice in half diagonally. In 6-quart container, layer lettuces, pea pods, green onions, celery, water chestnuts and carrots. Combine mayonnaise, mustard, garlic, lemon juice, salt and white pepper; spread over salad. Sprinkle with cheese. Refrigerate, covered, several hours or overnight.

To Serve: Gently toss salad; sprinkle with bacon. Arrange cherry tomatoes, cut side down, on salad.

*15 to 20 servings.*

# FRUIT PLATTER

*Refreshing and healthful, an attractive fruit arrangement is the ideal centerpiece on any buffet table. Select firm ripe fruits in season.*

| Fruit | Approximate Yield |
| --- | --- |
| 1 (3 to 4-pound) pineapple | 40 triangular-shaped chunks |
| 1 (4-pound) cantaloupe | 36 chunks |
| 1 (2-pound) honeydew | 36 chunks |
| 1 (4 to 5-pound) watermelon piece | 48 chunks |
| 1 pound seedless green grapes | 12 to 15 clusters |
| 1 pound seedless red grapes | 12 to 15 clusters |
| 1 pound strawberries | 20 to 25 large berries |
| 1 carambola (star fruit), sliced crosswise | Garnish (optional) |

With large knife, cut pineapple into fourths from base through green top. Remove core and loosen pineapple from shell using a grapefruit or paring knife. Slice each quarter into 5 triangular-shaped wedges; cut down center to make 10 wedges, leaving them in place in shell. Place a frilly cocktail pick in each wedge. Peel and cut melons into chunks. Snip grapes into clusters. Leave strawberries whole, stems on. Arrange fruit in interesting design on large platter. Garnish with star fruit. Serve with Almond Dip and/or Citrus Fruit Dip (below), if desired.

### *25 servings.*

**Almond Dip:** In small saucepan, stir ¼ cup cornstarch and ¼ cup sugar together. Pour in 1½ cups pineapple juice and 1½ cups orange juice. Bring to a boil over medium heat, stirring constantly; boil and stir 1 minute over low heat. Stir in 1 teaspoon almond extract. Refrigerate, covered, until 30 minutes before serving. Garnish with toasted almonds, if desired.

### *Amount: 3 cups.*

**Citrus Fruit Dip:** Combine 1 (8-ounce) carton reduced fat sour cream, 2 tablespoons sugar, 1 tablespoon fresh lemon or orange juice and 2 teaspoons grated lemon or orange peel. Refrigerate, covered, several hours or overnight to blend flavors. Garnish with lemon or orange zest.

### *Amount: about 1 cup.*

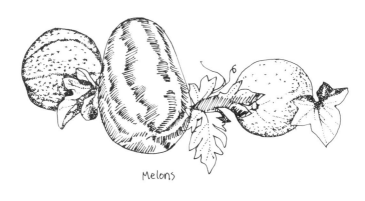

Melons

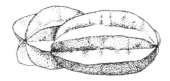

Carambola

# CARAMEL-FUDGE SUNDAE SQUARES

▼

*Who doesn't relish a divinely rich chocolate-caramel combination? After cooking and cooling step for fudge sauce, layering goes quickly for a fresh-from-the-freezer treat that's hard to beat.*

2 cups powdered sugar
1 (6-ounce) package semi-sweet chocolate chips
1 (12-ounce) can evaporated milk
½ cup butter or margarine
1 teaspoon vanilla

1 (9-ounce) package chocolate wafer cookies, crumbled (2½ cups)
⅓ cup butter or margarine, melted
1 (12.25-ounce) jar caramel flavor topping, divided
½ gallon brick style vanilla ice cream, slightly softened
2 cups dry roasted peanuts

In 2-quart saucepan, combine powdered sugar, chocolate chips, evaporated milk and ½ cup butter; bring to a boil over medium heat, stirring constantly. Cook 8 minutes, stirring constantly. Remove from heat; stir in vanilla. Cool 1 hour at room temperature.

Combine crumbled wafers and melted butter; press lightly in bottom of 9 × 13-inch baking pan. Pour about ⅓ jar caramel topping over crust; spread evenly. Cut ice cream into 1-inch slices. Arrange over crumb layer; spread evenly. Sprinkle with peanuts. Pour remaining ⅔ jar caramel topping over peanuts. Pour cooled fudge sauce over caramel. Freeze. When fudge sauce is frozen, cover with plastic wrap and foil. Freeze overnight.

To Serve: Remove from freezer about 5 minutes before cutting into squares.

### *18 to 20 servings.*

**Variation: Turtle Sundae Squares:** Substitute ½ cup pecan halves for peanuts.

# MINI FUDGE CAKES

▼

*Tiny morsels with a mighty rich fudge flavor require careful attention during baking to achieve their lovely moist texture.*

2 packages (1¾-inch) mini muffin foil baking cups
5 ounces semi-sweet chocolate
1 cup butter or margarine
1 teaspoon vanilla
1 cup chopped walnuts

4 eggs
1¾ cups sugar
1 cup flour
1 (16-ounce) container vanilla frosting with fudge swirl packet

Heat oven to 425°. Arrange foil cups about ½ inch apart on 2 baking sheets. Melt chocolate and butter together over low heat. Stir in vanilla and walnuts. In 2-quart bowl, combine eggs, sugar and flour; stir in chocolate mixture just until blended. Spoon batter into foil cups, filling half full. Bake until tops spring back when lightly touched with fingertip (13 to 14 minutes). Cool completely; store in covered container.

To Serve: Spoon 1 scant teaspoon frosting on each; top with small dot of fudge swirl.

### *Amount: about 5 dozen.*

**Tip:** About 4 dozen (2-inch) midget foil cupcake liners can be substituted for the mini muffin foil cups. Prepare as directed above; bake 12 to 14 minutes.

# SPUMONI TORTONI

▼

*These delightful individual dessert cups are a make-ahead freeze and forget dessert. Streamline preparation by using already-chopped pistachios from the produce department.*

24 (2½-inch) foil baking cups
10 (2-inch) flat coconut
    macaroon cookies, crumbled
    (2 cups)
¼ cup pineapple preserves

½ gallon spumoni ice cream,
    slightly softened
½ cup chopped pistachio nuts
¼ cup mini chocolate chips
24 stemmed maraschino
    cherries

Arrange foil cups in muffin pans. In medium bowl, combine cookie crumbs and preserves; divide evenly among cups, pressing in bottom. Place one rounded scoop of ice cream in each cup. Sprinkle with about 1 teaspoon pistachios and ½ teaspoon chocolate chips. Freeze until firm. Overwrap with heavy duty foil; return to freezer.

To Serve: Remove from freezer; garnish with cherries.

*Amount: 2 dozen.*

**Tip:** To soften ½ gallon ice cream, microwave (HIGH) in carton 40 to 50 seconds.

# KIWI SQUARES

▼

*The bright jewel colors of kiwi and strawberries glisten atop this do-ahead cheesecake-like dessert.*

1 cup butter or margarine,
    softened
2 cups flour
½ cup powdered sugar
¾ cup granulated sugar
2 tablespoons cornstarch
1 cup water
1½ teaspoons orange-flavored
    liqueur

2 (8-ounce) packages cream
    cheese, softened
⅔ cup granulated sugar
3 tablespoons orange-flavored
    liqueur
3 to 4 kiwi, peeled, thinly
    sliced
14 strawberries, halved or
    28 raspberries

Heat oven to 350°. Combine butter, flour and powdered sugar; pat evenly in bottom of 10 × 15-inch jelly roll pan. Bake until golden brown (15 to 17 minutes). Cool. Combine ¾ cup granulated sugar and cornstarch in small saucepan; stir in water. Bring to a boil over medium heat, stirring often. Boil and stir until clear (about 1 minute). Cool. Stir in 1½ teaspoons orange-flavored liqueur.

Beat cream cheese, ⅔ cup granulated sugar and 3 tablespoons orange-flavored liqueur until smooth. Spread evenly over crust. Refrigerate, covered, until set (45 to 60 minutes). Cut dessert evenly into 28 squares. Center a kiwi slice on each square; top with strawberry half. Pour and brush cooled glaze over surface of dessert. Refrigerate until glaze is set, then cover with plastic wrap.

*28 servings.*

**Tip:** Prepare crust and cream cheese filling 1 to 2 days before serving. Refrigerate, covered. Prepare glaze mixture and fruit the day of serving.

# CRANBERRY CHEESECAKE CUPS

*Mini cheesecakes can be prepared and frozen up to a month before needed. To serve, thaw and adorn with Cranberry Topping. What an ideal holiday dessert!*

48 (2-inch) foil midget baking
    cups
1½ cups graham cracker crumbs
  3 tablespoons butter, melted
  3 (8-ounce) packages cream
    cheese, softened

1 cup sugar
3 eggs
2 tablespoons orange-flavored
  liqueur or orange juice
– Cranberry Topping (below)

Heat oven to 350°. Arrange foil cups on baking sheets. Combine crumbs and butter; spoon a rounded teaspoonful into each baking cup. Beat cream cheese, sugar, eggs and liqueur until fluffy. Fill prepared baking cups. Bake until set but not brown (15 to 20 minutes). Cool. Spoon ½ teaspoon Cranberry Topping in center of each cheesecake. Refrigerate, covered, until serving time, several hours or overnight. Remove foil cups before serving.

*Amount: 4 dozen.*

**Tip:** Cheesecakes can be frozen up to 1 month. Thaw; spoon on Cranberry Topping.

**Cranberry Topping:** Dissolve 1 tablespoon cornstarch in 1 tablespoon water; set aside. Combine 1½ cups cranberries with 1 tablespoon water in small saucepan. Bring to a boil. Stir in ½ cup sugar. Cook, stirring and pressing berries, over medium-high heat until all berries have popped (about 3 minutes). Stir in cornstarch mixture. Cook, stirring constantly until mixture thickens (1 minute). Cool to room temperature.

# INDEX

▼

# The Best of Byerly's
# A Recipe Collection
## Volumes One and Two
### $25.00 EACH Includes sales taxes, mailer and postage

## ORDER FORM

**Print Full Name and Address Below**

NAME

ADDRESS

CITY, STATE, ZIP

**Gift order or ship to:** (use only if different from address at left)

NAME

ADDRESS

CITY, STATE, ZIP

| DESCRIPTION | QTY | PRICE EACH | TOTAL |
|---|---|---|---|
| Volume One | | $25.00 | |
| Gift Box | | $2.00 | |
| Volume Two | | $25.00 | |
| Gift Box | | $2.00 | |
| | | Total | |

*Mail to:*
**The Best of Byerly's**
**7171 France Ave. So.**
**Edina, MN 55435**

**Method of Payment:**

☐ Check ☐ Visa ☐ MasterCard

ACCOUNT NUMBER

—— —— —— ——   —— —— —— ——   —— —— —— ——   —— —— —— ——

____ / ____

Expiration Date      Signature (not valid without cardholder's signature)

Phone ( ) _____ Day ( ) _____ Evening

☐ I am sending a card to be mailed with my gift.

## ORDER FORM

**Print Full Name and Address Below**

NAME

ADDRESS

CITY, STATE, ZIP

**Gift order or ship to:** (use only if different from address at left)

NAME

ADDRESS

CITY, STATE, ZIP

| DESCRIPTION | QTY | PRICE EACH | TOTAL |
|---|---|---|---|
| Volume One | | $25.00 | |
| Gift Box | | $2.00 | |
| Volume Two | | $25.00 | |
| Gift Box | | $2.00 | |
| | | Total | |

*Mail to:*
**The Best of Byerly's**
**7171 France Ave. So.**
**Edina, MN 55435**

**Method of Payment:**

☐ Check ☐ Visa ☐ MasterCard

ACCOUNT NUMBER

—— —— —— ——   —— —— —— ——   —— —— —— ——   —— —— —— ——

____ / ____

Expiration Date      Signature (not valid without cardholder's signature)

Phone ( ) _____ Day ( ) _____ Evening

☐ I am sending a card to be mailed with my gift.

## ORDER FORM

**Print Full Name and Address Below**

NAME

ADDRESS

CITY, STATE, ZIP

**Gift order or ship to:** (use only if different from address at left)

NAME

ADDRESS

CITY, STATE, ZIP

| DESCRIPTION | QTY | PRICE EACH | TOTAL |
|---|---|---|---|
| Volume One | | $25.00 | |
| Gift Box | | $2.00 | |
| Volume Two | | $25.00 | |
| Gift Box | | $2.00 | |
| | | Total | |

*Mail to:*
**The Best of Byerly's**
**7171 France Ave. So.**
**Edina, MN 55435**

**Method of Payment:**

☐ Check ☐ Visa ☐ MasterCard

ACCOUNT NUMBER

—— —— —— ——   —— —— —— ——   —— —— —— ——   —— —— —— ——

____ / ____

Expiration Date      Signature (not valid without cardholder's signature)

Phone ( ) _____ Day ( ) _____ Evening

☐ I am sending a card to be mailed with my gift.